ADVANCE PRAISE FOR
Studies in Generalship

"Finkel's genuine research thoroughly analyzes on~ ~ ~ ost demanding military leadership positions ~~~ ~ decisions and actions of the IDF ch ~ ~plex
politico-military sphere—exem~ f the
senior military echelon in demo~ ~end
this book for statesmen, military ~

—Lt. Gen. Ehud Barak, ~inister and minister of
defense of Israel and ~~ ~ourteenth chief of staff of the IDF

"Finkel provides a lucid and analytic investigation of the role of the
chief of staff of the Israel Defense Forces, enriched by close exami-
nations of key historical moments, such as the Yom Kippur War, the
Lebanon Wars, and changes in the Golan Heights associated with
the Syrian Civil War. The volume has important lessons for scholars
of military history as well as for students of Middle East studies in
general."

—Russell A. Berman, senior fellow and director, Herbert
and Jane Dwight Working Group on the Middle East and
the Islamic World, Hoover Institution, and Walter A. Haas
Professor in the Humanities, Stanford University

"Everybody knows that Israel's armed forces have their own peculiar
operational style, so that their combat actions, large or small, very
often surprise their enemies as well as friends and bystanders. Meir
Finkel's book has finally uncovered how they actually work, by focusing with great precision on single episodes of generalship. It makes for
highly interesting reading."

—Edward N. Luttwak, historian, author of *Strategy: The Logic
of War and Peace,* and coauthor of *The Israeli Army*

STUDIES IN GENERALSHIP

STUDIES IN GENERALSHIP

Lessons from the Chiefs of Staff
of the Israel Defense Forces

Meir Finkel

Translated by Moshe Tlamim

HOOVER INSTITUTION PRESS

Stanford University | Stanford, California

hoover.org

Hoover Institution Press Publication No. 721

Hoover Institution at Leland Stanford Junior University, Stanford, California 94305-6003

First printing 2021
27 26 25 24 23 22 21   7 6 5 4 3 2 1

Manufactured in the United States of America
Printed on acid-free, archival-quality paper

Library of Congress Cataloging-in-Publication Data

Names: Finkel, Meir, 1968- author.
Title: Studies in generalship : lessons from the chiefs of staff of the Israel Defense Forces / Meir Finkel ; translated by Moshe Tlamim.
Other titles: Ramatkal. English | Hoover Institution Press publication; 721.
Description: Stanford, California : Hoover Institution Press, 2021. | Series: Hoover Institution Press publication ; no. 721 | English translation of: ha-Ramatkal. | Includes bibliographical references and index. | Summary: "The first in-depth comparative study on the role and performance of the Israel Defense Forces' chiefs of staff from 1948 to the second decade of the 21st century"—Provided by publisher.
Identifiers: LCCN 2021017938 (print) | LCCN 2021017939 (ebook) | ISBN 9780817924751 (paperback) | ISBN 9780817924768 (epub) | ISBN 9780817924775 (mobi) | ISBN 9780817924782 (pdf)
Subjects: LCSH: Israel. Tseva haganah le-Yiśra'el. Rosh maṭeh ha-kelali. | Generals—Israel. | Command of troops. | Israel—History, Military.
Classification: LCC UB225.I75 F56 2021 (print) | LCC UB225.I75 (ebook) | DDC 355.3/3041—dc23
LC record available at https://lccn.loc.gov/2021017938
LC ebook record available at https://lccn.loc.gov/2021017939

For my parents, Miriam and Yehuda

CONTENTS

Foreword *by H. R. McMaster*   xi

Preface to the English Edition   xiii

Acknowledgments   xvii

Glossary and Abbreviations   xix

Introduction   1

1   Identifying Change   17

David Elazar and the Announcement of the Blue and
White Alert, May 1973   18

Dan Shomron at the Outbreak of the First Intifada, 1987   23

Amnon Lipkin-Shahak and Hostilities in the Security Zone
in Lebanon, 1995   34

Shaul Mofaz Prior to the Second Intifada, 1999–2000   41

Dan Halutz and the Failure to Put the IDF on a War Footing
in the Second Lebanon War, 2006   47

Benny Gantz and the Change in Perception on the Golan
Heights, 2011–13   55

Chapter Summary   60

2   Developing Familiarity with All Military Domains   63

Yitzhak Rabin and the Plan for Operation Moked in the
1967 Six-Day War   65

David Elazar and the Tagar and Dugman Plans in the
1973 Yom Kippur War   74

Rafael Eitan and the Artzav 19 Plan in the 1982 First
Lebanon War   81

Dan Halutz and the Ground Force Plans before the
2006 Second Lebanon War   87

Chapter Summary   99

3   Losing Trust in a Wartime General   101

The Crisis between Moshe Dayan and Asaf Simhoni in the
1956 Sinai War   104

The Crisis between David Elazar and Shmuel Gonen in the
1973 Yom Kippur War   113

The Crisis between Dan Halutz and Udi Adam in the
2006 Second Lebanon War   123

Chapter Summary   141

4   Rehabilitating the Army after a Botched War   145

Mordechai Gur in the Wake of the Yom Kippur War   146

Gabi Ashkenazi after the Second Lebanon War   157

Chapter Summary   168

5   Leading a Change in Force Design   171

Moshe Dayan and the Transformation of the IDF's Fighting
Spirit Prior to the Sinai War, 1954–56   174

Dan Shomron, Ehud Barak, and the Development of
Precision-Guided Munitions for Use against Armored
Fighting Vehicles, 1986–94   192

Shaul Mofaz, Moshe Ya'alon, and the Diversion of Ground
Force Design to Low-Intensity Conflict, 1998–2005   204

Chapter Summary   216

6   Building Relationships with the Political Echelon in Force Design   219

Yigael Yadin and David Ben-Gurion on the Size of the Army, 1952   222

Moshe Dayan and David Ben-Gurion on the Use of Armor before the Sinai War, 1956   228

Mordechai Gur, Rafael Eitan, and Moshe Levi on the Establishment of the Mafhash, 1977–84   233

Dan Shomron and Yitzhak Rabin on the Lavi Jet Fighter, 1985–87   257

Chapter Summary   262

Conclusions   263

Précis of Each Chapter's Insights   264

Additional Aspects of the Role of Chief of Staff   267

An Integrated Analysis: The Role of the Chief of Staff in a Complex System and the Conditions That Aid in Success   272

Appendix A: Tenures of IDF Chiefs of Staff   279

Appendix B: Prime Ministers, Defense Ministers, and Generals   283

Notes   289

Bibliography   317

Photo Credits   327

About the Author   329

Index   331

FOREWORD

H. R. McMaster

This book explains the Israel Defense Forces (IDF) and its leadership in historical context. But *Studies in Generalship: Lessons from the Chiefs of Staff of the Israel Defense Forces* accomplishes much more than that. Soldier-scholar Meir Finkel also sheds light and understanding on the essential elements of effective military leadership in democratic societies at the highest levels. Finkel, who was once charged with designing the future IDF, combines impeccable research with lived experience. Of particular value is Finkel's framework for assessing leaders' records in fulfilling their critical roles. Those roles include providing the best military advice, determining the IDF's agenda, and shaping the IDF culture. Finkel's findings, illustrated with compelling historical vignettes of the IDF chiefs of staff grappling with myriad challenges, make this an important book for anyone interested in understanding the qualities citizens should expect in senior leaders. The book is also a guide for those who aspire to develop strategic acumen and leadership ability in themselves and others.

Studies in Generalship presents a well-developed theory of senior leadership, but that theory is grounded in actual historical experience and is eminently practicable. Finkel rejects buzzwords like *innovate* or *disruption* in favor of precise language. He describes how leaders identify and declare changes in reality and prepare the IDF to cope with those changes. The stories he tells illuminate the knowledge, skills, and abilities leaders need to serve successfully. Chiefs of staff, for example, require a high degree of competence not only in the air, land, or naval forces in which they served the bulk of their careers but across all domains of warfare, including space and cyberspace. They must hold subordinates accountable and be comfortable with making difficult personnel decisions. And leadership in extremis, whether due to a crisis or a perceived failure, requires leaders able to strengthen the moral as well as the physical foundations of their institution.

Leaders in any large organization will benefit from Finkel's analysis of leading change in force design. The cases he presents highlight the need to consider how to improve organizations culturally as well as effect concrete changes based on organization and technology. His examples caution leaders to consider continuities as well as changes and ensure that there are strong, respected advisers who can challenge assumptions. And, perhaps most important, his case studies reveal the importance of flexibility, and the need to constantly evaluate assumptions and to discard or modify plans if they are not producing the desired results.

Finally, *Studies in Generalship* holds lessons for how leaders might help organizations emerge from crises. The lessons Finkel identifies are as relevant to what the author describes as a "botched war" as they are to a pandemic. His recommendation to put education at the center of a recovery effort seems germane to the United States and other nations coping with multiple crises associated with pandemic, recession, social strife, and political polarization. The stories he tells about how IDF leaders took their organizations back to basics and set conditions for "healing on the job" are insightful and thought provoking. This is a book to be read and discussed, as Finkel's stories and analyses connect to a range of contemporary challenges and opportunities, and they are bound to spark creative ideas and an understanding of what it takes to implement those ideas.

PREFACE TO THE ENGLISH EDITION

The commander of the Israel Defense Forces (IDF), *Rosh Hamateh Haklali* (*Ramatkal*), which translates to "the chief of the general staff" or "the chief of staff," is an IDF institution and national figure. His decisions, advice, and persona are held in the highest regard by Israel's public and leadership (and have an impact indirectly on social, economic, and foreign affairs). Nevertheless, until now this institution has eluded methodical research. Although a number of autobiographies and biographies have been published, they each generally focus uncritically on one man.[1] Several picture albums have also appeared that are essentially chronological reviews of all the chiefs of staff, and in 2017 Israel's Channel 1 screened a series similar in nature.[2] But an in-depth comparative study on the role and performance of the chiefs of staff has been sorely absent, which is where this book steps in. In addition to closing this research gap, I have two goals:

- To enable senior role players in military organizations and security bodies to identify the chiefs of staff's patterns of actions and range of behaviors in various situations, in the belief that this awareness can assist officeholders in the political sphere as well as general staff and subordinate level officers
- To offer a critical look at the IDF's development and changes within the limitations discussed in the introduction

Comparative research on commanders and staff officers who filled a role similar to that of the Israeli chief of staff exists in world literature, but for the most part it presents the person's life story and compares it to the lives of his colleagues rather than analyzing and comparing his performance in specific areas of responsibility.[3]

This book looks at fifteen of the twenty-one chiefs of staff (serving until 2018), with some of them appearing in more than one chapter. Furthermore, the book is not chronologically structured or intended to assess the entire tenure of each chief of staff, but rather presents key events to highlight an aspect or aspects of the chief of staff's role and duties.

The main research challenge has been that while the book focuses on individual chiefs of staff, in reality this person is part of an exceedingly elaborate system. Above him are the defense minister, the prime minister, the cabinet, and other actors who try to influence him either directly or indirectly, while below him are the general staff—composed of professional staff officers and the commanders of the regional commands and services—and others who support and assist him. I deal with this challenge by providing short descriptions of the system as needed.

Finally, key elements in the chief of staff's command-and-control (C2) activity include knowledge development processes and other C2 measures, all of which are integral areas of the IDF's complex command system. Therefore, I have tried to describe both the chief of staff's performance and the command environment in which he operated. Although the chapters omit comparisons of learning mechanisms and C2 methods that the chiefs of staff developed in dealing with diverse situations, these issues are discussed in the conclusion.

The source material depends on the theme, area, or period under discussion. Much of the documentation deals with force employment in wartime. The research of Dr. Shimon Golan on the general staff's decision making in war has proved invaluable for my analysis of the veteran ground forces chiefs of staff's familiarity with the air force (and vice versa) and the chiefs of staff's loss of trust in the commander of a regional command. The IDF's History Department provided a large body of material on force employment in the interwar periods, and although it contained certain information gaps, I was able to close them with biographies and IDF memoir anthologies. In the area of force design, authorized IDF research is still in its infancy, so in addition to Ze'ev Elron's important studies I made ample use of IDF commanders' biographies.

Another obstacle, naturally, was the material's security classification—strictly classified material makes research difficult the closer the period of investigation approaches the present. For relatively recent events, such as the periods of chiefs of staff Gabi Ashkenazi and Benny Gantz, I turned to military correspondents for information but was also allowed to use classified documents. An additional challenge was the lack of after-action reports written by the chiefs of staff themselves that summarize their tenure and accomplishments (except those written by Yitzhak Rabin and Haim Bar-Lev). I wish to note that some of the material in this book comes from internal defense ministry and IDF sources that are being made public for the first time.

The advantage of comparative research is its ability to almost completely detach itself from the individual or the particular dilemma that he faced and chart basic patterns of action that future commanders and staff officers of all armies may find instructive. For readers familiar with Israeli military history and commanders, the book offers a robust and original comparative perspective on the performance of the chiefs of staff from 1948 to the second decade of the twenty-first century.

Brigadier General (res.) Dr. Meir Finkel
Head of Research, Dado Center, Operations Branch (Amatz)
April 2021

ACKNOWLEDGMENTS

This book was written with the help of scholars from the IDF History Department: Dr. Shimon Golan, an expert on strategic-level affairs, and Dr. Ze'ev Elron, an expert in force design. Both colleagues provided me with invaluable research material, advice on the choice of test cases, and incisive comments on large parts of the study. Gratitude is also extended to scholars Dr. Ohad Laslau and Ms. Chava Mudrik for their assistance in their fields of expertise. Special thanks are owed to the head of the History Department, Dr. Yigal Eyal, for our conversations that contributed to my understanding of the complexities and development of the chief of staff's role.

I wish to express my deepest appreciation to the people who took the time to read and comment on the entire manuscript. These include historians Professor Alon Kadish, Dr. Shimon Golan, and Mr. Shaul Bronfeld, and former and current IDF officers Chief of Staff Lieutenant General Gadi Eisenkot; Major General Tamir Heyman, the commander of IDF colleges; Major General Aharon Haliva, the head of the Technological and Logistics Branch; Major General (res.) Gershon Hacohen; Brigadier General Udi Ben Mucha, the commander of the Command and Staff College; Brigadier Generals (res.) Yoram Hamo and Itai Brun; Brigadier General Yakov Benjo, the commander of the Ga'ash Division; Brigadier General Motti Baruch, the head of the

Doctrine and Training Division (Tohad) in the Operations Branch (Amatz); Brigadier General Eran Niv, the head of the Manpower Division in the Ground Forces Command; Colonel Alon Paz, the head of the Strategic Planning Department in the Planning Branch (Agat); Colonel Hadas Minka, the head of the Behavioral Sciences Center in the Manpower Branch; the officers and researchers in the Doctrine and Training Division; Colonel (res.) Einat Gaffner; Lieutenant Colonel Matanya Tzahi; Lieutenant Colonel Eli Michelson; Lieutenant Colonel (res.) Dvir Peleg; and Lieutenant Or Glick.

In preparing the book I received excellent advice and encouragement from people in various fields based on their personal experience. Among them it is my privilege to mention Lieutenant General (and former chief of staff) Benny Gantz, Major General (ret.) David Ivry, Major General Shlomo (Sami) Turgeman, Major General Roni Numa, Colonel Eran Ortal, and Dr. Nimrod Hagiladi. My heartfelt thanks are given to the commander of Ma'arachot Publications, the late Effi Meltzer, who passed away shortly before the book went to press.

I am deeply indebted to Major Ramon, the information security officer of the Operations Branch, who read, constructively criticized, and approved the book's publication. I am also grateful to the librarian of the Command and Staff College, Chaya Shalom, and the librarian of the National Security College, Nava Grossman, for their unflagging assistance. Many thanks are owed to the secretaries in the Dado Center for typing the long quotations in the book.

Moshe Tlamim, my indefatigable translator, has made this book available to the English reading public. In that regard, I would like to thank Captain John Nisser of the Swedish Defense University for his valuable comments as a foreign reader and Lazar Berman of the Dado Center for his insights and for his guidance in crafting this book for an international audience.

GLOSSARY AND ABBREVIATIONS

Organizational Terms and Abbreviations

Agam: General staff branch (until 1999); operations department within Agam was headed by a colonel and from 1968 by a brigadier general.

Agat: Planning branch. Established in 1974 as part of Agam, headed by a major general. Autonomous branch since 1999, roughly parallel to the functions of J5 and J8 in US general staff terminology.[1]

Aman: Intelligence directorate.

Amatz: Operations branch (from 1999, succeeding Agam), roughly parallel to the functions of J3 and J7 in US general staff terminology.[2] The operations division within Amatz is headed by a brigadier general. (See figure 1.)

Armored Corps HQ: Headquarters responsible for armored forces design and in wartime operating as a divisional headquarters (1954–83); headed by a major general, unlike other corps headed by brigadier generals.

Chief of Staff (*Ramatkal*): Commander of the IDF.

COGAT: Coordinator of Government Activities in the Territories (West Bank and Gaza).

GHQ: IDF general headquarters. In wartime operates from the GHQ operations center (the Pit) in the Kirya (Hakirya) base in Tel Aviv.

Mafhash: Ground Forces Headquarters (1983–99 successor to Armored Corps HQ).

Mahad: Doctrine and training branch/department (1953–99); branch/department within the general staff branch (Agam) until 1999; headed by a major general.

Mazi: Ground Forces Command (from 1999; successor to Mafhash).

Shin Bet: Israel's internal security agency.

Tohad: Doctrine and training division (from 1999; successor to Mahad); a division within the operations branch (Amatz); headed by a brigadier general.

General Terms and Abbreviations

AFV: armored fighting vehicle

APC: armored personnel carrier

C2: command and control

C4I: command, control, communications, computers, and information

EBO: effects-based operations

HQ: headquarters

IAF: Israeli Air Force

IDF: Israel Defense Forces

ORBAT: order of battle: the number of units in the organization (IDF, IAF, or ground forces)

PA: Palestinian Authority

PGM: precision-guided munition

PLO: Palestine Liberation Organization

R&D: research and development

SAM: surface-to-air missile

UAV: unmanned aerial vehicle

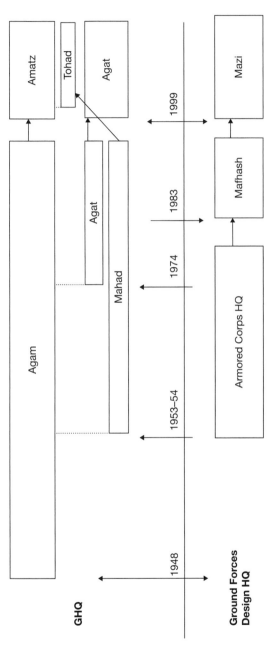

Figure 1. Timeline of GHQ operational branches and the body responsible for ground forces design, 1948–2019.

INTRODUCTION

The Israel Defense Forces' chief of staff (*Ramatkal*) is essentially the supreme commander of the IDF and fills one of the most important and esteemed positions in the nation's life. He determines long-term force design, makes operational decisions on a daily basis, and draws up strategic plans. His judgment is crucial in wartime. Surprisingly, a glaring gap exists in the academic literature on the dynamics of the chief of staff's role. This book comes as a first step toward closing the research gap by analyzing six aspects of the chief of staff's actions and decisions. This book's contribution has a wider aspect than the Israeli one, and it helps to break the deadlock of focusing singularly on biographical studies of past chiefs of staff, as well as other senior commanders in other countries.

The target audience includes generals and their staffs, university and military college students, and general readers who are interested in a fresh perspective on Israeli military history, strategic decision making, and political-military relations.

In order to make the book more accessible to an international audience, I begin with a short description of the IDF's structure and history and only afterward focus on the chief of staff.

In Israel everybody knows that the term "chief of staff" refers to the commander of the IDF. But choosing the term to be used in the English version presented a particular challenge. While "commander in chief" is used in some countries to refer to the commander of the armed forces, in the United States it refers to the president, so that was not an option. The same goes for the term "supreme commander," which usually refers to the political echelon. The commander of the IDF sounds straightforward, but it may confuse readers who have previously read Israeli military history where the term "chief of staff" is used. Taking all these considerations into account, I decided to stick with the term "chief of staff," although it does not exactly describe the essence of the office.

IDF Structure and History in Brief

The Israel Defense Forces came into being during the War of Independence (November 1947–March 1949) on the foundations of the Hagana, the unofficial military organization that existed before independence. The IDF was heavily influenced by World War II veterans of the British armed forces. Much of its structure—such as the organization of its general headquarters (GHQ), services, branches, fronts that became regional commands, and conscription method—is rooted in this war. (For today's organization, see figure 2.)

The IDF GHQ (*Hamatkal*) was stationed near Ramle, a small city east of Tel Aviv, until 1958, when it was moved to the Hakirya base in central Tel Aviv. Its organization initially followed the British model of three coordinating branches: (1) the general staff (*Agam*), which coordinates all combat and combat support arms; (2) the manpower branch; and (3) the logistics branch. But it soon shifted to the American model, based on a chief of staff coordinating directly more branches than the abovementioned three, such as intelligence and communications. In 1953, an independent intelligence directorate was created (*Aman*), separate from Agam. The same year, an independent doctrine

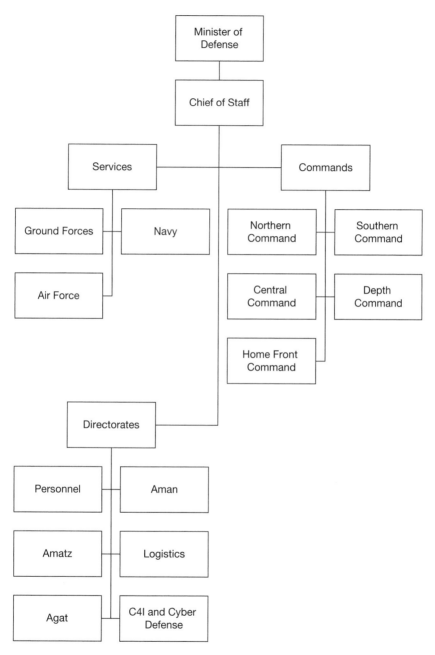

Figure 2. Organizational chart of the modern IDF, 2019. *Data source:* IDF Liaison Unit.

and training branch was created (*Mahad*). This branch was later degraded to the status of a department in Agam, but it was still headed by a major general until 1999, when it became a division within the newly organized operations branch (see below), headed by a brigadier general. Its name was then changed to *Tohad*. (See figure 1.)

After the 1973 Yom Kippur War, a new branch, responsible for strategic assessment and force design, was established (*Agat*), still under the head of Agam, whose title was then changed to deputy chief of staff and head of Agam. In 1999 Agam was dissolved and split in two: the operations branch (*Amatz*), which dealt with force employment, and Agat. The deputy chief of staff became in effect the chief of staff, in the sense of staff coordinator (it will be recalled that the chief of staff, although bearing this title, is effectively the commander of the IDF). Other changes in the GHQ branches were the establishment of a communication and computer branch in 2003, later developing into the current C4I (command, control, communications, computers, and information) and cyber defense directorate. Concerning ranks, the chief of staff is the sole lieutenant general in the IDF, while his deputy, the service commanders, commanders of the regional commands, and staff officers heading branches and directorates (intelligence, logistics, etc.) are all major generals. Until the Yom Kippur War, division commanders were mostly major generals, but from the mid-1970s onward they have all been brigadier generals. In the air and sea, the heads of staff divisions and major bases are brigadier generals.

As the IDF's fundamental mission is to defend the borders in peace and war, the ground forces are employed by three regional commands, each headed by a major general. In general, Northern Command is responsible for the Israeli-Syrian and Israeli-Lebanese borders; Central Command is responsible for the West Bank (in Israel often referred to by the biblical names Judea and Samaria) and the northern part of the Israeli-Jordanian border; and Southern Command is responsible for the Israeli-Egyptian border, the Gaza Strip, and the southern part of the Israeli-Jordanian border.

Over the years, the size, characteristics, and challenges of each arena have changed. For example, Southern Command conducted reprisal operations in the Gaza Strip in the 1950s; conquered Sinai in the Sinai War in 1956 and again in the Six-Day War in 1967; and defended the east bank of the Suez Canal in the War of Attrition (1968–70) and during the Yom Kippur War in 1973. After Israel returned Sinai to Egypt as stipulated in the Egypt-Israel Peace Treaty in the late seventies, Southern Command refocused on controlling the Gaza Strip until the disengagement from Gaza in 2005. In the last decade and a half, it has conducted ground operations against Hamas, which controls the Gaza Strip. Similar changes characterize the other two regional commands. In peacetime and in periods of low-intensity confrontation, which define most of Israel's history, the regional commands have defended the borders with regional regular divisions (for example, the 252nd Division during the War of Attrition on the Suez Canal and the Galilee Division along the Israeli-Lebanese border). When a large-scale confrontation emerges, GHQ allocates regular divisions as well as reserve divisions to the regional commands. The Home Front Command (for civil defense) was established in 1992 after Saddam Hussein targeted Israel with Scud missiles in the 1991 Gulf War, and the Depth Command (for operating behind enemy lines) was established in 2012. Due to the limited size of airspace and territorial waters, the Israeli Air Force (IAF) and the Israeli Navy employ their forces in a concentrated manner.

IDF force design is straightforward in the IAF and navy since these services both build and employ their forces, but it gets more complex with the ground forces. The IDF has witnessed a number of organizational changes regarding the authority and responsibility of, for example, ground force design, training, and manning. When the IDF was established in 1948, the ground corps (e.g., infantry, armor, and artillery) were directly subordinate to the chief of staff through Agam. In the mid-1950s, an Armored Corps HQ was established, which, based on the success of armor in the Sinai War and Six-Day War and its prominent role in the Yom Kippur War, preempted authority over the other corps in the 1960s and 1970s. In 1983, a new force design HQ (*Mafhash*) was established as a limited version of a service—the Ground Forces HQ—responsible for force design of the four combat corps (infantry, armor, artillery, and combat engineers). In 1999, Mafhash was upgraded to a full service and termed the Ground Forces Command (*Mazi*). From 2017 through 2020, Mazi assumed responsibility for the logistics command and also reorganized itself.

Designing and building the ground forces is not done by Mazi alone but also in certain areas by Aman, the C4I directorate, the IAF (which is responsible for helicopters and most of the unmanned aerial vehicles [UAVs]), and others. This structure makes coherent ground force design a formidable task.

The IDF is a conscription-based army with a limited number of career officers and noncommissioned officers.[1] Young women and men enter the army at age eighteen and serve for approximately two and three years, respectively. After serving in regular units, men and a small number of women continue to do reserve duty until the age of forty. In the ground forces, reserve units make up around 70 percent of the IDF order of battle (ORBAT). In the Air Force, all units are regular but many of the pilots are reservists. This kind of organization enables Israel to maintain a large armed force in terms of manpower and budget in comparison with its size.

The basic terminology of conflicts in the IDF has changed over the years but has always differentiated between periods of full-scale war and periods of routine security, when the forces engage in border security or "low-intensity" counterterrorism or guerrilla warfare. During the first decade of the twenty-first century, the accepted term was low-intensity conflict, or LIC, with some overlap with the term COIN (counterinsurgency). The last decade witnessed a new terminology in which operations in Gaza were referred to as "limited" or "deterrence" operations. The unceasing effort to disrupt the enemy's force buildup in Lebanon and Syria was described as a "campaign between the wars."

Table 1: IDF Chiefs of Staff

Ya'akov Dori	June 1947–November 1949
Yigael Yadin	November 1949–December 1952
Mordechai Maklef	December 1952–December 1953
Moshe Dayan	December 1953–January 1958
Haim Laskov	January 1958–January 1961
Tzvi Tzur	January 1961–January 1964
Yitzhak Rabin	January 1964–January 1968
Haim Bar-Lev	January 1968–January 1972
David (Dado) Elazar	January 1972–April 1974
Mordechai (Motta) Gur	April 1974–April 1978
Rafael (Raful) Eitan	April 1978–April 1983
Moshe Levi	April 1983–April 1987
Dan Shomron	April 1987–April 1991
Ehud Barak	April 1991–January 1995
Amnon Lipkin-Shahak	January 1995–July 1998
Shaul Mofaz	July 1998–July 2002
Moshe (Bogie) Ya'alon	July 2002–June 2005
Dan Halutz	June 2005–February 2007
Gabi Ashkenazi	February 2007–February 2011
Benny Gantz	February 2011–February 2015
Gadi Eisenkot	February 2015–January 2019
Aviv Kochavi	January 2019–present (as of September 2021)

Table 1 provides an overview of the IDF chiefs of staff, while Appendix A offers a more complex bird's-eye view of their tenures, the major engagements and major conceptual changes under their command, and the main headquarters and units mentioned in the book. Appendix B contains the personal aspects of their tenures and includes the prime ministers, defense ministers, and major generals who appear in the text.

The Evolution of the Role of the IDF Chief of Staff

The official definitions of the chief of staff's powers and responsibilities are vague and minimal. The Basic Law: The IDF (1976) defines the role as "the highest command position in the IDF" and states rather ambiguously that "the Minister of Defense is in charge of the IDF on behalf of the Government."[2] In a similar vein, the GHQ's directive dealing with the roles of the general staff affirms that "the chief of staff is the supreme commander of the IDF" and defines his role in one sentence: "The chief of staff commands and controls the employment of the IDF and oversees its force design by means of the main headquarters and the services."[3] The second half of the definition refers to preparing the IDF for war.

These documents reflect a minimalist definition of the chief of staff's role compared to that of the commanders of the regional commands, services, corps, divisions, and brigades. The sparsity of clarification may be intentional in order to give the chief of staff greater latitude in determining the scope of his role.

The authors of the IDF's strategic documents (IDF Strategy Papers) were aware of the need to define the chief of staff's functions in detail, especially where they relate to a war situation. Thus, the IDF's strategy document of 2002 (published during the tenure of Chief of Staff Shaul Mofaz) explains the chief of staff's role more precisely as "assisting the government by presenting war aims and specific goals, presenting the necessary conditions and modi operandi for achieving these goals, [and] outlining the implications and ramifications of war management."[4] The IDF's strategy document of 2015 (published during the tenure of Chief of Staff Gadi Eisenkot) defined the chief of staff's role as the "campaign commander [who] determines the idea and concept for mission accomplishment" and as a result "the efforts that the main headquarters must implement."[5] Although references in military literature (including military biographies) to the role of chief of staff are rare, they present a wide range of areas. Chief of Staff Dan Halutz noted that the role's multifacetedness is vast: it entails command and management, force design and its employment, an understanding of budgets, and a fair measure of political insight. The chief of staff is a media and social personality whose duties bring him into contact not only with those who appointed him but also with the general public. Halutz noted, "This was the challenge that I faced and that compounded the degree of responsibility that I bore, whose weight is a thousand times heavier than the added metal bars on the shoulders."[6]

Emanuel Wald of Agat described the enormous power that was invested in what he termed "the chief of staff institution" from 1967 to 1982. The chief of staff's almost unlimited power weakened the IDF in several ways. The first was the unprecedented surfeit of power that was concentrated in the IDF's "chief of staff institution." Norms of conduct and expectations of the person filling the role and his entourage created an unwritten definition of the role of chief of staff and produced the power base of the "chief of staff institution" and the conditions for its functioning. According to Wald, the chief of staff became a barrier to change and innovation, an obstacle on the path to self-reform that every healthy military organization needs to cultivate. Not only did the institution evolve into the center of radical conservatism in the IDF and its main bastion in this period, but it also led the IDF in the spirit of ultraconservatism. The tangible expressions of the overload of power that accumulated in the "chief of staff institution" were many and diverse. They weakened the general staff while strengthening the organizational status of the chief of staff.[7]

This book argues that despite Wald's profound and original insight into the "chief of staff institution" in particular, and the IDF in general, the generalizations are too sweeping and refer to specific chiefs of staff. Nevertheless, the excess of power given to the role of chief of staff appears to be closely linked to the immense security challenges that Israel faces compared to other countries. Furthermore, comparing the role of the IDF chief of staff to that in other armies is an elusive task. If we look at the US armed forces, the role of the IDF chief of staff combines those of chairman of the Joint Chiefs of Staff (a role that is part of the IDF chief of staff's duties) and commander in chief of the combatant commanders. By way of illustration, the role of the IDF chief of staff combined Gen. Dwight D. Eisenhower's role as Supreme Allied Commander in Europe in World War II with that of Gen. George C. Marshall, the head of general staff of the American army, who built the armed forces and sent them into battle. The second reason for the Israeli chief of staff's power stems from the two-pronged challenge that he faces: from Israel's coalition-based government, to which the chief of staff is subordinate by law, and which must agree on political-security matters; and from the relative weakness (as stated by the Knesset's Foreign Affairs and Defense Committee) of the National Security Council—the organization that is supposed to support the prime minister and government on security matters.[8]

The role of chief of staff, as we know it today, has evolved over the years. But its roots can be traced to the prestate period before the establishment of the IDF. Ya'akov Dori, the first chief of staff, continued his previous role as chief of staff of the Hagana (the main pre-independence paramilitary organization), but the essence of the role then was entirely different from what we are familiar with today. (Dori dealt mainly with the organization and structure of the IDF and manpower, and much less with the actual management of the IDF in war.) A complex triad existed in the early years of the state consisting of Prime Minister David Ben-Gurion, "the person responsible for security"; Yisrael Galili, the head of the Hagana's national staff (a position akin to defense minister, that is, an intermediary between the political leadership and the Hagana); and Yigael Yadin as head of Agam and the officers of the general staff. Ben-Gurion, who was averse to a middleman between him and the military, gradually scaled down Galili's status to the point of invalidating it and, ultimately, fired Galili. For the greater part of the period, Dori was convalescing at home due to illness. Under these circumstances, the general staff officers, first and foremost Yadin, complained to Ben-Gurion that they were unable to work effectively unless the role of the IDF's supreme commander was clearly defined. Ben-Gurion's solution was to ask Galili to return and pick up where he left off but without the same powers as the chief of staff of the Hagana.[9] The termination of that role was part of Ben-Gurion's plan to tailor the role of defense minister and limit the role of chief of staff.

The IDF's second chief of staff, Yigael Yadin, served three years and resigned after a budgetary disagreement with Ben-Gurion. Yadin's replacement, Mordechai Maklef, stipulated his acceptance on serving for only one year. Thus, the role of the first three chiefs of staff was basically similar to the role of chief of staff of the Hagana, whose limitations Ben-Gurion had determined. The first chief of staff to serve four years was Moshe Dayan, whose aggressive command style inspired the IDF during the 1956 Sinai War. His blend of charisma and public image was a significant factor in shaping the role of the chief of staff as we know it today.

After Dayan, the status of the role fluctuated, with the main variables (but not the only ones) being (and remaining) Israel's security reality and the degree of authority given to the defense minister. The chief of staff's relative personal influence versus that of the defense minister and of the prime minister varied; examples include Chief of Staff Yitzhak Rabin under Prime Minister and Defense Minister Levi Eshkol, when Rabin was regarded as the senior security figure—that is, until Dayan assumed the role of defense minister on the eve of the Six-Day War; Chief of Staff Rafael Eitan and Defense Minister Ariel Sharon in the First Lebanon War; Chief of Staff Mofaz and Prime Minister Ehud Barak in the withdrawal from Lebanon; Chief of Staff Dan Halutz and Prime Minister Sharon in the Gaza disengagement; and Chief of Staff Halutz and Defense Minister Amir Peretz in the Second Lebanon War. Various examples of the ups and downs in the chief of staff's status relative to the political echelon are illustrated throughout this book.

Methodology: Defining the Role of the Chief of Staff and Choosing the Aspects for Analysis

The role of the chief of staff is defined as follows: "The chief of staff commands and controls the employment of the IDF and oversees its force design by means of the main headquarters and the services."[10] For my research, this definition has been divided into three subsidiary functions in addition to the basic C2 roles.

The primary role is to interpret and mediate among the political sphere's understandings, decisions, and rulings, the IDF's structure (for example, scope, organization, and capabilities), and the manner of applying the IDF in diverse confrontations while developing directions of action and formulating recommendations for the political echelon's decisions. In other words, on one hand, the chief of staff must develop capabilities and plans of action that are suited to Israel's security needs; on the other hand, he needs to see that the political echelon's decisions are congruent with the IDF's capabilities (size, organization, and available resources). This calls for the creation and encouragement of an interechelon dialogue and development of a common language.

The second role is determining the IDF's agenda, which includes priorities for the entire organization, generating changes, and dealing with their outcomes. Examples are Dayan's focus on the offensive fighting spirit; Dan Shomron's plans for long-term military transformation; and Mofaz's efforts to prepare the IDF for a confrontation with the Palestinians (see chapter 5).

The third role is determining and directing the IDF culture. The term "IDF culture" here includes the values that IDF commanders and soldiers operate by and their rules of conduct (for example, determining the degree of devotion to mission accomplishment and combat ethics on the battlefield and the attitude toward disciplinary infractions and sexual harassment).

Another aspect of the chief of staff's role, which is briefly discussed, is the management of an immense organization that also requires the appointment of generals and colonels to various posts, the chief of staff's ceremonial duties, and so on. This area of management is certainly not unique to military organizations and is characteristic of other domains, such as the political sphere. Some of these managerial aspects, especially communicating messages to vast audiences, appear in chapters 1 and 5.

A comparative analysis of the chief of staff's role in the three subsidiary functions is extremely complex and calls for further breakdown. By way of illustration, the first role—mediating the political echelon's understandings and decisions for IDF operations—was filled by Prime Minister–Defense Minister David Ben-Gurion in the War of Independence; in the Sinai War it was carried out by Chief of Staff Moshe Dayan; in the Six-Day War on the Golan Heights by the commander of Northern Command David Elazar; and in the Yom Kippur War by Chief of Staff David Elazar. In the First Lebanon War, Defense Minister Ariel Sharon filled the role. In the last three limited Gaza operations it was probably Defense Minister (and ex–chief of staff) Ehud Barak (Operation Cast Lead, 2008–9, and Operation Pillar of Defense, 2012) and Defense Minister (and ex–chief of staff) Moshe Ya'alon in Operation Protective Edge, 2014. In light of the above, comparative research in this field is elusive—if not impossible—due to the substantial influence of unique circumstances.

The chief of staff's role in determining the IDF agenda—priorities for the entire IDF—also defies comparison, especially in areas that are nonoperational and unconnected to "hardcore" force design (organization and weapons). Insofar as the chief of staff deals with a wide range of areas, different priorities may be determined simultaneously in different areas. These decisions tend to be specific to the time they are made. For example, it is very difficult to compare Eitan's emphasis on the integration of soldiers from low socioeconomic backgrounds into the IDF ("Raful's boys") with Mordechai "Motta" Gur's lowering of the threshold of enlistment in order to expand the size of available manpower after the Yom Kippur War; or to compare it with the integration of ultrareligious Jews into the IDF, the integration of women into combat units, and changes in the reserve force that recent chiefs of staff have introduced. These topics are worthy of further study and are not included in this book.

In conducting the first ever research on the chiefs of staff, I have chosen patterns of action and elements of the role whose common denominator is performance under extreme conditions: war, strategic change, or shifts in force design. As stated, the chief of staff's duties in periods of quiet are immense and sometimes extremely complex to carry out, but given the focus of the research they are not analyzed here. Although my chosen perspectives on the chief of staff's performance offer only a partial look, they are sufficient for gaining an understanding of the chiefs of staff's patterns of action. The book is divided into six chapters, each based on a particular criterion and containing a number of test cases that illustrate patterns of performance and manner of functioning of selected chiefs of staff.

The third role—determining and directing the IDF culture—will not be presented directly but is illustrated through a few of the test cases.

The researched aspects as they appear in the book are as follows:

The role of the chief of staff in identifying and declaring a change in reality and generating changes in the IDF to cope with it. This is one of the chief of staff's main tasks: preparing the military force after he identifies a change in the strategic situation. He has to order the IDF to prepare for the developing change, and in many instances he has to convince the political echelon of the need for the change. Chapter 1 deals with the mechanism for identifying the change and the manner in which the chief of staff gets the IDF to adapt to the new reality.

The need for a chief of staff from the ranks of either the ground or air forces to become equally familiar with the other domain, including war plans and mode of fighting. The chief of staff is responsible for employing the IDF in a spectrum of scenarios. Therefore, it is only logical that he must be knowledgeable in the use of air, land, and naval forces. Chapter 2 examines the degree of the chief of staff's familiarity and influence on the services that he is less familiar with. This analysis has a growing relevance as warfare becomes more interservice and multidomain.

Crises of confidence. The chief of staff may lose confidence in a general in wartime. This phenomenon has been observed a number of times. On more than one occasion it was justifiably claimed that tension-ridden relations between the chief of staff and the commander of a regional command had a direct effect on the performance of the forces and even the results of the war. Chapter 3 focuses on the dynamics that created the loss of trust.

Command of the IDF in a crisis following a war perceived as a failure. A military organization in crisis, especially after a confrontation that is seen as a failure, such as the Yom Kippur War, can have a direct impact on the chief of staff's ability to function properly. This may require the chief of staff to rehabilitate the forces. Chapter 4 looks at the chief of staff's actions after such a war and discusses the price these actions exacted in view of a future confrontation.

Leading a change in force design. Every chief of staff engages in force design. Our comparative analysis focuses on cases in which the chief of staff changed the previous period's directions of force design. Chapter 5 deals with the factors that led to the change and the chief of staff's handling of opposition to change.

Working relationships between the chief of staff and the political echelon on force design. As noted, the interface between the chief of staff and the political echelon is beyond the scope of this book and has already been the subject of many studies. The perspective that I have chosen for chapter 6 focuses on relatively limited topics in force design and presents a gamut of relationships between the chief of staff and the political echelon.

The Test Cases

For each angle of comparison, suitable and sufficiently documented test cases were selected that enable in-depth analysis. The chapters are constructed as follows: (1) a brief theoretical outline of the subject examined; (2) the test cases; and (3) a summary. In each chapter the analysis is adapted to the criterion of its subject. For the sake of convenience, the test cases are presented chronologically. This book is geared toward professional military audiences, academics, and the informed general reader. Therefore, I have sufficed with a short historical background to each test case.

Unavoidable overlap naturally exists between the criteria. One example: the change that Dayan introduced in the IDF before the Sinai War exemplifies, to a certain degree, command of a military organization during a crisis. Another example: Gur's decision to block the creation of the Ground Forces Headquarters after the Yom Kippur War is discussed in the chapter on working relationships between the chief of staff and the political echelon, but the chapter also includes changes in force design and is another angle of commanding the IDF in crisis.

Another matter that appears in some of the chapters is the difficulty in attributing a particular action to a specific chief of staff. This is especially true regarding long-range processes that continue through the tenure of more than one chief of staff, such as force design processes and command of the IDF during (or after) a crisis. In these instances, one of two approaches is taken: either a description of the conduct of two or more chiefs of staff, as in the case of establishing the Ground Forces Headquarters (see chapter 6), or singling out and focusing on the conduct of one figure in the succession of chiefs of staff.

1

IDENTIFYING CHANGE

One of the roles of the chief of staff is to identify an unexpected strategic shift at as early a date as possible, announce the change, and see that the necessary steps are taken in the IDF to prepare for it. Many information sources are available for tracking the emergence of a new situation, such as the military intelligence directorate (Aman) and other intelligence sources, as well as the chief of staff's firsthand interaction with the reality in the field. Whatever the provenance, the chief of staff must be able to recognize that a change is taking place in the security reality and decide when to act so that the IDF will have sufficient time to prepare. The case studies in this chapter illustrate that in some instances the chief of staff identified the change and prepared the IDF in advance. On other occasions, the change was obvious and the chief of staff had only to reconceptualize the situation and proceed in the right direction. In yet other instances, the chief of staff apparently failed to grasp the change and thus reacted relatively late.

The following six cases are presented chronologically: David Elazar, who ordered the Blue and White alert in May 1973 five months before the Yom Kippur War; Dan Shomron's relatively slow response to the outbreak of the first intifada in late 1987; Amnon Lipkin-Shahak's definition of routine security operations in the security zone in Lebanon in 1995 as a combat situation; Shaul Mofaz's preparation of the IDF in 2000 prior to the outbreak of the second intifada in October that year; Dan Halutz's failure to shift the IDF from a routine security mindset to a war mentality in the Second Lebanon War in 2006; and Benny Gantz's definition of the response to changes in the Golan Heights in 2011–13.

The examples here are "clear" cases, meaning that—regardless of each chief of staff's successes or failures in identifying and defining the emerging threats—each had a significant impact on the IDF. The study does not examine instances in which the chief of staff initiated changes that occurred over a long period of time and are therefore difficult to capture and define.

In the conclusion to this chapter, I analyze factors that helped each chief of staff gain an early understanding of the change, those that impeded his understanding, and those that either assisted or impeded the implementation of a change in the IDF after the chief of staff recognized the need for such.

It should be emphasized that identifying a change in the region and launching the IDF on the path of change are not solely the chief of staff's responsibility. The political echelon is also under obligation. One example is David Ben-Gurion's swift realization that the soon-to-be-declared state had to prepare for war with the Arab armies and the measures he took to attain this readiness. Another is Defense Minister Moshe Arens's establishment of the Home Front Command, a regional command responsible for civil defense, when he recognized the emerging missile threat to the civilian population.

David Elazar and the Announcement of the Blue and White Alert in May 1973

In April 1973, two and a half years after the War of Attrition with Egypt ended in August 1970, Lieutenant General David Elazar announced the Blue and White alert—raising the state of military readiness for conflict with Egypt—which remained in effect until August. The alert had a major impact on the IDF in the Yom Kippur War, which erupted on October 6 that year, because it allowed the IDF to acquire new equipment, organize units, and move bases closer to the borders. This enabled the army to meet the challenge admirably despite the war's strategic surprise for Israel.

Elazar's decision to order the alert ran contrary to Aman's official assessment. On Passover Eve (April 16, 1973), the chief of staff assembled the general staff and cynically warned that the meeting was not called "to hand out the traditional Passover holiday reading passages." Major General Eli Zeira, the head of Aman, repeated his estimate that no substantial change had occurred in Egyptian strength since the previous year's situation assessment at the end of 1972, and that the Libyan Mirage and Iraqi Hunter jet fighter planes that Egypt had received were incapable of altering the balance of airpower. Zeira said, "The probability of war is low, almost nonexistent—but it still exists." Many of the participants in the discussion agreed. Ariel Sharon, the commander of Southern Command, said that he felt prepared for a war in Sinai: "All in all, we're in very good shape regarding control measures and communications systems, command posts, and access roads to the Suez Canal." The head of the doctrine and training branch (Mahad), Major General Shmuel Gonen, on the other hand, believed that the IDF did not have to proceed according to this information as though there were no danger, "because if something does happen we won't be able to explain to ourselves and others that we thought that war wouldn't break out." Elazar said, "We must consider the warnings [of an Egyptian surprise attack] we've received with utmost seriousness and take full advantage of the coming month for intensive preparation." He focused on developing bridging equipment to cross the Suez Canal, refreshing operational plans, and elevating the state of readiness. He summed up the situation thus: "If war erupts next month or month and a half, we'll be able to respond with maximum effect." Prime Minister Golda Meir consulted with Elazar on April 18. Afterward, the chief of staff called another situation assessment meeting in which he said: "This time the warning—unlike the warnings of October, November, and December 1972—is more serious. If previously the probability was estimated at 'close to zero,' this time the likelihood seems higher, regardless of Aman's assessment that [Egyptian leader Anwar] Sadat won't open fire at this stage."[1]

Elazar judged the probability of Egypt opening fire sufficiently high to commence preparations, all of which would be in the form of updating plans. The chief of staff stipulated the implementation of practical preparations on additional intelligence signals that he anticipated in the coming days.[2]

In the ministerial committee on security affairs on April 24, the chief of staff stated:

> Even if I agree with the assessment of the head of Aman of low likelihood to this possibility—and I'm referring to the second part of the sentence, "low likelihood"—I still think that it is more likely than the two last [intelligence] warnings, in late 1972 and late 1971. And despite the low likelihood, we are forced to maintain a certain level of alert, which is what we're doing. The current alerts do not include troop mobilization or movement, but we're doing many other things.[3]

The Blue and White alert consisted of various steps to accelerate force buildup on the eve of war that had to be taken. The following are the main points:[4]

> *Organization.* The dates for establishing the following units were significantly advanced to the second half of 1973: the 210th Division (originally scheduled for March 1974); the 418th Ivry Missile Unit; the 440th Division Task Force Headquarters; three reconnaissance battalions (originally slated for August–November 1973); two assault roller bridging units; and two reserve engineer battalions.

Operational infrastructures. In the Golan Heights, anti-tank ditches, dirt roads, and landline communications systems were constructed, and two reserve brigade bases were moved closer to the Heights; in Sinai, reserve bases were established close to the Suez Canal. (The Agranat Report—the official postwar investigation committee on the failure in war preparations—found that Northern Command's early establishment of bases for reserve armored brigades closer to the border played a decisive role in their arrival in time to the Golan Heights to block the Syrian attack west into Israel.)

Equipment. Significant additions were made in communication systems, water-bridging equipment, and rocket launchers. R&D on tow bars for pulling the roller bridges (two-hundred-meter-long bridges for crossing the Suez Canal) at the steep lateral angles in the sand dunes in the Suez Canal area received top priority (regardless of cost) but failed to reach a suitable answer in time for the war.

Training. The early formation of units doubtless had a marked effect on the amount of training being carried out. Various training exercises were held, such as canal bridging for designated units. For example, the first training session for the 257th Armored Reserve Battalion/421st Brigade (established in April 1973) lasted ten days and was followed by a scaled-down divisional exercise in August. The 257th was originally scheduled to receive the tanks and equipment in 1974.

Alert. Calling an alert is not considered an element of force buildup. But in order to complete the picture, it is important to mention that on May 25, 1973, Agam began preparations for the mobilization of the reservists, which included checking emergency mobilization procedures; ordering regular army headquarters to test the call-up of reserve units and confirm home addresses; readying emergency stores units; dispatching mobile artillery units to Sinai; and hastily deploying bridging equipment.

Discussions were held on operational plans. In two meetings in late April and early May, the chief of staff affirmed all the operational plans. They were later presented to the defense minister and prime minister.[5] All these preparations took place while Israel was celebrating its twenty-fifth Independence Day in a mood of prosperity and confidence, oblivious to the rumblings of the approaching war. A summary of this intensive activity was presented in GHQ on May 8, one day after the gala Independence Day military parade.[6]

The Blue and White alert lasted four months (April to August) and ended without any hostile action or increased tension at the border. The price tag of 69 million Israeli lira (approximately $73 million in 2019 US dollars) improved significantly the IDF's preparedness for the Yom Kippur War, October 6–25, 1973.[7] Major General Israel Tal commented on the alert's effectiveness: "The IDF entered the Yom Kippur War stronger than what was planned for 1974–1975."[8]

In concluding this section, it should be stressed that the chief of staff issued the alert without Aman's backing. The head of Aman viewed with overt skepticism all of the possible scenarios that Elazar had laid out in detail. He regarded the outbreak of war as most unlikely and said that, as hard as he tried, he failed to find any signs of an increase in its likelihood. The discussions lasted over three weeks. GHQ assumed that Sadat may have had a "motive" and the threats should not be underestimated (an assumption shared by the ministers Dayan and Galili), but a significant difference existed between the assessments of the head of Aman (who also reports directly to the prime minister) and those of the chief of staff, a gap that remained throughout the period. Elazar also said that, based on available information, he agreed with the estimate that a low likelihood for war existed—but not a "very" low likelihood. On the contrary, he believed that "the likelihood is higher than at any time since 1967. All of the signs point to war—the intention to go to war and the preparation for war. Arab efficiency may lead to one or more postponements, but war is coming."[9]

Summary of the Test Case

Here is a positive example of the chief of staff's performance concerning identifying a change and acting upon it. Elazar's opposition to the head of Aman's recommendation began a process that included elements of force buildup—from the immediate renewal of emergency mobilization procedures to planning steps and finally to pushing up the date for establishing units and expediting weapons procurement—all of which had a crucial impact on the IDF's victory in the war. Since the intelligence analysis was conveyed directly to the political echelon (Prime Minister Meir, Dayan, and Galili), Elazar was allegedly "covered" (i.e., he was not required to act), and in this light his initiative to raise the level of alert was commendable.

One major issue that would later have an impact on the IDF's ability to contain the October 6, 1973, surprise attack by Egypt and Syria that launched the Yom Kippur War was the relative strength of the chief of staff's position compared to that of Zeira, the powerful head of Aman. As it turned out, war did not break out during the Blue and White alert, a fact that bolstered Zeira's views vis-à-vis Elazar and the political echelon when Zeira repeated that the likelihood of war in the autumn was low. This is an example of the relations between the chief of staff and the head of Aman, which will be dealt with briefly in the book's conclusion.

Dan Shomron at the Outbreak of the First Intifada, 1987

The first Palestinian intifada (Arabic: uprising) began in December 1987 after twenty years of Israeli occupation in the West Bank and Gaza Strip. The intensity of the insurrection waned by 1991 and formally ended with the Israeli-Palestinian Oslo Accord in 1993. The focus here is on its beginning. Before initiating our discussion on the conduct of Chief of Staff Dan Shomron in the first intifada, it is important to note that this type of conflict—mass civil rioting—was an unprecedented challenge for the IDF. Little wonder that the vocabulary employed in describing the IDF's actions in the December 1987 events included "surprise," "consternation," and "confusion," especially as the unrest in Gaza spread to the West Bank. When Defense Minister Yitzhak Rabin returned from abroad, Shomron and General Shmuel Goren, the Coordinator of Government Activities in the Territories (COGAT), were waiting at the airport to update him on events. The general staff did not consider the riots of December 9–10 as something out of the ordinary and still believed that order would be restored in a few days.

The outbreak of the intifada caught all of the security forces off guard. The deputy head of Agam, General Giora Romm, publicly acknowledged this: "The IDF was surprised by the riots in the West Bank and Gaza." Aman, too, was caught off balance. It had not focused on dealing with an uprising, mass disturbances, or civil disobedience but rather on preventing terror. The IDF and the Shin Bet (Israel's internal security agency, also called the Shabak) argued over who was responsible for gathering data and providing intelligence, since no one had defined which party was in charge of a general assessment in this area and no entity existed for dealing with it. The commander of Southern Command, Major General Yitzhak Mordechai, was the first to grasp what was happening in the Gaza Strip. He demanded immediate reinforcements. He wanted regulars sent to Gaza to deal with the new phenomenon. He was worried that the situation might deteriorate because of the lack of sufficient manpower. He did not want the troops on the ground facing thousands of rioters, lest they be forced to open fire. Mordechai transferred to the Gaza Strip a battalion of regulars from the Givati (Infantry) Brigade that was on training, despite the order that training could not be halted without permission from the chief of staff.[10]

In an interview, Mordechai claimed, "It took Shomron some time to realize that a basic change had occurred on the ground." According to Mordechai, Shomron "made every effort to keep the troops to their training schedule and maintain their operational capability for war." Mordechai felt that Shomron's misreading of the situation compelled the commanders of the regional commands to pressure him to allocate troops and resources to quelling the intifada.[11] The attitude of the Southern and Central Command generals vis-à-vis the chief of staff's attitude toward the suspension of training and military education courses became an issue of contention. Shomron wanted to see the regular units prepare for war. He opposed any curtailment of the IDF commanders' training programs because of routine security operations and unrest in the West Bank and Gaza. Furthermore, he regarded the events in the Gaza Strip as part of the Palestinians' periodical letting off steam. During his tour in Gaza on December 15, he spoke with commanders and soldiers and came away with the impression that the wave of rioting would soon pass. But Mordechai doggedly pressed Shomron for more reinforcements.

Even the Shin Bet's support of Southern Command's requests failed to convince the chief of staff. In the general staff meeting of Sunday, December 20, most of the participants felt that the riots were only a case of disorderly conduct. The head of Aman, Amnon Lipkin-Shahak, who had previously served as the commander of Central Command, visited Bethlehem on Saturday, December 19, and left with the impression that the situation was indeed severe. All the shops were shuttered, even though Christmas was approaching. Nevertheless, the general staff considered Lipkin-Shahak's description and warnings as exaggerated.

On Friday, December 18, the chief of staff helicoptered to the Gaza Strip. The visit came in the wake of a heated conversation with the previous defense minister, Ezer Weizman, who rebuked Shomron, "You seem to have lost control over there!" Shomron assured him that he had not but decided to see for himself. At this point he changed his position and ordered the immediate reinforcement of men and material.[12]

The commander of Central Command, Major General Amram Mitzna, was of the same opinion. Mitzna, like Shomron, had assumed at the start of the intifada that he could contain it without recourse to additional strength. Romm, the deputy head of Agam, accompanied Shomron on a tour of the army units. He recalled how in the meeting with Mitzna someone slipped a note into the room stating that a Palestinian had been killed in the Jenin area (northern West Bank). Thirty minutes later the chief of staff received a report that riots had erupted in Wadi Ara (a major east-west axis inside Israel with Arab villages lining both sides of the road). Romm said later, "Shomron's countenance fell. Only then did it hit him that the intifada was not a fleeting phenomenon." Romm recalled that on the flight back "we saw flags of Palestine draped on all the roofs, and it finally dawned on us that something was taking place much deeper than the usual riots we had been accustomed to quelling according to routine procedures."[13]

In retrospect, not sending reinforcements at the beginning of the intifada was a mistake. Events spiraled out of control, the IDF lost its deterrent strength, and violence in the West Bank and Gaza spiked. The small forces that were operating on the ground found themselves in precarious situations and opened fire when they felt their lives threatened. In the first month of the intifada this often happened. As a result, twenty-six Palestinians were killed, which only exacerbated the rioting.[14]

Shomron's difficulty in defining the situation as a new reality that demanded a new answer, and the subsequent gaps in the troops' preparation for new tasks, can be seen in the general staff's discussions in the first days of the intifada. In a GHQ meeting on December 14, Shomron said:

> This produced a rising wave of demonstrations. The IDF should put an end to them and restore the previous state of affairs rather than reach a situation in which it has to enter the refugee camps.

This had to be completed by the end of the week as the Christmas holidays were fast approaching with Fatah Day [named for the largest faction of the Palestine Liberation Organization, or PLO] coming after them. Since we have to suppress the riots before the holidays, we brought in additional forces. Difficult as this is, we have to release forces from training and instruction. We will then concentrate large numbers of troops and deploy large-scale units since most of the [Palestinian] fatalities occurred when a small force found itself up against a crowd and had to open fire to protect itself.[15]

Nevertheless, Shomron ordered his deputy Major General Ehud Barak to upgrade crowd dispersal methods. On the same day, Barak called a meeting to discuss weapons for crowd dispersal in the West Bank and the Gaza Strip. The summary of the meeting states that Barak approved the proposal of the head of the operations division (within Agam) for the acquisition of concussion grenades, tear gas projectiles, and rubber truncheons for crowd dispersal, and ordered some of the weapons to be immediately purchased. An order was also given for the immediate production of tear gas grenades, barriers, and roadblocks.[16]

On December 18, Shomron held a meeting to discuss the situation in the West Bank and Gaza. The meeting opened with the report that three locals had been killed and several wounded during rioting in the Gaza Strip. Shomron spoke about the events in the West Bank and Gaza and admitted that he honestly thought that the discussion would focus on "the next stage," but because of "the reports coming in from Gaza today, at this very moment, it seems that things have taken a step back." He expressed his disappointment over the failure to prevent deaths during riot dispersal and his apprehension that the situation would spin out of control.

Shomron summed up the meeting by saying that the IDF had to deal with events that had attained a new level of intensity. "We can't simply disengage from the problem-infested West Bank and Gaza. We have to maintain law and order in the whole of the Strip, not only on the main road, otherwise the mobs will take over." In his opinion, a curfew had to be enforced in the riots' hot spots and the instigators arrested. "The problem is that we don't have much time. External pressure is mounting and causing very great damage," the chief of staff emphasized.

The entire discussion was held under the pressure of the events and of the minimal time allotted for discussion. The chief of staff appeared impatient throughout the hour-and-a-half meeting and apologized, "I have a flight [to the Gaza Strip] waiting for me." On other occasions he even asked the speakers to keep their comments short. His approach is astounding against the background of the reality on the ground and the need for an in-depth discussion. Be that as it may, during the meeting no one dared to warn of the danger of a popular uprising or civil rebellion, even though the shadow of the threat permeated the air.[17]

Three days later, on December 21, the situation in the West Bank and Gaza was again raised in a general staff meeting. And again the participants expected the return of quiet to be close at hand. The chief of staff summed up the meeting: "A basic discussion on the situation in the West Bank and Gaza will be held in the general staff forum at the first opportunity after things calm down; the main problem right now is to create that quiet."[18]

On December 28, a general staff meeting was held on events in the West Bank and Gaza. It was clear that Shomron's perception of the phenomenon had changed and that he was now aware that "something different" was brewing in the West Bank and Gaza. Shomron stated that after the previous day's tour of Gaza and his talks with the troops, he realized that the soldiers' mindset had to be dealt with (the soldiers had been trained to think in terms of attack and defense, and withdrawal as beneath their dignity). He emphasized that they had to be made aware that they were no longer involved in strictly military operations but in policing assignments. A police officer doesn't fight the people, he said; his job is to maintain law and order. The troops have to be taught that in order to prevent the streets from exploding in violence, they often have to avoid killing the enemy and allow the demonstrators to let off steam. Later, after the riots, they can make arrests. "We're up against a new kind of situation, [and] given the large number of IDF forces in the streets, we have to disperse the riots swiftly," Shomron said.[19]

Barak, however, perceived the situation differently. On January 7, 1988, in the weekly situation assessment chaired by the deputy chief of staff, the discussion signaled a turnabout in the general staff's position on the situation in the West Bank and the Gaza Strip. Barak agreed with Brigadier General Ilan Biran (head of the operations division within Agam) that although the events in the West Bank and the Gaza Strip were the main issue, the weekly situation assessment created thinking solely in terms of terror attacks and tactical intelligence warnings instead of a broad estimation of the strategic situation. Therefore, Barak ordered that starting next week Aman would also present its estimate of the situation: "If the head of Aman sees this as a departure from Aman's mandate, then a representative from the Shin Bet will join the forum and present its data and assessment of the riots, subversion, demonstrations, etc., in the West Bank and Gaza."[20]

In the January 10 forum, chaired by Defense Minister Rabin, Barak defined the level of unrest as critical. Its main features were (1) massive demonstrations that included fatalities that inflamed the rioting and (2) media documentation that fueled the motivation for turbulence and hurt the security system's image, detracting from its ability to maintain control—all of which caused long-term damage resulting from the need to deploy large numbers of forces for suppressing the uprising. In order to comprehend the situation better, Barak said, "we need an integrated situation assessment based on input from Aman, the Shin Bet, and COGAT."[21]

On January 18, 1988, more than a month after the start of the events, Shomron appeared to finally come around to realizing that they should be seen as a deep-seated conflict, although he hoped that the clashes would end soon. In his summary of the discussion, Shomron stated that the outbreak of the intifada was the result of a rupture in the balance between the Palestinians' desire for statehood and their economic situation. From IDF's point of view, he said, "[since] the balance was upset, military deterrence was needed to restore it."[22] The January 25 general staff discussion illustrated the contrast between the chief of staff and his deputy's understanding and definition of the situation. Shomron expressed his satisfaction that the soldiers had been briefed as ordered and knew what was expected of them. He said that the coming period would be a test of the force that the IDF was employing and the use of collective punishment to create deterrence in the West Bank and the Gaza Strip: "Since the curfew has been lifted in most areas, we can check if deterrence is working and if it's possible to return to a normal way of life." Barak claimed that the current situation was the result of a process, part of which had been going on for two decades (since the occupation of the West Bank and Gaza in the Six-Day War) and some of which had been manifested in the last ten years, triggered by various events. The current situation, he said, was a national-social-political expression led by youth and backed by massive support of the general public. This situation could be expected to continue in ups and downs in the coming years. Shomron said that the struggle against the riots in the West Bank and Gaza was having a serious impact on Israeli society and other circles, such as friendly countries, the Arab world, and Israel's Arab citizens. Thus, the army had to restore quiet. The IDF had no lack of manpower to carry out the mission but was strapped by the way Israeli society perceived itself and the world's expectations of the country. The government was responsible for the lives of the people in the West Bank and Gaza; therefore, it decided at the initial outburst of disturbances not to crush them with overwhelming force but to let the exploding energy run its course. At one point, quiet did return briefly, and when the rioting rebounded the only alternative was to prevent the consolidation of the demonstrations. This required the use of force to disperse the rioters and the imposition of curfews wherever a rock was thrown. On the other hand, those who wanted to go to work and open their shops had to be allowed to do so. According to the chief of staff, this was the correct policy. At this stage Shomron thought that deterrence was restored in the West Bank, and Gaza was close to calming down.[23]

Major General Yossi Peled, the commander of Northern Command, stated that the IDF's surprise and confusion and the chief of staff's failure to appreciate the seriousness of the situation were sensed in Northern Command: "We weren't immune to it." The command was ordered to send a large number of its units, stationed on the Lebanese border, to the West Bank and Gaza and to cut back on the training of regular army and reservist units. Peled recalled:

> When I look back on this period I see mainly confusion. Today I know that we weren't prepared to deal with this type of uprising. We simply failed to read the map correctly. That's why we weren't ready for what happened. How could so dramatic an event spring up from under the ground we stood on without our perceiving it? There was also a moral indecision. How does a modern army cope with women and children?
>
> Bewilderment was the reason for the general staff's behavior. I don't remember whether we held a single marathon meeting. I can't recall any systematic thinking on the matter. I remember the chief of staff distributing a dry, condensed report in Monday meetings. I remember the reports of the unit commanders. That's all.[24]

In a March 1989 television interview, Shomron himself admitted that he had been caught by surprise and had misjudged the events: "During the first weeks of the intifada I hoped and believed that economic conditions would eventually bring most of the people back to the path of normalcy. But their tenacity and willingness to endure economic hardship was greater than I thought."[25]

Harsh criticism of Shomron's and Barak's conduct in defining the situation and its implications was written by Major General Moshe Bar-Kochva, a member of the general staff and the assistant chief of staff for lesson learning from the First Lebanon War: "It was the chief of staff's duty in the first days and weeks of the intifada to grasp the operational situation correctly. He should have recognized more precisely its true nature and inherent dangers and not have related to the initial events lightly and disparagingly as merely local incidents that would quickly subside." And later, "As an alternative to the concoction of improvisations that the troops had to carry out, the chief of staff should have devised a comprehensive operational plan for terminating the uprising, as a basic guideline for the commands and divisions in drawing up their plans. . . . The befuddlement that surrounded the intifada came to symbolic expression in the endless uncertainty in the military campaign in choosing a term for what they were up against. For months they didn't know what to call it: a rampage, disorder, riots, unrest, civil revolt, rebellion, war, etc."[26]

Journalists Ze'ev Schiff and Ehud Ya'ari summed up the period, writing that several days after the start of the uprising it was obvious that the IDF was unprepared for this type of challenge. Its rich military experience lay in an entirely different realm of fighting. The numerous wars it had fought, the commando operations, and the extensive military actions, including those against terrorist organizations, had produced an exceptionally seasoned army whose skill was gained from the decades-old conflict with regular armies and terrorist organizations. Its successes as well as its blunders and failures were taken as lessons and passed on from one generation of commanders to the next. In this way, commanders learned from past experience. "And now, for the first time in many years, the IDF is suddenly faced with a situation unlike any it had ever experienced: a civil uprising of the masses," they wrote. "Not a war against tanks, airplanes, artillery or terrorists, but of coping with rocks and Molotov cocktails, without recourse to live ammunition." They noted that for some reason this possibility had never been conceived in the scenarios that Israel had planned for. The twenty years of Israeli occupation in the West Bank and Gaza had witnessed waves of rioting, but they had never encompassed such huge crowds that included women and children in so many places simultaneously. They never persisted for so long and in view of globally connected television cameras. This time the IDF was confronted with an entirely different kind of threat, ironically in a theater that until now was considered only a marginal nuisance. The general staff was stuck in confusion. At first the military command was reluctant to put more boots on the ground. When it finally did, it did not know how to employ them against the throngs of civilian demonstrators. The army was simply at a loss as to how to disperse the demonstrations professionally. The soldiers had never trained for this type of assignment.[27]

Barak, the deputy chief of staff, stated in an interview that to the best of his knowledge, Shomron understood one very important factor: that he had to keep Palestinian casualties to a minimum. Therefore, he refrained from sending untrained forces on crowd dispersal missions. As a result, small contingents of soldiers were frequently caught in situations in which they had to open fire. It took time until the IDF acquired the necessary equipment for crowd control and more time until the equipment was tested and authorized for use.[28]

Summary of the Test Case

In summing up the period, we can say that the violent demonstrations that erupted on December 9, 1987, surprised the security forces in general and Chief of Staff Shomron in particular, who, at the outset, seem to have expected the disturbances to run out of steam quickly. But this was not to be. In the first stage, the army lacked the proper tools and skills for suppressing the demonstrations. Small units found themselves facing large-scale rioting and had to use live ammunition to extricate themselves. These actions led to fatalities on the Palestinian side, expanded the dimensions of the riots, and put Israel in an unfavorable light in the world's eyes. As the clashes continued, the army developed effective tools and methods of action for grappling with the new reality. Examples included strengthening the troops in the West Bank and the Gaza Strip by shifting regular forces from training and courses and sending reservists to reinforce the regulars; introducing a designated training program; procuring the necessary equipment; restructuring headquarters; and implementing a policy of curfews, arrests, and expulsions.[29]

Shomron's conduct exhibits a certain degree of repression of reality, wishful thinking that things would work out and the situation would return to its former state. Why did it take him so long to identify the phenomenon if the commander of Southern Command, Yitzhak Mordechai, and the deputy chief of staff, Ehud Barak, clearly stated that a different answer was needed? It seems that Shomron's undeniable experience in conventional combat and in special operations against terrorists may have clouded his perception of the rising Palestinian violence. His inexperience in the Palestinian arena also hampered his understanding of the depth of the change, contrary to the perceptions of Barak, a former commander of Central Command. To Shomron's credit, it can be said that he identified the emerging trends in ground warfare and introduced an important change in this area (see chapter 5) despite significant opposition in the army. This change may have occupied a great deal of his time and caused him to downplay the developing situation.

Another difficulty in identifying and analyzing the events in the Palestinian arena may have stemmed from the lack of meaningful dialogue between the political and military spheres. The absence of direct communication, as well as the absence of war games, for example, dealing with a popular uprising in the West Bank and the Gaza Strip, could have been the reasons why the IDF stumbled into the intifada vortex without adequate plans of action and with a glaring deficiency in preparations for such a contingency.

Amnon Lipkin-Shahak and Hostilities in the Security Zone in Lebanon, 1995

Little research has been done on the eighteen years of fighting that began with the First Lebanon War in 1982 and ended with the IDF's withdrawal from Lebanon in 2000, and the gaps in this case study limit its scope. Nevertheless, enough evidence can be found to illustrate the manner in which the chief of staff did (or did not) identify major shifts in the Lebanese arena, including the change in the enemy and the change in the nature of the fighting.

In the decade between the IDF's withdrawal in 1985 (and the establishment of the "security zone" in southern Lebanon), and Amnon Lipkin-Shahak's promotion to chief of staff in 1995, hostile events in the security zone escalated. The Shiite Hezbollah organization developed a wide range of capabilities by 1995, including anti-tank missiles, sophisticated mining methods, high-trajectory fire, and assaults on Israeli strongholds. Before Lipkin-Shahak became chief of staff (that is, during the period of Shomron and Barak), the military activity in the security zone was seen as "routine security operations" that did not require a special effort on the part of the general staff regarding intelligence orientation and the development of designated units and weapons. When Lipkin-Shahak stepped into the office of chief of staff, he announced that the "routine security" mindset was over and that the IDF was now engaged in "combat" against a terrorist and guerrilla organization.

The summary of the March 27, 1995, routine security conference, chaired by the newly instated chief of staff, offers a look at the IDF's understanding of the issue. Lipkin-Shahak emphasized the importance and vast resources invested in routine security activity on the northern border, in the West Bank, and in Gaza, as well as in other sectors. He stressed that in some outposts in the security zone in Lebanon, "the soldiers feel as though they're in combat, and their feedback is very similar to that of troops in wartime, yet somewhat different, but the situation can definitely be defined as war." To better deal with this scenario, he ordered the Ground Forces HQ (Mafhash) to put more money into weapon systems designated for the fighting in the security zone, to instill lessons learned from this fighting in the military schools and training bases, and to update doctrine and disseminate it to the forces. From the air force he demanded an improvement in cooperation with the ground forces in the form of joint air-ground fighting during routine security activity.

Lipkin-Shahak reiterated the importance and centrality of routine security, which was, in effect, "our daily war and which will undoubtedly impact our performance in an all-out war if the need arises." He added, "Routine security has an influence on deterrence. All our successful and unsuccessful routine security activities affect the general deterrence, especially on deterring Hezbollah and Hamas." He said he considered "routine security to be our most critical combat assignment today, therefore it will receive top priority in the IDF's activity. If the necessary attention, thought, and resources are invested in improving routine security, better results will surely follow."[30] Although the chief of staff opened the meeting using the term "routine security" for the operations on the northern border and in the West Bank and Gaza, it seems that the example he brought from the Lebanese front reflected his understanding of the need to improve military activity there.

The practical result of the change in definition was that activity on the Lebanese front would be defined as combat operations in four areas: intelligence, organization, taking the offensive, and weapons and replenishment.

> *Intelligence.* Several commanders mentioned that a significant improvement appeared to have been achieved in Aman. The brigade commander of the eastern sector of the Israeli-Lebanese border, Moshe Tamir, found that vital intelligence was received and the results felt in the field only after Lipkin-Shahak defined security activity in the fighting area as "combat" and enlisted the entire army to the campaign.[31]

> General Tamir Yadai said that upon becoming commander of the Golani Brigade's 13th Battalion in 1997, he encountered an entirely different reality from what he had known only two years earlier (when he served as military assistant to the

deputy chief of staff). He recalled that one such change was intelligence's capabilities and the dissemination of information to echelons in the field. During his tenure as deputy battalion commander, he had the impression that intelligence was only at a general level and presented mainly scenarios of existing threats in the whole region, without a specific focus. When General Effi Eitam assumed command of the Galilee Division in 1997, the force's method of operation was changed by making greater use of Aman's available intelligence.[32] Eitam stated that, at first, the head of Aman refused to convey primary source intelligence to the divisional level, fearing it would be leaked, and therefore it remained solely at the regional command level while relevant information failed to reach the division in time. A major change was introduced, and the division began receiving primary source material.[33]

Organization. On becoming chief of staff in February 1995, Lipkin-Shahak established the Egoz commando unit for the war against Hezbollah. The unit, consisting of fighters from other crack units, was led by Lieutenant Colonel Erez Zukerman of Shayetet 13 (Israel's Navy SEALs). Egoz's mission was to carry out commando operations in the security zone, develop counterguerrilla tactics, and become expert in all aspects of infantry warfighting against Hezbollah.

According to Yadai, the unit was designed to bridge the gap between the regular infantry battalions and the elite Golani reconnaissance unit. The Egoz unit quickly accomplished its goal and transformed the fighting methods through widespread ambushes. The unit also served as the spearhead for the entire IDF in improving capabilities and testing combat techniques.[34] Major General Moshe Kaplinsky, who also commanded the Galilee Division, said, "Egoz's actions influenced the rest of the units and altered the perception of fighting in Lebanon with an emphasis on counterguerrilla warfare."[35]

Training was transformed regarding the length of time and quality of preparation needed for line duty in Lebanon. Nitzan Nuriel, the Northern Command's Eliakim training base commander from 1992 to 1994, recalled that he recognized the importance of tightening the link between the Galilee Division, responsible for guarding the border, and the liaison unit in Lebanon (a unit designated for commanding the Israeli troops within the security zone and overseeing cooperation between the IDF and the South Lebanese Army, which Israel funded and supported), so that lessons could be circulated swiftly. In the early 1990s, predeployment training suddenly became longer as training for war was shortened due to the intensive deployment of units in the West Bank and the Gaza Strip.[36]

The guerrilla school that opened in Nachal Si'on—in addition to Northern Command's Eliakim training base—prepared battalions for special in-depth operations, extended operations in enemy territory, ambushes in dense vegetation, and deployment in extreme conditions.[37]

Taking the offensive. A more offensive approach began in 1994 under the commander of Northern Command, Major General Amiram Levin. The period of Levin's command witnessed the intensive use of special forces against specific targets. Hitting the terrorists on their own turf, sometimes in depth, was one of the principal features of Levin's operational concept. The general brought his vast experience in commando operations to the war against Hezbollah and spurred the units to raise the threshold of their operational abilities.[38]

Weapons and replenishment. Weapons went through many changes and improvements. The multiyear Mirkam 2000 plan, which emphasized an answer to the terror threat, characterized Lipkin-Shahak's tenure as chief of staff, during which investment in routine security increased severalfold. The steps taken included: providing stronghold protection in Lebanon against mortar fire and anti-tank missiles; equipping troops with protected vehicles and improved protection on armored combat vehicles (ACVs); beefing up the intelligence effort; and procuring intelligence-gathering equipment. The investment in routine security was adapted to the more offensive approach.[39]

Eitam also pointed to the growing need for protection against Hezbollah's anti-tank threat and its high-quality explosive devices. The heavy armored personnel carrier *Nakpadon* was developed with the help of the deputy chief of staff, Major General Matan Vilnai, and the head of the Merkava Tank Administration, Major General (ret.) Israel Tal. Because of Hezbollah's improved high-trajectory fire, the IDF had to stiffen protection in the strongholds and construct reinforced roofs. The improvements in intelligence collection assets included deployment of sensors linked to tactical operations centers, deployment of the Nurit mortar fire spotting system, and artillery capability for closing the circle.[40] Eitam received command of the division in 1997, but the bulk of the changes that he described began earlier when Lipkin-Shahak focused the IDF's attention on the fighting in Lebanon.

Another change in this period was the installation of special anti-tank protection on the Merkava tank. Changes in the protection of the Merkava Mark IIB—a relatively advanced, improved version of the Mark II—were introduced in the hull and turret. At first, Ground Forces HQ (Mafhash), under the command of General Amos Malka, rejected the proposed improvement, because Malka believed that a reduction in casualties would be achieved not only by reinforced protection but also by a change in the operational approach. After the bid to protect a limited number of tanks engaged in routine security was postponed due to cost, the assistant defense minister, Tal, designed additional protection and a routine security kit for the Merkava Mark II until approval for the model was granted. Only when several tanks were hit did the chief of staff realize the urgency for a limited number of tanks to be equipped with improved protection kits adapted to the Lebanese theater and authorize their installation. The Mark III was also provided with an advanced protection kit. Since the Mark III was designed on the modularity principle, it was relatively simple to introduce changes in the kit. Subsequently scores of Mark IIs and Mark IIIs were installed with advanced protection kits.[41]

Lipkin-Shahak had the support of Defense Minister Rabin, who took a personal interest in the creation of the Egoz unit, approved the upgrade of stronghold protection, and ordered an improvement in the intelligence effort.[42]

Summary of the Test Case

In the decade between the staged pull-out from Beirut (which the IDF had partly occupied in 1982) to the security zone in south Lebanon (February–June 1985) and Lipkin-Shahak's appointment to chief of staff, the IDF regarded its routine security procedures and capabilities as sufficient for defending the border.[43] A variety of assumptions and constraints, some of them political, dictated the fighting. Only after Lipkin-Shahak announced that the IDF "is engaged in a stubborn protracted war in several sectors, [and that] routine security is today's most important combat mission and will receive top priority" were changes introduced and improvements made in such areas as intelligence, organization, and replenishment. The trigger was probably Hezbollah's slow but continuous improvement in fighting capability that caused the IDF an increasing number of casualties and the embarrassing incident at the Dla'at outpost (October 29, 1994), when Hezbollah photographed its fighters hoisting the Hezbollah flag on the outer perimeter of the outpost. The key agents of change were the commanders of Northern Command, the Galilee Division, and brigades, without whose tenacity and perseverance change would have been impossible.

Shaul Mofaz Prior to the Second Intifada, 1999–2000

The seven years between the Oslo agreement in 1993 that formally ended the first intifada and the beginning of the second intifada in 2000 were characterized as multiple rounds of "two steps forward and one step back" between the Israelis and the Palestinians. While Israel transferred authority to the newly established Palestinian Authority (PA) in Jericho and Gaza, allowed Palestinian leader Yasser Arafat to return from his exile in Tunisia, and signed follow-on agreements including the Oslo 2 Accord in 1995 and the Hebron Protocol in 1997, Hamas suicide attacks in Israeli cities took a heavy toll on Israeli civilians. Arafat mildly condemned the attacks but did next to nothing to stop them. Israel hesitated in moving forward with the process but was fundamentally committed to its implementation.

This case study describes what happens when the chief of staff's understanding that war is about to erupt runs contrary to political and public sensibilities. The chief of staff, the generals of Central and Southern commands, and others on the GHQ realized that if the peace process with the PA fell through, a major confrontation would follow. It must be noted that Shaul Mofaz had firsthand experience in the Palestinian arena as commander of the Judea and Samaria (West Bank) Division and as commander of Southern Command. The IDF had a relatively long time to prepare for the confrontation. In 1999, because of Mofaz's insight, notwithstanding the promises of peace being touted by the Barak government, 600 million shekels (about $213 million) were diverted in time to close the replenishment gap for fighting in the West Bank and Gaza. When the clash did erupt, the army had already completed the mental preparation for formulating its modus operandi and penetrating the Palestinians' rationale for action. Nevertheless, in later periods of the fighting, serious shortages were apparent in certain areas.[44]

In the first weeks of the confrontation, when it became clear that the Palestinians intended to inflict casualties on Israel, the IDF took pride in its preparations. The cliché that the army always plans for the last war seems to have been off the mark in this case. The correlation between the scenarios that the army was ready for and the prompt identification of deficiencies enabled the IDF to score pinpoint victories over the enemy.[45] Moshe Ya'alon, the commander of Central Command before the confrontation and deputy chief of staff during it, describes the incongruity between the public atmosphere and the chief of staff and his generals' discernment of events:

> The public atmosphere made an about-turn that year. It was awash in euphoria, it sensed the end of the conflict and that peace was around the corner. A wide gulf was created between the IDF's preparations, especially in Central and Southern commands, and the public mood. Later they blamed us that war broke out due to our preparations, as though it were a case of self-fulfilling prophecy. . . . But during the year 2000 I found myself girding the army for war and expecting war even when at the same time a large part of the public was preparing for peace.[46]

Mofaz, the general staff, and especially Ya'alon of Central Command and Major General Yom Tov Samia, the commander of Southern Command, crystallized their realization as the events of September 2000 approached. This understanding already began to form in the years preceding the outbreak of the second intifada.

According to the December 22, 1997, situation assessment for the coming year, Agat laid out the expected scenarios in the Palestinian arena. It raised the possibility of violent clashes with the Palestinians that might lead to an all-out confrontation and Israel's reoccupation of Area A (Palestinian Authority autonomous areas). The commander of Central Command, Major General Uzi Dayan, brought up the question of readiness for a prolonged engagement with the Palestinians in

1998: "I can't say what's really needed for such a situation. . . . I'm not adequately protected. . . . I don't think our security is up to par. . . . I want it understood that the likelihood of confrontations like these in the West Bank needs only some kind of trigger. . . . In my opinion our intelligence-gathering coverage of the Palestinian autonomy is flawed."[47]

The head of Agat, Major General Shlomo Yanai, wanted to keep the budget allocation as it was. In his opinion, the Burning Steel plan for a confrontation with the PA already envisaged and took into consideration a major flare-up in the PA that would require the use of force and the proper means to "provide the command with an answer to its needs." Mofaz, deputy chief of staff at the time, called for "another round of preparations in 1998 . . . including designated training for increased readiness and preparation." In a summary of the discussion, Lipkin-Shahak said: "I believe that a confrontation with the Palestinians will have repercussions on our entire region, but even if it doesn't affect our work plan, it could still impact it with implications for wider areas." Thus, we see that Mofaz's understanding paralleled that of the commanders of Central and Southern commands but differed from that of the chief of staff and the head of Agat.

On July 9, 1998, Mofaz was promoted to chief of staff. The peace process continued with peaks and troughs. In April 2000, the Forward Drive exercise was a milestone in the IDF's preparations. The exercise was designed to test the army's general readiness, understandings, deployment, and responses if violence erupted in the Palestinian arena, and to present the general staff, the commands, and the divisions in the West Bank and the Gaza Strip with probable scenarios of deterioration in view of the political processes. The exercise gave practical expression to the impact of all the processes on the Palestinian population and leadership: the intensification of violence, Israel's counterresponse, escalation, and the culmination that would come with Arafat's declaration of Palestinian statehood.[48]

The summary of the exercise highlighted the need to formulate and determine all aspects of forces employment. The Judea and Samaria Division realized that communication between the command and general staff had to improve, and understandings and terminology had to be clarified (like "containment" and "road networking"). A uniform knowledge map was prepared for the Burning Steel, Field of Thorns, and Fortress operational plans.

The exercise exposed manpower shortfalls and equipment deficiencies. Central Command's internal summary also pointed to the absence of contingency plans such as priorities for retaining locations in areas A and B; a list of springboards and targets; and road networking in the area. At the general staff level, the summary of Forward Drive served as the knowledge basis for strategic readiness and preparation for the next likely confrontation—the declaration of Palestinian statehood in September 2000. In the generals' forum, Mofaz discussed the need to keep in mind that "some of the [lessons] had already been assimilated from Nakba Day 2000" (the violent outbreak on Palestinian Remembrance Day that commemorated their loss of homeland in the 1948 war), such as deepening knowledge of low-intensity conflict (the warfighting doctrine), dealing with civilian violence, exacting a price from the Palestinians, and being aware of the cost of confrontation. The chief of staff attributed importance to slashing the Palestinians' ability to injure troops and civilians based on his realization that the number of casualties and the price of confrontation would be key factors in decision making. He brought up the issue of mutually comprehensible terminology and orders for opening fire, especially as regarded tanks and attack helicopters.

The May 5, 2000, Nakba Day was a "rehearsal" for developments later that year. In the July 4 general staff summary of April's Forward Drive exercise, Mofaz called attention to the fact that since the general staff assessment had taken into account the deterioration in the situation, the work year of 2000 would henceforth be called "the year of preparation," with an emphasis on training for operational deployment in the West Bank and Gaza, upgrading the training facilities, creating a doctrine workshop for expanding a common language, and carrying out preparatory exercises at the regional brigade level. The chief of staff estimated that, in light of the political crisis, "a showdown with the Palestinians would probably occur in the coming weeks."[49]

The Judea and Samaria Division, which bore the main brunt of the friction with the Palestinians, worked on honing its readiness and capabilities as the target date of an expected clash in September 2000 approached (the estimated date of Arafat's declaration of statehood). Preparations according to the Magic Melody plan included merging the Burning Steel and Field of Thorns plans; adding infantry ORBAT to the Binyamin and Etzion brigades; enhancing anti-tank capabilities; and adding mechanical and engineering equipment for road networking. A model was designed for dealing with armed riots and other events.[50] Moshe Ya'alon, the commander of Central Command until August 2000, described his part in preparing the command:

> I realized that we had to prepare for a war in September 2000. It was obvious that the forces had to be trained and made ready for a new type of conflict. This required erecting a mock Palestinian village in the Beit Guvrin training base, where regular army and reservist battalions could train prior to their posting in the West Bank. In May 2000 I convened all the commanders of the regular army and reserve units, from battalion level up, at the Ammunition Hill Memorial Site [in Jerusalem] and announced that we're going to war. I explained the nature of the confrontation and what we had to prepare for. I informed them that we'd be operating in a civilian environment with the possibility of being ordered to regain control and occupation of Palestinian cities.[51]

In the July 24 general staff meeting, Mofaz outlined a number of scenarios noting "signs of a preconfrontation atmosphere and the likelihood of a clash and region-wide escalation." The chief of staff ordered all necessary preparations to be diverted to a limited confrontation: "All units must be readied. . . . This goes for all regular army units and special forces [and Northern Command units]. . . . The forces will be used in a limited confrontation before we call up the reserves."[52] According to Gal Hirsch, the Judea and Samaria Division's operations officer and commander of the Binyamin Regional Brigade at the outbreak of the events, from Nakba Day in May 2000 to August 24 he feverishly wrote the lessons of the battle and prepared lesson plans for various courses in coordination with the chief infantry and para-trooper officers' headquarters, trained and oversaw exercises for many units, and personally led the development of new fighting concepts in controlling "armed demonstrators." He attested that the division and the command accepted his rush forward with the doctrine and training.

According to Hirsch, division commander Shlomo Oren and Yitzhak Eitan, the commander of Central Command, did their best to obtain a huge amount of equipment and protection for the forces, issuing rapid procurement procedures, prioritizing allocations for sniper courses, preparing intelligence means, and upgrading plans. On August 24, he led a study day for 1,400 regular army and reserve officers, from the company commander level up, at Central Command's training base in Beit Guvrin, where the new doctrine and equipment were presented, including live displays of different steps in fighting and riot control, the use of special forces and counterterror teams, air assistance, and the use of tanks for escorting border police jeeps. The high point of the day was the presentation of the capture of a mock-up Palestinian town, although not many in the audience were happy to hear about this pos-sibility. Later, Hirsch noted that preparations consisted of all elements of force design, such as headquarters exercises and the development of warfighting doctrines and combat techniques geared especially for the Palestinian theater—a complex urban environment of civilians and popular resistance (cold weapons, rocks, firebombs) where threats of live fire, improvised explosive devices (IEDs), anti-tank weapons, and sniper fire abounded. The air force was integrated into the battle preparations; replenishment was provided; study days and briefings were held in military schools.[53]

Summary of the Test Case

This case presents a positive example of the chief of staff identifying deep strategic change and preparing the IDF in time as comprehensively as possible through doctrine, training, and weapons (limitations and shortfalls notwithstanding). This was done even as the political echelon and some of the members of the general staff were verbally or diplomatically involved in the peace process. Still, it must be noted that while the IDF prepared for mass rioting with the Palestinians using live fire, it did not prepare for urban combat, a pattern that the IDF would shift to in early 2002.

Unlike the first case study of Elazar and the Blue and White alert, in this case the chief of staff was not alone in recognizing the change. The identification and announcement, or at least the implementation, of the appropriate steps, was shared by other commanders, some of whom were members of the general staff. Nevertheless, Mofaz played a key role in the preparations, as Central Command could not have taken all of the steps necessary for meeting the approaching confrontation without the support of and explicit orders from the chief of staff. Mofaz's experience with the Palestinians when he was the commander of Southern Command and the Judea and Samaria Division may have been key references for the change he sensed. The general staff Forward Drive exercise and the lessons learned from Nakba Day also contributed to the IDF's readiness. These were decidedly critical factors in the Central Command and general staff's formulation of the picture.

Another noteworthy point is the time element. It is true that Napoleon said, "You can ask me for anything you like, except time," because a few more hours, days, or months are always needed to prepare for a military engagement. But the IDF's success in identifying changes in a reasonable amount of time allowed it to take the proper action that proved invaluable in the early stages of the confrontation.

Dan Halutz and the Failure to Put the IDF on a War Footing in the Second Lebanon War, 2006

During the Second Lebanon War between Israel and Hezbollah in the summer of 2006, the chief of staff tried from the start of the confrontation to define it as a war, but for various reasons he failed to put the IDF on a war footing. The Winograd Commission report said this after the war:

> We investigated the management of the war that ended without a decisive victory, which is also the opinion of those in the army who conducted the war. A major factor was that until the fighting actually ended—and afterward—no clearly stated expression had been internalized by the command echelons that the country was indeed in a wartime situation, that the rules of engagement were different from those in high-intensity routine security activity. . . . The military and political echelons' failure to perceive that they were dealing with a war situation was responsible for managerial details along the chain of command whose aggregation contributed to the results. This ambiguity prevailed, even though from the start there were those who avowed that the IDF was in a state of war. But their warnings failed to serve as the basis for precise instructions and decisive action.[54]

In several places in his memoir, Dan Halutz explains his growing awareness of the situation and his attempt to impress it upon the army.[55] On July 12, 2006, Hezbollah attacked an IDF border patrol, killing three soldiers, wounding three, and abducting two IDF soldiers. This action occurred after a failed similar abduction attempt in November 2005 in Ghajar. The abduction ignited what would later be known as the Second Lebanon War. Halutz wrote that immediately after the event, he already realized the implication of the event but failed to act on it:

> I couldn't say exactly how long the battle would last. What I did know—and this is the message that I conveyed to the general staff and Northern Command—is that it would be relatively long. The word "war" was on my mind and I asked myself how I could convey the message that we had to alter the forces' awareness that

they were no longer in routine security activity but in war. The mental shift was crucial. The operational significance meant a sweeping transformation of the rules of the game for our forces and regarding the enemy.[56]

Later that day he urged IAF commander Eliezer Shkedi and head of Amatz Gadi Eisenkot to get rid of routine security mentality, terminology, and procedure and help him to overcome the fact that "no one in today's generation who's doing staff work has ever fought [in a real war]. All they're used to is the Gaza Strip and the West Bank; that's all that their military experience amounts to. . . . They think in terms of routine security—they have to make a mental switch."[57]

In the July 13 situation assessment, Halutz underscored the new state of affairs: "The truth is we're still using routine security terminology as though this is a border incident. Gentlemen, this is not a border incident, we're at war in Lebanon. This is how it must be seen. Maybe our forces will wake up after a couple of surface-to-surface missiles land in Haifa, maybe then everything will fall into place and they'll realize that."[58]

The chief of staff's tirade shows he was fully aware that the current engagement went beyond routine security, and, like the head of Aman, he criticized the now obsolete routine security mindset that had to be updated into terms of a full-fledged war. Responding to another comment he said: "We're not fighting in the south, we're not fighting in the West Bank, we're at war, that's what this is all about. This is how I define what we're doing, and it's according to these rules that we're operating."

Regarding the need to change the operational and conceptual framework, the head of Amatz noted that many meetings, often with the defense minister's participation, were held for approval of cross-border operations and sorties (peace-time procedures) and those procedures should have been scrapped. Halutz also ordered that only he or his deputy would attend forums with the defense minister: "We're not sitting down and working in a routine security mode now and checking which window which missile will sail through." In his opinion, the general public would change its outlook the moment heavy rocket barrages began landing on the home front.

The head of the operations division within Amatz, Shlomo "Sami" Turgeman, recalled that after he saw the chief of staff fuming over the routine security mindset, he decided to take an extraordinary step for someone in his position. On the night of July 14, he flew to Northern Command and met with the command's intelligence officer, chief artillery officer, head of the air force's forward command post, and other intelligence and fire coordination officers in an attempt to learn what the general staff was doing that prevented them from implementing the fire plans and other assignments in a situation defined as war. He noted that the Friday evening flight gave him a better understanding of the IDF's current situation.[59]

In the situation assessment on the evening of July 15, the chief of staff viewed the INS *Hanit*, a missile boat damaged by an anti-ship cruise missile on July 14 after its captain failed to engage its missile protection system, as an example of IDF units that still hadn't internalized the change in their operations, that still hadn't awakened to the fact they were no longer engaged in routine security activity: "The most sophisticated naval vessel in the world, all of whose systems are designed to deal precisely with this type of threat, is on patrol, crossing the line, with its switches off. What were the ship's officers thinking— that they're on a holiday cruise and not in a war?"[60]

Halutz insisted that he struggled in vain to instill an understanding in the IDF that Israel was in a state of war. As he saw it, the mental shift from routine security operations to wartime actions lagged, creating a serious challenge to convert an organization as vast as the IDF from one mindset to another. He realized that the residue of years of routine security in which the IDF was involved in policing had exacted a price, as evidenced by the *Hanit* strike.[61]

Halutz claimed that from day one he voiced his view in the general staff discussions that the IDF was in a wartime situation, but his exhortations fell on deaf ears. He saw that the internal orders of Northern Command, the navy, and air force not only omitted mention that the situation had changed, but they also imposed unnecessary restrictions and unrealistic constraints on the forces operating in the field. On the other hand, he admitted that this phenomenon could be explained against the background of expectations that developed in the army over the years: society exhibited a lack of patience or tolerance for casualties; commanders were expected to accomplish their missions with zero losses to our side; mission accomplishment had ceased to be a sacred tenet; and so forth. "If this is the case, what's there to criticize?" Halutz asked.[62]

On July 20, Halutz brought up another case in point. During an IDF situation assessment, Shkedi, the air force commander, said that caution was needed when employing the air force in the proximity of ground forces. Halutz recalled, "He meant that we had to maintain the safety restriction of routine periods in the use of airpower. For a second time I made it absolutely clear to him, and to the others, that 'the current situation is closer to war than to routine security.'" The fact that Shkedi said this over a week into the war demonstrates the colossal cognitive barricade that commanders in all the services had to overcome in assimilating the new reality.[63]

The Winograd report states that during the fighting Halutz failed to get his understanding across to the IDF. This is also expressed in the testimonies of the ground and air forces commanders. According to Gal Hirsch, the commander of the Galilee Division, Hirsch and the commander of Northern Command had a row over the number of casualties after the attack on Maroun al-Ras in the afternoon of July 20, during which five soldiers were killed.

"Gal," Udi [Major General Adam, commander of Northern Command] said, "We are losing too many people in this fight." I thought that he must still be processing the scope of our casualties, and the transition from routine to war. "This is not true," I tried to reply, "This is war and there are casualties."[64]

Later he wrote that when he returned to his HQ that evening, he said, "We're at war," and ordered a sign put on the wall behind him that read "WAR" so that everyone who was watching the division HQ in the video conference would get the message.[65] Later that evening Hirsch had a furious wrangle with Adam over the number of casualties, during which Hirsch erupted: "Listen to me and listen well—we will have 250 fatalities and fifteen hundred wounded soldiers in this war. Let those numbers sink in—that's what happens in war."[66] In concluding the chapter on the battle, Hirsch wrote:

> All Northern Command wanted was raids leaving dead Hezbollah operatives. I believe that even at this point, the command had not yet shifted to a mindset of war. They may have perceived the situation as a collection of "battle days," or as prolonged clashes and no more. From my point of view, it was a war from day one. The result was that the command and the division were operating under completely different operational logic. I was finding it extremely difficult to combine the two.[67]

Hirsch argues that Northern Command's headquarters didn't relate to the events as war and continued to employ routine security procedures for quite some time. The division had to go through a mesh of red tape to get approval for every action, contrary to the principles of C2 in wartime. Transitions between modes of action were the main issue—from routine security to battle day, to counterattacks, to defense, to first brigade battle, then first division battle, and full division campaign, and finally to full command campaign.[68]

The problems with shifting the ground forces to a war mentality were also felt at the brigade and battalion levels, and not only because the norms of routine security activity had taken root during the successful suppression of terror in the West Bank and the Gaza Strip.[69] The situation in the air force was similar. During the postwar debriefing on the mental shift from routine security to war, problems were raised akin to those in Northern Command. Pilots complained about the elevation they had to fly at and the definition of lines that limited the flight path—definitions that were used in routine security—and the wrong state of alert in the air force. Air force headquarters did not really switch from routine security to war, and as a result neither did the rest of the air force. Like Northern Command, the problem was in differentiating between levels: the strategic level and the operational level considered the event a "large" routine security incident.

Further down the line, the need to shift came into sharper focus in the fighting units, and the tension escalated between the organization's approach to events and what was happening on the ground. One study found that the ambiguity in defining the situation also caused the various branches of the general staff, such as logistics and C4I, to continue operating for a relatively long time as though nothing out of the ordinary had happened in terms of availability of replacements, hours of activity, and procedures.[70]

Why did the chief of staff's repeated declarations and attempts to define the situation as war never have the intended effect? From the second day of the confrontation, his pronouncements sounded more like disciplinary reprimands rather than orders to be obeyed, which may have been because of the dichotomy between what he said and his conduct as the commander of the army. One mode of action that had an effect on the perception that this was not a war was the limited use of the GHQ underground command post in Tel Aviv and the fact that situation assessments were dealt with in the chief of staff's office rather than in the underground wartime command post.[71] The second pattern was the peacetime cross-border operation and sortie approval procedure forum (that operated during periods of routine), which functioned until a relatively late stage in the fighting, notwithstanding the head of Amatz's declaration to the contrary on July 13. For example, in a July 26 action in the Lebanese border village of Keela, the destruction of a number of dwellings was conditioned on permission from the defense minister.[72] And in the case of authorization for the 98th Division's plans on August 3, the chief of staff said, "Although this is a matter of peacetime cross-border approval procedure—I'm extending it a bit."[73] Other shortcomings were the slow and fragmentary pattern of mobilizing the reserves that did little to instill the sense of urgency in the ground forces that is so necessary in wartime and the slate of prohibitions on the use of various means.

The last problematic pattern also appeared in Northern Command. Adam placed many restrictions on the forces, such as the entry of armored personnel carriers (APCs), limited night action, and adherence to the routine security "mode" in intelligence, logistics, fire, and home front arrays.[74] As stated, the problems in this field filtered down to the battalion and squadron levels.

Summary of the Test Case

This case is unique since it is the only one in which the chief of staff knew that the definition of the situation had to be changed but failed to implement his understanding. Halutz's determined statements in general staff discussions did not correspond with his patterns of action as commander of the army, and for various IDF bodies they did not communicate "war."

Why was it so hard for Halutz to convey his message? His personal experience in the War of Attrition and Yom Kippur War may have skewed his perception toward a war that was less severe than the earlier ones he was familiar with, leading him to manage it not as a "real" war but more as a large-scale routine security operation. Another explanation is that he may have remained locked in the air force mentality where missions can be rerouted minutes before a strike, and he extrapolated this modus operandi to the ground forces. However, the ground forces regarded sudden and constantly revised directives as symptomatic of "nonessential" limited-scale operations and not as war.

Declarations on the change in the situation are not enough to disseminate a change in the organization, and it requires actual actions like mobilizing the reserves, changing the rules of engagement, shifting to wartime C2 procedures, or using code names of war plans in order to push forward this transition.[75] On the other hand, the chief of staff is expected to be capable of persuading the political echelon that the new reality is indeed a "war" situation, one that the political level is often hesitant to declare.

Benny Gantz and the Change in Perception on the Golan Heights, 2011–13

Syria's civil war and subsequent disintegration began in 2011 and, as of this writing, are still ongoing. Benny Gantz, the chief of staff from February 2011 to February 2014, realized the ramifications of the Assad regime's loss of Syrian control on the Golan Heights and therefore instructed the IDF to prepare for trouble by strengthening the defense system in 2011. Following this he stepped up preparations by establishing the Bashan Regional Division, designed for border operations in place of the multipurpose Ga'ash Armored Division, which had been deployed for decades on the Heights opposite the Syrian army threat.

Gantz said that events in the Arab world, especially the Syrian regime's failure to suppress the riots in Dara'a (southern Syria) in March 2011, confirmed his understanding that the Syrian arena was changing. Furthermore, the events of the May 11 Nakba Day, when thousands of Syrian civilians stormed the border in the northern Golan Heights and several dozen crossed into Israel, convinced him of the power inherent in the fluid situation and the need to introduce fundamental changes in the IDF.[76] In June 2012, he informed the government's Foreign Affairs and Defense Committee that the IDF had identified robust Iranian and Hezbollah involvement in Syria and that the Golan Heights had become increasingly unstable because the events in Syria and on the border could reach the level of terrorist activity. He made it clear that "we are concerned about the possibility of Syrian weapons being transferred to Hezbollah, especially if the Syrian government disintegrates."[77]

The commander of Northern Command, Major General Yair Golan, recalled that Deputy Chief of Staff Yair Naveh presented the general staff with the idea of setting up an obstacle, a multisensor system that General Golan was familiar with from his previous role as commander of the Judea and Samaria Division. As he requested, the IDF's most advanced border defense system was integrated into the obstacle.[78]

According to a report from November 2012, the IDF was expected to complete the deployment of its most advanced radar network on the Syrian border in the coming weeks, thereby upgrading observation, area control, and information-gathering capability. The new system, which included optical fiber deployment, radars, and new cameras, enabled integrated daylight/nighttime observation into Syria in depth and was intended to revolutionize the IDF's cross-border data-collecting ability. At the same time, an obstacle enhancement project along the border was carried out for the first time since the 1974 ceasefire agreement with Syria. The report also cited IDF estimates that global jihad and al-Qaeda teams were already based on the Syrian Golan, exploiting the governmental vacuum created in the wake of the civil war, and that the IDF was concerned that terrorists would carry out attacks against civilians and soldiers along the Golan border fence, similar to the attack carried out by Salafi jihadists on the Sinai border in August 2011.[79]

Despite official policy forbidding wounded Syrians from being brought to Israel for medical treatment, General Golan supported Brigadier General Tamir Heyman, the Ga'ash Division commander, who decided in view of the events on the ground to transfer the first wounded Syrians into Israel in February 2013. Gantz also agreed, and in the coming months Israel treated additional wounded, with the chief of staff and the political echelon allowing increasing numbers to enter. General Golan regarded this step as a way of maintaining border security with the cooperation of Syrian organizations affiliated with the wounded. In mid-2013 Gantz decided to set up the Bashan Division on the Golan Heights. Its main job was to prevent terror attacks from the Syrian side of the border. The new division was based on the headquarters and some of the units of the Netiv Ha'esh (Path of Fire) Reserve Armored Division under the command of Brigadier General Ofek Buchris. Gantz ordered the Ga'ash Division, the IDF's largest division, which had been responsible until then for the Golan line, to concentrate on other assignments. "In his [Gantz's] view, the Golan Heights has become an active front because of the civil war in

Syria and Syrian military activity against the rebels in Kuneitra [one kilometer from the border] . . . and other villages on the line. The area needs a headquarters to concentrate on routine security. Also, a home front command district will be established on the Golan," journalist Amir Oren wrote. Some members of the general staff were concerned about the impact that the 200-million-shekel price tag for the new division would have on budgetary priorities, which, regardless of the cost, were scheduled to be curtailed. "Gantz decided in favor of the division and ordered staff work undertaken to set it up. In this way the IDF will be adequately prepared at the onset of a hostile move and not have to wait, as often happens, until it's a fait accompli."[80]

Gantz appears to have realized the developing threat earlier than others in the IDF and provided preemptive action. He explained that the creation of the Bashan Division was the synthesis of an earlier idea for restructuring the IDF's divisions and the new development on the Golan Heights. Two earlier events had convinced him that the divisions had to be restructured: (a) the employment of the entire Ga'ash Division during the disengagement from the Gaza Strip in 2005 (another division replaced it on the Golan Heights); and (b) the use of Ga'ash's brigades (the Seventh and Barak armored brigades and Golani Infantry Brigade) in the 2006 Second Lebanon War, while at the same time the division's headquarters commanded other units on the Golan Heights.[81]

In light of these events, he drew the conclusion that if the relatively full complement of regional divisions had to deal with a significant challenge on the borders, they must be separated from the reservist divisions (that would specialize in one arena) and the standing army divisions (that would be multipurpose or multi-arena).[82] According to Gantz, the events of Nakba Day 2011, which revealed the deteriorating situation on the Golan Heights, justified his earlier understanding and led to his decision to establish a regional division on the Golan Heights and convert the Ga'ash Division into a multi-arena force. His understanding was reinforced after Operation Pillar of Defense in December 2012, when a standing army division that had completed a divisional exercise in the north was transferred to Gaza for deployment during the operation.

Heyman, Ga'ash's commander at the time, claimed that a main factor in Gantz's realization that the situation on the Golan Heights had changed was his frequent visits to the Heights and, as they traveled in a jeep, Heyman's presentation of his own developing understandings.[83] According to Heyman, Gantz perceived things differently from Yair Golan, the commander of Northern Command, who viewed the separation of divisions as diverting attention from the challenge of the Shiite axis (the alliance of Iran, Syria's Assad, and Hezbollah). Heyman claimed that the head of Aman, Major General Aviv Kochavi, also realized the need for restructuring the units on the Golan Heights in view of Aman's focus on the global jihad challenge. Speaking at the graduation ceremony of intelligence officers in July 2013 a few months before the Islamic State (ISIS) became rooted in Syria, Kochavi termed the country "the center of global jihad" and declared that "Syria attracts thousands of the global jihad activists and Muslim radicals from the region and beyond, who establish themselves in the country."[84] In this case, Gantz seems to have relied on a combination of Aman assessments and his tours of the area.

Buchris reorganized the Netiv Ha'esh Reserve Division into the Bashan Regional Division in late 2013–early 2014 and served as its first commander. He recalled that when he was commander of the Golani Brigade, he met with Gantz on July 2012 at the conclusion of a military ceremony and told him, "Ga'ash can't be a regular army armored division responsible for a large regular army ORBAT and at the same time perform routine security in a sector that has changed and demands greater attention than in the past." In early 2013, a few months after Buchris assumed command of Netiv Ha'esh, he sent Gantz a detailed proposal for converting the reservist division into a regional division on the Golan. He believes the proposal fell on receptive ears. Gantz, as noted, had considered the idea himself and was looking for a solution to the storm brewing on the Golan. The commander of Northern Command dismissed the need to take the Ga'ash

Division off the Heights and insisted that the establishment of another regional army division, in a period of budgetary drawdown, would be the ultimate misuse of resources.[85]

General Golan contended that as a general staff officer, his opposition was based on a different view from Gantz's regarding the management of the IDF's shrinking resources. As commander of Northern Command, he believed that the creation of a standing army regional division rather than a reservist division would strengthen the command.[86] Gantz accepted the fact that General Golan disapproved of the proposed change, but from the moment the decision was made he carried it out to the best of his ability.[87]

Buchris said that the first factor in the change (as he saw it) and the adaptation to the new situation occurred in early 2012, when the plans for defending the Golan Heights (that the troops had been drilled on for years) were replaced by plans and exercises designed to meet the global jihad organizations that were now entrenched on the Heights.

The new division was also designated as a center of knowledge for the entire IDF on developments on the Golan Heights. Gantz acknowledged that his earlier experience as commander of the Lebanon Liaison Unit contributed to his understanding of this key element in the new division's knowledge development role.[88] Buchris added that when he presented the division's raison d'être and reorganization to the chief of staff, the latter stated that one of the division's new functions would be to generate knowledge on the Golan Heights for the chief of staff, too.[89]

Summary of the Test Case

Here is a positive example of the chief of staff's early identification of a change in the situation. The change led to the restructuring of the theater that included new technological means for border defense and a reinforced regional division on the Golan Heights while converting the Ga'ash Division into a multi-arena division. Gantz combined his own and his subordinates' insights—Heyman, the division commander, and Golan, the commander of Northern Command—on humanitarian assistance to wounded Syrians, which probably contributed to the preservation of quiet on the border.

Chapter Summary

Many factors influence the chief of staff's ability to identify a strategic shift and define it as such. Two main yet somewhat contradictory factors are the chief of staff's personal experience and his ways of learning. Personal experience seems to be of equal significance in both identifying and defining the changed situation.

Elazar was the commander of Northern Command in the Six-Day War (much of the Blue and White alert's preparations were influenced by his experience in the command). Mofaz had a wealth of experience in dealing with the Palestinians as commander of the Judea and Samaria Division in 1993–94 and as commander of Southern Command in 1994–96. Gantz was familiar with the Golan Heights and the Syrian army from his tenure as commander of Northern Command prior to the Second Lebanon War, and as chief of staff he closely followed the changes in the region. Lipkin-Shahak, the head of Aman and deputy chief of staff between 1986 and 1995, was familiar with the fighting in the security zone. As a pilot in the Yom Kippur War, Halutz experienced the difficulty in shifting from routine security to war, but he failed to apply his understandings during the Second Lebanon War because of the gap between his announcements and the management of the general staff and its branches.

Shomron's prior military experience with the Palestinians (unlike Yitzhak Mordechai's, for example) seems to have been very meager, which limited his ability to deal cognitively with the new situation. His military postings had all been geared to warfighting against regular armies. His personal experience included wartime combat, retaliatory raids, and special operations, but not quelling a civilian uprising as in the Palestinian case. His main service was in the paratroopers (as commander of the 890th Battalion, and later as chief infantry officer), in armor (as commander of the 401st Brigade in the Yom Kippur War and commander of the 162nd Division in 1976–78), and a combination of the two as commander of the Ground Forces HQ. During his tenure as commander of Southern Command in 1978–82 he oversaw the evacuation of Sinai, the growth of the ground forces' capabilities, and large-scale exercises in the event of another war with Egypt, but at no time did he come into significant contact with the Palestinian population in the West Bank or the Gaza Strip. In this case, Shomron's focus on all-out war would seem to have created a cognitive block that prevented him from correctly reading the developments on the ground.

Be that as it may, previous experience can sometimes limit the ability to recognize a new situation. Over the years, Halutz developed the concept that the effective way of dealing with Hezbollah was by air operations against the dual-purpose infrastructures in Lebanon, whereas ground action was an insignificant factor against this foe. The method of operation that was eventually devised and applied in Lebanon included large-scale ground action. His clearly stated definition of the situation as war appears to have been of greater importance for the ground units than for the air force. The peacetime cross-border operations and sorties approval procedure was better suited for commando units and may have been part of the reason why he failed to shift the army from one level of situational awareness to another.

The second major factor is the chief of staff's learning patterns. When a new reality lies outside his personal experience, he can still take steps to compensate for it. Gantz, for example, toured the area, observed the changes, and gained firsthand knowledge. He read the Golani Brigade commander's letter, listened to the Ga'ash Division commander relate his insights, and received assistance from the head of Aman. Other chiefs of staff received (or could have received) assistance from the generals of the regional commands and the heads of the services and branches that make up part of the general staff's formal learning group. Sometimes routine situation assessments are sufficient for recognizing the change; in other times exercises and war games are needed to illustrate the anachronism of the prevailing concept or response. The chief of staff must develop diverse learning methods to enable him to identify a change at as early a stage as possible.

Regarding the challenge of moving the IDF from one mentality to another when the chief of staff identifies the need to change the army's perception of events, Sami Turgeman, the head of the operations division/Amatz in the Second Lebanon War, claimed that the difficulty in switching from routine security to wartime in that war was unlike anything in previous wars and seemed more like the challenge in recently fought limited operations in Gaza (and may remain so in the future). The problem is the differential transition of certain elements in the IDF to a war (for example, all or part of the air force), while other elements are operating in a state of routine or emergency. The current alert scheme, which applies to the entire IDF during a confrontation, impedes a differential transition. Another problem that Turgeman noted is that today's relatively single-value link between a war situation and code names for large-scale operational plans complicates matters when the plans are adapted to a specific context at the onset of a confrontation. In this situation, changing the plan's name complicates matters for the commander in shifting from routine security to war.[90]

The introduction of changes is not a trivial matter; it demands of the chief of staff an understanding of the tangible elements that signal the shift from one mental state to another. Examples of this, as we have seen, are the mobilization of the reserves and the implementation of a plan whose code name the IDF immediately recognizes as war.

2

DEVELOPING FAMILIARITY WITH ALL MILITARY DOMAINS

Chief of Staff Rafael (Raful) Eitan is claimed to have quipped that the Israeli Air Force (IAF) is "a foreign army, but a friendly one." The comment rings true because of the notion that ground force commanders are only partially familiar with the air force, and that the same probably describes their knowledge of the navy, military intelligence, and other services.

Before examining the chief of staff's degree of familiarity with the various services, let it be noted that in the IDF hierarchy the chief of staff is also the commander of the ground forces. Unlike the air and naval services, whose commanders are responsible for force employment, the ground force design is the responsibility of the Ground Forces Command (Mazi), with the assistance of most of the general staff branches, and its employment is the direct responsibility of the commanders of the regional commands.

This means that the chief of staff's responsibility for the ground forces is greater than it is for the air force and his expertise in ground forces employment has to be greater than for IAF employment. Be that as it may, I claim that because the IAF plays so decisive a role in IDF war plans, the chief of staff whose career has been in the ground forces must acquire an expert's knowledge of the air service, or at least have as much understanding of it as he has with the ground forces' plans. A short introduction is in order regarding the chief of staff's relationship with the air force in general and its commander in particular.

Historically, the IAF's force design shows that the chief of staff has little say regarding its organization or aircraft replenishment (the type of planes—not their quantity, which depends on the IDF's resources). This stems from a number of reasons, including (1) the IAF's ability to perform exhaustive staff work and present its case effectively, whereas the chief of staff's personnel—today the planning (Agat) and operations (Amatz) branches—would be hard-pressed to challenge the IAF's arguments; and (2) the IAF's standing as a strategic service whose chief has direct access (relative to the other services) to the political echelon, and thus is given an edge over the commanders of the other services. Also, since the IAF is perceived as a tower of excellence, the chief of staff has no intention of interfering with its decisions; and in view of the last factor, the IAF commander has a special status on the general staff. An exception to this is Chief of Staff Benny Gantz's decision, on the basis of the staff work of his deputy, Gadi Eisenkot, to establish the Depth Command (responsible for employing airborne and seaborne forces in operational and strategic depths), despite the IAF's contention that this HQ is superfluous since in-depth operations are the air force's turf.

In that light, this chapter focuses on the chief of staff's degree of familiarity with the IAF's plans and their impact on subsequent events. The test cases include Yitzhak Rabin's familiarity with Operation Moked in the Six-Day War; David Elazar's familiarity with Operations Dugman and Tagar in the Yom Kippur War; and Rafael Eitan and Operation Artzav 19 (Mole Cricket 19) in the First Lebanon War. The chapter concludes with a discussion of Halutz's familiarity with the ground forces plan in the Second Lebanon War. Four levels of familiarity are defined and the test cases are analyzed in light of the first three:

> **General.** Did the chief of staff sufficiently understand the IAF's capabilities and basic requirements for air supremacy, weather, visibility, and other variables to enable its employment?

The plan. Did the chief of staff have full command of the inputs that went into the plan regarding alternative possibilities, estimated strategic outputs, the price of potential errors, and the political implications of implementing the plan?

Possible changes. Was the chief of staff knowledgeable in the priorities, the consequences of the plan, and similar issues if the plan went awry?

The fourth level of familiarity has never occurred in the IDF: when the chief of staff introduces changes in the IAF's concepts and plans, including changes that the air force is dead set against. The IAF's independence, which its sixth and highly influential commander, Ezer Weizman (1958–66), insisted on and which still remains in effect, inhibits the chief of staff's involvement, although we may assume that in certain cases the chief of staff's involvement is necessary. Furthermore, the air force develops its own concepts for dealing with evolving challenges in-house (relative to the development of knowledge in the regional commands that are more open to other participants) and reaches the chief of staff with "done deals" that are nearly impossible to question professionally, let alone oppose, without an external examining staff (which is almost never found in Agat or Amatz).

Yitzhak Rabin and the Plan for Operation Moked in the 1967 Six-Day War

The idea of a preemptive air strike on the Arab air force bases probably germinated during IAF commander Dan Tolkovsky's time as a lesson learned from the Sinai War, developed during Ezer Weizman's stint as IAF commander, and was brought to fruition by Major General Mordechai "Motti" Hod in Operation Moked (Focus) at the very outset of the Six-Day War. Chief of Staff Yitzhak Rabin became deputy chief of staff in late 1963 (after serving as head of Agam). Coming from this wealth of experience, he should have been very familiar with the operation's plan. However, in Hod's account, quite the opposite picture emerges:

> I found it rather strange, but most convenient, that no one took any interest in the air force's plans. One of the great paradoxes of the war is that so many people were worried sick over the armored force in Sinai that air issues didn't interest them. The chief of staff knew that the air force had a plan, but as far as I know he was unfamiliar with it and uninvolved in it. At any rate, he didn't relate to it during presentations with the same intensity that he did to the other plans. I explained the air force's plan in very general terms so it was always assumed that the first thing we'd do is go after the Egyptian air force.[1]

Hod continued:

> Given his state of mind, he accepted whatever we said or did—no questions asked. If somebody presented a plan and was prepared to carry it out, it was given the green light. . . . The funny thing is that all the other IDF plans were spread across walls with diagrams, curves, and arrows while the IAF's plan consisted of [a few] tables and a list of airfields. I remember that the first person to be uncomfortable with the plan when I showed it to him for the first time was the defense minister [Moshe Dayan, from June 1], because he didn't understand which kind of IAF plan this was.[2]

Hod offered this perspective of the general staff's work style, saying that practically no one could have criticized the IAF's meticulously designed tactical plan that had been drawn up by the sharpest minds. In fact, he said, the IDF's organizational structure—in which no level in the general staff is more capable than the air force in time of war to evaluate if the air war is being fought properly—is the right one. Only the air force can assure absolutely essential decision making on air matters in wartime, unlike Agam's time-consuming control over the ground forces.[3]

Hod described the heavy burden he felt after receiving absolute responsibility for decisions "that he hadn't thought would remain solely on the shoulders of the IAF commander." As he saw it, the lack of supervision only increased his freedom of action. In response to the question whether his statements could be construed as meaning that at no time were the air force's plans presented to the general staff for a discussion, he replied:

> For discussion—no, only a presentation. For discussion—never. . . . Nobody objected to the method of attack, the techniques, or anything like that. The chief of staff determines the goal of the ground plans and the ground forces show him their assignments and timetables. The air plans were never presented this way to the general staff; instead, the IAF did all the planning and the IAF commander showed the general staff the finished product. The only time the plan was explained in greater detail to the chief of staff was when he toured the Ekron Airbase. That was the only time the chief of staff received an explanation of how the attack on the airfields would be carried out. It wasn't for him to review the plan but to learn and support it.[4]

The commander of the Mirage squadron that Rabin toured recalls his impression of the chief of staff's visit on June 2, three days before the war:

> Immediately after the light aircraft carrying the chief of staff and air force commander touched down, the control tower directed it to the alert area. I saluted Rabin and shook Motti [Hod]'s hand. As we walked to the building, I told the chief of staff that he was about to surprise six fighters who were on interception alert—three lead captains and three lieutenants (numbers two [second aircraft in the flight formation])—a typical cross section

of the squadron's pilots. We walked into the room and the six pilots jumped to attention and snapped a salute. "Good morning, gentlemen, be seated," Rabin said in his gravelly voice, and immediately began tossing questions at them as though he came prepared with them.

"If war comes, where are your targets?"

"At Inshas."

"Where's that?"

"On the outskirts of Cairo, east of the city," came the reply.

"What's there?"

"Forty-two MiG 21s."

"Where are they parked?"

"They're positioned on the runways on parking areas spread across the base's operational sector adjacent to the hangars."

Rabin pressed on, asking about the location of anti-aircraft cannons, types of cannons, enemy deployment, and the pilots' feeling about the air force's ability to successfully carry out the mission in the opening strike on the initial flyover if war erupted. The missions the IAF headquarters presented to the chief of staff earlier appeared complicated and difficult to accomplish, and this was probably why he wanted to learn firsthand the pilots' feelings, their degree of preparedness for the missions, and their confidence in winning the war. It was a crucial twenty minutes of Q&A, a lively discussion between the old warhorse and the young fighter pilots.[5]

Rabin's questions seem to indicate that he was privy to the IAF's plan, but in light of Hod's account, it appears that during his visit to the Ekron Airbase he received a detailed explanation of the plan for the first time. Lending credence to Hod's version is the head of air intelligence, Brigadier General (ret.) Shaike Bareket, who confirmed Hod's depiction of Rabin's minimal knowledge of the plan.[6]

Further evidence of Rabin's low level of familiarity with the use of the airpower is his conduct in two events in which significant airpower had been employed independently under exceptional circumstances when he was chief of staff. The first was during the "War over the Water" against the Syrian attempt to divert the Jordan River sources. On November 13, 1964, in response to Syrian fire on Israeli settlements and IDF forces, IAF commander Ezer Weizman dispatched fifty planes, nineteen of which attacked Syrian strongholds and artillery positions.

Prime Minister–Defense Minister Levi Eshkol had been kept in the dark about the unprecedented and seemingly cavalier use of dozens of warplanes. There had been no prior formal discussions, only a phone conversation, so he probably thought that a small number of aircraft would be involved (a four- or two-plane formation). Rabin's instructions to Weizman over the phone probably did not go into details or put a cap on the number of planes or types of munitions to be used. This is backed by the record of Colonel Motta Gur, the head of Agam's operations department, in his debriefing of the event: "No limit was put on the firepower that the air force employed. There were no restrictions on the use of bombs, napalm, strafing, or anything else; everything was left to the IAF commander's discretion." In the end Eshkol probably thought it sufficient to give the chief of staff his vague approval to call in the air force, without determining the nature or limit of its employment. This was how the chief of staff generally issued orders to the IAF commander. Thus, Weizman was at liberty to decide the size of the force and the scope of the mission.[7]

Two and a half years later, on April 7, 1967, a border incident escalated into a "battle day" (a concentrated clash lasting a few hours) two months before the Six-Day War. The air force, now under the command of Motti Hod, was sent into action. The action was "unprecedented." All of the fighter squadrons—over half of the IAF's first line planes—took part. The squadrons carried out 171 sorties (including eighty-four attacks and fifty-two intercepts and patrols) and dropped sixty-five tons of bombs, which casts heavy doubt on whether Chief of Staff Yitzhak Rabin, who remained in Northern Command's forward command post in Poriya (a ridge to the west of the Sea of Galilee) during the event, had control over the large-scale employment of the air force. This case seems to repeat the pattern of the November 13, 1964, incident. Again, the IAF commander decided on the size of the employment, the missions, and munitions without conferring with the chief of staff.[8]

Therefore, we see that Operation Moked in June 1967, despite its phenomenal success, was the third event in Rabin's tenure when the IAF went into action while the chief of staff remained aloof of the details of its employment and their ramifications. Without in-depth knowledge of the IAF plans and in light of Hod's and Weizman's over-arching self-confidence, two issues kept the helmsmen of the state awake at night: one, the success of the operation, and two, air defense of Israel's skies, which, according to the plan, was supposed to be carried out by only three finger-four formations (6 percent of the IAF's ORBAT). Some considered this a calculated risk; others saw it as a reckless gamble. As for "those who receive the goods"—the leaders— the idea was accepted but only with great reluctance; most of the time they were skeptical about the IAF's optimism. Rabin urged dispatching special forces to enemy airbases on sabotage missions to back up the air force if the attack fell short. In early June, in line with Southern Command's plans, Deputy Chief of Staff Haim Bar-Lev admitted, "The plans are certainly impressive, but I have a major problem with them— they're based on the assumption that the IAF succeeds, and this is far from certain." Accompanying the sense that they were rushing ahead with the plans was another grave concern. The matter of air defense had fallen by the wayside. Hod stated that he made the rounds of all the ministerial forums and participated in the general staff discussions carrying a small Bristol board (sketch pad) on which he presented the IAF's plan "due to field security." Regarding air defense, he quipped, "They didn't quite ask the questions and we didn't exactly provide the answers."[9] Hod elaborated in a later interview:

> I explained the basic idea to Yitzhak [Rabin]. The first thing was
> to convince him that it wasn't a greater risk to concentrate the

effort on Egypt and leave Syria and Jordan for later. Everyone was in a panic over what the Egyptian air force and Jordan's planes would do. That's why I had to devise a technique based on a number of factors: (1) real-time intelligence; (2) the enemies' response capability; (3) our analysis of how we'd accomplish the plan.

Hod explained that according to the IAF estimate there was a very strong likelihood that in the event of a successful tactical surprise, the Arabs would take three hours to respond, based on the time needed by the Egyptians to figure out what happened and relay the information to the Syrians and Jordanians, who would require time to work out what to do and prepare to take off.[10]

As for the defense of Israel's skies, Hod was not especially forthcoming. He refused to give details on the number of aircraft that would remain to defend Israel's skies. Some claim that he was playing with fate. "I didn't say whether we'd keep ten planes or twelve planes behind. I didn't want to involve them in our plans. The truth is I didn't think we had to leave any planes for air defense. But we did leave some lest they accuse us of taking a foolhardy risk. I kept two finger-four formations in the air and one on the ground, and the minute the Mirages—our best planes for air defense—returned, they would attack relatively close by targets and forty-five minutes later would be ready to reinforce the planes that we hadn't used in the attack."

After the war he said that he was called to Prime Minister–Defense Minister Eshkol's office a few times to assure him that not a bomb would fall on Tel Aviv. He promised that Tel Aviv would not suffer a major bombing but neglected to tell Eshkol or the chief of staff outright that according to the Moked plan the entire Israeli Air Force would be taking part in the attack, and only twelve planes were being held back for air defense.

I preferred to present the matter in half a sentence [otherwise] it might encounter opposition. . . . Yitzhak [Rabin] was won over. Now we had to convince the government. Rabin wanted to be sure that Eshkol knew exactly what we were doing. I accompanied him to Eshkol and we explained that we were concentrating our strength—while leaving a minimum for air defense—and that we had reasonable information to assume that until [the enemy] knew what happened, we'd have already finished with the Syrians and the Jordanians. A few days later Rabin and I were called to Eshkol's office. . . . Eshkol asked, "Young man, can you guarantee that not a single bomb will fall on Tel Aviv?" I replied, "Eshkol, the last time a bomb fell on Tel Aviv was in 1948. The Egyptian air force came over with a single Dakota that dropped a few bombs on the Central Bus Station. They exploded and that was the last time bombs fell on Tel Aviv. What I can promise you is that Tel Aviv won't come under a massive air attack."[11]

Rabin appears to have had only the barest information necessary to reply to the government's questions. For example, in the May 23 government meeting, Minister Zalman Aran asked, "How many [of our] planes will be hit in the air operation?" Rabin estimated between fifteen and twenty-nine out of a total of 180. Weizman confirmed Rabin's estimate and added, "We believe we can open with a tactical surprise using a certain technique that will enable the first wave to destroy the Egyptian airfields without being detected until a few minutes before reaching the target."[12]

In the June 2 government meeting, Hod conveyed details on the Arab air forces, their recent penetrations into Israeli territory, and his absolute certainty that "the IAF was ready for immediate action." The ministers grilled him at length. For example, Minister Ya'akov Shimshon Shapira questioned him about the air defenses of Israeli cities, and Hod answered that "the IAF's deterrent capability has always been its best defense." Rabin added that "the best defense against an attack is to smash the Egyptian air force."[13] Nevertheless, Rabin seems to have been deeply concerned over the IAF's ability to achieve what it promised. For just such a contingency the general staff had prepared the Blue Bird plan, which called for special forces sabotaging Egyptian airfields and headquarters in Sinai.[14] Rabin noted that the

May 21 general staff preliminary discussion group decided "that airborne troops would receive top priority in assisting the IAF to accomplish its mission: annihilating the Egyptian air force, incapacitating its airfields, and disrupting communications and transportation."[15] As for his doubts about Moked, Rabin wrote that Hod radiated optimism and confidence in the IAF's ability to carry out its mission and predicted that the Egyptian air force would be destroyed before the other air forces were ready to attack. "I confess that I doubted our objectives would be achieved in the time set out by Motti Hod. But I also assumed that even if gaining air superiority took a whole day, it would still be a magnificent achievement."[16]

Another account of Rabin's qualms and perhaps other priorities in the May 15–June 5 waiting period comes from Ezer Weizman, who claims that Rabin didn't believe in an attack on the airfields and the benefits that would supposedly accrue because he felt that the air force would not be free soon enough to link up with the ground forces in the breakthrough into Sinai, which involved frontal attacks on fortified objectives. In other words, the air force would be too involved in its own missions at this point to interdict the enemy in Sinai's depth.[17]

The only issue that the general staff did review in depth was the timing of the attack, because of the ground forces' demand to begin the breakthrough at night and the air force's insistence on attacking in daylight. Yitzhak Hofi, the head of the operations department in Agam, claimed that Rabin did have a basic understanding of the IAF's needs. According to Hofi, for many years GHQ had deliberated over the timing of the IAF attack, whether the IAF's "H" hour would be the cornerstone of the plan, and whether the ground forces' "H" hour could be advanced to coincide with the IAF's operation. This thorny issue remained on the agenda from the day the attack plan for Sinai was devised. The big question was whether the IAF would open the war with a morning attack or the ground forces would advance into Sinai at night, thus creating a time gap. For years, Hofi insisted, the general staff knew that the price of this interval would be the loss of the most valuable hours, in terms of time and space. Discussions were also held on the possibility of the air force commencing the attack in the afternoon and the ground forces at night, which brought up another problem: would the air force have enough time? The last thing the general staff wanted was to shortchange the air force by having the ground forces open the war first, thus usurping the element of surprise. Furthermore, in the original Kilshon (Pitchfork) plan, the attack was scheduled to begin at night, not in daylight.[18]

Scholars on the subject of the chief of staff's (and general staff's) familiarity with IAF plans have reached the same conclusions. "The Defense Minister trusted the chief of staff, and the chief of staff trusted the head of Agam and the air force commander. Hod's freedom of action was (and not for the first time) absolute. The [modus operandi] was very successful, but not by the book," wrote historian Ami Gluska.[19] "In contrast to the general staff's intensive work on the details of the ground operation plans, it approved the air force's plan en bloc without studying it in depth," wrote IDF's historian Shimon Golan.[20]

Summary of the Test Case

Rabin appears to have understood the basic needs and principles of employing the air force, and therefore he realized its conditions for delivering a preemptive strike. This explains why he gave priority to the IAF's demand to begin the war in daylight. His level of familiarity with the plan probably would not have stood the test in the event of a change or disruption in the plan that would have forced him to determine a new set of priorities for attacking the airfields (as was done by Motti Hod after the third flyover of the attack took off) or diverting the air force to other missions, such as close air support, which did occur to a limited degree.

David Elazar and the Tagar and Dugman Plans in the 1973 Yom Kippur War

The IAF encountered great difficulty in dealing with the Russian-made Egyptian SAM (surface-to-air missile) array on the Suez Canal during the air campaign in the War of Attrition (1968–70). Between 1970 and the Yom Kippur War (1973), the IAF developed the Tagar plan for attacking the SAM array on the Suez Canal and the Dugman plan for attacking a similar array on the Golan Heights. On the night of October 6, 1973, only hours after the surprise Egyptian and Syrian invasion, Chief of Staff David Elazar ordered Tagar for the next morning. Reports of the precarious situation on the Golan Heights, where Israeli lines had been breached, compelled him to change his decision. After the first flyover of Tagar he instructed the air force to reorganize and implement Dugman.

An argument has been made that Elazar failed to grasp the true meaning of his decision on the morning of October 7. In the opinion of IAF scholar Shmuel Gordon, which I intend to refute, the typical chief of staff generally has a DNA of "ground commander." Most of his career has been spent commanding ground troops. On the other hand, his experience in staff work is limited, and his working experience with the air force is even more limited. He lacks expertise, understanding, and familiarity with the advantages and disadvantages of the air force and large-scale air operations. When the chief of staff is not an expert in the use of certain military services, an unbridgeable gap develops between his professional and operational paucity of knowledge and the almost unlimited authority he wields in making and implementing decisions. While Elazar issued orders to the air force from the IAF's main control center, previous chiefs of staff would enter the center only to track the operations, not to interfere with the complex, professional control of all the IAF aircraft in real time. Gordon claims that Elazar's intervention had critical flaws at key junctures in the air war decisions. When the flaws accumulate at a given moment, a false situation picture and deceptive situation assessment emerge devoid of ground and air staff work and resting on the chief of staff's limited expertise. In this case, the results were catastrophic. The decision to switch to attacking the missiles in Syria (Dugman) had grave strategic consequences for the air force and the IDF throughout the war. A few minutes later, after his return to the general staff, Elazar all but boasted in great detail that he'd ordered the air force to shift to

Dugman. Following his elaborate description of the decision-making process and the main people involved in it, Gordon placed responsibility on the chief of staff and the commander of the air force, who was the first to initiate the shift, didn't object to the decision, didn't try to argue against it, and didn't evaluate its consequences correctly.[21]

I contend (see below) that in this case the chief of staff, despite being a ground commander, was well acquainted with the IAF's plans and had a deep understanding of the need to attain air supremacy by attacking the SAM missiles as a condition for providing the ground forces with air assistance. Elazar's understanding came to expression before and during the war. In his summary of the July–August 1972 Battering Ram war game, he clarified his concept of how the air force should operate and defined its role in the blocking doctrine:

> Air supremacy is a condition for blocking the enemy. All our moves depend on it. It is also a condition for a defensive mission. It justified force design and the prioritization of the IAF over artillery for the next five years. I believe we'll have a forty-eight-to-seventy-two-hour warning before the Suez Canal crossing. When it begins, we'll order the armored brigades to engage and block [the enemy] with less [than the necessary] artillery support and without air assistance in the first stage. We'll have to make do with what we've got. In this stage we'll launch the large air offensive against the missile array, as we assume it will take a few hours. By eliminating the missile array we'll gain freedom of action that will contribute to our blocking effort. This is the solution at the start of the battle: the IAF destroys the missiles and gains freedom of action.[22]

When Benny Peled replaced Motti Hod and assumed command following the heightened state of alert, the IAF's operational plans were presented to the general staff. The presentation began on May 9, 1973, one day before Peled stepped into his office. The orders included Tagar, the plan for attacking the Egyptian SAM array on the Suez Canal;

Dugman, the attack plan for the SAM array on the Golan Heights; Negicha (Ramming), the attack plan on the airfields in Egypt and Syria; and Sreeta (Scratch), the master plan for the unfavorable situation in which the air force has to assist the ground forces to block the enemy before the SAM array is neutralized. Master orders were also presented for attacking strategic targets in Egypt and Syria and for air defense.[23]

The main dilemmas that were discussed were:

- The air force's ability to operate and assist in blocking before it attained air supremacy—that is, before eliminating the SAM array and achieving freedom of action in the air.
- The IAF's requirements for employing its strength to the greatest effect in the all-out war: the intelligence alert; political authorization for a preemptive strike; focusing on one front (Suez Canal or Golan Heights) before moving to the other.

Peled believed that the air force could achieve a decisive victory over the SAM arrays within forty-eight hours, but to do so the bulk of its strength would have to be allocated to the mission. Afterward it could assign finger-four formations to assist the ground forces by exploiting the Skyhawks, which were less suited to the difficult task of neutralizing the SAM array. Elazar approved this approach and promised that he would do everything possible to provide the air force with the vital forty-eight hours.

The major flaw in the IAF's prewar plans was expressed in the likelihood and level of detail in employing Sreeta in case of an Egyptian surprise crossing, whereby the IAF would be diverted to assisting the ground forces. It has been noted that the plan, for all purposes, was inoperative and uncoordinated with any ground maneuver plan. Elazar, like his general staff, apparently failed to apprehend the difficulty involved in applying the ground forces' defense plans to the situation on the canal at the end of the War of Attrition, i.e., the IAF's loss of air supremacy.[24] Before the Yom Kippur War, Elazar had observed an F-4 Phantom "loft" bombing display at the air force's firing range, the attack method the air force intended to apply against the Egyptian anti-aircraft cannons, as a first flyover to clear the way for the second flyover against the SAM batteries.[25] He testified to his positive impression.[26]

On August 20, 1973, a month and a half before the war, Elazar called a special meeting to evaluate the reinforced SAM array on the Golan Heights and the countermeasures that had to be taken. At the conclusion of the meeting, Agam issued orders to plan Operation Valerian: Northern Command's application of artillery to knock out the SAM bases on the Golan Heights up to thirty-five kilometers from the border.[27] This is another example of Elazar's familiarity with and involvement in the impact of surface-to-air missiles on the air force's operational ability.

In a postwar meeting, Elazar explained the concept that he discussed with Peled at 4:40 a.m. on October 6 when he instructed the IAF commander to prepare a preemptive strike:

> We spoke about the concept that we'd formulated, which may help clarify the question: What exactly is the air force supposed to be blocking? We always considered the air force to be of paramount importance in holding [the enemy]. In other words, it had to play a key role in the blocking or containment stage. And we'd recognized the IAF's contribution over the past year, especially in the April–May [Blue and White] alert that was based on the assumption that the air force needed sufficient time to initiate an attack on the Egyptian and Syrian missile arrays. Once it gained freedom of action it would be able to provide an invaluable contribution. Since this is the concept that we'll be using, I'm looking for a way to begin [the fighting] according to the model that we want. In other words, a model that will enable the IAF to overpower the enemy's missile array and air forces so it can be free to assist the ground forces.[28]

The chief of staff appears to have been fully aware of the air force's needs before the war and informed of the details of employing airpower.

During the October 6 nighttime meeting on the IAF's mission the next morning, Peled presented the IAF's plan of action for the next day. Taking into account the weather conditions, he recommended that the first flyover be directed against the anti-aircraft cannons in the canal sector in preparation for Tagar. Simultaneously the airfields in the Nile Delta would be attacked. What happened next would depend on the ground forces' situation in the Canal Zone. If the blocking succeeded, the air force would continue preparations for the two options. Peled presented Elazar with a plan: at approximately 7 a.m. the first flyover would attack the anti-aircraft cannons in preparation for Tagar, attack eight airfields and air defense and control centers in Egypt, assist in the fighting in the Suez area, and provide air defense. The second flyover would be a continuation of Tagar: attacking airfields and assisting the ground forces in the canal area and providing air defense. The third flyover would also be a continuation of Tagar and a continuation of the attack on the airfields. The chief of staff approved the plan. He also approved unmanned aerial vehicle (UAV) photography to pinpoint the exact location of the missiles before attacking them. He said that he would be in the control center at 6 a.m. the next day to make the final decision regarding air operations.[29]

Later that night Elazar said that the effect of a nighttime air strike would be marginal and that as of that moment few Egyptian forces had crossed the canal. If the Egyptian Fourth Armored Division crossed the canal, then IDF ground forces would be given assistance. He also said that he was aware of the problem of attacking the missiles and had ordered a number of measures to be taken: the area would be photographed by a UAV before the attack in order to obtain updated information on the location of the missile batteries, and the first flyover would target the anti-aircraft cannons, not the missiles. When the defense minister expressed his concern over the number of tanks the Egyptians might bring to the battlefield in two nights, the chief of staff said that he would be with the IAF commander at approximately 5 a.m., at which time he would be able to assess the situation and possible courses of action. The defense minister stated that if the situation in the morning looked dire regarding the tank crossing into Sinai, it would be wiser to attack the tanks and bridging equipment regardless of the anti-aircraft defenses, then attack the airfields and missile array, which wouldn't have an effect on the battle. Past chief of staff Lieutenant General (res.) Haim Bar-Lev added: "Attacking the missiles if we don't intend to cross the canal will be a costly undertaking."[30]

Two approaches appear in this discussion. The chief of staff and the defense minister wanted the air force to assist the outnumbered ground forces in interdicting the enemy that was pouring across the canal. The defense minister believed that the enemy tanks had to be destroyed first and prevented from crossing so that Israel could preserve the balance of armored forces at as early a date as possible. Therefore, he favored employing the air force against enemy forces and bridges even before destroying the missiles, whereas the chief of staff placed greater importance on air supremacy in the canal area, which would render air support more effective. Elazar's order to the IAF on the night of October 6–7 to cease "loft" bombing is further evidence of his intimate knowledge of the air force and its limitations.[31]

As noted, a significant gap existed in Elazar's familiarity with the IAF's plans for assisting the ground forces, but this was not because he had not studied them. Rather, it was due to the basic concept that assistance would not be available for forty-eight hours until air supremacy was attained and the ground force reservists were mobilized—all of which would occur after a warning had been received.[32] Furthermore, Southern Command's prewar certitude that the regular armored units would successfully block an Egyptian crossing attempt without recourse to air support created a situation in which the air force was without a plan for assisting the ground forces in thwarting the flow of Egyptian forces across the canal.

Summary of the Test Case

Elazar seems to have had a deep understanding of the air force's mandatory conditions for a preemptive strike against the SAM array. He was well acquainted with the plans that were frequently shown before the war and with the "loft" bombing method. During the war he was able to hold an in-depth discussion with the IAF commander on the prioritization of missions and ORBAT. His decision to shift the air effort from Tagar in the south to Dugman in the north does not indicate gaps in Elazar's knowledge or understanding, since Peled had explained the ramifications of discontinuing Tagar and the time needed to halt the operation and shift to Dugman, though he had not made it clear that Dugman would be executed without an updated intelligence picture of the missile batteries' location, including the mobile SA-6 batteries. (It is possible that Peled too was unaware of the ramifications.)

Rafael Eitan and the Artzav 19 Plan in the 1982 First Lebanon War

Operation Artzav (Mole Cricket) 19—the June 9, 1982, destruction of fourteen Syrian SAM missile batteries and two SAM brigade HQs in the Beqaa Valley in the First Lebanon War, conducted on the fourth day of the war—represents the third instance of the pattern for achieving air supremacy before assisting ground forces. This case study examines Chief of Staff Rafael Eitan's familiarity with IAF plans.

The SAMs had become a strategic issue by the spring of 1981, more than a year before the war began. In spring 1981, the Lebanese theater changed when the Christian militias in Lebanon asked for Israel's aid against the Syrians, following which the IDF announced the Air Summit alert. Attention was partially channeled to dealing with problems created by the missile deployment. Given the concern that the IAF would be denied freedom to gather intelligence and strike at terrorists, the elimination of the missile batteries was deemed vital. When the operation to destroy the batteries was canceled because of inclement weather, Israel agreed to the American request to embark upon a diplomatic track to remove the missiles.[33]

In a series of discussions between April 28 and May 10, 1981, IAF commander Major General David Ivry listed all the considerations that the chief of staff had to weigh before ordering an attack on the Syrian SAMs in Lebanon or the Osirak nuclear reactor in Baghdad. For example, Ivry said, one of the dilemmas was whether to attack the entire SAM array or only part of it: "The chief of staff agrees with me that the entire missile array has to be taken out, otherwise the batteries that haven't been hit will target the aircraft that attack the neighboring batteries. Isn't this what they're there for? In other words, a partial attack is more dangerous than an attack on the entire array."[34]

In the Knesset's Foreign Affairs and Defense Committee meeting, Ivry repeated in detail his reasons for recommending an attack against the entire SAM array in the Beqaa valley and Lebanon mountain ridge rather than in just part of it, while avoiding being dragged into an all-out war with Syria. His analysis included the possibility, however unlikely, that America's special representative would succeed in securing a partial withdrawal of the batteries. If freedom in Lebanon's skies was not achieved, then assistance to the Christians would certainly be limited.

Two cardinal military reasons were presented. One, an attack on part of the array is a greater risk than an attack on the entire array; and two, the destruction of the entire array could be a major deterrent in staving off an all-out war and could force the Syrians to spend several years in preparations before launching another adventure. The main argument was that revealing the IAF's latest capabilities meant exploiting the full potential of the surprise element. Their partial use would probably hasten Syria's development of countermeasures that would prevent Israel from prevailing in the next confrontation. "The ministerial committee naturally accepted my recommendation, as did the prime minister."[35]

These testimonies prove that the chief of staff, who, by Ivry's admission, was a partner in the deliberations and decisions, had a thorough understanding of both the strategic significance of an attack against the missiles and the operational consequences of an attack against the entire SAM array as compared to only part of it.

Ivry recalled that the question of employing the systemic capability—a new C2 apparatus, various types of missiles and bombs, electronic warfare systems, and sophisticated intelligence acquisition systems that had been developed as a surprise weapon in the wake of the flaws in the Yom Kippur War and had been designed basically for a large-scale war—was discussed only in internal IAF forums and not with the chief of staff.[36] This type of discussion should have been held jointly with the chief of staff and the political level. This appears to be a clear case of overindependence of the IAF and a failure to involve the chief of staff in air decisions.

In the course of formulating the Oranim plan for war against the PLO in Lebanon, the issue of attacking the SAM array was brought up again. This time it was agreed that "the timing of the attack . . . would be determined professionally and objectively close to the start of or during the operation, and the decision would depend, among other things, on whether or not to pursue the fight with Syria."[37]

In March 1982 the chief of staff conducted the Shoshanim (Roses) war game. One of the questions that arose was the timing of an attack against the Syrian SAM array. The head of the IAF staff claimed that a confrontation with the Syrians was unavoidable. Since target acquisition required swift action, the IAF had to be allowed to attack quickly, as this would enable the ground forces to advance rapidly. The IAF commander recommended attacking at "H" hour plus two to six hours, that is, in the early stages of the operation. The head of Aman, Yehoshua Sagi, also recommended attacking the SAMs at an early date, either before or immediately after the commencement of ground operations, as this might lead to dogfights that would gain the IAF air supremacy and enable the annihilation of enemy armor, as in the Six-Day War.[38] When the generals met on May 13 to discuss the plans for Lebanon, Ivry expressed his views. The IAF pushed very strongly to open with an attack on the SAM array, but for strategic-political reasons Ivry didn't think this was practical, since it meant declaring war on Syria: "True, the IDF would be drawn into attacking the SAMs during the operation, and from a military point of view it would be preferable, ironically, to begin the campaign like this, but such a gambit that immediately pulled the Syrians into the fighting meant that Oranim, whose objective was to alter the Israel-PLO terrorist equation, would not be achieved."[39]

The reports from the general staff discussions reveal that Chief of Staff Eitan was very well informed about the nature of the problem and the plans for its solution. During the fighting, Defense Minister Ariel Sharon held a three-hour discussion (from 11:30 p.m. June 8 to 2:30 a.m. June 9) that demonstrates his and Eitan's high level of understanding of the dilemma and their ability to relate to the air force's plans. An unresolved question was the Syrians' Third SAM Division and 82nd SAM Brigade's destination. The key to every Syrian armored maneuver in the Beqaa Valley was the SAMs' protection of the Syrian forces. Thus, the question was whether the IDF should first remove the SAM umbrella and then attack the ground forces from the air and in armor battles. And if so, the 82nd SAM Brigade had to be stopped before it reached its deployment site or at least located and attacked before it had time to deploy. Before June 8, thirteen batteries were already positioned in the area, and on June 8 another battery arrived. The 82nd with its five SA-6 batteries was making its way to the fighting zone, bringing the number of batteries up to nineteen—fifteen SA-6s and four heavy batteries. Therefore, if the brigade deployed in the Dahr al-Baidar area (high ground twenty kilometers east of Beirut), the IAF's operational ability would be reduced in the whole area as far as Jounieh (fifteen kilometers north of Beirut).

After the commander of Northern Command's presentation, Sharon and the deputy chief of staff discussed various issues dealing with the air force. Regarding Syria's reaction to losing their planes, IAF deputy commander Brigadier General Amos Amir told Sharon that it didn't matter much since the Syrians were used to it. The deputy chief of staff asked whether the arrival of another SAM brigade would hurt the IAF's ability to attack the SAMs. Amir answered that it would. The head of Aman interjected and said that he believed the greatest threat was not the reinforcement of the missile array in the Beqaa Valley, but the brigade's deployment at the edge of the missile-saturated zone on the mountain ridge (he may have been referring to the Dahr al-Baidar area), which would create another missile-saturated zone. Amir pointed out that although on the day after the brigade's long trip its operability would be limited, its deployment site would still have to be identified as early as possible. He then stated that what he was about to say represented his own view, as he had not spoken with the IAF commander yet. It was his opinion that Operation Hafarperet (Mole)—an air attack against the SAM array—had to be carried out on June 8. The original operation against the SAM array deployed in Lebanon would be carried out as planned. The arrival of the 82nd Brigade had altered the situation, but in this case the "first-day effect" needed to be taken into account, as it would effectively hinder the brigade and thus facilitate the task of dealing with it. The air force had to locate it in the morning, exploit the first-day effect, integrate the attack plan into the general plan, and hit the entire array in one strike.[40]

Eitan summed up the discussion:

> Let me say this about the attack on the SAM array: preparing for it doesn't interfere with the air force's other activities. The planes can be on alert every day, in all kinds of weather and conditions: visibility, angles of the sun, shadow, and other influences. Electro-optics enables this. For example, the SAMs could be attacked on June 8 between 10:30 and 15:00. Since June 8 a method has been adopted: the planes remain on alert for attacking the SAMs the same day. For example, if at 09:00, June 8, we decide to carry out an attack, this can be done at 11:00.[41]

The defense minister asked that he be informed whether the Syrian 82nd Brigade had deployed in Lebanon when he arrived in Jerusalem at 9 a.m. The chief of staff replied that it might be impossible; if the brigade moved into position without deploying, it would be hard to detect. It could even reach Dahr al-Baidar and set up an ambush that would be discovered only after its radar was activated, which meant only after it detected Israeli planes. In the chief of staff's opinion, the IAF should not attack the SAMs from the air unless there was no alternative, because hitting the missiles would add new dimensions to the fighting and force the sides to mutual responses. Nearly all the SAM batteries were within range of IDF artillery. When six 175 mm guns arrived, which had already landed from the sea in the 162nd Division's Awali sector, the SAM batteries on the Syrian-Lebanese border would be in their range of fire. The missile array could be attacked in echelon, first with artillery and then with planes, or first with planes followed by artillery fire to keep it paralyzed. He pointed out that on June 8 he had ordered preparations for a joint plan of action.[42]

According to Eitan's memoirs:

> That evening we had to make two decisions: one concerned assessment and the other operations. After reviewing all the scenarios, we realized that after the first armor battle, Syrian involvement was unavoidable and would have to be taken into consideration in all subsequent actions. And if this is how things were, then the Syrian missile array in the Beqaa had to be taken out, otherwise the safety of our planes would be compromised and their freedom of action severely reduced. Differences of opinion revolved around the question of when to attack the missiles. The defense minister wanted it done immediately. I was against it. This would be a complex and difficult operation. It had to be planned down to the minutest detail like work in a laboratory, calculated from A to Z, getting all the fine points down. We'd had a bad experience with missiles in the Yom Kippur War when circumstances forced our planes to attack where the SAMs were operational.[43]

It should be noted that the disagreement between Eitan and Sharon was on principle more than it was about practical arrangements for the operation that Eitan spoke about. Sharon pressed for an attack against the Syrians, whereas Eitan tried to avoid, or at least postpone, the clash, which explains why he insisted on attacking one battery and not the entire SAM array. In light of the chief of staff's reservations, in his discussion with the prime minister on this matter, Sharon brought along General Amir, who spoke passionately in favor of the action.

Summary of the Test Case

Eitan appears to have been well acquainted with the IAF's plans. He displayed a deep understanding of the air force's strategic and operational requirements for carrying out the plan and appeared solidly informed on the technical-operational details. Eitan had developed close professional ties with the head of the IAF operations department, Colonel Aviem Sella, who planned the anti-SAM operations, and deeply trusted him. This probably affected his decisions. Furthermore, Eitan attested that he joined, as a navigator, a Phantom training sortie focused on SAM attack, which convinced him of the IAF's capability to conduct the mission successfully. He had also participated in a test flight before Operation Opera (the Israeli attack on Iraq's Osirak nuclear reactor in June 1981).[44] It is also worth mentioning that Eitan was an amateur pilot and his son an IAF pilot. This too undoubtedly contributed to his familiarity with air operations.

Dan Halutz and the Ground Force Plans before the 2006 Second Lebanon War

On the face of it, this test case is a negative example of a chief of staff's familiarity with the plans of a service that he has not spent his career in, but the matter is more complex and contains elements that do not relate solely to Chief of Staff Dan Halutz, who grew up in the IAF.

The first element is the fact that ground fighting is more complicated than air combat. There are several reasons for this—among them, the integration of different corps and disciplines; the large number of forms of battle that must be mastered in order to wield them in coordination; the various fighting methods linked to field conditions (open area fighting, urban warfare, mountain warfare, and others); and the relatively large number of echelons. The aggregate of these factors makes an understanding of the nature of ground fighting, and its capabilities and needs, more demanding for an air commander to learn than vice versa.

The second element deals with the cutbacks in ground force training and the relatively little time spent by the general staff discussing the ground forces' operational plans in the Lebanese theater in the years before the Second Lebanon War (when Shaul Mofaz and Moshe Ya'alon served as chiefs of staff). When Halutz served in different roles on the general staff he could have familiarized himself with the employment of ground forces (even if only to a limited degree, as stated). Under the circumstances mentioned above, he had no opportunity to learn the intricacies of their employment in a war scenario, mainly because almost no exercises of this type were held. Even in the IDF's yearly Fire Stones 9 exercise in June 2004, which focused on the northern theater (when Halutz was on standby between IAF commander and deputy chief of staff), Chief of Staff Ya'alon decided not to use the maneuver plan that Northern Command proposed.[45] In addition, general staff discussions on operational plans for employing ground forces in the northern theater were relatively limited in this period.

The third element is Halutz's conviction that a large-scale ground maneuver was not a relevant option. This meant that during his tenure as chief of staff little or no planning went into the large-scale employment of ground forces in a confrontation in Lebanon.

The combination of these factors, together with the political echelon's rejection of Halutz's airpower-based pressure concept for action in Lebanon, created a situation in which during the Second Lebanon War Halutz made relatively large-scale use of the ground forces without knowing the characteristics of a major ground action and the basic needs for ground combat in an arena such as Lebanon. This section examines Halutz's degree of familiarity with the ground plans from two perspectives: familiarity with the ground forces' "DNA" and knowledge of their plans for Lebanon.

In his book *At Eye Level*, Halutz describes his efforts to familiarize himself with the ground forces' units, capabilities, personnel, professional culture, and so forth. He writes that during the year that he served as assistant head of Agam (2000) and the six months as the first head of Amatz after the organizational changes were introduced, he became increasingly involved in the processes, initiatives, and decisions dealing with the entire IDF organization, especially with the ground forces. During this period, he and others prepared the IDF for the possible renewal of Palestinian terror and the possibility of pulling out of Lebanon: "I participated in numerous ground forces exercises and got to know many of the people who, in the coming years when I served as chief of staff, would become my subordinates and colleagues on the general staff."[46]

Regarding familiarity with the units, participation in exercises, and acquaintance with the ground force language, he testified that from the end of his tenure as IAF commander in April 2004 to the time he became deputy chief of staff in July, he devoted all his energy to learning the basics of the IDF organization, especially the ground forces' corps. He took part in dozens of individual and group meetings, toured units and army bases, and participated in ground force exercises at various levels. He also held meetings with government officials. He described the reason for choosing his bureau chief, Major Yaron Finkelman, who had completed his tour of duty as deputy commander of the 890th Paratrooper Battalion: "I felt I needed a quality officer next to me who could clarify the concepts and jargon of the ground forces."[47]

As for his choice of deputy chief of staff, he wrote that his first meeting on the composition of the general staff was with Major General Moshe Kaplinsky on February 22, 2005, prior to his formal nomination. He told Kaplinsky that if he [Halutz] were chosen to be the next chief of staff, he wanted him as his deputy. "He seemed the perfect choice to fill in my knowledge gap on the ground forces."[48]

Halutz describes the differences between the air force culture and ground forces culture and relates how Eisenkot, the head of the operations branch (Amatz), enlightened him on the cultural gap with respect to orders.[49] Halutz recalled a September 2006 lesson-learning meeting in Northern Command after the Second Lebanon War, where it was said that the working assumption should be that when an order is given it won't be obeyed—therefore, the person giving the order is responsible for seeing that the order is carried out. Halutz admitted that upon hearing this he was blown away by the honesty and matter-of-factness of such a revelation. "I'd been accustomed to a different operational culture where an order is sacred, and after it's issued, the person who issued it hasn't the slightest doubt that the person who received it will fulfill it to the letter. What two senior officers were telling me corroborated what General Eisenkot had said during the war."[50]

Halutz's description of the ground forces culture does grave injustice to reality and seems to be rooted in a basic misunderstanding of the ground forces' command culture, where a relatively wide berth is given to interpretation and discussion of a mission and the manner of accomplishing it because of the high complexity of land warfare. This takes place during battle procedure, mainly at the senior command levels, where debates often become heated. This phenomenon is fundamentally different from the specific and detailed attack missions that are characteristic of the air force's C2 method, which cuts across the echelons. Here the mission is target based and the operation is orchestrated from above, which leaves less room for discussion.

On the diminished capabilities of the ground forces as a result of cutbacks in training, Halutz claimed that he was aware of the growing gap, which had begun during his predecessors' tenure, and had even warned others of it. During the standing army's Ga'ash Division exercise he witnessed firsthand the byproduct of lack of training. "I jotted down: 'The number of mockup enemy vehicles doesn't fit a divisional exercise. Divisional headquarters is a mess. The division's headquarters and its centers have to be reorganized. The relationships between the field corps headquarters and the division headquarters confuse commanders. No one's given any thought about integrating the air force's capabilities into the divisional effort.'"

In Halutz's opinion, his criticism was proven by the fact that 2004 saw a trend of making do with headquarters training because of budgetary constraints that precluded full-scale divisional exercises. This type of training had an irreparably adverse effect on the senior commanders, who lost the ability to appreciate the true significance of moving brigade- and division-size forces, especially with regards to time and space, and of combining multiple efforts of fire and maneuver that would fulfill the division's mission. The results of the Second Lebanon War speak for themselves. In places where the commanders were supposed to operate large formations, they had a hard time integrating the various efforts (air, artillery, engineers, armor, and infantry) into a synergetic push directed toward the division's mission.[51]

Halutz's account contains a contradiction. On the one hand he admits to participating in ground units' exercises at various levels, and on the other hand he notes the growing trend in the IDF of sufficing with headquarters training.[52]

A look at the ground forces' training graph of 2004–6 shows that the standing army brigades carried out skeleton exercises without exception, rather than partly skeleton and partly full-strength exercises, as was the norm before the belt tightening that preceded the Second Lebanon War, so Halutz's claim that "the cutbacks effectively canceled full-scale divisional exercises" testifies to his lack of familiarity with the nature of a divisional exercise (a skeleton exercise even after the Second Lebanon War). Two skeleton divisional exercises were carried out in 2004 (one of which Halutz described), and such exercises were held for four regular army brigades.[53] In 2005—the year of the Gaza disengagement—not a single divisional exercise was held and only one skeleton brigade exercise occurred.[54] In 2006 (up until the war) there were no divisional exercises and only two reserve brigades underwent skeleton exercises.[55]

Regarding his awareness of Northern Command's war plans, Halutz wrote that from the beginning of his tenure as chief of staff he dealt extensively with the northern theater at the military level and in talks with the political echelon. He claimed that in the very first discussion on June 27, 2005, he began to formulate a policy of action in the north, based on military intelligence that Israel was heading toward a confrontation with Hezbollah. The next day, Defense Minister Mofaz and Halutz arrived in Northern Command for a working visit. The command headquarters reviewed the situation on the border and presented recommendations for directions of action. Halutz said, "In the course of these talks, ideas began to crystallize for a policy change that I would recommend to the political echelon."[56]

Halutz's policy change was to leverage the damage on "assets" in Lebanon as a means of pressuring Hezbollah. Actually he appears not to have adopted a new approach but to have returned to the one that he presented in 1996 when he was IAF chief of staff.[57] In 2000, as IAF commander, he stated that "airpower alone is capable of deciding a war, and can definitely be a senior partner in a battlefield decision. This is possible on condition that the ORBAT is sufficient and appropriate, that its employment is calculated and not merely a search for targets, unless it has already chosen the requisite ones."[58] It seems that Halutz meant attacking Lebanese "assets" as "the requisite targets" (medium- and long-range rockets and multipurpose military-civilian targets) for achieving the goal, as opposed to searching and "hunting" for targets (the elusive short-range rocket launchers). This statement was probably a result of the IAF having learned from the US Air Force about effects-based operations (EBO).[59]

Needless to say, Halutz was not the only one in the IDF who saw airpower as the answer to the Lebanese problem. The approach had been developed during the tenure of his predecessor, Chief of Staff Moshe "Bogie" Ya'alon, who applied it in the general staff Fire Stones 9 exercise in June 2004 without a ground maneuver, even though there was a plan for one.[60]

According to Halutz, after the Gaza disengagement in the summer of 2005, the IDF was able to devote more attention to events in the north, "which in a certain sense resembled a volcano just before it explodes. Jets of smoke and steam occasionally spewed skyward like a warning to everyone to get ready for the eruption."[61]

The fact is that Defense Minister Mofaz's instructions to Chief of Staff Halutz in March 2005 (before the Gaza disengagement) to revise the plans for Lebanon by the end of 2005 were not carried out.[62] Halutz describes how he developed his familiarity with the northern theater, recalling the visit in Northern Command of Ehud Olmert, the acting prime minister, in February 2006; the discussion that Olmert chaired in early March 2006; and especially the general staff meeting with Northern Command on March 13. The meeting lasted several hours, during which the Northern Command presented its operational concept for action in Lebanon. Changes in the operational plans were agreed upon and were later code-named Mei Merom (Sky High Water) and Shoveret Kerach (Icebreaker). In brief, the plan was a three-stage operational action: first, massive and lengthy air, ground, and sea fire; second, Icebreaker's limited ground moves (raids by ground forces); and third, Sky High Water—a larger-scale ground maneuver across Southern Lebanon from the Israeli-Lebanese border to the Litani River. The shift from stage to stage depended on the previous stage's degree of success in achieving its goals and required authorization from the political level.[63]

Colonel (res.) Boaz Cohen, Northern Command's operations officer, avows that, to the best of his recollection, at the end of the meeting the chief of staff said, "Get this straight, one division is enough to solve the problem in Lebanon."[64]

According to the Winograd report, the chief of staff lacked a solid operational plan for the Lebanese front. The working plan was called Country Defender (which suited the situation where the Syrian army was stationed in Lebanon, before the massive strengthening of Hezbollah's defense array in South Lebanon). The battle procedure for maintaining this general staff plan was halted about a year and a half before the war. Although most of the senior officers had moved on to other positions, the plan was jettisoned without a replacement.[65]

The Galilee Division exercise that was a part of Northern Command's Joined Arms exercise took place in June 2006 and dealt almost exclusively with fighting in the Northern Command theater. The command exercised the operational plans that were still in the draft stage but in advanced stages of receiving authorization. All of the IDF services took part in the exercise, but it mainly consisted of headquarters and skeleton forces. As Halutz stated: "This was an additional step in elevating the command's level of readiness for combat in its sector, and part of the annual training plan that was based on the assessment that Israel would probably be in a confrontation with Hezbollah in the summer."[66]

Again, we find a contradiction in Halutz's statement. If such an assessment had been made, then he was duty-bound to execute a set of urgent actions to hone the army's readiness for war (as Elazar did in May 1973). The chief of staff seems to have been referring to the multi-year intelligence assessment of May 2006 that found "the potential for deterioration on the northern front had risen."[67] This is the type of vague evaluation that influences long-range force design and preparation. Halutz's interest in the exercise focused on C2 issues under the renewed operational concept according to which the commander of Northern Command was supposed to be the "campaign commander." This issue, and not the operational concept for fighting Hezbollah, headed the agenda in senior-level discussions both before and after the exercise.[68] Cohen, Northern Command's operations officer, claims that "the 'campaign commander' issue remained unresolved and unacceptable to the air force, as far as I know." During the Joint Arms exercise, other aspects of the campaign commander's role—the lack of coordination and agreement—and matters related to it developed into full-blown issues.[69]

Regarding the regional command role in the war, Major General Udi Adam, the commander of Northern Command, insists that Halutz didn't have a clue as to "how the regional command works. He asked me 'why the command headquarters doesn't sit on the general staff,' a question that reflects his utter lack of understanding of the regional command and the meaning of regional responsibility [the headquarters' responsibility for the entire area]. This is the clearest expression of the IAF mentality [responsibility for the mission, detachment from the area context]."[70]

This failure to comprehend the true nature of the regional command and its responsibility seems to have been a key factor in the employment of the ground forces in the war.

Regarding the plans for the Lebanese theater, Halutz said that the war in Lebanon was not a hypothetical scenario. The IDF had been dealing with this possibility since 2000. Plans were drawn up and training was carried out. The air force had been training to destroy the long-range missiles since 2001. The commanders of Northern Command came and went, and each one updated the orders in view of the developing capabilities and intelligence reports. Concerning his views on the role of air power in a future war in Lebanon, Halutz admitted that as the IAF commander in 2000–2004, he endeavored to convince the general staff to give the air force a major role in combat operations, but "I never said that the IAF alone could achieve a decisive victory if war broke out. . . . In fact, the opposite was said. The air force repeatedly stated that there were currently no operational solutions from the air for short-range Katyusha rockets. This was true for Lebanon as it was for Gaza." He emphasized that when hostilities began (July 12), a comprehensive written operational idea had already been formulated for war in Lebanon, the product of thought and discussion in Northern Command and the general staff (the Icebreaker and Sky High Water plans).[71]

Halutz appears to have strongly believed that pressuring Lebanon to force Hezbollah to stop was the answer, as he suggested when serving as IAF chief of staff in 1996. Regarding the ground maneuver, he claimed that from day one of the war he perceived an unwillingness to implement it. This was based on an assessment of the cost relative to the expected benefit. The experience of eighteen years in Lebanon (1982–2000) was the most compelling evidence of the exorbitant price Israel paid for meager returns. He further attested that he perceived that the question was not how to enter Lebanon, but how to leave it. The spirit and rhetoric in the meetings with the political echelon were unequivocal: there was no desire or intention to engage in a wide-scale ground maneuver. Nevertheless, two people who consistently opposed this position were Meir Dagan, the head of the Mossad, and Amos Gilad, the head of the political-security staff in the defense ministry.[72]

As the fighting developed, Halutz appears to have been surprised by the political opposition to his idea of attacking targets in Lebanon as a means of applying pressure on Hezbollah. Even though the main point in his prewar concept had been preempted, in several places in his book he claims that he considered the entry of ground forces into Lebanon a mistake. When he was denied permission to implement his concept, he felt that he'd been put in the worst situation possible.

Colonel Roni Numa, the chief of staff's personal aide, asked Halutz what would happen if the political echelon vetoed an attack on Lebanese infrastructure targets.[73] Halutz answered that it wouldn't happen, and therefore he didn't order Amatz to prepare an alternative plan for the use of ground forces. Numa thinks the reason is that "copying and pasting" the IAF's relatively simple and very flexible C2 pattern onto the ground forces is what led Halutz to think that when the need arose, he could employ the ground forces relatively quickly even if there were no plans for it. Apparently, he was unaware of the critical role that in-depth battle procedure demanded before a ground forces operation. It included discussions on key issues and voicing differences of opinion, should such exist, especially concerning complex and ambiguous situations, not to mention the time needed for the ground forces to prepare for operations in an environment as complex as Lebanon. One example from the general staff's July 18 situation assessment illustrates Halutz's miscalculation of the need for early planning in the employment of ground forces. Halutz rejected a large-scale ground maneuver, saying, "It would be a waste of valuable time in planning, period! If we have to plan for it, there'll be time enough. . . . We may have to plan for it, but then again, maybe we won't. I want an effort made not to [introduce large-scale ground forces into Lebanon]."[74]

The chief of staff's overinvolvement in the command's activities is described in the Winograd report (see chapter 3 of this book, which deals with Halutz's loss of trust in Adam but also discusses the issue at hand).

As Cohen noted:

Put simply, the command has to be given a goal, a mission, along with the resources and constraints, and it must achieve results.

The commanding echelon has to monitor it in reasonable time slots (for Northern Command this was reckoned in days). In reality the general staff gave us the tactical definition of "how" [to carry out the mission] from day one, but the "how" was not always related to the goal or the mission. But jumping headfirst into the tactical matters and demanding an hourly achievement report illustrates more than anything else the chief of staff's lack of understanding of waging a ground force war.[75]

It seems that the definition of "how" and the high rate of required reports stemmed not only from the perception that this was not war, even though, as the first chapter showed, Halutz defined the situation as war. But again, it should be emphasized that Halutz tried to force on the ground action those elements in the IAF's C2 that define specific missions for aircraft. The discussions express the constant tension between Northern Command, which was trying to apply its earlier plans gradually to the developing stages of the maneuver, as agreed upon before the war, and the general staff, which focused on a pattern of limited raids whose final goal Northern Command often found incomprehensible.[76] The raids were managed like the raids in the West Bank and the Gaza Strip—by the general staff's direct control, which did not conform to the situation.

Summary of the Test Case

In this case three elements merged to create a uniquely unhealthy situation. The first was Halutz's unwillingness to employ ground forces although such plans had been drafted (this explains the absence of discussion before the war). Added to this was the command-procedural concept of the chief of staff's role as strategist-in-chief and the command's role as "campaign commander" (as noted, the command had practiced the role in exercises, but its role had not been made absolutely clear). According to this concept the chief of staff is not supposed to be involved in the command's plans (and not even be especially familiar with them). We may add that during Halutz's tenure, between his assuming the role and the outbreak of war, not a single general staff exercise was carried out that could have provided him with knowledge of C2 processes in the GHQ.

The last element is the IAF's approach of C2, where attack missions are assigned relatively quickly and without recourse to discussion between the echelons. Furthermore, Halutz's ignorance of the need for battle procedure for clarifying missions and defining their importance stemmed from this, as well as from the IAF's centripetal C2 culture.

The merging of these elements led Halutz and the IDF into a situation where the use of the ground forces in Northern Command suffered not only from problems of capability and aptitude but also from decision-making and extremely problematic C2 processes at the general staff-command level. Kaplinsky, the deputy chief of staff (whom, it will be recalled, Halutz had appointed as "the most suitable person to fill the gaps in his knowledge of the land army"), contributed to the discussions but failed to bridge the holes in Halutz's understanding.

From Halutz's description of decision making during the fighting, it seems that because of his disappointment with Northern Command's performance (see chapter 3) he was forced to descend to a lower echelon of ground maneuver planning and designate sectors to the divisions on July 19.[77] On August 1, he found himself forced to speak about tactical matters that a chief of staff was not supposed to deal with, such as building hasty defenses for infantry and armored vehicles, a topic that he never imagined he would have to deal with in wartime.[78]

Halutz had no experience in this type of planning, and it frustrated him that Northern Command "was dragging him down," a feeling that had a major impact on his loss of confidence in the commander, Major General Udi Adam.

To sum up the test case, Halutz was partly at fault because of his inherent belief that a wide-scale ground maneuver would not be a major factor in defeating Hezbollah and partly because of the intrinsic difficulty in learning and acquiring experience in ground fighting (due to the ongoing decline in training that had begun with his predecessors).

Under these circumstances he had the minimum knowledge of the nature of ground fighting and the conditions for applying it and was barely aware of the recent plans for the Lebanese theater, since the general staff, which he was in charge of, had not gone over them in depth.

Chapter Summary

The ground force chief of staff's familiarity with the air force's abilities, needs, and limitations was and will remain a critical factor. It seems apparent that when the IDF employs relatively large-scale fire campaigns in urban and populated areas, as it has done in recent years, it does so with the sensitivity required of this type of action. The analysis has shown that David Elazar and Rafael Eitan understood the need for the chief of staff's familiarity with the air force and its plans—and were sufficiently knowledgeable of them. The reason for this may be the excellent results of Operation Moked (1967), when the air force had almost absolute freedom of action. The chief of staff realized the importance of the air service and his need to acquire an in-depth understanding of the IAF's plans.

The common link binding the three ground force chiefs of staff whose familiarity with the air force is analyzed here is that all of them appreciated its strategic importance. On the other hand, Halutz's lack of familiarity with the ground forces' plans seems to have stemmed from a combination of two external factors—an inherent difficulty in understanding complex ground fighting and the absence of a "learning environment" in the years before the war—and two internal factors—his approach that significantly diminished the need for ground maneuvers, and limited preoccupation with the planning for war against Hezbollah.

Looking ahead, it is clear the ground forces–oriented chief of staff must be familiar with the air force's plans and the nature of air operations to a degree that enables him to determine priorities in an emergency for air force missions, evaluate and redirect missions, and act in other decision-making capacities. Beyond this, in a rapidly changing environment where the demands on the air force are reinvented at an increasingly rapid rate, the chief of staff would be well advised to be a partner in the development of knowledge of air force concepts and plans so that he can add meaningful input to them at the start of his tenure and not simply give his stamp of approval to their products.

This chapter has focused on the familiarity of a chief of staff who came up in the ground forces with the air force's plans (and vice versa), but its conclusions are relevant for every area where a leader is not well versed because of the nature of his previous roles. Naval operations, for example, is another domain that the ground forces–oriented chief of staff is not deeply familiar with. The sinking of the INS *Eilat* in 1967 and the *Dakar* submarine in 1968, the capture of *Karin A* in 2002, the damage to the INS *Hanit* in 2006, and the case of the *Marmara* in 2010 are examples of incidents that the chief of staff has had to deal with. The defense of gas-processing rigs may soon be added to his agenda; therefore, he would be well advised to expand his knowledge and understanding on the maritime dimension. Knowledge can be acquired from joint command and staff education (which was enhanced after the Second Lebanon War) and continues throughout an officer's career. But the type of understanding the chief of staff needs can probably only be acquired by supervising naval operations from a command ship or the navy's headquarters, for example, or from IDF GHQ during small-scale operations and by conducting debriefings.

Cyber is another field that is developing at an accelerated pace, but its military history is both limited and classified, which makes learning from it difficult. In the coming years, the chiefs of staff will undoubtedly have a knowledge gap in this dimension because of the abovementioned constraints and also because of the generational gap between them and the younger, cyber-savvy professionals. The rules that have been proposed in this chapter are equally valid for cyberwarfare.

3
LOSING TRUST IN A WARTIME GENERAL

The loss of trust between the chief of staff and a general is a common, probably unavoidable, phenomenon among senior officers who have clashed more than once during their careers.

A brief recall of a few tension-laden relationships in Israel: Moshe Dayan and his deputy Haim Laskov (see chapter 6); Laskov and his deputy Tzvi Tzur (Tzur could not bear working under Laskov, and therefore he asked Ben-Gurion to relieve him of his post and he was sent to France for military studies until his promotion to chief of staff); Shaul Mofaz and his deputy Uzi Dayan (whom Mofaz sought to remove from his position as deputy chief of staff lest he remain a relevant candidate for chief of staff); and Rafael Eitan and Moshe Levi and their attempt to create a scandal by spreading rumors that Dan Shomron was a homosexual. In periods of quiet, these relationships can hamstring staff work, impede decision making, postpone the promotion of capable individuals, and stain the good name of the IDF. In wartime, the chief of staff's loss of trust in the commander of a regional command has far greater consequences. Chief of Staff David Elazar and commander of Southern Command Shmuel Gonen's acerbic relationship in the Yom Kippur War is linked in the public's memory to the grievous shortcomings of that war. But this kind of falling out is a recurring issue, as the Winograd report pointed out in the case of Chief of Staff Dan Halutz and Major General Udi Adam:

> We would have avoided this issue altogether if we thought it solely a personal matter. . . . We comment on it only because it seems that faulty work procedures were the cause of much tension and that the flawed organizational culture must be examined and rectified so that breakdowns like this will not repeat themselves and the IDF will be better prepared to meet future challenges. As we have seen, conceptual gaps and tensions emerged in the interface between the general staff and Northern Command almost from the onset of the fighting. But conceptual differences and perceptional gaps are expected and need not have been an obstacle. The rules for discourse and dialogue, together with military hierarchies, were supposed to be efficient mechanisms for handling such differences properly. The problem that emerged in the war in Lebanon was that the rifts, the differences of opinion, and the distrust that developed were dealt with so ineffectively that they negatively impacted the management of the entire war and its results.[1]

I contend that the recurring dynamics that create such distrust are traceable and analyzable. The elements of these dynamics, which are described in detail at the end of this chapter, can be divided schematically into two types of gaps: (1) prewar differences in approaches, knowledge, and a common language; and (2) disagreements that evolve during wartime, such as gaps in expectations, the intermediation of information by staffs, and problems with reporting.

The three test cases in the chapter are from different periods but are similar in essence. They feature a commander of a regional command who was appointed by the chief of staff and the rifts that developed between them because of the abovementioned factors. The first case discusses Chief of Staff Dayan and the commander of Southern Command, Asaf Simhoni, in the 1956 Sinai War; the second case concerns Chief of Staff Elazar and the commander of Southern Command, Shmuel Gonen, in the Yom Kippur War; and the third case involves Chief of Staff Halutz and the commander of Northern Command, Udi Adam, in the Second Lebanon War.

The question of the chief of staff's trust in his subordinates is also connected to the professional issue of the regional commander's authority and responsibility. The 2006 IDF strategy considered the idea that the regional commander is essentially the "campaign commander." The 2015 IDF strategy turned this decision around and stated that the chief of staff is "campaign commander."[2] The issue itself harbors unresolved tension between chiefs of staff and regional commanders, especially in a one-front campaign as in Sinai in 1956, Lebanon in 2006, and the three major Gaza operations in the first two decades of the twenty-first century. The Dayan-Simhoni case seems to involve this issue more than others, because Israeli airpower at the time was very limited and the operation was carried out primarily by Southern Command ground forces. In the case of Elazar and Gonen, the regional commander's independence does not appear to be the heart of the matter, nor does it in the Halutz-Adam case, despite the definition that was formalized before the war that the regional command is the "campaign commander."

The source of the interechelon tension between the general staff and regional command in wartime seems to originate in two connected gaps. The first is the paradigmatic difference in perspective. The general staff's approach is a strategic-political view of events, whereas the regional command's approach focuses on operational-tactical matters. The second is that in war, the knowledge gap between the two bodies widens, since the attention and focus of each relates to different dimensions of the campaign and, given the time constraints, they find themselves hard-pressed to engage in dialogue to clarify common issues.[3]

The problem in bridging the gap stems from the chief of staff's relative difficulty in exerting his authority over a regional commander who sees himself as the expert on his theater of operations; the difficulty in developing common knowledge, which leads to critical information gaps; and the standard communication channels (orders, instructions, restrictions, visits, plans, conversations between commanders) that produce only a limited dialogue between the two bodies, as not all the knowledge and gaps are apparent. These and other reasons lie at the heart of the following case studies.

The Crisis between Moshe Dayan and Asaf Simhoni in the 1956 Sinai War

During the Sinai War (October 29 to November 5, 1956) the IDF routed the Egyptian army and occupied the Sinai Peninsula. The year leading up to the war witnessed an arms race between the two countries, and it is widely accepted that Israel escalated the situation in order to conduct a preemptive war before Egypt could fully utilize its newly acquired superior planes and tanks. Israel aligned with Britain and France in a coalition before the war and was the land actor in a campaign designed to overthrow Egyptian president Gamal Abdel Nasser.

After the armored units' inadequate maintenance status was revealed and the likelihood of war increased in 1956, Dayan made a list of urgent appointments on July 17. Haim Laskov, the deputy chief of staff and head of Agam, was appointed commander of the Armored Corps HQ. Meir Amit, commander of Southern Command, moved to the head of Agam, and Asaf Simhoni, who was on leave to study in Britain, was chosen to replace Amit at Southern Command. Dayan sent off two telegrams to London. The first, dated July 17, ordered Michael Bengal, the IDF liaison in London, to "put Asaf Simhoni on an El-Al flight back to the country as soon as his studies were over." The second, dated July 19, was a frantic message labeled "most private" and was also delivered to Bengal. In it, Dayan informed Simhoni that he was being promoted to commander of Southern Command and his immediate reply was required. This was a year and a half after

Dayan dissolved Southern Command and a few months after he realized his error; he ordered its reestablishment as the possibility of war loomed on the southern horizon. Furthermore, he had to choose the most qualified officer to command it. Only eight years had passed since the War of Independence. No senior IDF colonel had more wartime command experience than Simhoni. It is important to note that Dayan wanted Amit next to himself in Agam, thus leaving Amit's post as commander of Southern Command vacant. In addition, Simhoni had served successfully for a year as the temporary commander of Northern Command, a post he appears to have received on Dayan's recommendation. In this capacity he worked in close coordination with Dayan, who was the head of Agam.[4] However, personal tension arose in the Dayan-Simhoni relationship as both officers competed for Ben-Gurion's favor. Still, Dayan valued Simhoni as a commander. According to Uzi Narkis, Dayan created "a semi-official advisory body consisting of officers whose opinions he respected, among whom were Asaf Simhoni, Meir Amit and myself."[5]

Simhoni was Dayan's choice to command Southern Command, but this did not prevent Simhoni from criticizing the chief of staff when he felt necessary. For example, in a general staff meeting after the October 10, 1956, Qalqilya reprisal raid fiasco (in which eighteen Israeli soldiers were killed and sixty-eight wounded, while eighty-eight Jordanian soldiers were killed and fifteen wounded), Simhoni leveled harsh criticism against the plan that Ariel Sharon, the paratroop commander, had formulated with Dayan's authorization.[6]

Another source of tension developed between Dayan and Simhoni over Sharon. Sharon was accustomed to reporting his border operations directly to the chief of staff, but Simhoni, the newly promoted regional commander, demanded that Sharon report to him on actions in his sector. He even ordered a regional command operations branch staff officer, equipped with a radio, to accompany Sharon's force on every retaliatory raid. Dayan was forced to agree to this arrangement.[7]

The differences between Dayan and Simhoni on the use of armored forces boiled down to two issues: one, a conceptual gap on the basic manner of their employment; and two, the specific manner of employing the Seventh Armored Brigade (regulars) in the Kadesh plan to conquer Sinai in 1956.

Regarding the conceptual gap between the chief of staff and the regional commander, the commander of the Seventh Brigade, Uri Ben Ari, wrote, "[In] a September 1, 1956, operational discussion on the manner of employing armor [presented in detail in chapter 6], Dayan stated that armor would remain a support branch for the infantry." According to Ben Ari's notes on the chief of staff's visit to the brigade on September 26, Dayan had not changed his mind. In the operational discussion, Simhoni agreed with Dayan and rejected an alternative suggestion of concentrating armor. He also stated that in the event of war the Seventh Brigade would have to split up, since two tank battalions in an armored brigade were superfluous in wartime.[8]

But over the next two months Simhoni changed his attitude, telling Ben Ari, "After all the talk about 'how armor will fight' and after a penetrating look at a map of Sinai, I realize that you were right in your approach to armor. If you'll be allowed to operate according to your doctrine, there's an excellent chance we'll win this war."[9]

Simhoni, the commander of the forces in the field, viewed the delay in using armor as a distorted approach to the battlefield reality and the mistaken employment of his forces. Dayan may have been motivated to delay armor's entry into action partly due to his prewar negative evaluation of its maintenance status.[10]

As for the correct use of armor, the chief of staff and the regional commander were divided on the issue. The conceptual gap had remained under the radar before the war, when it was neither discussed nor clarified, and may have been a key factor in Simhoni's opposition to Dayan's decision concerning the employment of the Seventh Brigade in the Sinai War plans.

The second element in the gap between the chief of staff and the regional commander undoubtedly stemmed from Dayan's micromanagement in the planning and supervision of the Sinai War. Simhoni harbored a host of professional misgivings over the plan, such as the need for the 38th Division headquarters, which had been hastily set up (without any field exercises); its commander, Yehuda Wallach, with whom Simhoni was unfamiliar; and the subordination of two brigades (the Ninth and 202nd) to the direct command of the general staff.

But the crux of the breach between Dayan and Simhoni revolved around the manner of deploying the Seventh Armored Brigade. Simhoni's basic argument against the Kadesh 1 order will probably never be known, but from his various statements he seems to have opposed the disparagement of Egypt's fighting capability and vociferously complained that as commander of Southern Command, he hadn't been a partner in the formulation of the order. Zonik Shaham, one of the few officers to whom Simhoni divulged the secret of the expected developments in early October, recalled the atmosphere that pervaded Southern Command's headquarters when Kadesh 1 was issued. "For all practical purposes the general staff dictated it to us," Shaham said. "It allotted forces to Southern Command, but the general staff called all the shots, and Simhoni reared up on his hind legs, and roared, 'I'm in charge of Southern Command. Tell me what to capture, give me the troops and it'll be "mission accomplished." If you get what you ordered, then good; if you don't, then sack me. But don't tell me how to do it.'"

This wasn't a case of a commander jealously guarding his turf but the way Simhoni expressed his opposition to the remote-control campaign management from the GHQ hundreds of kilometers from the fighting theater. This trend was the antithesis of Southern Command's and the IDF's warfighting doctrine that recognized the responsibility and importance of the opinions of the operating echelon. Given Simhoni's combat experience as a commander in the War of Independence and the professional knowledge he had acquired since, he was certain that this kind of management could not be a substitute for a situationally aware command close to the front. This was especially true considering that the IDF's shoddy communication equipment hampered the GHQ's activity in real time.

This attitude toward dictates from above, and the way information reached the chief of staff, did not work in the regional commander's favor. "Anyone who knows Dayan," Shaham recalled, "knows that you don't say to him 'don't tell me what to do.'" This too is what probably precipitated the highly charged discussion on the Seventh Brigade. Shaham remembered the long-standing friendship between the two when Dayan was commander of Northern Command and Simhoni commander of the Golani Brigade: "The first time I sensed that something had soured between them was after one of the orders groups for the Sinai War, when Simhoni's request to have a free hand in employing Uri Ben Ari's 7th Brigade, which the general staff had designated as its own reserve force, was denied."[11]

A factor whose importance cannot be overstated in the context of the interechelon gap over the employment of the Seventh Brigade was the need for strict secrecy about the political pacts with the French and British. This tripartite coalition formed the basis of the new plan—Kadesh 2—that was presented to the general staff on October 25. It included a maneuver in northern Sinai in a later stage than what was planned in Kadesh 1 and provided an answer to Ben-Gurion's political concern that the British and French would renege on their part in the plan. The plan called for an Israeli parachute drop into the mountain passes of western Sinai and a British-French operation on the Suez Canal in the opening round of the war. This would facilitate the IDF's activity in northern Sinai and its thrust south to Sharm el-Sheikh. Dayan brought a few members of the general staff into the secret but not the regional commanders, including Simhoni.

Dayan stated:

Everyone will be updated on only the essential details of his mission, even if he doesn't understand the overall moves. Given the political objectives, curious orders will be issued that seem to defy what we've planned till now, and they may appear counter to military logic. Nevertheless, staff officers and combat officers must obey them without reservation, whether in practice or in talk among yourselves. Absolute discipline is required . . . especially for the unconventional decision to begin the war by conceding the air initiative and operational surprise.[12]

Thus, Simhoni and others were not privy to Dayan's plans.[13] In the ensuing days, in the same vein, Dayan ordered the commanders of Southern Command and Laskov's 77th Division "not to argue with the general staff."[14] When Simhoni returned from the general staff to the command's headquarters, he told his senior officers that "the chief of staff has gone nuts." He opposed Dayan's idea that the Egyptians would interpret the remote paratrooper drop and the movements of the three brigades as a raid and therefore transfer their forces to the fortified facilities in eastern Sinai. Simhoni also questioned the rationale behind the operations of the 202nd Paratrooper Brigade and the Ninth Brigade.[15] Dayan's meeting with Southern Command's senior commanders on October 27 testifies to the divide between the chief of staff and the regional command. Dayan denied the request by Simhoni and Wallach, the commander of the 38th Division, to deploy the Seventh Brigade at the start of the fighting.[16] In disregard of the general staff's instructions on the use of the Seventh only on the third day of the war, Simhoni ordered Ben Ari to prepare to move out the moment the fighting commenced.

The day after his message to Ben Ari, Simhoni tried to convince Dayan to engage the Seventh Brigade in action as soon as the Fourth Brigade captured Kusseima on the first night of the campaign (the capture had been moved forward from stage 2 to stage 1)—and was denied. The chief of staff demanded that he not move the Seventh Brigade into Sinai except in the event the Fourth Brigade ran into severe trouble. According to Elad Peled, Southern Command's operations officer, Simhoni said in the October 28 orders group, "This is the plan! In the end I'm the one who'll be in the field and I'll decide [what has to be done]." Peled saw this not as an expression of overweening pride but as part of the norm expected of every IDF officer, especially of a regional commander. In Peled's eyes, Simhoni read the battlefield correctly and his sense of the field was outstanding.[17]

Leaving Simhoni uninformed of the secret political conditions undoubtedly contributed to the disagreement with Dayan. On the morning of October 30, when the Fourth Brigade was stuck on the

Kusseima Road, Simhoni sent the Seventh Brigade into action, a move that apparently infuriated Dayan, even though he adopted Simhoni's initiative without change.

Dayan's diary entry reads:

> Yesterday I had a stiff contretemps with the commander of Southern Command who, contrary to GHQ orders, sent the 7th Armored Brigade into action before their appointed time. Despite the specific orders that armored forces were not to be employed before October 31 and explanatory reasons for this, commander of Southern Command considered that not a moment should be wasted and immediately at the start of operations initiative and surprise should be exploited to advance and capture whatever he could. He accordingly resolved to send into action, already on D-Day, all the forces at his command. As for the instructions of the general staff's and the military-political considerations that had called for a different approach, he, the commander of Southern Command, was not prepared to rely on the possibility that "someone else"—i.e., Anglo-French forces—might go into action, and he therefore saw no justification for holding up our main attack for forty-eight hours. He felt that the GHQ orders on this matter were a political and military mistake for which we would pay dearly.[18]

Mordechai Bar-On, the head of Dayan's office, who naturally supported his commander's position, wrote that Simhoni's decision to enter the Seventh Brigade on Tuesday morning, October 30, was a hasty move that stemmed from a lack of discipline and a limited understanding of the strategic planning: "Dispatching the 7th Brigade was a command error and flagrant act of irresponsibility."[19]

It is difficult to know all of Dayan's thoughts, beyond his anger at Simhoni's insubordination in wartime. Was it envy at Simhoni's prewar approach that proved correct, Simhoni's personal relations with

Ben-Gurion, or Dayan's desire to reap the victor's laurels for himself? Whatever the reason, his charges against Simhoni touched on issues of substance.

There were several events that the general staff interpreted as Southern Command's loss of control during the fighting. First and foremost, obfuscation surrounded the whereabouts of the Seventh Brigade, not only in its premature deployment but also in the later stages of the fighting. Furthermore, Dayan received a bitter impression from an array of blunders, such as the 10th Brigade's dithering, which led to its commander's removal; the 37th Brigade's hasty and failed actions; and the air force's attacks on IDF troops because the pilots were not given the location of advancing IDF units. Observers from the IDF history branch, ensconced in the GHQ's operations center, wrote on October 31 that Southern Command Headquarters had begun to lose control of its forces.[20]

In various parts of the chief of staff office's log, Bar-On compiled statements with Dayan's consent denouncing Simhoni. For example, one version describes the Dayan-Simhoni falling out on October 30:

Yehuda Wallach [38th Division commander] appears to have completely lost control of the situation, and functions at best as Simhoni's pageboy. Simhoni runs the whole show in partisan-like fashion, issuing orders without coordination or logical order, although he has decision-making skills and is a dynamo in employing and driving his forces in battle. However, it seems that little benefit will come from this duo in the complex organization of running the entire campaign.[21]

Wallach claimed that Simhoni took over his division's main communications equipment so he could issue orders to the Seventh Brigade while bypassing the 38th Division's headquarters.[22] In the afternoon of October 30, Dayan finally found Simhoni in the company of the 38th's commander at the Fourth Brigade's headquarters in Be'erotayim (on the Israeli-Sinai border) after failing to locate him in Southern Command's headquarters in Beer Sheva, and later failing to catch up with him in the command's forward command post in Shelah west of Shivta. Dayan canceled the orders group that Simhoni had planned for the 38th's commanders, postponing it for an hour until he arrived and gave orders that overrode the ones that Simhoni had planned.[23] Thus, the premature deployment of the Seventh Brigade seems to have been only one issue that caused Dayan to lose trust in Simhoni.

The dazzling success of the fighting precipitated a struggle among those seeking to be recognized as the father of victory. On November 4, after the picture became clear, the chief of staff wrote in his diary:

> Asaf Simhoni walks around drunk with victory. His right to boast is extremely limited. Most of the time he was occupied with minor matters in a narrow sector, while Southern Command as a regional command was completely paralyzed . . . and at best he served as a liaison between the general staff and the brigades. . . . Moshe also criticizes Gandhi [Rehavam Ze'evi, the Southern Command chief of staff] . . . for not exerting control over his staff. . . . Gandhi claims that he can't work with Simhoni, who makes a mess out of every piece of orderly work, flings illogical commands at him, and, in short, is intolerable.[24]

The chief of staff's diary documented a meeting between Dayan, Meir Amit, and Haim Laskov on November 5: "Moshe says that in his opinion Simhoni has shown himself to be a blatant failure as commander of Southern Command and regrets this very much, because he believed in his ability." After Simhoni's death in a plane crash on November 6, Dayan tried to delay Ben-Gurion's twin demand to promote Simhoni posthumously to the rank of major general and award him the Distinguished Service Medal. Ben-Gurion finally gave up on the idea of the medal. Dayan's disgruntlement over the laurels that Ben-Gurion and others awarded Simhoni came to expression in the chief of staff's diary.[25]

Summary of the Test Case

The first test case in this chapter is different from the others in that it does not deal with a general's failure of performance in the eyes of the chief of staff but with the lack of discipline that resulted in an overwhelming success. The success of the campaign resulted from Simhoni's order to Ben Ari to advance with the Seventh Brigade, from the 38th Division's push forward, and from other issues that were not under his direct supervision but nonetheless proved successful. The root of Simhoni's insubordination seems to have been a combination of basic differences left unaddressed regarding the proper way to employ armor and openly stated differences regarding the campaign's C2 structure. These two issues, together with Simhoni's self-confidence and accessibility to Ben-Gurion, who regarded him as his protégé, appear to have resulted in Simhoni's decision to deviate from Dayan's instructions, the act that led to the crisis in trust. Other contributing factors were Simhoni's and his headquarters' C2 problems and Simhoni's withholding from the chief of staff updated information on the location of his forces.

The Crisis between David Elazar and Shmuel Gonen in the 1973 Yom Kippur War

Chief of Staff David "Dado" Elazar's loss of trust in the commander of Southern Command, Shmuel "Gorodish" Gonen, during the first days of the Yom Kippur War contains all the elements that were mentioned in the introduction to the chapter: the absence of a common language; faulty management unbecoming of a major general, such as frantic reports and requests; unauthorized changes in understandings that had been reached with the chief of staff; and lack of control over division commanders. In June 1972, six months after becoming chief of staff, Elazar appointed Gonen as head of the doctrine and training branch (Mahad, which was part of Agam). Gonen's rise was controversial, and sharp criticism was voiced after the war by senior commanders who felt that the high posting was above his capabilities, while others noted that Gonen did an outstanding job as head of Mahad. Elazar regarded Gonen as the model of a daring armor commander who would perpetuate the IDF as a fighting body. The critics charged that Elazar gave the man too much credit and underestimated the demands of the role.[26]

On July 1, with Ariel Sharon's retirement from the army, Elazar appointed Gonen the commander of Southern Command in the belief, as Elazar's biographer Hanoch Bartov writes, that Gonen would have time to "grow" into the role. The chief of staff felt that just as Gonen had succeeded in his last role as head of Mahad, he would probably "ripen" as commander of the largest and most complex of regional commands. What may have tilted the decision in Gonen's favor was that the changes in command were made on July 1, just as the apprehension over the Blue and White alert had abated and war seemed to recede into the distance by at least two or three years—time enough for Gonen's "maturation" or for finding a replacement.[27]

The basic plan, code-named Dovecote, for defending the Israeli strongholds (*ma'ozim*) along the Suez Canal in the event of either a limited Egyptian attack or full-scale war, was to send the platoon-size armored forces of the 14th Brigade's regulars on the front line to aid the strongholds and interdict the crossing. In the rear, two regular armored brigades (the 401st and 460th) would wait to be ordered forward to places where the Egyptians had been successful. The three brigades were under the command of the Sinai 252nd Division. At a later stage, two armored divisions of reservists—the 143rd, commanded by Major General (res.) Ariel Sharon, and the 162nd, led by Major General (res.) Avraham Adan—would cross the canal to the Egyptian side.

The following passages illustrate the ingredients that led the chief of staff to lose trust in his subordinate. Already at the outbreak of hostilities on the southern front, Gonen had changed the command's Dovecote force deployment plan, contrary to what he had agreed on with the chief of staff. In the senior command meeting that summed up the war, Elazar said:

> I know that there was a short circuit somewhere: Dovecote wasn't executed. In the general staff meeting on Saturday [October 6], the commander of Southern Command and I thought we were preparing for Dovecote. I know that for all practical matters we weren't prepared for Dovecote. I know that somewhere in the pipeline Dovecote had become Little Dovecote and Little Dovecote was postponed to four o'clock, and Dovecote never took place.[28]

Elazar claimed that Dovecote's deployment had been agreed upon in the meeting. Gonen did not deny this, but he planned to alter his force deployment without informing the chief of staff. He did not intend for the armored brigades to remain concentrated in the rear in Refidim and the Bir Tmada area, about eighty kilometers from the Suez Canal, but to advance them closer to the canal. In effect, when the war erupted the 401st and 14th Brigades were in these positions but the chief of staff was unaware of it, because Gonen had failed to convey his reasons to him for bringing them forward earlier than the original plan envisioned.[29]

October 7

On the morning of October 7, twenty hours after the start of the Egyptian attack, Gonen unleashed a wave of rapidly changing reports and requests. At 9:25 a.m., for example, he informed the chief of staff that he would try to hold on for a few hours without air support, but twelve minutes later he requested air support.[30] At noon the chief of staff announced that Gonen had acted against his instructions, and Elazar ordered Gonen to stabilize the line and not to plan a counterattack yet.[31] At 3:30 p.m. Gonen proposed crossing the canal, and the chief of staff vetoed the proposal. Elazar thought it dangerous to

throw the 143rd Division, one of Southern Command's two fresh reserve divisions, into a night battle in a sector forty to fifty kilometers
long against two hundred enemy tanks and without IAF assistance,
as the Egyptian SAM array was still intact. In his opinion, even if
most of the enemy force were destroyed, the division would still suffer losses, the Egyptian crossing would continue, the division would
engage in containment battles, and the air force would still be unable
to provide substantial support. In effect, nothing would be gained.[32]

October 8

At 10 a.m. the chief of staff was seated in a government meeting. The
senior officer on duty in the Pit (the GHQ operations center in the
Kirya, Tel Aviv) was General Rehavam Ze'evi. During the meeting a
counterattack in the south developed, whose handling convinced the
chief of staff of Gonen's lack of control and poor situation assessment
ability.

Reports came in from Southern Command announcing the 162nd
Division's success and requesting permission to cross the canal
and commence the next stage in the offensive plan: bringing the 143rd
Division across for an attack in the southern sector. At 9:55 a.m., Ze'evi
received a report from Gonen that the 162nd's spearhead was inside
the Hizayon stronghold and the area was relatively clear of any enemy.
General Gonen explained that he intended to cross the canal with a
small force in the Hizayon area because of an Egyptian bridge there
and engage the enemy forces in the Chinese Farm area. Gonen also
stated that he had ordered the commander of the 252nd Division to
engage the enemy and pressure him in the direction of the canal and
reported that he was holding the 143rd Division in reserve for the canal crossing. At 10:15 a.m., Gonen contacted Ze'evi and informed him
that he had ordered the commander of the 252nd to remain in his place
and create pressure. He made two requests: first, to continue receiving
air assistance because without it, it would be difficult to approach the

canal; and second, to receive permission to capture Egyptian bridges and hang onto territory at a depth of two hundred to three hundred meters beyond the canal in order to prevent the bridge's sabotage.[33]

In light of Gonen's rosy and totally unsubstantiated situation reports, the chief of staff issued the following instructions for bridge crossing: not too small a force that could find itself cut off and not too large a force lest it create a commitment. He also wanted to know the number of places where the crossing would take place. Gonen's answer, which Ze'evi conveyed to the head of the chief of staff's bureau at 10:25 a.m., stated that at this stage the commander of Southern Command requested only an "option" to cross in four or five places. The only place where Gonen had already ordered a crossing was at the Hizayon stronghold, and as for his next moves, he requested only an "option." Regarding the crossing itself, Gonen explained that he would conduct matters according to the chief of staff's instructions—crossing only at a spot that was clear of enemy and in a force not too small so as not to be cut off and not too large so as not to create an obligation. At 10:35 a.m., Gonen made another request. In light of Elazar's order not to send the 143rd Division into battle unless he personally gave permission, Gonen requested authorization to move the division to the Gidi Roads and thus save four hours. That would put the division in position to attack in the southern sector at as early a time as possible and to cross the canal in the vicinity of the city of Suez. The request was conveyed, and Elazar granted permission. At 10:40 a.m., Ze'evi informed Gonen that approval had been granted. About half an hour later, at 11:05 a.m., Gonen requested permission to move the 143rd Division farther south. The division would move on Lateral Road, enter from the Mitle Pass, and engage the enemy from south to north. It would also attempt to capture the bridge in the vicinity of the Nisan stronghold and cross the canal toward Suez. Ze'evi relayed this request to the chief of staff at 11:15 a.m., when he returned from the government meeting. At 11:25 a.m., Elazar spoke with Gonen and heard the reason that he was requesting to act contrary to the original plan, which was based on a north to south attack. The chief of staff approved the plan, and in view of Gonen's clarifications he ordered Ze'evi to report his approval to Agam.[34]

Given these seemingly upbeat developments, the chief of staff decided to publish a statement that the war had reached a turning point. But later that day the whole episode turned out to be a pipe dream. By the afternoon, Elazar realized what happened and spoke with Defense Minister Dayan about the 143rd's attack:

> [Elazar:] "A whole day with the division has been wasted! It was supposed to attack in the morning; and would attack in the evening, and that was it! . . . I gave him permission to go out by degrees at noon, then Shmulik [Gonen] told him [Sharon] to go out at 10:00; then at 14:00 he [Sharon] still hadn't left." "Couldn't they have gone out in the morning?" asked the minister. "No. He wasn't ready!" the chief of staff answered. "No sense in crying over this," Dayan replied. "Okay, we didn't attack today, maybe tomorrow we'll be able to."[35]

This event brought home to Elazar the extremely problematic nature of Gonen's performance. In seventy minutes—from 9:55 to 11:05 a.m.—the commander of Southern Command had called the chief of staff no fewer than five times requesting permission for moves that deviated from agreements they had made the previous evening. In other words, every quarter of an hour, developments occurred that required policy changes at the general staff level. This was an unacceptable rate in the general staff–Southern Command interface. One reason for the requests was that the chief of staff had stipulated certain changes could be made only after he granted permission. The conversations between Elazar and Gonen in the critical hours of the counterattack took place through the mediation of General Ze'evi and Lieutenant Colonel Avner Shalev, the head of the chief of staff's office. Yet during this time the chief of staff was engaged in government meetings; thus, General Gonen conveyed his requests to General Ze'evi, who passed them on to Shalev, who then conveyed them to the chief of staff, whose return answer went through the reverse procedure. The whole process repeated itself without any monitoring on the part of the general staff, while the chief of staff granted permission to the regional commander almost automatically.[36]

October 9

Defense Minister Dayan, too, realized that Gonen's performance was at issue, partly due to his inability to control Sharon. He discussed the matter with Elazar in the afternoon of October 9. During their talk, the possibility arose of appointing Haim Bar-Lev, the previous chief of staff, in place of Gonen. The defense minister reached the chief of staff's room following Elazar's request to discuss a change of personnel in Southern Command. It will be noted that at daybreak, when the defense minister returned with the chief of staff from a tour of the southern front, he suggested replacing Gonen. The October 8 events left no doubt in his mind that Gonen had lost control of his forces. Elazar was not keen on removing him. He felt, as he admitted to others that day, that Gonen lacked the vision of a regional commander, but Elazar preferred at this stage to send his deputy, General Tal, to the southern front. Tal arrived in the south at 4:30 p.m. and intended to remain only until the night of October 9. On that day another incident occurred in Southern Command that proved that Gonen was failing to exert his authority over the commander of the 143rd Division. While remaining in contact with enemy forces facing him toward the Suez Canal, Sharon convinced Gonen to request a crossing, although it went against the chief of staff's instructions. This cemented Elazar's resolve to replace Gonen. In the evening it became clear that the 143rd's forces had reached the waterline. At 6:45 p.m., the chief of staff phoned his deputy, Tal, who was in Southern Command's forward command post. After the conversation, he immediately repeated to everyone in the room what he'd just heard: "Arik [Sharon], contrary to my orders, has taken the division, attacked here and reached there . . . he made it [to the canal] against my orders. They told him [Gonen] that they didn't intend to cross, yet he brought his division over." After speaking with his deputy, the chief of staff conferred with Bar-Lev, who was also in the room, about the possibility of appointing him commander of the southern front. He tried to reach the defense minister and was told that Dayan was with the prime minister.[37]

Elazar finally contacted Dayan and discussed the replacement of Gonen:

"Is Gorodish [Gonen] doing a good job?" the defense minister asked the chief of staff. Elazar replied that General Gonen was "an outstanding fighter . . . he has to stabilize the situation . . . and pursue the fighting as expected. The problem is he still hasn't shown that he has what it takes to be a regional commander. He's running it like a division commander, focusing on what's happening now instead of the next stage. . . . I know what regional command demands from personal experience. You become adept at it when you start thinking in terms of 'what's happening is out of my hands, it's the divisional commanders' show now. . . . Let's talk about tomorrow—that's my job.' . . . He [Gonen] isn't there yet. . . . That's his only drawback."

"This isn't something to be treated lightly," Dayan said. "We need a creative mind to get us out of this mess." They both agreed that a commander had to be sent south not to "replace" Gonen but "in addition" to him, and one of higher rank. "In that case there's Haim Bar-Lev," the chief of staff said. "But is he willing to go?" asked the minister. "I've just spoken with him. . . . He's willing," Elazar replied. "Bar-Lev is a very good choice," the minister agreed, "I can appreciate his willingness."[38] Bar-Lev's prestige and the fact that he "was able to think outside the box" and solve Southern Command's problems by being there decided in his favor. The chief of staff contacted Lieutenant General Bar-Lev by phone. As they waited for the line to get through, the minister returned to the problem of the 143rd: "What are you going to do about Arik [Sharon]? . . . They told him to move his forces out, and he did just as he was ordered, isn't that true?"

"That's the reason I wanted to speak with you," the chief of staff said. "Nothing in this war has pissed me off so much as what he did." . . .

Hearing this strengthened Dayan's opinion that "Bar-Lev had to be sent south to take control so they could devise a plan."[39]

At 5:00 p.m., Dayan met Bar-Lev, who agreed to assume the role. Afterward, Prime Minister Golda Meir gave her approval. Elazar worried about the effect Bar-Lev's appointment would have on morale in the IDF and among civilians. Bar-Lev wanted to know if the chief of staff had already informed Gonen of the matter. Elazar answered that he had not spoken with him but he believed that Gonen would not be against it. There is an option, he said to Bar-Lev, that Gonen will immediately receive command of the 143rd and Sharon will be sacked.[40]

The attempts to persuade Gonen to remain in his role under Bar-Lev were complex and occupied a great deal of Elazar's time. Gonen regarded the appointment as a vote of no confidence in his abilities. Asked whether his management of the battle was disappointing, the chief of staff replied, "It wasn't bad. It definitely wasn't bad, but in this situation we're concentrating all our resources so it will get even better." Gonen was deeply offended and announced his intention to quit. Elazar tried to dissuade him, arguing, "Bar-Lev is a lieutenant general, a former chief of staff; it won't look bad for you." But Gonen wasn't swayed. His firm opposition to Bar-Lev's appointment came as a surprise to Elazar. A frightening thought suddenly struck him that once the public learned that Gonen had been relieved of command, it might interpret it as a sign that the southern front had collapsed.

Immediately after Elazar's meeting with the generals in the south, he received a call from the defense minister, who hadn't set out for the north yet. Elazar confided in Dayan, "I'd like to say to Gorodish and to Haim [Bar-Lev] that Haim is the commander of the command—he's the commander, but without revoking Gorodish's appointment."

Dayan said, "You're the clever one—get us out of this." Elazar looked for a solution that would satisfy all the parties. When Bar-Lev returned from the government meeting, the chief of staff asked all those present to leave the room and let the two of them speak privately. He described Gonen's reaction—"It was murder." He admitted to Bar-Lev his concern over the possible negative impact from publicity if the switch in commanders in the south were interpreted as firing Gonen, although it was obvious that commanders in Southern Command would perfectly understand that Gonen was subordinate to Bar-Lev. Bar-Lev did not like the looks of the proposal and suggested consulting with General Aharon Yariv (special assistant to the chief of staff). The three generals put their heads together. Elazar contacted the prime minister's military secretary and asked to postpone the publication until an appropriate formal wording was found. If Gonen's resignation were made public it could have a disastrous effect, he repeated. The impression would be that the IDF had failed to give the Egyptians a shellacking due to the incompetence of the commanding general in the south. Therefore, a solution had to be found that Gonen could accept.[41]

Elazar seems to have repressed the real situation due to his fear that Bar-Lev's appointment would hurt morale more than the actual results of the battles would. A heated discussion among Elazar, Tal, Bar-Lev, and Gonen on the morning of October 10 lasted until Bar-Lev was finally installed as assistant chief of staff or, in other words, the general staff's appointment to special tasks.

Summary of the Test Case

Elazar's trust in Gonen deteriorated rapidly from day one of the fighting. It included all of the elements that were mentioned in the introduction: a gap (hidden from eye up until the war) in a common language (regarding the Dovecote plan), shoddy management (of what was expected of a commanding general—frenzied reports, cries for air assistance, and the canal crossing issue), deviation from agreements with the chief of staff in the form of moves taken without his permission, and the problem of asserting control over the divisional commanders (in this instance, Ariel Sharon). No doubt that the poor marks for Gonen's performance as the commander of a regional command resulted from his lack of experience and Elazar's overconfidence that he would quickly grow into the role.

The case illustrates the chief of staff's leadership-command challenge when he is forced to solve the operational problem of a general whose performance is flawed.

The Crisis between Dan Halutz and Udi Adam in the 2006 Second Lebanon War

This test case is more complex than the others, as the loss of trust includes a number of factors that have not appeared until now. They include Dan Halutz's limited knowledge of the basics of ground force employment, the absence of an agreed-upon and exercised plan for the northern theater (see chapter 2), and the problem of shifting the IDF from a state of routine security to a state of war (see chapter 1). On the basis of these factors, additional gaps developed in the common language, in expectations regarding the speed of implementation, in senior command collegiality, and more, leading to the crisis of trust.

Obviously Halutz's feelings were based on reality as he perceived it. Even though the factual basis of some of these feelings was mistaken, the loss of trust is a highly subjective matter, and much can still be gleaned from this case. There are two important points on the research methodology. One, the description is based primarily on Halutz's autobiography (with all the caveats that this poses); and two, even after a careful reading of the records of the discussions, the participants' feelings are still hard to identify, compared to the other cases where personal memoirs or testimonies shed light on the participants' views of the events.

Halutz claims that in his first week as chief of staff he decided to appoint Udi Adam as commander of Northern Command, as he considered him a superb officer and human being, loyal to the system, honest and trustworthy. He had rich experience as an armor officer and as a commander: he had commanded a regular army armored division and served as head of the logistics branch, and over the years had accumulated vast operational command experience.[42]

Before the war, Halutz and Adam were already divided by conceptual gaps, some open, others veiled. The Winograd Commission's interim report dealt at length with the differences in their approach to Israel's policy concerning Hezbollah and especially to a future abduction attempt. The defense ministers and the heads of government in the interlude between the pullout from Lebanon in 2000 and the war in 2006 adopted a "containment" approach. While some senior military figures contended that this approach was most questionable and argued against it, others approved it. After the war, Halutz stated that he had opposed this policy but waited for the political echelon to stabilize after the 2006 elections.[43] The commission's report describes the discussions in the newly elected Olmert government in January 2006 on the likelihood of a soldier's kidnapping and Israel's response. Halutz backed the containment approach in principle and noted that the IDF had prepared a number of steps in response.[44]

The report states that the situation reached the point that the routine security concept reflected "expanded containment" even as Hezbollah was operating brazenly along the border in preparation for a hostile act, and the IDF was still prohibited from responding. Thus, for example, three days before an attempted kidnapping in the border town of Ghajar in November 2005, the commander of Northern Command requested permission to employ precision fire in order to eliminate enemy teams that were deployed along the border. The chief of staff expressly forbade it.[45]

Halutz and Adam interpreted the Ghajar kidnapping attempt differently. As commander of Northern Command, Adam viewed it as an escalation in terms of place and scope, whereas Halutz regarded it as another incident in a series of routine Hezbollah actions. During a visit to Northern Command by newly inaugurated prime minister

Ehud Olmert and new defense minister Amir Peretz, the conceptual gap dividing Adam and Halutz was revealed again, this time over the prospect of war breaking out in the north.[46]

The contrasting approaches of the chief of staff and the commander of Northern Command to the containment policy are understandable since the chief of staff is supposed to have comprehensive situational awareness and the ability to answer the political echelon's needs, while the regional commander's considerations are more strictly military. The point here is not who was right but that conceptual gaps separated the two senior figures on so fundamental an issue as the manner of response to a kidnapping.

As for war plans in Lebanon, the gap between them widened but was left unspoken. Adam, like Halutz, regarded an Israeli operation in Lebanon after the Syrian exit as taking place in stages.[47] The Winograd report and Halutz note that the first stage—the Icebreaker war plan—was based on massive standoff fire and commando raids (both under the direct command of the general staff) and that the second stage—Sky High Water—was the command's plan for a relatively large ground maneuver up to the Litani River that naturally included the occupation of areas close to the border in order to improve defense.[48] The difference between the positions of the chief of staff and the commander of Northern Command lay mostly beneath the surface, and much of it developed before the war, when Adam proposed integrating the command forces within Icebreaker—the general staff plan—as brigade-size raids a few kilometers across the border.

Before the war Northern Command's proposal was neither discussed in depth nor approved; in fact, it became another element in the interechelon conceptual rift. Regarding Sky High Water before the war, both the commander of Northern Command and the chief of staff seem to have consigned the plan to "lowest-level priority."[49] During the first days of the conflict, a prewar latent conceptual gap came to light. Adam viewed the staged approach as including maneuvering, even if relatively limited (which he considered the correct action), whereas Halutz approved of the staged plan, but did not see the point in having a stage consisting of a limited ground operation other than response with fire. Therefore, he did not study Adam's plan in detail. (It should be noted that the political echelon also did not study the plan too closely.) Halutz and Adam also held opposing views on the basic logic of the plan that was still being worked out and receiving formal authorization: the logic being that Icebreaker's failure would necessitate the implementation of Sky High Water, not in an intermediate stage but as a large-scale maneuver that included the encirclement of South Lebanon.

These conceptual differences were not clarified in discussions, exercises, or war games before the war (see chapter 2), nor were other issues such as the distinction between "gaining control of an area" and "capturing or occupying an area," so that their unresolved status persisted during the war.

In the Northern Command's Joined Arms exercise in June 2006, which was focused on a war in Lebanon, the focus was on C2 structural issues in order to determine the general staff's concept that the regional command is the "campaign commander" in wartime, whereas the concept of fighting Hezbollah was shunted aside.[50]

Thus, beset by unresolved conceptual gaps, the chief of staff, the general staff, and Northern Command stumbled into a conflict that came to be known as the Second Lebanon War.

Halutz described the development of his loss of trust in Adam. Unlike Elazar, who changed the C2 structure on the southern front after three days, Halutz needed three weeks to make the move. On July 12, 2006—the day of the abduction of two IDF soldiers by Hezbollah—Halutz sensed that something was amiss in the command but admits that he was confident that "General Adam would swiftly regain his composure and return to full command, and this is what I communicated to him in our conversations."[51]

Halutz's feelings about the turmoil in Northern Command are naturally subjective. However, during the discussions in Northern Command HQ that day, Adam ordered preparations for limited ground actions—capturing areas adjacent to the border to improve defense and drawing up plans for brigade-size raids, which had not received the general staff's approval in the previous period—as the first stage of actions. At any rate, Adam proposed his moves to the chief of staff.[52] In a joint conference call Halutz refused permission to cross "the blue line," the UN-recognized border between Israel and Lebanon, or initiate any ground action. Brigadier General (res.) Alon Friedman, Northern Command's chief of staff in the war, claimed later that the gaps in evaluating the July 12 kidnapping, which had already appeared in the November 2005 Ghajar event, became even more pronounced.[53] Under these circumstances Halutz's aide-de-camp, Colonel Roni Numa, suggested that Halutz fly to Northern Command and speak privately with Adam. On July 13, the chief of staff landed in Northern Command.

The question of a ground move was brought up in the meeting. Adam expressed reservations, and Halutz's impression was that Adam's self-confidence had waned, but he "decided to give Udi as much backing as necessary."[54] Numa says that when he asked the chief of staff how the meeting went, he was told "excellent." Later Adam met Numa and said that the chief of staff's concept in the meeting was mistaken to the core and would result in many casualties. Numa remembers the huge gap between the two generals' feelings about the meeting. From his experience, as commander of Central Command a decade later, Numa insists that this was only one of many cases when two senior officers leave a meeting with antithetical or radically divergent understandings. The results of the meeting that Halutz believed had reconciled expectations with Adam seem to have only increased the gap between them.[55]

The main conceptual divide, which was revealed immediately after the July 12 abduction that set off the war and which remained throughout the fighting, was between the commander of Northern Command, who from the beginning of hostilities tried to implement what he understood as the earlier agreement with Halutz for employing his forces in stages, and the chief of staff (the loyal representative of the political echelon's position), who tried to avoid the first stage of ground force deployment by rejecting the initial proposal for ground operations. He finally approved the moves, albeit unwillingly and at a relatively late point in the war, which forced Northern Command to carry out hasty planning.

On July 15, Halutz weighed in on Northern Command's proposal, saying that a ground move was "an opportunity to leave dead IDF troops on Lebanese soil as a result of our penetration." He insisted that a ground move was not in anyone's interest—the government, the Israeli public, or the world. He explained that in his view, a ground move into Lebanon would shorten Israel's legitimate time for action and force it to compromise.[56]

In the July 16 senior design forum that was chaired by the chief of staff, the head of Amatz proposed battalion-size raids on certain villages near the border.[57] The next day, July 17, he brought up the subject again. A third discussion around this matter on July 18 illustrates the conceptual gaps and the development of the idea of raids as the main pattern of action in the war. That morning the head of Amatz stated that Northern Command's focus on brigade-size raids and the relatively lengthy battle procedures that they would require best illustrated the command's misunderstanding of time and space. He also noted that battalion-size raids following four to eight hours of battle procedure would achieve the limited gains that the IDF needed and in a shorter time.[58] The Winograd report elaborates on the discussion that was held that afternoon. The head of Amatz opposed Northern Command's idea to implement brigade-size raids and presented his battalion-size raids option. According to the head of the operations division (within Amatz): "The maximum alternative is Sky High Water that we rejected, and you [the chief of staff] vetoed. I think we were justified in not considering it an option. There is the simple option that Northern Command began . . . employing small forces to capture the ridges along the border."[59]

In the end the chief of staff approved the head of Amatz's position. He ordered: "Nothing larger than battalion-size-plus operations . . . I don't approve of a large-scale ground move at this point. It's a waste of time to plan it now. Period! If we get to that stage, there'll be time enough to plan for it. . . . [But] I'll make every effort not to reach that stage." That evening, in a situation assessment meeting headed by the chief of staff, tensions flared up again between the commander of Northern Command and the head of Amatz regarding the size of the forces and timetables needed for the action.[60]

Regarding staff work during July 19, the commission noted that Halutz's order changed the strategic concept for the first time since the start of the war. The strategic idea was defined as "a joint coordinated strike (onslaught) in an operational 'maneuver' [quotation marks in original] with all means available to undermine the Hezbollah organization's operational capacity, increase the effectiveness of the target hunting effort . . . and create conditions for freeing the captives."[61]

Here we see that the battalion-size special forces or designated troop raids that were carried out a few days after the kidnapping were a kind of compromise between Amatz and Northern Command (which favored a brigade-size raid) and the special forces raids of Icebreaker, which relied to a degree on the pattern of raids in the West Bank and the Gaza Strip of the previous years. Amatz planners may have believed that they had managed to bridge the gap between the unwillingness of the chief of staff and the political echelon to employ ground forces and the prewar plans that Northern Command thought were still standing. The size of the force to be used in the raids was a matter of dispute between Adam and the head of Amatz, since the time needed for battle procedure in planning a brigade-size raid was greater than for a battalion-size one. The gain in the shorter time, which Amatz considered to be crucial, was not appreciated in Northern Command.

The Winograd report summarized the development of the raid concept, finding that despite the original operational plans and despite the growing realization that a fire offensive would not attain the expected goals, the IDF preferred not to reexamine the operational concept. It instead avoided a decision on whether to continue the fighting (which would entail preparations for a large-scale ground move at the very least) or make a quick end to the fighting and bring the matter to a forthright decision before the political echelon. The IDF also refrained from issuing a major call-up of reserve units and preparing for the possibility of a wide-scale ground action (designed to exert pressure on and deter Hezbollah). The report stated, "Thus, the IDF entered a protracted intermediary period. In what seems like a compromise more than a sound and solid strategy, it decided to carry out a series of limited ground moves and raids of limited scope, limited depth, and limited goals."[62]

A situation was created in which the commander of Northern Command felt that no one was listening to him, and at the same time the chief of staff was disappointed by the results of his forces' action. Adam says that the gap between the command, which was struggling to keep to its earlier plan of a brigade-size action, and the more limited raids that the chief of staff had approved in the initial days of the fighting stood at the heart of the tension that later burst into a full-blown crisis of trust.[63] The chief of staff visited the Galilee Division on July 15. At this stage, his criticism was aimed primarily at the command's loss of control over events in the field and communication problems with the general staff. Halutz wrote:

> My overall impression of the visit is that the operational system in Northern Command is in shambles. The reports are inaccurate; inconsistency reigns supreme between what's said and what's done. The command's reporting system is out of whack, and . . . the commander and his staff haven't a clue as to what's going on, therefore they convey unsubstantiated, unreliable information to the GHQ. Only in retrospect did I realize the magnitude of the gap. But more than faulty reporting, what worried me was the lack of knowledge that had led to erroneous decision making. This feeling caused me much anguish over the best way of dealing with the problem. On the one hand I tried to bolster the commander of Northern Command; on the other hand, I needed better information—the kind I was getting from the GHQ, the head of Amatz, and from the deputy chief of staff.[64]

Northern Command's internal debriefing after the war listed the reasons for the gaps in the command's reports that had bolstered Halutz's convictions: gaps in operational reports appeared at all levels; the reports were fragmentary and failed to reflect the entire situational picture (location, ORBAT, capturing Hezbollah POWs) which impeded decision making and created mistrust and the sense of ineptitude.[65]

Regarding C2 processes in the two echelons, it will be recalled that the GHQ operations center in Tel Aviv (the Pit) was only partially in operation (see chapter 1), whereas the Northern Command's command post was manned around the clock (but the quality of its work was far from satisfactory). The lack of coordination between the two headquarters contributed to the negative dynamic of personal (Halutz-Adam) and interechelon loss of trust. On July 18, Halutz noted Northern Command's difficulty in executing its missions. The command presented its plans that were based primarily on the employment of special forces units. Halutz wrote:

> It was unfortunate that I didn't know then what I knew at the end of the fighting: that a gulf had been drawn between the command's statements on its performance and its action in the field. The picture that it presented was fallacious. I vetoed its request to use cluster bombs against the [rocket] launch areas until I received further clarification from the legal advisers on their legitimacy.[66]

In reality, Northern Command did employ complex munitions from the outset in accordance with Adam's decision, and after the war the chief of staff claimed that he knew nothing about it. On July 19, Halutz elaborated on C2 problems and the partial use of the forces allocated to the command. Northern Command was ordered to employ its ground forces to push the missile launchers to the north, which would diminish the rockets' effectiveness and put some Israeli settlements out of their range. The dissatisfaction with the command's performance was glaring. The top brass on the general staff felt that the

Northern Command headquarters had misinterpreted the orders and, worse, had failed to ask questions or take the initiative. The command had complained about the lack of engineering equipment for clearing the contact line, but the deputy chief of staff reported twenty-seven D9 tractors standing idle in the command's area. Things of this nature heightened the distrust over what was said and what was being done in Northern Command. Halutz attested that matters reached a point where two senior staff officers suggested that he replace both Adam and the commander of the Galilee Division, Gal Hirsch. "They believed that no progress would be made while these two commanders stood at the helm because they still hadn't recovered from the shock of the kidnapping."[67]

Halutz described the gulf in expectations that was revealed by the July 21 situation assessment. While General Adam's morning update sounded almost optimistic, Halutz thought its connection with reality was wishful thinking and that Northern Command seemed oblivious to the time dimension. "I felt that instead of the command galloping forward and pushing for innovative operational ideas, the tables had turned, and it was the general staff that was trying to spur the command forward."[68]

The expectations of Northern Command in commanding the campaign may have increased in proportion to Halutz's prewar concept that the regional commander was the "campaign commander" (this was the accepted term used in the 2006 IDF Strategy that had been published just before the war) while the general staff focused on the strategic level.

Be that as it may, Halutz's statement that the "tables had turned" regarding the command's initiative was far from accurate. From the first day of the war until the last, the command had urged the employment of ground forces in stages, which, it thought, had been agreed upon. The gap in understanding probably stemmed from the general staff favoring battalion-size raids by designated units as a kind of compromise between leaving the ground forces idle and making wide-scale use of them (an option the chief of staff did not want to discuss).

Halutz appears to have viewed battalion-size raids as the correct form of force employment while the command failed to see the logic behind them (which explains why it took no initiative in that direction). It perceived them as an intermediate stage in a wider action rather than the effective action to end the war. The general staff included the discussion and authorization of the raids under the conceptual framework of routine security, where it was termed "operations and raids," which required approval for every action from both the general staff and the defense minister, a procedure that fired up the tension between the command and the general staff to the boiling point. Halutz seems to have been unaware of this growing interechelon rift; therefore, his frustration with Northern Command over the raids intensified.

Halutz described how he tried to resolve the problem by speaking with Adam, who complained about the general staff's overinvolvement and the way senior officers on the general staff were bypassing Northern Command headquarters and directly contacting the commanders of Northern Command forces in the field and, worse, were issuing instructions that countermanded the command's policy. Halutz said that he found no evidence for this. But the fact that such accusations were being made forced him to deal with them, clarify them, and order the entire senior staff to cease this pattern of conduct.[69]

On the one hand, Halutz seems to have taken no notice of the visits to the Galilee Division units by his deputy, as well as by the commander of the Ground Forces Command, Benny Gantz; the head of the technological and logistics branch, Avi Mizrachi; and others. He may have turned a blind eye to their visits because of his air force culture background, where the commander is the undisputed authority. On the other hand, the conduct of Northern Command's deputy commander, Major General Eyal Ben Reuven, who made suggestions to the defense minister and the prime minister when they visited the command—suggestions that Halutz deemed irrelevant—infuriated the chief of staff and added to his unfavorable feelings toward Adam.

Halutz described the criticism that was voiced in the discussion: that Northern Command's plan was defective, that the command had failed to make full use of its forces, that it had proved incapable of shifting mentally from routine security to war (albeit the general staff too had not "shifted mentally"—see chapter 1). Halutz also mentioned the command's mediocre employment of special forces (which forced him to place Brigadier General Tal Russo in charge of their employment).[70]

Regarding the July 22 daily situation assessment, Halutz wrote that it reinforced the sense that the GHQ had to deal with almost every aspect of Northern Command's responsibility because its plans were incompatible with the operational concept. He had to ensure that basic matters were made absolutely clear, such as keeping strictly to the timetable of a GHQ order and the need to define in unequivocal terms mission, goals, and other matters. "The time spent on these issues frustrated me and I felt that instead of devoting my attention to the strategic level, I was bogged down in work on tactical matters."[71]

A key issue that contributed to Halutz's loss of trust is closely tied to the gap in the common language concerning ground forces' achievements. The Bint Jbeil affair apparently had a powerful impact on the relations between Halutz and Adam: On July 22, the commander of Northern Command declared that "no one is allowed to enter Bint Jbeil under any circumstances. The mission called for encircling Bint Jbeil and not occupying it."[72] The attack began on the evening of July 23. Five days later, July 28, Adam estimated that the mission was accomplished and the forces could withdraw from Lebanon. They pulled out on the morning of July 29. However, it turned out that serious communication gaps existed in the common language over the nature of the fighting. At this stage, Halutz, who was disappointed by the command's achievements, ordered Adam to gain control of the town, and Adam replied that he was in control of it and asked if the chief of staff meant that he should occupy it.[73]

The Winograd report states that the absence of a common language proved detrimental in the battle for Bint Jbeil. The chief of staff had noted "the communication gap between the general staff and the regional command over the definition of the term 'capture' in the case of Bint Jbeil." In a nutshell, mutual understanding and agreement were lacking. Also missing was a clear definition of what had to be done in Bint Jbeil in the first round of fighting. The main flaw was that the goal and the nature of the mission had been vaguely worded and left without the basic tool to remedy this misunderstanding: clearly written operational orders from Amatz that should have been adapted and detailed while formulating the command's orders. Herein lay the root of the problem: sending large forces to accomplish a poorly defined mission. "We view this as the perfect formula for colossal misunderstandings in expectations and the resultant sense of failure."[74]

The following explanation was given in Northern Command's postwar debriefing for the orders' muddle and vagueness. The orders at all the levels were insufficiently clear; missions, resources, and constraints were poorly defined; and the overall language was only occasionally accurate by any professional standard and often allowed ample room for interpretation that deviated from the superior level's intention. For example, the term "gaining control" was understood differently in each echelon, and the absence of timetables for mission achievement in the orders also contributed to the confusion.[75]

The Winograd report found that GHQ orders seemed to mirror the general staff's uncertainty about the aims and the form of the fighting, which added to the problems that cropped up in the conduct of the fighting. For example, the orders failed to clarify, let alone reduce, the gaps in the campaign's operational concept between the general staff and Northern Command over ground moves.[76]

The orders' ambiguity was a key factor in the general staff's distrust of the command and vice versa—the same lack of trust that we have seen between the chief of staff and the command, as Boaz Cohen, Northern Command's operations officer, noted:

What best explains the lack of communication and trust is that sometime between ten and fourteen days from the start of the war the general staff turned the "mute" switch on when situation assessments were being discussed in the GHQ conference room. . . . [In other words] the commander of Northern Command was left out of the discussion (he could lip-read if he wished). . . . The regional commander was linked up only when he was asked to convey his description of the events. As I see it, this was the epitome of lack of communication.[77]

The Winograd report summed up as undeniably inadequate the communication and coordination between the general staff and Northern Command in general, and between the chief of staff and the commander of Northern Command in particular, on the basis of the reasons presented above, emphasizing the micromanagement of Northern Command's operational decisions by the chief of staff and GHQ while paying too little attention to overseeing the big picture and devising a strategy for the campaign. The general staff felt that the command had failed to live up to expectations in the execution of its missions. Furthermore, the chief of staff's expectations that the command would make suggestions and would initiate and implement attack plans were not realized. Referring back to the conceptual gaps cited by the Winograd Commission in the introduction to this chapter, "The important question from our point of view has been to identify why an effective way was not found to seal the gaps and create a joint command system that conveyed clearly worded messages to the different command echelons that could then be translated into operational language that enabled monitoring their implementation. This is what should have been done from the beginning. Why was not a better and faster way devised to rectify the situation when it was obvious that something had gone awry?"[78]

On the morning of August 2, Halutz visited Northern Command headquarters and learned that it had not kept to the timetable and that the rate of advance was slower than expected. After the visit he realized that he had to find a solution to the command problems in Northern Command. He ruled out the possibility of replacing Adam as long as the fighting was in progress. The plan that he came up with was to appoint a senior commander to Northern Command on his behalf to confirm that coordination was being maintained between what was said and what was done. Two names came to mind: the commander of the Ground Forces Command (Mazi), Benny Gantz, and his deputy, Moshe Kaplinsky. The groups close to him on the general staff insisted he do something, and he began to check the possibilities: "I knew that it would have to be done before a major ground offensive commenced."[79]

On August 6, Halutz attested that after a series of conferences and consultations, and against the background of the growing likelihood that a large-scale ground move would be needed in South Lebanon, he decided not to dismiss the commander of Northern Command but to introduce a change in his headquarters.[80] Halutz considered, as stated, appointing Gantz or Kaplinsky as his representative in the command. On August 7 he informed Adam of his decision to send a permanent representative to the command's headquarters. After Northern Command presented its plans, he asked to speak privately with General Adam:

> [I] informed him that I'd decided to appoint a permanent representative on my behalf to the command. . . . "Who?" he demanded. "There's two possibilities," I said. "Benny [Gantz] or Kaplan [Kaplinsky]. I prefer Benny because Kaplan is overloaded with assignments right now and there's no one to replace him. Also, Benny's very familiar with the command and the people in it." I meant to say something else but Udi cut me short. "If it's Benny—I quit on the spot!" Nevertheless, in the midst of his negativism, I caught a positive note and intuited that he was willing to accept Kaplan. Immediately I said, "Okay, Kaplan it is." It was important for me not to break his spirit and to take his opinion into consideration as much as possible under the circumstances. We spoke about the working framework with Kaplan. I made it clear that Kaplinsky would be the GHQ representative and the senior authority for Northern Command's force employment. Udi would remain the regional commander and be in contact with the commanders of the forces.
> We parted with a handshake.

Later he took Kaplinsky aside and told him that the next morning he would present himself in Northern Command and assist both Adam and him in getting the command's missions accomplished. When he returned to his office in Tel Aviv, he and his staff struggled to find the appropriate wording for the announcement, which on Tuesday morning, August 8, became a reality.[81]

That morning, Halutz approved Adam's plans for the divisions. He tells of an event that occurred in the headquarters of Erez Zukerman, the commander of the Netiv Ha'esh (Path of Fire) Division, which bolstered his judgment that Adam was plagued by command problems. As soon as Zukerman began laying out the plans, Adam abruptly stopped him, saying:

> "These aren't the plans you showed me and that I approved!"
> A pall of embarrassment blanketed the room. The division had decided on its own initiative, after the approval of one plan by the commander of Northern Command, to change the plan, and had neglected to consult with the command's headquarters or trouble itself to update it.

This event glaringly illustrated the relationship between some of Northern Command's senior officers and its commanding officer. Halutz justifiably regarded this as additional evidence to what he had already witnessed during the fighting—that Adam's authority and control were not to be taken for granted.[82]

The gap between Adam and Zukerman probably stemmed from a visit by Kaplinsky the previous evening, when the latter advised Zukerman to modify the plan. Whatever the reason, Halutz was further convinced of Adam's problematic conduct. It should be noted that Moshe Kaplinsky, the deputy chief of staff, who, as stated (see chapter 2), Halutz had appointed as "the person best suited to fill in his lack of knowledge in the ground forces domain," seems to have assisted him in the employment of Northern Command just by his presence in the decision-making sessions. At any rate, Kaplinsky's meeting with the division commanders contributed little and may have even disrupted the interechelon, division-command-general staff hierarchy that was complex even in the best of circumstances.

The "subversion of collegiality" among senior commanders also proved instrumental in creating interechelon distrust. This is a recognized phenomenon. After the Yom Kippur War, it received the moniker "the war of the generals" in the wake of mutual accusations between Ariel Sharon and Avraham Adan, the two leading divisional commanders in the battles on the Suez Canal. The public media were the main theater in which the "war of the generals" was fought. In the Second Lebanon War, however, for sundry reasons, "the war of the generals" raged on during the fighting. Gal Hirsch's book describes his colleagues' and fellow division commanders' suggestions for his replacement, and Halutz mentions the recommendations he received to replace Adam. The lack of collegiality added to the mutual distrust between the chief of staff and the commander of Northern Command. Adam's response to Kaplinsky's appointment as the chief of staff's representative in the command was restrained. In three different television interviews Adam gave variations of the following comment:

> The question is: How does one look at [Kaplinsky's appointment]? The chief of staff told me that he wanted to appoint Kaplinsky.... This is legitimate assuming that the main effort is in the northern theater.

Adam added that he still sees himself as responsible for what is happening.

> The troops are fighting courageously and giving all they've got. I feel duty-bound and answerable to them. This is a war. Things are happening that are more difficult than [Halutz's decision] right now. I'm not going to keep quiet about this. [But right now] I'm trying to focus my mental energy on making the right decisions in the northern theater.[83]

The deputy chief of staff sat in Northern Command as the chief of staff's representative for only a very short time and was meticulous about not appropriating the role of its commander for himself. There is no evidence that he made a significant impact on the conduct of the war.[84]

Halutz summed up the loss of trust:

> It's not a simple matter when the chief of staff decides to appoint a representative on his behalf in a regional command, let alone his deputy. The decision to send Major General Kaplinsky to Northern Command was one of the most difficult decisions I had to make during the war in Lebanon. I had recommended Udi Adam as commander of Northern Command. I valued his personal qualities and was familiar with the posts that he held. . . . I could have chosen from various options: transfer him elsewhere and appoint someone in his place; leave the situation as it was; or send the command a representative on my behalf. I chose the last option. You could ask why I didn't assume command. Look, I didn't have the advantage of an experienced ground force general like Kaplinsky or Gantz, and someone had to manage the IDF in the other theaters, and last but not least my informal meetings with the political echelon were crucial.
>
> The effort to back the commander of the Northern Command was not made by remote control; it took place behind the scenes. My contact with General Adam consisted of lengthy conversations in his office, which I often visited during the fighting [unfortunately, these talks have no official documentation], and many telephone calls so I could learn what was happening in Northern Command from a primary source.[85]

Summary of the Test Case

As in the previous test cases, here too is a person whom the chief of staff implicitly trusted and appointed to his current position. From the beginning of the conflict numerous factors reached a point after more than three weeks that led to Halutz's decision to subordinate Adam to Deputy Chief of Staff Kaplinsky. All of the elements in the introduction to the chapter appear here: conflicting interpretations and a conceptual gulf between the chief of staff and regional commander regarding the operational response to another kidnapping attempt and on the "stages approach" in force employment in a case of war; a conceptual gap over the improvisatory pattern for raids during the fighting; a basic divide in expectations that sprang from the chief of staff's minimal background in the nature of ground action (the importance of preplanning and early preparation; see chapter 2); GHQ instructions that were too often vague and whose rationale, as stated, was frequently ambiguous; psychological difficulty in adapting to a new situation (see chapter 1); faulty coordination between staffs; intervention by parties who were outside the chain of command; the breakdown in collegiality in the senior command; and C2 problems and the difficulty in asserting authority. Halutz's impression of Northern Command, as well as pressure from other parties, finally clinched his decision act on that issue. After three weeks of deliberation and dithering, all of these factors culminated in Kaplinsky's appointment as the chief of staff's personal representative in Northern Command. The case also highlights the roles of the regional command's and the general staff's headquarters in exacerbating the rift between the chief of staff and his generals.

Chapter Summary

The loss of trust in a commander in the course of fighting is a universal phenomenon. Abraham Lincoln's removal of commanders in the US Civil War and Winston Churchill's replacement of British commanders in the Western Desert campaign in World War II are just two of many examples. A number of lessons can be learned from this chapter.

First, the importance of the interechelon development of concepts, doctrines, and common language while preparing for war cannot be overstated, as it builds the mutual trust that is so vital during the fighting. A shift in the IDF's geopolitical and operational environment must be brought to the attention of all echelons—the regional command or service, the general staff, and the political echelon—in order to maintain constantly updated, relevant, and synchronized knowledge of the challenges the IDF has to cope with and develop mutually acceptable operational concepts and plans among the echelons. This is a Sisyphean task in periods of quiet. Conflicting approaches to concepts must be ironed out in the open rather than suppressed for the sake of "industrial quiet." Otherwise conceptual gaps will preponderate and invariably engender the loss of trust at the onset of the confrontation. Discussions of military language—the proper definition of various levels of operational achievements—are a key factor in building a common concept.

But early preparation is not enough. Sami Turgeman, the head of the operations division in the Second Lebanon War and commander of Southern Command in the Cast Lead campaign in the Gaza Strip in 2014, learned from his own experience that a major lesson in precluding the loss of trust is to hold joint learning sessions between the general staff and the regional command at as early a date as possible after the fighting begins, aimed at identifying and sealing interechelon gaps that may have developed. According to Turgeman, even if joint understandings are created before a confrontation, the new context will unfailingly cause the earlier understandings to unravel. Therefore, the developing gap will have to be remedied as early as possible, even at the cost of interechelon quarreling over professional issues during the fighting.[86]

Joint learning sessions, which should be less formal than design discussions and situation assessments, must focus on the "soft" elements, as described in this chapter, that cause the dynamics leading to a loss of trust during the fighting. These may include the following:

- Gaps in expectations that develop during the fighting, such as performance level and achievement speed
- Imprecise reporting, irregularities in requests due to their frequency and content, and changes in implementing what has already been agreed on with the chief of staff

- Gaps in interechelon staff work due to natural interechelon differences in perspective and the "broken telephone" phenomenon in communications: commander to commander; commander A to staff A; staff A to staff B; staff B to parallel commander B; etc.
- The chief of staff's feeling that the regional commander has lost control of his subordinates (divisional or field corps commanders)
- The intervention of senior commanders from outside the regular chain of command exacerbating the breach in trust that developed because of the abovementioned factors

The last point is the chief of staff's need of a defense minister whom he can talk to and discuss sensitive issues involved in the loss of trust. We have seen the case of Dayan's assistance to Elazar regarding Gonen, as well as Halutz's lack of a partner at the political echelon with whom he could have consulted about his misgivings about Adam.

4

REHABILITATING THE ARMY
AFTER A BOTCHED WAR

Over the years the IDF has weathered numerous crises. The two worst crises came after the Yom Kippur War and the Second Lebanon War. Another accompanied the failed retaliatory raids of the early 1950s (see chapter 5) and still another (not discussed in the book) followed the First Lebanon War, when rifts widened among both the public and the army over the war's justification. The crisis within the IDF after the First Lebanon War developed into a bitterness felt by junior- and middle-level commanders over the army's performance and a decline in officers signing up for career service. At this point, Deputy Chief of Staff Moshe Levi appeared as the right man in the right place at the right time. He was appointed chief of staff mainly because it provided maximal managerial continuity in the IDF.[1] (Before his appointment, Levi was known as a solid staff officer and less as a field commander.)

The crises after the Yom Kippur War and Second Lebanon War are similar in many respects, although their geopolitical contexts are quite different. From the IDF's standpoint, both crises generated a commission of inquiry (Agranat and Winograd), the resignation of the chief of staff, and a long period of rehabilitation. Mordechai "Motta" Gur, after the Yom Kippur War, and Gabi Ashkenazi, after the Second Lebanon

War, became chiefs of staff when their predecessors left the post prematurely in the wake of perceived failure. Gur's and Ashkenazi's advantage over other candidates was that they were not tainted by the failure of the poorly conducted wars because they had not been actively involved in them.

As chiefs of staff, their mission was to rehabilitate the IDF. Their methods were surprisingly similar and may be termed a "back to basics" approach that included a comprehensive overhaul of the army's training (whether it had undergone training before the war, as in the case of the Yom Kippur War, or suffered from the lack of it, as happened before the Second Lebanon War); the expansion of the ORBAT or putting the brakes on its reduction (regardless of whether this was related to the results of the war); the cancellation of organizational changes that were decided before the war or the nonimplementation of changes that appeared necessary after it; and the dilemmas involved in appointing senior commanders. Toward the end of their tenures, both chiefs of staff were forced into small-scale, successful operations that the IDF leveraged to show its rehabilitation.

The most important point is that these steps focused on rehabilitation (one may say they were aimed at winning the last war), but in effect they exhausted the IDF's organizational energy and delayed the IDF's much-needed reform after those wars. The lesson here is how to combine rehabilitation with an in-depth discussion and implementation of steps as early as possible in order to shorten the period until reform begins.

Mordechai Gur in the Wake of the Yom Kippur War

Nature of the Crisis

Israeli society and the IDF underwent a crisis in the wake of the Yom Kippur War. Although the fighting ended with an almost unparalleled military victory, considering the initial strategic surprise, several facts merged into an overriding sense of anguish and failure that still haunts the national psyche. These included the fact that the IDF had been caught by surprise; the fact that blunders were made (the October 8 counterattack in Sinai, the IAF's battle against the SAMs); the fact that an exorbitant casualty toll (by Israeli standards) had been exacted; the fact that the Agranat Commission published blistering findings that precipitated the resignations of the chief of staff, the commander of Southern Command, and the head of Aman; and—last but not least— the reservists' protests.

The postwar biographies of senior commanders reveal the depth of the crisis. Defense Minister Moshe Dayan wrote that "this political-military chapter in the history of Israel is stamped with failure because of political myopia, neglect, and inexcusable complacence [that preceded the war]."[2]

Avraham Adan, the commander of the 162nd Division, was more discreet, writing, "Not only was the war not conducted as we envisioned, but indications are that many things were flawed."[3] The IDF's morale plummeted to an unprecedented low in the postwar period. This was the first time the IDF and individual commanders came under scathing public criticism. As a result, some commanders decided not to enforce basic military norms in their units. "Some of us preferred to avoid antagonism, while others made concessions or compromises rather than harsh demands that could have swiftly restored the IDF's professionalism."[4] The IAF sensed it had failed to live up to prewar expectations, and after the war concentrated all its effort on solving the SAM issue.

As the postwar chief of staff, Mordechai Gur felt that "public sensitivity had seeped into almost every corner of military life—from proper attire, to the quality and quantity of the fighting equipment, and finally to the prevailing desire not to take risks."[5]

Gur had to cope with this labyrinthine crisis. He had been the military attaché in the United States during the war. After the war he returned to the post of commander of Northern Command and after Elazar's resignation was immediately appointed chief of staff.

The Formula for Crisis Resolution

Increasing the Number of IDF Units

Gur summed up the April 15, 1974, general staff meeting, his first such meeting since becoming chief of staff:

> In the next six months an assault force will be built that gives the IDF more "teeth," therefore all discussion on establishing a Field Forces HQ and introducing basic structural changes in the IDF is forthwith postponed. I informed those present that the brunt of our efforts would be channeled toward force design, training, and lesson learning from the war.[6]

A year later, Gur's answer to a journalist's question on the possible dearth of American equipment expressed the importance of the quantitative increase in quality ORBAT (from American acquisitions):

> If there's a "drought" [in acquisitions] it will be very bad. Let's hope there won't be any misunderstandings. If the flow of spare parts and ammunition starts but we're left without the main fighting equipment, we're in trouble. Let's not kid ourselves, if AFVs [armored fighting vehicles], artillery, planes, ships, new missiles, not to mention the latest word in electronics, don't arrive, this will be unfortunate. It means we'll pay a heavier price in war.[7]

The postwar surge in strength was due to the massive influx of American aid. Herzl Shafir, the head of Agam after the war, commented on the multiyear Etgar (Challenge) plan:

> Speaking candidly, after the surge [in acquisitions] you might say that [Prime Minister] Rabin blamed me. We began with the assumption that after the war—trauma or no trauma—we'd rebuild the army to as large and strong a fighting force as possible. We'd expand it no matter what, and if it turned out that we erred, then we'd trim it down.[8]

In his memoirs, Rabin notes that by late June 1977, the IDF had doubled in size since the Yom Kippur War. The number of tanks increased by more than 50 percent; mobile artillery by over 100 percent, including advanced weapons; AFVs by 800 percent; aircraft by 30 percent, including some of the most sophisticated planes attainable. "At first we had a problem with establishing a large number of military units that sometimes detracted from adequate performance because of the unprecedented arrival of weapons from the United States. But as the level of training and organization improved, we were able to bridge the quantity-quality gap."[9]

According to Gur, the government's and military leadership's goals after the Yom Kippur War were to rebuild the army in a way that provided the government with full political and military freedom of action without imposing dictates on the government. This was done to avoid the situation that occurred during the war, when IAF commander Benny Peled said that he had only two days left to operate freely because of the attrition of combat-ready planes.[10]

A critical report prepared by Agat officer Colonel Emanuel Wald found that the huge economic investment in military force design in the 1970s had, by the mid-1980s, yielded a significant quantitative increase in the IDF's ORBAT and arsenal. The number of armored divisions almost quadrupled (from three to eleven); the number of tanks more than tripled in a decade (from 1,075 to 3,600); the number of fighter planes rose by 60 percent (from 374 to 600); the standing army's manpower more than doubled (from 75,000 to 180,000); the reserves increased by 60 percent (from 225,000 to 370,000); and the overall investment in arms acquisitions during the decade came to $16 billion. The surge in security procurement naturally reached the ground forces too. Ground force manpower nearly doubled between 1973 and 1982 (a cumulative increase of 75 percent), even though active-duty manpower rose by only one-quarter (a cumulative increase of 26 percent).[11]

The dramatic increase in strength, which was a main factor in the response to the postwar crisis, came at the price of development of other capabilities and alternatives to the units based on heavy platforms.

Equally alarming, Israel's economy tanked, inflation skyrocketed, and the state's finances were brought to the brink of disaster.

Uzi Eilam, the head of R&D during and after the war, wrote that Buried Treasure (the American equipment's acquisition plan) was an expression of the war's trauma:

> Today we realize that the trauma was the reason for the nearly unlimited increase in the defense budget that went to brigades and divisions (especially armored divisions). Today we also know that the unbridled strengthening weighed heavily on the national economy. Today we can evaluate the degree to which this quantitative effort diverted attention from progress in the qualitative elements of future defense systems. The sin of a greedy appetite for the voluminous quantity of hardware that flooded the IDF after the war like a tsunami was the heavy price we had to pay for many years.[12]

Iftach Spector, a squadron commander during the war and later the head of the IAF operations department, tried to develop alternative solutions to the quantitative panacea: "Naturally I focused on the UAVs that I wanted us to acquire and develop instead of 'superfluous' airplanes (as I perceived them). This is where I clashed with agreements and vested interests. The dominant logic—the general thinking—led in the opposite direction: obtaining more planes for our arsenal."

Since the Yom Kippur War, the IDF supreme command, headed by Gur, believed that the army's preparation for the next war lay in its expansion. With the war's catastrophe still fresh in mind, the IDF and the defense ministry were given power that they duly wielded. Israel's defense budget, which was classified information, became the topic of open discussion at universities and among the foreign press. Spector described how, during his studies in the United States, he learned the actual figures for the first time. Israel was spending 30 percent of its annual budget on defense—twice as much as before the Yom Kippur War and five times as much as a powerful country with "normal" security needs spends. Israel was fixated on accumulating military strength and striving for independence in this area. The IDF and the defense ministry, with the enthusiastic assistance of the defense industries, galvanized the country into developing and producing fighter planes, ships, tanks, and other costly projects while taking risks that very few superpowers allowed themselves. Spector said, "In this atmosphere, to suggest a cutback on the number of planes and development of 'toys' [UAVs] in their place was tantamount to talking to a wall."[13]

Increasing the Size of the Manpower

Another side to force enlargement was the increase in available manpower. Gur introduced changes that enabled this. In a general staff meeting in April 1974, immediately after he assumed his post, a key issue was the conscription of people with deferments due to health, age, or family situation reasons. He ordered all men in civil defense professions to be reclassified and called up for military service—especially those who were skilled in restoring combat vehicles to operability.[14]

In April–May 1975, Gur announced the IDF had nearly reached the limit of quantity and quality. Additional sources of manpower involved basic questions about the country's educational and social systems. "Nevertheless, we were able to induct almost four thousand people above this year's planned number from sources the IDF had never reached before," Gur wrote. "Looking at the prospects of an enemy attack, there's no question about the need for additional manpower."[15]

Wald examined the IDF's rapid growth and found that the manpower sources that contributed to the rise in the ground units' quantity in this period had a strong influence on the nature and quality of the ORBAT. About two-thirds of the manpower that was added to the regular army units over the decade was the result of lowering compulsory conscription standards to include subgroups of lower qualifications than the average conscripts in the annual quota. Furthermore, shortening the military education period made more soldiers available for military activity in the regular units but harmed proficiency. These steps gradually eroded the quality of the standing army.[16]

Senior commanders' appointments are another aspect of manpower development. Gur described the January–February 1974 talks that Defense Minister Dayan held on senior-level appointments. Participating in the talks were the heads of the branches and the commanders of the regional commands. "In retrospect, it was in these discussions that I learned of the defense minister's intention to retire veteran commanders and advance to senior positions relatively young field commanders who had distinguished themselves in combat." Gur thought that even if this was the accepted approach, and under certain circumstances some of these promotions were justified, it would be difficult to carry out a comprehensive turnover throughout the army. The defense minister's withering criticism of senior commanders, who, many felt, had performed admirably in the war, left the unavoidable feeling that Dayan was motivated more by personal sentiment than by objective vision for the good of the army. Elazar wanted to protect the army from unnecessary shocks and requested that each officer and position be discussed on an individual basis.[17]

Later Gur wrote:

After the Yom Kippur War the officer cadre that had led the IDF for fifteen years suddenly left the army in one fell swoop! In my eyes, as chief of staff, I would have preferred to see them depart gradually—but this was not to be. Some quit because of events in the war, and others resigned because they felt uncomfortable in the new postwar conditions. As I said, they were the group that had led the IDF for decades, and almost all of them suddenly disappeared! It wasn't easy to rebuild the senior cadre quickly with people who were willing to bear the burden. A considerable amount of time is needed for a senior commander to acquire self-confidence in his "doctrinal truth" and his ability to make an impact on the units.[18]

The appointment of Shlomo Gazit as head of Aman after the Agranat Commission sacked General Eli Zeira occurred because he, like Gur, had not been involved in the intelligence fiasco that resulted in a strategic surprise at the start of the war.[19] When it came time to appoint Aman's assistant head of research in place of Aryeh Shalev, who had been removed, it was decided that neither of his two deputies fit the bill since both had been active in the prewar assessments, and that an officer who was not tainted by the intelligence debacle, Yehoshua Sagi, would be promoted.[20]

Emphasizing Education and Training

In April 1974, during a general staff meeting, Gur spoke of the need to educate and train armor officers. He ordered the rapid conversion of as many infantry and paratrooper officers to armor as possible. Two goals motivated this decision: one, to replenish the recently depleted armor officer roster; and two, to advance the combined arms battle concept. He believed that the more commanders with two-pronged experience—infantry and armor—the smoother and less strained the employment of combined forces would be.[21]

The following year Gur discussed the mutual effort that was needed to enlarge and man the tank inventory. The measures to be taken would include the conversion to armor of elite Nahal (infantrymen) soldiers and religious-military programs (military service combined with religious study). It would also be necessary to strengthen these soldiers' professional knowledge and lengthen their service time in the armored units in the coming year:

> If we build up the number of units, which is imperative given the ratio of forces between our side and the enemy's, then we'll have to come up with social, educational, instructional, and training solutions, such as simulators and additional training time in the field. The instruction array will be expanded and undergo a thorough process of modernization, sophistication, and efficiency. Only at the end of the year will we know if the effort has succeeded, if it's produced better forces. I believe that this is our problem! In the coming work year we'll have more than enough equipment. Agreements have been signed for the supply of tanks,

artillery, and AFVs, though the arrival date isn't certain. Maybe there'll be a slowdown, but the goods will eventually get here. Now the troops have to be trained—and this we will do.[22]

In a meeting with the defense minister in December 1977, Gur ordered Mahad to display the latest training methods and systems. Commanders of the training bases and divisions were invited. He pointed out that the size and quality of the army demanded the continuous upgrade of fighting skills with minimum resources in the shortest possible time.[23]

Immediately after the war, Yossi Peled received command of the 460th Training Brigade for junior armor staff. Too many armor commanders had been injured in the war. The 460th Brigade was tasked with rehabilitating the corps' command backbone. Peled said, "I'll never forget the experience of instructing commanders not only in professional matters but also in educational and ethical areas. I met many former infantry officers in the brigade who had gone through professional retraining to armor." After the war, the IDF realized it had a large surplus of highly trained infantry officers and a shortage of armor officers. Moreover, one of the lessons of the war was that the armored corps had to be expanded. The IDF looked to infantry officers to become armor officers. Although most of them were reserve officers who had served a long and stressful stint during and after the war, their response was very good. Most of them quickly integrated into veteran armored units and new formations.[24]

As deputy commander of the armor school immediately after the war, Avigdor Kahalani, who as a battalion commander on the Golan Heights had fought gallantly in the war, presented a completely different view of the former infantry officers and soldiers. As he saw it, the changeover to armor involved a lot more than just a few months of learning a new profession. It demanded a basic mental change that called for a special effort in tanker training. He showed General Adan, the commander of Armored Corps HQ, the condensed plans for officer instruction and tanker training, and then was told to cut the training period in half. The Haruv Reconnaissance unit in the Jordan Valley was also one of the candidates for professional reeducation, but its staff was vigorously opposed. General Dov Tamari (deputy commander of Armored Corps HQ) and Kahalani had a heart-to-heart talk with the men. "What I heard nearly floored me. The reconnaissance fighters, donned in their red berets, refused to convert to armor because of the high number of casualties the Armored Corps had incurred. And they had no scruples about saying this out loud."[25]

Kahalani, now a full colonel, recalls that Gur took a personal interest in furthering the training infrastructure for combined arms in Tze'elim training center in the Western Negev desert.

I explained to Gur the need to bring infantry, combat engineers, and artillery officers to the facility.

"The area isn't big enough for everyone," Motta said.

I showed him a map and drew an imaginary circle around the area.

"It's not a question of space, it's a question of will and vision," I insisted.

Motta agreed and ordered Mahad to take care of it. Now we had to deal with robust opposition from the chief of the infantry and paratroopers, General Dan Shomron.

"Over my dead body!" Shomron swore. "I'll lie down on the road and stop the whole show!"

A few days later the name of the facility was changed to "Field Units Training Base." The infantry units marched into the base in full glory, the combat engineers were proud to be counted among the units training there, and the artillerymen, whose main base wasn't far from Tze'elim, closed the circle. I couldn't hide my pride at the sight of the facility teeming with life. The classrooms hummed with reservists who were learning doctrine, tanks were revving up their engines and instilling a new spirit in the training areas.[26]

Kahalani's successor, Colonel Nathan Nir, who had commanded a reserve brigade in the Yom Kippur War and was now the first commander of Tze'elim Training Base, described the high priority that Gur, who often came up with original ideas, gave to the facility. Gur wanted to demonstrate the importance of the new training facility to the commanders and decided that a general staff meeting would be held at Tze'elim. He also invited the chief of infantry and paratroopers, Dan Shomron, on three occasions to visit the sprawling desert site and in effect harnessed him into cooperating with the base's establishment by ordering him to send instructors to the facility's headquarters to coordinate combined arms exercises. He also ordered the chiefs of other corps to go south. And lo and behold, they began to take the change seriously. Gur kept close tabs on activity at Tze'elim. He observed exercises, witnessed training drills, and inquired about the types of exercises, the number of officers who underwent training, and their professional skills.[27]

No Organizational Changes Made

As stated, in his first meeting with the general staff Gur got down to business: "In the next six months an assault force will be built that gives the IDF more 'teeth,' therefore all discussion on establishing a Field Forces HQ and introducing basic structural changes in the IDF is forthwith postponed."[28]

Chapter 6 shows that talks on setting up the Field Forces HQ were shelved for an even longer period, and when they were finally renewed Gur set to work vigorously and successfully to stymie it. However, he did introduce some relatively limited organizational changes, such as the creation of Agat.

Operation Litani as Proof of the IDF's Rehabilitation

In 1976 Operation Entebbe (the daring rescue of hostages from Uganda's international airport) uplifted the national morale, as did the March 1978 Operation Litani (named after a prominent river in southern Lebanon), the first large-scale operation since the 1973 war.

The operation was a response to Palestinian terrorists' massacre of thirty-five civilians in a bus on the coastal road near Tel Aviv. The government decided to attack the PLO's terrorist infrastructures in south Lebanon. In a week-long operation, four brigade-size combat teams captured the area south of the Litani and carried out combined arms operations in rural and urban terrain, killing approximately three hundred terrorists. The IDF lost eighteen soldiers. Before Gur was replaced by the incoming chief of staff, Rafael Eitan, on April 16, 1978, a senior command conference focused on the lessons of the recent operation. "At the end of the meeting the chief of staff and defense minister summed up the IDF's four years of rehabilitation and development since the agreement on disengagement after the war. Operation Litani was perceived as the culmination of this process, despite its limited scope and the asymmetry of the opposing sides—a standing army versus a terrorist organization."[29] Whether Operation Litani was "the completion of the rehabilitation process" or not, we may assume that the IDF commanders regarded it, even partially, as the rectification of the mistakes made in the Yom Kippur War.

Gabi Ashkenazi after the Second Lebanon War

Nature of the Crisis

When the Second Lebanon War ended in the summer of 2006, Israel was plunged into a crisis similar to that which occurred after the Yom Kippur War. The IDF performed far below expectations, and the home front proved to be poorly prepared. In the wake of the war, reservists took to the streets in protest and bereaved families voiced angry criticism, followed by the resignations of Chief of Staff Dan Halutz; Udi Adam, the commander of Northern Command; and Gal Hirsch, the commander of the Galilee Division. The Winograd report's blistering appraisal stated that "after thirty-four days of combat the IDF could claim neither a decisive victory nor even a win on 'points.' Hezbollah fire on the Israeli home front ended only because of the ceasefire. Israel did not win the war."[30]

Gabi Ashkenazi's tenure as chief of staff witnessed a period of relative consensus on the IDF's disappointing performance in the war and the limited results. As time passed, the notion took hold that the war had been more successful than previously assumed.[31] Be that as it may, this understanding took hold after Ashkenazi's term as chief of staff.

After the publication of the Winograd report, Ashkenazi discussed the IDF's rehabilitation:

> The IDF had learned the lessons of the war even before the report was made public and will continue to apply them. The IDF is a strong army; it doesn't need to rehabilitate. Correct itself, yes—rehabilitate, no. It continuously upgrades its capabilities and preparedness to provide answers to any threat facing us from near and far.[32]

Whether or not Ashkenazi intended "to rehabilitate the IDF," at the end of his tenure, and after Operation Cast Lead (December 27, 2008–January 18, 2009), the IDF was perceived as rehabilitated (see below). The political-security elite expressed as much with regards to Ashkenazi's efforts. In the words of former chiefs of staff:

> [Amnon] Lipkin-Shahak: Gabi can hang up his uniform with a great sense of satisfaction. The army he inherited four years ago—after the Second Lebanon War—has been restored to its former strength under his command. . . .

> [Shaul] Mofaz: The IDF was fortunate to have an outstanding commander like Gabi in one of its most challenging periods. All of us—commanders, soldiers, and citizens—thank you. During your tenure you brought terms back to the IDF lexicon that we were all familiar with—victory, responsibility, personal example, operational discipline. . . .

[Moshe] Ya'alon: As chief of staff, Gabi Ashkenazi restored the confidence that the IDF lost in the Second Lebanon War and led the soldiers and commanders in Operation Cast Lead. The people in Israel regained their confidence in their army, and our enemies are again deterred.[33]

President Shimon Peres praised Ashkenazi for rehabilitating the IDF after the Second Lebanon War: "Looking at all eighteen former chiefs of staff, Ashkenazi's contribution to Israel's security has been unique and exceptionally gratifying. You were one of the IDF's finest chiefs of staff."[34]

Before describing the steps that Ashkenazi took after the war, it is important to note that some of the decisions on necessary changes had been made during Halutz's period in office between the end of the war and his resignation.

Response to the Crisis

Maintaining ORBAT Strength and Rescinding the Prewar Decision to Shorten the Length of Service Time

The IDF prewar multiyear plans Kela (2003) and Keshet (2006) introduced reductions in various areas of ORBAT. Kela called for a cut of approximately 20 percent of ORBAT, but this lasted only until 2005, when another reduction in security expenses was called for. When Halutz became chief of staff, he discovered that most of the budget had been earmarked for certain uses by previous decisions and contracts and was unavailable for future needs. Therefore, the plan had to be discarded and a new one formulated (Keshet).[35]

In the week that the Second Lebanon War broke out, the IDF was supposed to decide on a significant reduction in the tank inventory during 2007–11, as the Kela plan stipulated. The five-year Tefen plan that was drawn up after the war canceled the proposal to close tank brigades and instead continued with Merkava Mark IV tank production.

The cutback in ground units, which the IDF had been pursuing since the end of the previous decade, was terminated. Units that had been disbanded on the eve of the Second Lebanon War—for example, field corps headquarters on the Lebanese and Golan fronts—were reestablished in a condensed framework.[36]

In the September 2007 Tefen plan conference, Chief of Staff Ashkenazi announced that the key factor in the IDF's strength was the size of the ORBAT. Every effort would be made to safeguard the current scope of the main units, he said. The multiyear plan emphasized the strengthening of ground maneuvers by building an offensive capability based on the balanced integration of maneuver and fire capabilities along with maneuver-supporting elements. Ashkenazi stressed that given the cutbacks that were supposed to have commenced the year before, preserving the ORBAT in its present size was a significant step in itself and required appropriate resources and financial input. For the ORBAT to remain at its present size, its employment would have to be more flexible:

> Before we sum up the plan, the following ideas for enlarging the ground ORBAT will have to be examined and the ramifications presented for . . . converting the Kfir Formation into a regular army infantry brigade and assigning the independent Givati Brigade to a division. We also have to look into the creation of designated units for routine security duty that is based on border police companies or another solution. The current reestablished corps headquarters will also have to be reinforced.[37]

Despite the earlier intentions to slash the ORBAT, the possibility of preserving it stemmed from the approval of the budgetary framework that the Brodet Committee on the security budget drafted in 2007. This framework paved the way toward a generous multiyear plan that avoided painful reductions and enabled a buildup in various arrays without special prioritization.[38]

The Cancellation of the Shortened Service

Reminiscent of the period before the Yom Kippur War, the question of scaling back the length of compulsory service was on the agenda before the Second Lebanon War. The Ben-Basat Committee that Defense Minister Shaul Mofaz had appointed on the eve of the war (February 2006) studied the ramifications of reducing compulsory service by having combat troops and personnel engaged in special professions serve two years and four months (instead of three years) and receive a significant financial compensation. Implementation of the plan was supposed to take several years.[39]

Shortening the length of service implied a major reduction in the combat forces and the number of battalions, a condensed military education period, and other limitations. In July 2007, the government voted to put off a decision on shortening the length of service to an unspecified date. Postponing the decision was, in effect, a condition for keeping the ORBAT at its current level (see above).[40]

Emphasis on Military Education, Training, and Inventory

The cutback in the training of ground units in the prewar years was the main reason for their slipshod performance in combat.[41] After the war, Ashkenazi gave top priority to reintroducing training programs for regulars and reservists, stressing education, and reopening advanced courses for brigade commanders and division commanders.

His emphasis on returning the army to combat fitness was discussed publicly shortly after he assumed his post. On his first visit to the Knesset Foreign Affairs and Defense Committee in late March 2007 (a month and a half after he assumed office), it was reported that in regard to evacuation of an Israeli settlement on the West Bank, which usually required many forces, the IDF announced that it would commit a minimum number of troops to the operation so as not to detract from their infantry training. Ashkenazi would also cancel the system according to which officers (brigade commanders) served in two roles, thus freeing officers to concentrate all their time and energy on one position. For example, officers who commanded both a training facility and a reserve unit would now have more time with their units.[42]

A few days later (early April 2007), another article noted that the cancellation of training was possible only with the chief of staff's personal approval and that the chief of staff forbade calling off training at the battalion level and higher without his personal approval. Furthermore, the training format had been changed. Soldiers were now trained primarily for war and only secondarily for anti-terrorist operations in the West Bank and Gaza. An article on the *Ynet* website stated, "Ashkenazi considers the training of units, including basic instruction, a vital element in force building and preparing for various scenarios in the Middle East. As he sees it, this issue is of paramount importance."[43]

In May 2007, the IDF reopened the division commanders' course with three division commanders who fought in the war: Guy Tzur, Eyal Zamir, and Erez Zukerman.[44] At the same time a brigade commanders' course opened.

In the conference on the Tefen multiyear plan, the chief of staff made it clear that the level of training (in quantity and quality) was the key element that would not be compromised. A general staff workshop document stated, "As early as 2007 we saw a quantum leap in the scope of training throughout the IDF, with an emphasis on the ground force reserves." In the coming years, Ashkenazi said, in accordance with the multiyear plan, the level of ground training would expand even more than in 2007. The budget slotted for training the reserve component would be a major part of the plan. "Despite its shortcomings the plan provides a satisfactory solution for training the ground forces and is a radical departure from last year's situation and even a significant improvement over today's plan. One of the main lessons from the recent fighting has been that there's no room for compromise in readiness." The IDF's ORBAT, he said, must be equipped, trained, and in tip-top shape. "Last year we made a giant leap forward in this area and we will continue to strengthen the army in the next multiyear plan too."[45]

Another decision of far-reaching consequences for the ground forces made after the war was to determine the proficiency level of regular army and reserve units, as the air force had been doing for decades. In 2010, in a major improvement, the general staff began monitoring the proficiency of each unit, a procedure that aimed at eliminating "surprises" as in 2006's revelations of low ground forces competency. The IDF's training plan had been consistent since 2007, and every battalion underwent training for at least thirteen weeks a year. Only the highest echelons were authorized to approve a postponement or cancellation in the schedule. Regular army units returned to training with live ammunition, which had been denied them in the years before the Second Lebanon War.[46]

A commander of a reservist infantry battalion related that a year after the war, during a Northern Command study day on the fighting in Lebanon, Ashkenazi called him aside and asked him if his instructions on resuming organized training and returning to clear military language had filtered down to the field echelons.[47]

At the end of Ashkenazi's tour of duty (February 2011), Giora Eiland (previously the head of the National Security Council, Agat, and Amatz) wrote that the army's preparedness had vastly improved by every measure. The reservists underwent better training; the stocks had been replenished; the frequency of senior-level exercises had increased; and operational plans, some of which were brushed aside on the eve of the Second Lebanon War, had been refreshed, updated, and made available.[48]

One of the main lessons of the Second Lebanon War was the need to boost spare parts and ammunition stocks. A few months after the war, a significant effort was made to fill the IDF storerooms, which included closing the Port of Ashdod for an entire month to enable the unloading of huge arms shipments. These deliveries raised the level in the stocks above the prewar level.[49]

No Organizational Change: Upending Chief of Staff Halutz's Prewar Decisions

In 2006, approximately half a year before the Second Lebanon War, Halutz instituted sweeping organizational transfers. Chiefs of combat support corps (manpower and personnel administration, ordnance, logistics, and C4I) were transferred from GHQ to Ground Force Command (Mazi). The reinforced Mazi now received responsibility for posting units in the regional commands' sectors for routine security operations and for administering the budget for this activity. Mazi also oversaw the maintenance department and ground forces technological division (until then part of the Logistics Command) and force design authorities for regional command headquarters.

Ten thousand standing army and compulsory service positions were transferred from the general staff to the ground forces, and a new mechanism was created for manning the general staff with officers from all the services. Thus, the general staff no longer had to concentrate on the ground forces, which left Mazi free for the first time to decide on force design since it was now given most of the authority to do so.[50]

Mazi received the four abovementioned corps, and in order to cope with the addition of the corps' schools to those already under Mazi, a "ground forces training and instruction array" was established within Mazi under the command of Major General Meir Klifi. Another change was the focus of the deputy chief of staff on force design along the lines of the air force's force design model, and the head of Amatz assumed responsibility for force employment. But when Ashkenazi stepped into his new role as chief of staff, he rescinded all of these changes (excluding the transfer of the ground forces technological division).

In the aftermath of the Second Lebanon War the realization of the need to be continually prepared for war, as much as was possible, stood at the heart of the cancellation of Halutz's organizational reforms. Discussion revolved around the arrangement of responsibility and authorization for ground force employment. Yet Ashkenazi decided that the regional commands would remain under the direct authority of the general staff. In other words, the reorganization of 2007 merely confirmed the traditional hierarchy: the GHQ remained the commander of the ground forces, thus canceling the need to establish an additional headquarters between the general staff and the regional commands. This meant that senior roles, authorities, and staff bodies that were crucial for the employment of the ground forces returned from Mazi to the general staff. As a result, Amatz received authority to order routine security duties (which had been transferred to Mazi in 2006), and a C4I division was established in the C4I branch that would be responsible for employing C4I. The chief of staff made it clear that the corps would be the supreme professional authority. The upshot of all these decisions was that the IDF was more or less organized along the same lines as before the 2006 changes.[51]

The Gap in Senior Commanders

After the Second Lebanon War, as in the case of the Yom Kippur War, the sudden resignation or retirement of senior commanders forced the chief of staff to fill senior positions. For example, General Dan Harel, the Israeli military attaché to the United States, was recalled to Israel to serve as deputy chief of staff. When General David Ben-Besht, the commander of the navy, and other senior naval commanders retired prematurely, Ashkenazi brought back to active service senior commanders who had already entered civilian life: General Eli Marom as commander of the navy and General Rani Ben Yehuda as Marom's deputy and naval chief of staff. Gal Hirsch, the commander of the Galilee Division, was replaced by General Yossi Bahar, who had just been appointed chief of infantry and paratroopers. Other appointments also seem to have been made by force of circumstance, such as that of General Avi Mizrahi, who fulfilled all of his previous posts in Northern Command, as commander of Central Command; and of General Sami Turgeman as commander of Mazi (in his first role as major general, after the two previous Mazi commanders, who had been seasoned major generals).

The Return to Doctrinal "Basics"

Ashkenazi gave priority to professionalism as well as to military doctrine, which had been shunted aside in the prewar years in favor of the lexicon of "effects" and routine security jargon (see chapter 5). The Winograd report elaborated on the impact of ambiguous operational language before the war and the years of fighting terror. Ashkenazi appears to have set as a goal the reinstatement of proper military language in the IDF. Four years after the Second Lebanon War, not a trace remained of the concepts and terms that had been the vogue in the IDF on the eve of and during the war. Terms such as "effect" (as part of the EBO approach) and "burning the enemies' consciousness" (make the enemy leadership stunned and confused) vanished from the military discourse. In their place basic terms like "deterrence," "warning," and "decisive victory" returned. The IDF strategy that had been in use in the three months before the war was put on hold and effectively eliminated.[52]

At the same time, the Winograd report warned of the blanket negativism toward all the ideas that developed on the eve of the war in the name of "back to basics." A senior officer complained that since the end of the war "it's as though an order had been issued from above to stop thinking."[53]

In a 2008 television interview, Ashkenazi was asked about the issue of military language. His approach seems more balanced:

> I think we have to be strict about proper military language . . . and assure that the terms are clear and familiar. . . . I'm not opposed to developing knowledge, I'm not against new concepts. The nature of war is constantly changing, and the tools of the past aren't always suited to it. . . . I'm only saying that we must do this methodically and thoroughly.[54]

On the danger of suppressing openness, Eiland wrote that the atmosphere in the army, especially the top brass, was problematic. True, morale and self-confidence were gaining momentum, but the atmosphere at the senior level failed to transmit encouragement, let alone criticism and innovation. Ashkenazi did the right thing in his first two years when rehabilitation demanded discipline and less room for a profusion of opinion. It may have been possible to increase development in the last two years, but this didn't happen. One of an army's (especially a general staff's) major pitfalls is "group think," and it seems that too little attention was channeled to this dimension.[55]

In this test case, too, areas can be identified where "back to basics" delayed changes that could have begun earlier under Ashkenazi but began only when Benny Gantz became chief of staff. These include conveying information that Aman collected and processed to ground forces' tactical echelons (code-named "intelligence-oriented combat"), and relevant fighting methods focused on engaging an asymmetric enemy like the Hezbollah (Ashkenazi's first years as chief of staff focused on a war with the Syrian regular army).

Operation Cast Lead as Proof of the IDF's Rehabilitation

Operation Cast Lead in Gaza (2008–9) provided the IDF with an opportunity to demonstrate the lessons it learned from the Second Lebanon War. The IDF employed air strikes and four brigade combat teams. The Palestinians suffered 1,300 casualties (500 to 700 Hamas fighters and the rest civilians), while Israel lost three civilians and ten soldiers.[56]

The operation took place more than two years after the war and a little less than two years from the time Ashkenazi became chief of staff. The media, military, and political leadership perceived Cast Lead as a chance to prove IDF's recovered ability, in command and staff procedures at all echelons, in combined arms tactics, in close air support, and in intelligence support. Many observers justifiably viewed the operation as a corrective experience: the IDF perceived the war in Gaza as a second chance, an opportunity to redress the failure and humiliation that Israel had incurred in the war in Lebanon in the summer of 2006. The conditions made it easier this time, not only because Hamas proved a weaker foe than Hezbollah, but also because of the improved performance of IDF officers, from the chief of staff, Gabi Ashkenazi, and the commander of the Southern Command, Yoav Galant, to the brigade commanders who pushed forward, far from their computer screens, to the logistics personnel. In an article in *Ha'aretz*, Avi Issacharoff and Amos Harel added, "But before we criticize those who led the fiasco in Lebanon, it's worthwhile to remember the supreme command's predicament, which was partially their own fault, at the outbreak of the last war."[57]

Chapter Summary

The crises after the Yom Kippur War and Second Lebanon War are similar in many ways, although the enemies that Israel faced and the consequences of the wars were quite different. Similar steps were taken by the two chiefs of staff who were appointed after the crises, with an emphasis on training the army (whether it was well trained as it was before the Yom Kippur War or inadequately trained as before the Second Lebanon War). They also included increasing the ORBAT while halting its reduction and canceling the organizational changes that had been decided before the war or delaying changes that seemed necessary after it. All in all, both chiefs of staff adopted the "back to basics" approach, which had its own ramifications: a decline in innovative military thinking in favor of quantitative expansion with equipment that was missing in the last war, and curbing concepts of innovative force employment.

The two test cases deal with the relatively lengthy initial stage of emergence from the crisis and can be termed "healing on the job," which is based on training and education. It took a decade from the crisis (during the tenure of the third chief of staff after the war) for the

IDF to cultivate more open thinking on future challenges, the type of mental freedom that can produce conceptual and technological break-throughs. The US Army experienced a similar phenomenon after the withdrawal from Vietnam.

Thus, in order to shorten the "lost decade" as much as possible, I would recommend that military organizations that are struggling to recover from failure create a mechanism that enables new ideas to ger-minate in a period of "back to basics." This will move them forward relatively quickly when the conditions are right for change.

5
LEADING A CHANGE IN FORCE DESIGN

All of the IDF chiefs of staff have implemented force design processes, including doctrine, organization, education, training, and weapons acquisition. They have also introduced changes in other fields—normative, organizational, and conceptual. There are many reasons for the differences in the nature and scope of the changes: political decisions, resource availability, the evolving nature of threats, open-mindedness or opposition in the IDF to change, and each chief of staff's proclivity toward conservatism or innovation.

A key factor in the chief of staff's decision to institute change is his assessment of the IDF's ability to absorb it without being overly shaken up. Major organizational changes, such as the establishment of the Ground Forces HQ (Mafhash) in 1983, the merger of the Ground Forces Command (Mazi) and the Technological and Logistics Command (Atal) in 2015, the attempt to create a cyber service, and massive cutbacks over the years, have had ramifications not only for the IDF's effectiveness but also for the level of career security of those serving in it, which affects their degree of trust in the organization. As discussed in chapter 4, chiefs of staff Gur and Ashkenazi, neither of whom intended to institute major changes, performed a volte-face when they realized that a crisis in the IDF, after what was perceived as a failed war, warranted the stabilization of the system rather than further convulsions. Another major factor in deciding on the extent of the change is the level of operational risk the chief of staff is prepared to take if a confrontation erupts while the change is underway.

Historically the chief of staff does not reverse a major change that his predecessors initiated. The reason seems to be that in most cases, the chief of staff served in a senior position on the general staff during his predecessor's tenure and was partner to the change. Therefore, one could say he is duty-bound to see to its implementation. On the other hand, he is also aware that should he backtrack, his replacement may do the same to his changes. An exception to this pattern occurred when Ashkenazi overturned the decisions of his predecessor, Dan Halutz, regarding the IDF's organization. It appears that the two-pronged crisis that roiled the IDF after the Second Lebanon War (the IDF's performance and the collapse of Halutz's prestige in the public's eyes) enabled Ashkenazi to make this exceptional move.

My analysis focuses on the way the chiefs of staff handled a change: how it was perceived and explained; which measures they took in order to accomplish it; if there was resistance, how they coped with it; and lastly, how they dealt with the risk factor during the change.

The cases chosen for analysis in this chapter focus on major changes in force design. Thus, cases where the number of units increased or decreased will not be looked at, but cases where significant changes in force design occurred will be examined, such as a major shift in the IDF culture, the creation of a vital capability, or the diversion of force design from one war scenario to another.

These changes present a wide area of transformation, starting with normative-conceptual changes of an existing force to large-scale changes in weapons, organization, and training. At no time did a chief of staff institute a change *ex nihilo*. The completion of the process generally required more than one chief of staff's tenure.

The first case is the change in the IDF's fighting spirit in the years before the Sinai War (1954–56), when Moshe Dayan served as chief of staff. Dayan's challenge was to introduce the fighting principle of devotion to mission accomplishment in offensive actions. This came in the wake of a string of failures in limited ground operations. Dayan's solution was to raise the IDF's standards by exploiting the successful operations of Unit 101, which he inherited from Chief of Staff Mordechai Maklef, and later the 890th Paratrooper Battalion as inspirations for emulation throughout the IDF. Afterward he expanded the use of Nahal infantry (combined military and agricultural settlement troops) and other units in offensive actions. He also conveyed messages through training events and operational debriefings and forced commanders to set personal examples through compulsory parachuting courses. Dayan had to overcome the opposition of the powerful lobby of the Kibbutz Movement (which comprised a kind of social-political-ideological elite at the time) for the increase in offensive manpower at the expense of regional defense by Nahal infantry.

The second case deals with the change in the approach to the IDF's main challenge in the aftermath of the Yom Kippur War—the enemy's large quantity of armored fighting vehicles (AFVs). Chiefs of staff Dan Shomron and Ehud Barak carried out the changes from 1986 to 1994. Their efforts focused on the development of intelligence-gathering systems and precision-guided munitions (PGMs). This development was resourced in part by the cutbacks in the IDF's tank inventory that had burgeoned after the Yom Kippur War (which began during Chief of Staff Moshe Levi's tenure). These weapons eventually merged into an integrated system designed to destroy enemy AFVs, especially before they reached the front line. The goal was to block enemy armor under acceptable attrition rates even as the IDF stood at a quantitative disadvantage, as it did in the Yom Kippur War on the Golan Heights. The change included the development of new weapons, the creation of designated units, and the adoption of an operational concept for applying the new capability. Shomron and Barak had to cope with veteran armored corps personnel who viewed the change as a threat to armor's supremacy.

The third case looks at chiefs of staff Shaul Mofaz's and Moshe Ya'alon's changes in force design between 1998 and 2005, especially in training, organization, and weapons acquisition for a limited confrontation with the Palestinians. This was the first time that the main scenario for force design shifted from war against regular armies to confrontations with guerrilla and terror organizations. Opposition in the IDF to the change was relatively low-key.

The test cases present how the operational or resource-based need for change was perceived; the chief of staff's intentions and implementation; internal opposition (if there was any) to the change and the chief of staff's tactics for overcoming it; and finally the results of the change (the degree of success or failure).

Moshe Dayan and the Transformation of the IDF's Fighting Spirit Prior to the Sinai War, 1954–56

Research on the changes in the IDF between 1952 and 1955 focuses on the tangible elements of force design: weapons, organizational changes, budgets, and manpower data. In light of the incompatibility between actual force design and the statements of senior officers, the conclusion is that the measure of improvement was not as great as the interested parties presented it to be. Conversely, during Mordechai Maklef's and Moshe Dayan's tenures as chiefs of staff, improvement can be seen in areas that are difficult to measure and quantify, such as morale, pride, confidence, and fighting spirit—areas that contributed inestimably to the IDF's victories in the coming years.[1]

One writer discussed "Dayan's efforts to enhance the fighting ability."[2] Another scholar studied the paratroopers' performance, which Dayan had emphasized, in instilling the fighting spirit.[3] This test case looks at Dayan as chief of staff and the changes that he introduced, in particular the fighting spirit and offensive approach. Dayan was not the first to take up this challenge. Unit 101, which played a major part in the change, was established during Chief of Staff Maklef's tenure when Dayan, as head of Agam, opposed the creation of an elite unit in the belief that a more comprehensive solution was needed (see below). But the one year that Maklef served as the chief of staff was too short to upgrade the IDF's competency. It should also be pointed out that the basis of the change was the improvement in manpower that took place between the end of the War of Independence and the period under discussion, which was chiefly the result of higher numbers of immigrant recruits going through Israel's education system before conscription.[4]

The Need for Change

Until 1953, the army's organizational infrastructure had crystallized under chiefs of staff Ya'akov Dori and Yigael Yadin. The IDF was in the midst of procurement, instruction, and training, but it still lagged in many areas, such as its fighting spirit. Dayan put his finger on the IDF's condition after the War of Independence:

> To our credit, the War of Independence bequeathed us a tradition of the highest degree in the defensive battle and the willingness to engage an enemy that possessed superior equipment and manpower. But I'm sorry to say that in most of the offensive battles we fought in the War of Independence, the willingness and aggressiveness [of our fighters] were less than in the defensive battles. The "unconditional defense" of every settlement and position, regardless of the topography, balance of forces, or whatever else, brought us victory in the campaigns. But the War of Independence's legacy was not enough in itself to bolster and guarantee the army's level of fighting for what came next. The soldiers and commanders who are now educated in the army are tested not in defensive battles but in offensive ones; and all the stories of the dazzling exploits in the War of Independence are not enough to ensure that the next war will be fought in the same tradition. A soldier who serves in the army today is educated on battles that he and his comrades are fighting.[5]

It is important to note that Dayan exaggerated his disparagement of the army's performance in offensive battles in the War of

Independence. He seems to have forgotten operations Yoav (repulsing most of the Egyptian Army from the Negev and encircling its remnants), Horev, and Hiram (recapturing the Lower and Upper Galilee from the Syrian Army and Arab Liberation Army, and then crossing into southern Lebanon and seizing fourteen villages), probably because he did not take part in them.

Dayan described the IDF's low-level competency between 1951 and 1953 and his conclusions regarding the need for change, stating that many tasks that the forces were assigned in this period were left uncompleted. Upon entering a village, if the forces encountered guards or were discovered, they would abort the mission. Preparations were insufficient, information on the area was outdated, and even the elite units that were designated for special operations, such as the paratrooper battalion, demonstrated inexcusable incompetence. This was in the face of an enemy who was not a trained and equipped regular army but a "national guard"—Arab villagers who were guarding their homes, without machine guns and hand grenades, armed only with rifles. "Still, many of our operations fizzled. . . . I'm determined to put an end to the outrageous results of our engagements with the Arabs and to the IDF's apathy throughout the chain of command that leads to bungled episodes and the lame excuse of 'we weren't able to,'" Dayan said. "I saw three factors at the root of our shortcoming: the soldiers' reluctance to risk their lives to accomplish a mission; the role and location of the units' commanders during the battle; and GHQ's basic attitude toward these matters."[6]

Dayan elaborated on the failed actions during 1952 and 1953 (albeit there were some successes): the Fifth Brigade in the Jordanian village of Falama in January 1953 (a company under the battalion commander's direct command aborted the mission); the Seventh Brigade's failure in its mission to lay mines on roads in the Gaza Strip in April; and the paratrooper battalion's botched diversionary attack on the Jordanian village of Idna. Ariel Sharon recalled the IDF's low morale as a catalyst for the establishment of the special-forces unit, Unit 101: "The first problem I faced was finding people for what was being called

Unit 101. With the army as demoralized as it was, not many soldiers were volunteering for this kind of venture. There was a general feeling that nothing effective could be done."[7]

The retaliatory raids included cross-border activity involving transportation disruption, mine laying, and, at a later stage, incursions into villages and army posts to wreak havoc and inflict losses on the enemy. Colonel Mishael Shaham, the commander of the Jerusalem District, who established Unit 101, stated in an interview that the retaliatory actions had been floundering and were embarrassing senior general staff officers. "In one case a mechanized infantry battalion was ordered to conduct a retaliatory raid against the Jordanian village of al-Safi, south of the Dead Sea. The unit failed to reach the target and backtracked the way that it came. The failure was a stinging blow and left a stain on the IDF's armored forces for a long time."[8]

The year 1952 witnessed a series of failures. IDF troops were lax in mission accomplishment and demonstrated disgraceful professional conduct on retaliatory raids or in places where a raid was supposed to take place: Beit Jala, Beit Sira, Idna, Wadi Fukin, Furiq, Dir Balat, and others. These small-scale incidents were kept from the Israeli press. The government thought that citizens should assume the IDF was maintaining a policy of restraint for political and other reasons, rather than learn the truth of the military fiascoes that contributed nothing to the IDF's prestige.

The security situation and the IDF's disappointing capabilities headed the agenda at the general staff meeting on July 27, 1954, during which Defense Minister Pinhas Lavon admitted that nearly all the actions initiated between January and June 1953 appeared to have ended in failure. Perhaps one case alone ended relatively successfully. He also noted that in general the soldiers failed the performance test for many reasons, and each case had its own reasons. Once it was because of poor planning; another time the intervention of force majeure was blamed for messing up the plans; a third time it was because of fear, a substandard, ragtag force, and the commanders' inability to control their men; and on still another occasion it was simply due to the commanders' ineptitude. Every time there were extenuating circumstances, "but if you look at the whole picture, the conclusion is obvious that for quite some time—and in this period we carried out ten initiated actions—almost all of them were military blunders."[9]

Lavon was aware of the new unit's successes—Unit 101—but he made it clear that more was needed:

> Beginning in June 1953 a tangible rise was felt in combat proficiency. . . . On the other hand, as I see it, what is more serious and requires more thought on our part, is the fact that if I make a rough comparison between the more or less successful operations and the ones we botched, then the successes were the product of one IDF unit—and the failures of the rest of the IDF.[10]

The sense of crisis and need for change seems to have been shared at the tactical level (Sharon and Shaham, for example), with the heads of Agam (Dayan and Amit), and with the political echelon (Defense Minister Lavon and perhaps less so Prime Minister Moshe Sharett—see below).

Creating a Change

Dayan believed that a transformation in the fighting spirit would have to include the following: small, successful offensive actions as the spearhead of the entire IDF; an upgrade of infantry units' competence in carrying out complex battle assignments; strict demands for mission accomplishment; the use of symbols (such as paratrooper wings) with an emphasis on personal courage; and commanders' examples. The change began while Dayan was still the head of Agam, under Maklef's command, and continued during his tenure as chief of staff. The change also included various material elements for strengthening the IDF's offensive capability, but these will not be discussed, except for the diversion of quality manpower of the collective farming settlements from the Nahal infantry and regional defense tasks to offensive units, a move that sparked robust opposition to Dayan, and which he was forced to deal with (see below).

Enhancing the Fighting Spirit through Retaliatory Actions: Unit 101 and the Paratroopers

During Shaham's struggle to establish Unit 101, he met with David Ben-Gurion's military adjutant and penned a memo, as Ben-Gurion requested, proposing the appointment of Ariel Sharon as commander of the unit. And so it was.[11] The unit's success stemmed to a marked degree from the special relationship between Dayan and Sharon. Between the two flowed a mutual understanding regarding the essence of the army, its goals, training, and education. Above all, they saw eye to eye on the retaliatory strategy, which helped forge the strong connection between them that overcame many an irregularity and misunderstanding. In these years, Sharon had an enormous influence on Dayan, who admired the young officer's skills and saw him as the commander who would revolutionize the faltering army.[12] Dayan wrote that changing the general staff's approach was not difficult. In a meeting with the regional commands' general staffs, he announced that from then on, if a unit commander said he wouldn't carry out a mission because "he's unable to overcome the enemy forces," his excuse would not be accepted unless 50 percent of his men were incapacitated. The term "I can't" is relative, Dayan insisted, the question is how much of an effort was made to accomplish the mission despite enemy resistance. Unless the unit lost its fighting strength, it must pursue the attack: "As you can see by my facial expression, I'm deadly serious. Every commander must be fully aware that if he doesn't accomplish his mission he'll find himself facing an unsparing investigation. And if I'm not satisfied, he'll be judged accordingly." However, he continued, Unit 101 turned the ship around. It was a volunteer unit designated for special cross-border operations and led by Sharon. It comprised a select group of soldiers, joined by reservists. Dayan wrote later, "In May 1953 when the idea was first broached for setting up the unit, I was against it. I felt that it wasn't a question of 'what to do to hurt the Arabs' but rather how to raise the IDF's level of fighting. In the end the unit achieved what I'd hoped for—a boost in the general level of fighting. The 101's action was invaluable." Its performance set an outstanding example for the rest of the IDF and proved that missions could be accomplished successfully where other units had failed.[13]

According to Dayan's memoirs, the IDF's operational capability, type of activity, and conceptual change of commanders and units could be divided into two stages: stage 1, before the establishment of Unit 101 in August 1953; and stage 2, the establishment of the unit and its merger with the paratrooper battalion.

Until 1953 IDF activity was predominantly passive. This was expressed in border patrols, ambushes, and observation missions. Cross-border activity included disrupting road traffic, planting mines, and making low-level responses to Arab actions. In early 1953 the IDF escalated its cross-border operations to include penetration into villages to cause the enemy casualties and property damage. The infantry battalions involved in these operations were unmotivated. This seems to have stemmed from the units' lack of confidence in their strength and ability to carry out risky assignments. Commanders who exhibited lack of leadership and indifference to mission accomplishment were not brought to trial. Explanations were always given for their failure. When a unit entered a village and encountered a guard or was detected, it often retreated before finishing the job. Preparations for an operation were shoddy and incomplete. Intelligence on the area and the objectives was invariably outdated and pointless. Failing to reach the target or chancing upon "surprises," such as fences or an alert guard, all but guaranteed mission abort. This was the situation until other fighting methods and a much higher standard of performance were instituted.

The reversal came about mainly thanks to Unit 101. The unit's initial achievements, followed by the paratroopers' operational successes, restored the IDF's confidence in its capabilities. Its operational proficiency rose. The Israeli army proved that it was capable of carrying out daring missions, in both small and large formations, in the enemy's depth and against regular army troops. The drawback in employing only one unit for these assignments was that other infantry units missed out on the experience and training that can only be gained in actual combat.

After these initial successes, other IDF units seemed more ready. Their commanders were eager to go on cross-border missions. In-depth patrols were performed successfully and demonstrated improvement in other units' operational ability. The IDF commanders' assessment of what could be accomplished in enemy territory changed for the better. After the Yarkon patrol (an in-depth action in Sinai in preparation for the Sinai War) and paratrooper missions, things were seen in a different light. Nevertheless, the lesson from the retaliatory raids had still not been internalized to the fullest, Dayan noted. "The Officer Candidate School still puts insufficient emphasis on the lessons that should be learned from the retaliatory raids."[14]

Meir Amit, who served twice as the head of Agam in Dayan's general staff, recalled the exaggerated support that Dayan gave Sharon even when the latter overstepped his authority and embroiled the IDF and the State of Israel in unfortunate episodes. Yet Dayan seems to have been willing to pay the price of Sharon's "indiscretions" if they meant putting the mettle back into the IDF's fighting spirit. Amit wrote later, "You could say that Dayan shut his one eye [he lost his left eye in a military operation in Syria in 1941] and forgave the combat units for their whims. Even if he steamed and fumed at times, you could see that he tended to condone their peccadilloes and commend them on their valor, imagination, and creativity." The main problem facing GHQ was how to implant a change in conduct in the IDF units. The botched Falama operation in January 1953 was the turning point. This was when the GHQ decided—in no small way due to Dayan, who coined the slogan "no retreat if less than 50 percent casualties"—that the situation had to be amended. The question was how to instill this goal in the combat units.[15]

For two years, until December 1955, Dayan assigned every combat mission to the 890th Paratrooper Battalion. "The unit became a 'hothouse of heroes,' as Ben-Gurion put it, and inspired warriors with spirit of the Maccabean [second-century BCE Jewish rebel warriors]," according to Shabtai Teveth's biography of Dayan. Dayan let them operate with a free hand, supported and encouraged them with expressions of personal affection, waited at the border for their return from raids, welcomed them back with grapes, watermelon, and candy that he brought in his car, showered them with praise, and addressed them by name. This was how he kindled envy in the commanders and soldiers of other units. And it worked. Haim Bar-Lev, commander of the Givati Brigade at the time (later chief of staff), remembered that Dayan managed to arouse resentment in him: "I objected to all of the good stuff going to the paratroopers. When they went out on a mission to Gaza, we'd come and hold the line on the Gaza Strip. But we never received cross-border actions. I commanded Givati for almost two years, and all we got was a couple of patrols." The commanders of other units felt the same.[16]

The envy of the paratroopers created a powerful platform for impressing the spirit and standards of combat into other units by way of emulation. This was accomplished by having every action by the paratroopers accompanied by a general staff observer and commanders from other units who then returned to their units and conveyed what they learned. Later the commanders of the 890th Paratrooper Battalion were transferred to other units and to assignments in the training branch. For two years, the IDF formulated its infantry combat doctrine in the 890th Battalion.

Employing Nahal to Expand the IDF Offensive Ability

When Dayan served as head of Agam, he vetoed the establishment of an elite unit for retaliatory operations, explaining that all of the combat units must become competent for such assignments.[17] But when Unit 101 was established and its activity began to bear fruit, he leveraged the opportunity to advance his goals. The merger of Unit 101 with the paratroopers contributed to the expansion of the sphere of offensive activity, but Dayan was aware of its limitations. In early 1956 he said that one of the major shortcomings was that the Paratrooper Battalion couldn't be turned into a kind of hatchery for all IDF units. The battalion had set a high standard for combat but included only a few career officers. "I'm not worried about its officers not being career soldiers," Dayan wrote. "What worries me is that many career officers rotate through posts without serving in the battalion or in other combat units."[18]

Dayan's diary entry for August 14, 1956, states that he happened to bump into Sharon and told him that it was inconceivable that the battalion with the most combat experience didn't send any instructors to the officers' school and company commanders' course and didn't cooperate with other units. And it was also inconceivable that the battalion was built entirely on the personality of Arik Sharon and of lads who were always there "on condition" that a war broke out. The army, even the paratroopers, can't be built on this type of service. The paratrooper unit must become like all the other units and integrate into the IDF and inspire the entire system by its achievements and spirit. In the same vein Dayan noted, "Arik [Sharon] too must become an officer like any other officer, go through rotations, and serve in various posts."[19]

Dayan's solution to strengthening the IDF's fighting spirit was to use the Nahal Infantry. His diary notes a discussion with Ben-Gurion in November 1955 about the idea of beefing up the regular army infantry brigades with Nahal companies. Dayan explained to Ben-Gurion that not only the paratroopers but every battalion mission had to be preceded by a breakthrough action. Afterward it was simpler. There had to be an elite force for the breakthrough, one whose fighting ability was far above that of the average battalion. He claimed that if all the standing army infantry battalions had one crack company, this elite force would be assigned the breakthroughs. They didn't have to be paratroopers, who needed to be used for special operations. When

Ben-Gurion asked, "In that case, who?" Dayan's reply was, "Sorry to say—Nahal." Ben-Gurion asked why, and Dayan replied: because of Nahal's outstanding human material. Those who joined Nahal came from the kibbutzim, or were highly motivated high school graduates, or members of a youth group. "As of now these are better units than the others. There are currently 4,000 guys in Nahal. I want 1,700 of them attached to the Golani and Givati Brigades as well as the paratroopers."

Ben-Gurion persisted, "Can't the infantry battalions be trained to make the breakthrough?" Dayan's reply:

> You've asked me this five times already. The technique's not the main point, but the willingness to charge forward and assault is. Every day the paratroopers demand more action. In other units the soldiers want somebody else to run forward [and risk their lives]. Among civilians, too, there's a divide. Not everyone is equal. The same thing goes for soldiers. The army's cut from the same cloth as the public. If Nahal was dispersed among all the other units, then the units would develop a higher degree of combat proficiency. Each battalion can receive a quality Nahal company as an assault force. If war is on the horizon then this is what has to be done.[20]

Dayan ordered the Nahal's training base converted into an airborne infantry battalion. Nahal's training program was changed to include jump school, beach landings, and guerrilla warfare. This enabled the IDF to make maximum use of high school graduates and conscripts from the collective farming settlements since only a small percentage of Nahal soldiers had been sent to command courses until then.[21] The use of Nahal aroused opposition in the Kibbutz Movement (see below).

Extending the Offensive Capability to Other Units

Examples of extending the offensive capability in reinforced battalion-size operations include Operation Volcano (or Operation Sabha,

November 2–3, 1955), which was carried out by the Golani Brigade and 890th Paratrooper Battalion; and Operation Olive Leaves (or Operation Kinneret, December 11, 1955) in which paratroopers, Nahal, Givati, and paratrooper reservists took part. One study on the operations in Gaza and Israel's retaliatory policy in the 1950s described an IDF official's account of the operational activity in 1955–56, which stated that a peacetime army that sees no possibility of operational action becomes stultified. Units that were assigned operational activity saw it as a gift and used it to sew the units' fabric. This was the first time since the end of the War of Independence that the IDF demonstrated its prowess as a true fighting organization. "This year's operations wiped out the bitter taste of Falama and Mutila [a controversial battle fought between Israeli and Syrian units north of the Sea of Galilee] with daring missions being carried out by the same units," the account stated. The year also witnessed the reinforcement of material, in numbers and quality, in weapons diversity, and in combined arms cooperation. Unfortunately, not all the corps gained equal combat experience. What stands out is that if in previous years the force that was sent on a mission was limited to a company, now battalion- and brigade-size operations were carried out against fortified positions and regular armies. While the unit performed its task, its staff also gained invaluable experience. As the account emphasized, "As stated, these actions are differentiated from actions in the past in terms of force size, which sometimes included an entire brigade, and in terms of artillery, armor, and aircraft. The use of different types of weapons is undoubtedly the result of the lessons that we learned from the actions of the year before last."[22]

Conveying Messages through Exercises, a No-Nonsense Attitude to the Conduct of Commanders, and the Glorification of the Paratroopers and Unit 101

Dayan employed many methods, including training exercises, to get his messages across. When Dayan was the head of Agam, he laid out guidelines to the commander of the Command and Staff College and other commanders to prepare tactical exercises without troops for forging a breakthrough into a fortified area. Dayan's instructions were unique: there would be no outflanking, surprises, or hitting the target from the rear. He did not want any "smartass Jewish gimmicks." Mission accomplishment would entail a breakthrough, fighting for the objective regardless of casualties. These instructions caught his people off guard. Yuval Ne'eman, the head of the planning department in the GHQ, recalled that the directive "disturbed" him. "I had just returned from the École de Guerre, where I was taught solutions such as the one Moshe wanted, but I always found a 'Jewish way,' the kind that finds a substitute for hard fighting on the objective. But here Moshe, of all people, the master of stratagems, demanded the kind of solution accepted abroad, a non-Jewish solution."

Dayan told the exercise planners how deeply the Falama fiasco had affected him, and that the habit of always trying to cut the number of casualties would lead to many more stinging failures unless the fear of a frontal attack was overcome. For the sake of the exercise, a mountain pass in the Negev was chosen. About a hundred commanders whom Dayan selected, everyone whom he believed had something to say about the IDF's fighting, were invited to take part. Indeed, all of the commanders without exception tried at first to come up with an elaborate, "crafty" solution (in the language of the time) of the kind that had heretofore been encouraged. But the exercise advisers insisted that nothing less than a breakthrough and actual battle for the objective would be allowed. At the conclusion of the exercise, Dayan said, "Mission accomplishment shouldn't be influenced by casualties." One of the participants asked, "How many casualties, what's the limit?" Dayan replied, "20, 30, even 50 percent losses." Thus, in an answer to a question, a guideline crystallized that was never issued as a formal actual order. The same exercise was repeated with other commanders in other places. Dayan's goal was to condition the commanders to think in terms of *ayn breira* (there's no alternative). "You must kill, be killed, and not try to outflank."[23]

Dayan was uncompromising with commanders who failed to measure up to the expected standard of conduct in the face of the enemy.

At an officers' graduation ceremony on May 30, 1955, he stated that he had dismissed a career officer who ordered a driver to carry out an act in the face of enemy fire while he crouched behind cover. Dayan stressed that "IDF commanders don't send solders into battle; they lead them at the head of their units."[24]

The transformation in the IDF's fighting spirit included sending commanders to jump school. In July–August 1954, Dayan toured the United States with Yitzhak Rabin (the head of Mahad) and Matityahu Peled (the chief instructor of the Command and Staff College). The three senior officers were duly impressed by the requirement that American combat officers go to either jump school or a guerrilla warfare course. Dayan ordered the IDF to adopt the same format. In October, the defense minister approved the plan. A condensed parachuting course for senior commanders began in November. Among the first to jump were Dayan, Rabin, Chief of Armor Yitzhak Pundak, and Chief of Infantry Zvi Zamir.[25] The general staff met on November 1 and decided "to make it compulsory for career combat officers up to the rank of captain, as well as to soldiers of the brigade reconnaissance platoons, to undergo a parachuting or commando course."[26]

The last issue was the desire to advance young commanders. This was Ben-Gurion's initiative, as realized in his appointment of thirty-two-year-old Yigael Yadin to chief of staff. Dayan continued this trend by promoting "talented young officers with combat experience in the War of Independence,"[27] apparently in the belief that the commanders' age would bolster the IDF's offensive spirit.

Opposition to Changes That Dayan Faced

Between January 1954 and November 1955, Dayan served as chief of staff under Prime Minister Moshe Sharett. Sharett, it will be noted, disapproved of Dayan's activist, escalatory approach, but his opposition was deflected by the activist defense minister Pinhas Lavon, who sided with Dayan. This remained the state of affairs until Lavon's resignation in February 1955, despite the consuming tension between Sharett and Dayan on questions of authority.[28] Sharett stated that on January 18,

1955, he "scotched" Dayan's plans for a retaliatory operation in response to a flock of sheep being stolen from Kibbutz Ein Hashofet, to which Dayan responded with a furious outburst.[29] On January 23, he canceled an operation, even though Lavon argued this would infuriate the army.[30] On February 28, Sharett was shocked by the news that thirty-seven enemy soldiers were killed in the Gaza operation, after he had given it his approval with the explicit understanding that the death toll would be no higher than ten.[31] Lavon's replacement as defense minister in February and later Sharett's replacement as prime minister in November was none other than David Ben-Gurion, who backed Dayan's aggressive efforts to buttress the IDF's offensive spirit. Nevertheless, Dayan had to struggle with opposition directed at him from outside the army, in particular from leaders of the border settlements. Members of the Kibbutz Movement and their political supporters assumed that the coming war would be like the initial stages in the War of Independence. "If there's war, it'll erupt around the settlement areas," wrote one member of the Kibbutz Hame'uchad Movement. "I mean, the areas surrounding the settlements will most likely become the front lines [and] . . . the settlements' tenacious resistance will again prove itself to be the attacker's 'weak spot.' He won't be able to advance into the heart of the country if his positions are stuck in the rear. . . . The settlements' obstinacy will be the savior of the country."

Dayan thought otherwise. Despite the political decision, he was unwilling to give up his basic stance. "I want to correct a very common misperception," he said to a gathering of writers and intellectuals in late January. "It is impossible to win by defense alone. Of course a war can be lost without proper defense. But a war that is defensive only is a lost war. . . . The point of war is offense, not defense. In our war against the enemy we must reach his territory."[32]

In order to steer the situation to the benefit of the IDF's offensive potential, quality manpower had to be diverted from one of its largest reservoirs—the collective farming settlements—at the price of regional defense and Nahal seed groups (core groups serving in Nahal while establishing or strengthening a kibbutz). Mordechai Bar-On wrote, "Over the anticipated opposition of the politically powerful Kibbutz Movement, Dayan decided to change this situation."[33]

His solution was to change the classification of territorial defense settlements. Dayan told of a meeting with Defense Minister Ben-Gurion on February 1, 1956, regarding territorial defense. The topic of the discussion was the new classification for kibbutzim that had been border kibbutzim in the War of Independence but were now located in the "middle of the country." The two leaders also reviewed the settlements' opposition to the change in classification, which would result in people being away from the farm in wartime, since they would be serving in offensive combat units. Dayan recalled this exchange:

BEN-GURION: Which is more pressing, manpower for farming or the defense issue?

CHIEF OF STAFF: Defense has become an ideology. Those against the change of classification seem to think a war can be won by defending a settlement. The sane among them know that this is bullshit. Instead of sitting in Ein Harod and waiting for the enemy to attack, it'd be better if they went out and fought the enemy in Beit She'an. The new classification will bring five thousand men into the reserve units.[34]

Dayan's transformation of Nahal in order to enhance the IDF's offensive potential also generated opposition. Nahal went rapidly from a unit designated primarily for land settlement to a unit of crack troops. As expected, these changes raised the hackles of the Kibbutz Movements' leaders, who tried to enlist parliamentarians and government ministers to their side and who exerted heavy pressure on the prime minister. But Ben-Gurion supported Dayan, and the plan came to fruition almost in its entirety.[35]

Another party that opposed the change was that of the "veteran" commanders, former Hagana fighters, whom Dayan got rid of by not promoting them. Thus, we see how Dayan dealt successfully with the political opposition to the changes and with the internal military opposition—except for the merger of Unit 101 and the 890th Para-trooper Battalion, which resulted in the departure in protest of fighters from the unit and officers from the battalion.[36]

Ramifications of the Change—the Offensive Fighting Spirit of the Ground Forces in the Sinai War

The changes in the IDF's offensive approach and fighting spirit that Dayan instituted were tested under fire in the October 1956 war in Sinai. Dayan recalled the impact of the prewar changes in the IDF on the war results:

> We were about to embark on the Sinai War after numerous repri-sal actions, in which the army registered a notable achievement—the ability and readiness of small units to carry out tough and daring missions. In Sinai we shall need to exploit this achieve-ment to the full—though I am aware that most of the reprisal actions were carried out by a small group of picked officers and men, mostly the paratroopers, whereas now the entire army will be facing the test. The most serious question is whether we may not be mistaken in expecting that army regulars and reserves will attain the same fighting levels as those of our picked units in re-prisal operations. I hope they can, and I have no doubt that the key lies in the hands of their commanders.[37]

In the third Command and Staff College graduation ceremony on August 15, 1957, Dayan said that the Sinai War provided the army with greater confidence in itself and its fighting ability, which proved to be an advantage over the enemy. The successes in the war were due to the IDF's organization, training, replenishment, and fighting spirit, qualities that it cultivated from the first day of its founding. But in the period before the war, it increased its demands on field commanders' responsibility in an offensive battle. "We decided that a commander would be justified in not completing a mission only if more than half of his force was lost, in which case he would have to explain not only what he ordered his men to do but also what he himself did to guarantee mission accomplishment."[38]

The following year, he wrote that whatever the reasons were, in retrospect, the standard of fighting in the offensive battles of the War of Independence was not as high as it should have been; then came the retaliatory raids, and the standards rose. Although this was the work of crack units, the whole nation heard about it. He emphasized "the whole nation," because in his view not only the army was aware of it, "but a thousand sixteen-year-olds who listened to the radio and read *Bamahane* (the IDF magazine) were educated on this. And the unit itself, when it returned from a retaliatory action, felt that the praise and glory showered on it in the wake of its deeds were the capital of the greater public."[39]

Half a year after the war, speaking before paratrooper brigade commanders, Ben-Gurion said that the chief of staff and his talented and loyal assistants played a vital role in boosting the IDF's capability. But, he said, let no one be mistaken—it was the paratrooper unit that had been the key factor during the last three years for both the IDF and the nation. Naturally, the entire nation didn't take part in the Sinai War, but it exhibited an impressive degree of calm and confidence. There were almost no signs of fear and anxiety.

"I believe," Ben-Gurion said, "that the unit's successful operations over the years instilled in the nation an abiding trust in the IDF." This is an asset to be treasured whose value cannot be overstated, he noted. "But of no less importance was this unit's impact on the entire IDF. If the reservists—and the army is an army of reservists, which means civilians, laborers, shopkeepers, journalists, teachers, and office workers who are mobilized, report for duty, and go off to battle—if they go with confidence in their strength and perform deeds that dazzle the whole world," then it was due to the paratrooper operations over the last years that played a major role in the IDF's abilities and self-confidence. These seemingly minor operations, especially in Gaza, Sabha, Kinneret, and others, are not to be underestimated. "The IDF's main purpose is to prevent war, break the enemy's will to fight, and preserve the peace. . . . But the ability that you displayed in the minor operations and in the Sinai War planted in the heart of the entire nation—not only in the State of Israel but in the Jewish people all over the world—the confidence in the IDF's proficiency and in your superb skill as a crack unit to ascend to higher summits from year to year that elevates you and the IDF, and in doing so instills fear into the heart of our enemies and forces them to think twice before provoking us."[40]

Summary of the Test Case

During Dayan's tenure as chief of staff, the IDF underwent a genuine revolution of the spirit. Even if the material changes were controversial, no one denies the conceptual transformation and improved morale.[41] Dayan employed various methods to inculcate the high standards needed in the IDF: declarations of devotion to mission accomplishment, the emphasis on Unit 101's operations, his decision to send commanders to jump school, and his personal example of attending the school. This was accompanied by many material changes, such as the increase in combat manpower in offensive units, which forced him to overcome the opposition of the leaders of the Kibbutz Movement. Here too he succeeded in facing down the naysayers thanks to Ben-Gurion's unflagging support.

Dan Shomron, Ehud Barak, and the Development of Precision-Guided Munitions for Use against Armored Fighting Vehicles, 1986–94

The Need for Change

The lessons of the Yom Kippur War compelled the IDF to strengthen the armored ORBAT (see chapter 4 on Chief of Staff Mordechai Gur). The severe budgetary crisis in the 1980s was caused, among other factors, by the general increase in ORBAT as well as by macroeconomic factors. Given the advances in military technology, the heads of the general staff demanded changes in the composition of the IDF's strength. The IDF embarked upon the development of "beyond-the-line-of-sight" intelligence systems, long-range precision fire, and, as those matured, an integrated system of PGM-targeting intelligence designed to destroy enemy AFVs before they reached the front lines. The goal was to block enemy armor in the event of a disproportional balance of forces and at an accepted rate of attrition. The two chiefs of staff who promoted this change were Dan Shomron and Ehud Barak.

Dan Shomron: The Development of Weapons and Initial Organizational Changes

Shomron was aware that a change had to be made. As division commander (1976–78), he had demanded real-time intelligence during exercises and later, as the commander of Southern Command, he promoted the use of UAVs.[42] The Zahavan (Scout) UAV system was then in trials in the IDF, and Shomron, as commander of Southern Command, was tasked with developing a suitable employment concept for the new asset. He ran it through a test in a regional command–divisional exercise in whose preparation Southern Command's weapons chief, Gershon Paztal, took part and oversaw. In May 1981, during the exercise in the vast tracts of Sinai, with Ehud Barak's 252nd Division taking part, the system's enormous potential was befittingly recognized. Eventually, Elbit, an Israeli defense electronics company, proposed developing a small mobile UAV kit called Pazit. Shomron put the UAV to test again, this time with the elite artillery Moran unit, followed by submitting operational requirement and development assignment documents for the weapon.[43]

Shomron was a lead player and firm believer in the development of PGMs and successfully rebuffed its opponents. He spearheaded the development of the PGM doctrine and the organization that dealt with the weapon. He looked forward to the day when every brigade would be reinforced with a PGM company.[44] Colonel Benny Beit-Or, the officer in charge of developing the Tamuz system, an anti-tank missile with a twenty-five-kilometer range (see below), recalled that "he invited himself" to Shomron's office in Southern Command and presented him with a theoretical idea that Shomron immediately seized upon, and even took part in writing the chapters on the weapon's combat application in the development assignment document.[45] As the commander of Southern Command, Shomron coined the slogan "a small, smart army," and it remained his byword when he became chief of staff.[46]

As the first commander of the Ground Forces HQ (Mafhash), Shomron continued promoting the Tamuz. In a lecture to the graduates of the Command and Staff College in 1984, he said that the PGM revolution in the IAF and navy was already underway, and in his opinion it had finally reached the ground forces, who would be making a technological leap forward when they acquired long-range PGMs. These missiles would enable the forces to fire without closing the distance with the enemy and without deploying in firing positions. It did not mean that the tank had lost its supremacy on the battlefield, "but in the field of enemy target destruction, we'll be capable of knocking out targets at long ranges. We'll be able to hit headquarters, tanks, and AFVs at fifteen-to-twenty-kilometer ranges with television-guided PGMs integrated into the C2 system, and in conjunction with UAVs. Today's warfighting has undeniably entered another dimension."[47]

The change that Shomron, now as Mafhash commander, pushed had its share of opponents in the corps' chief officers, where the new weapon was perceived as a threat to their status and resources, and its battlefield contribution considered still unproven. In a study on the Tamuz's assimilation into the IDF, Beit-Or, the first commander of the PGM unit, claimed that the chief infantry and paratrooper officer said that the Tamuz was unsuited to the corps because the infantry "sees the white of the enemy's eyes" when it fights. The chief artillery officer charged that the PGM didn't fit a corps that operated a "statistics weapon" (artillery), and the commander of the armored corps wasn't interested in a platform that wasn't protected like a tank. In the end it was decided that the Tamuz would be developed in conjunction with the infantry, though infantry invested no resources in the development of an employment concept until it obtained the first launchers.[48]

In a lecture at the National Defense College in 1986, Major General Ehud Barak weighed in with his view:

> In these things we don't have to go far, it's enough to look at ourselves. Take the Midras missile [the former name of the Tamuz] for example. . . . When it was brought up for discussion under the aegis of the Armored Corps (the predecessor of Mafhash) there was a strong tendency to limit its range to seven kilometers. This was considered enough. Let's not blow things out of proportion. There's a sense (perhaps unconscious) of threat that [if the missile has] a longer range and is [capable of] indirect fire it will be transferred to the artillery. A strong tendency was revealed to add protection to it that would enable the missile launcher vehicle to cross fire-swept areas while assaulting an objective, that is (and this seems to be the message in discussions with Kuti [Deputy Chief of Staff Yekutiel Adam]), that it simply has to be part of the last five hundred meters of the assault. "A missile tank," ironically. . . . We also saw the opposite tendency that the minute the artillery gets it, it will try to extend the range so it can "dominate" the field, and make the ranging and fire indirect and in an extended loop so as to derail any chances that the missile goes to armor or infantry.[49]

David Ivry, the deputy chief of staff from 1983 to 1985, says that he looked for a suitable base to set up the new Moran unit, but all he got was the cold shoulder. Finally, he turned to the commander of the Ramon Airbase, who agreed, and a facility was established there.[50]

According to Shomron, the problem was that most commanders with tenures of two or three years felt that such a weapon, no matter how sophisticated and accurate, would become operational only in five years at the earliest, and therefore it was not their problem. They had to provide answers to the current platforms.

> How can they be expected to stand at the forefront of a conceptual revolution? Every brigade or division commander would be

delighted to take a company of ready-for-fire PGMs into battle. They'd be willing to forego another unit in their division just to get their hands on an operational PGM unit. But if it's a case of two or three more years, then this is outside the realm of their responsibility and they'd say, "Sorry, not interested in something two years from now."[51]

Shomron made the connection between the "technological revolution" and the establishment of the Mafhash. He was aware that the "generals' wars" (a term that described the public wrangle between Arial Sharon and Avraham Adan over their respective divisions' performance in the Yom Kippur War) and the parochial interests of the corps bred a lack of coordination, let alone a comprehensive operational concept. He realized that unless the Mafhash was established, the technological revolution would never reach the ground corps and be made available to the forces. Clearly, this was not a matter for short-term timetables.[52]

As deputy chief of staff, Shomron had to deal with reductions in the IDF's size due to cutbacks in the defense budget. At the same time, he was cognizant of the PGMs' inherent potential to shrink the armor's ORBAT. He countered the criticism of armor officers who blamed him for scaling down the tank's battlefield status because of the precedence accorded to building a PGM capability:

> I visualize the land army in another few years with half the number of divisions it has today, poised at the "tip of the spear" with the most advanced weapons. We have the know-how, we have the technological advantage, and we can attain our goals before anyone else in a few years. In my opinion, this is worth any price. And if we decide to do it "at any price," then it will be accomplished.[53]

Shomron had to prioritize the army's resources. In order to realize his concept, he as deputy chief of staff closed one Merkava tank production line temporarily in 1986 and funneled the budget to PGMs.[54] He also dealt with the human resources required for operating the intelligence-fire array, as a crucial factor in the assimilation and development of advanced technologies. He emphasized, "It would be wrong to think that in the future battle all a soldier will have to do is pull the trigger. Operating a sophisticated weapon calls for highly professional operators, just as an advanced C2 system requires first-class human resources for its operation and command."[55]

In 1988, as chief of staff, Shomron merged the Moran unit and the IDF Anti-tank Center into the David's Sling unit and made it responsible for formulating a combat doctrine and an educational and instructional plan for the continued assimilation of the new array's weapons in a somewhat surprising framework: subordinate it directly to Mafhash. Thus, in 1991 it came under the command of the artillery corps. Beit-Or, the first commander of the newly established David's Sling unit, attested to Shomron's personal involvement in the process.[56]

The instructions for developing the Misgav multiyear plan stated:

We reaffirm the direction of his emphasis on strengthening quality weapons, on areas and orientations that will provide us with a significant advantage over the enemy and achieve a swift victory with minimal attrition ratios, given the focus on the following orientations: Attaining a level of ground target destruction that is relevant to both land and air battles and that is significantly higher than what we are currently capable of, with a focus on the ability to conduct operations in the initial days of war without depending on air superiority . . . C2 systems and real-time intelligence for attaining maximum effectiveness of the inherent potential of the force being built in the years planned for.[57]

It should be noted that at this stage, fire and intelligence elements were mostly developed separately, and their integration into an intelligence-fire system occurred when Ehud Barak was chief of staff.

Ehud Barak: The Development of a Concept
That Would Maximize Capability

Ehud Barak recalls that his first conversation with Dan Shomron on the need for a change in the ground forces as a result of their encounter with Egypt's Russian-made, wire-guided Sagger anti-tank missiles occurred during a lull in the fighting on the western bank of the Suez Canal.[58] At the time, Shomron was commander of the 401st Brigade and Barak was commander of the 100th Improvised Tank Battalion. The answer went through innumerable changes over the years, while Shomron and Barak worked alongside each other as commander and subordinate for over a decade and a half. According to Barak, their solution was to exploit the missile's range to the IDF's advantage. After the Yom Kippur War, the Israeli defense technology company Rafael began developing weapons, including long-range anti-tank missiles, for the ground forces.[59] This led to the idea of establishing units with anti-tank missiles mounted on the backs of jeeps (an idea that would materialize into the anti-tank brigade, which operated successfully against the Syrian army in 1982). These ideas were designed, first and foremost, for future combat against hordes of AFVs in Sinai. Barak had experience in the use of UAVs in the War of Attrition (1968–70) when he carried out Sayeret Matkal (special operations unit) reconnaissance operations across the canal. Later, Barak gained further experience with them as a division commander under Shomron's command. Another element was the development of PGM capability in the armored divisions (such as the Moran unit). A third element was air capability.

Barak became chief of staff in a period when the idea of a PGM-based standoff campaign (especially from the air) was first employed in the 1991 Gulf War, followed by a global discourse on the technological revolution in military affairs. Barak took the revolution a step further and transformed the developing capability into the basis for an entire concept.

He made it clear that at the heart of the concept was the idea that the offensive strike rate—masses of targets that were made short shrift of—would contribute to two areas: dramatically improving acceptable attrition ratios and knocking the enemy off balance.[60] As ground PGM capability matured, two issues came into focus: first, a large quantity of this type of munitions came at a high cost; and second, closing the circle between target-locating UAVs and ground-launched PGMs was still too slow and cumbersome. These two realizations sped up R&D on a suitable aerial capability.

The concept was tested in a series of large-scale experimental exercises, the first in 1993. Barak set up an exercise administration and introduced a novel pattern of wide-ranging experiments and exercises for developing an operating concept for the new weapons. The 1993 exercise was one of four conducted until 1999.[61]

In a 1986 study day devoted to the future battlefield, Barak (in the capacity of commander of Central Command) presented a detailed account of the IDF's need to change and the difficulty armies experience while undergoing transformation:

> Is this change or agglomeration of land, sea, and air changes really revolutionary? I think it may be, and that's the most we can say at this early stage. Another question: Perhaps we still don't perceive the full potential inherent in this change and don't grasp its full impact? I'll put it differently, in a way that has less to do with us: Can a good or even excellent military leadership, sharp as a razor and not under pressure, commit basic errors in its judgment and overlook the need to introduce essential changes? In my opinion, the answer is a resounding yes, and this can be seen throughout the history of weapons development.[62]

After a lengthy discourse, replete with historical examples of the difficulty in transforming a vast organization, Barak summed up his key ideas:

Despite the limited ability to assess the required changes, I would like to present my position in the clearest language possible. I won't deny that it's the product of a subjective evaluation that I can't prove. In a nutshell: the combination of state-of-the-art, long-range PGMs with the capability of collecting "target intelligence" in real time and local inexpensive "situational intelligence" together with swift local data processing and modern communication channels has the potential to transform the battlefield, which is basically the same as, and no less revolutionary than, the introduction of tanks as a combination of machine guns and pillboxes [in World War I]. . . . Last but not least, the necessary changes will have to be made proportionally and gradually for a number of reasons that I'll discuss later. However, Israel must undertake this change vigorously, with a keen understanding of exactly where we're going and with no qualms about making harsh economic, ORBAT, and organizational decisions.[63]

In the summary of the 1991 multiyear Mirkam plan seminar, Barak, as the chief of staff, detailed the conceptual changes and stated that the IDF was dealing with a change in the force employment concept based on the opportunities that the new weapons presented. The combined arms formation that depended on the tank's dominance would continue to be the ground forces' backbone and main offensive element. The change lay primarily in boosting the fire element based on PGMs and an employment concept that made maximum use of their potential. Strengthening the fire element would allow the force to bring the maneuver element to expression in the right timing in all forms of battle. The main goals were a high strike rate, continuous fighting ability, real-time intelligence, and C2. An extended battlefield would have to be created that provided a continuous, day and night, high strike rate at various depth levels in a way that did not depend on air superiority. In general, he said, these were the main points of the services' plans and they appeared to be correct. At any rate, in order to achieve a critical mass at the conclusion of Mirkam A and to identify the inherent advantages of the weapons' potential, an effort would have to be made beyond what was proposed in the services' plans.[64]

Opposition to Change

The opposition to change came primarily from two parties. The first, which was discussed in the analysis of Shomron's tenure as chief of staff and mentioned by Barak, were armor officers who considered Shomron's and Barak's ideas a big mistake. (These were officers who had grown up in the armored corps from day one of their conscription and not those who were absorbed into it later, like Shomron and Barak.) General Israel Tal argued against the idea of downsizing the army. While he criticized PGMs, he did not appear to explicitly reject them:

> Not a small, smart army, but a "smart army" is what the IDF needs. . . . It's a mistake to think that just because weapons are becoming more accurate and capable of pinpointing a target, that war is becoming "mathematical" and precise. War has always been "statistical." . . . Changing the arsenal is a very long and costly process.[65]

The other party opposed to change was the IAF, some of whose commanders had avowed over the years that the development of ground PGM capability did not have to come at the price of reducing the air force and that despite PGM development, the ground forces still needed close air support within the range of ground PGMs.[66]

Barak claimed that the IAF was against the change for financial reasons: it feared that the expansion of the ground arm's PGM and UAV capabilities would come at the price of aircraft replenishment.[67] The actual developments prove this opposition does not seem to have seriously impeded Shomron and Barak from pushing their concept forward.

The Result of the Change

The result of the change was the development of the IDF's ability to attack AFV targets deep in enemy territory. Because much of the material is classified, we can only discuss a limited number of weapons that were developed. The ten-kilometer-range Midras missile, as mentioned, evolved into the Tamuz with a twenty-five-kilometer range. As part of the Tamuz missile array, designated AFVs were created for launching the missiles. This was the Hafiz armored vehicle built on the chassis of an M-113 APC and later the Pereh (Onager) launcher on the chassis of a Magach tank (based on US Army M48 and M60 Patton tanks).[68] Airborne observation systems that began with the Zahavan and Pazit expanded over the years into a broad array of airborne sensors. Intelligence arrays and fire-delivery weapons supported by advanced C2 systems were developed under Shomron and Barak; their development continued under their successors. Later, during Mofaz's tenure, one could say that the IDF had developed a concept called "offensive defense." Essentially, it consisted of fire capabilities that enabled a simultaneous attack on the enemy at different depth echelons at a high strike rate in order to disrupt and sever all levels of the enemy's attack. It also facilitated the fighting effort of the frontline defense forces.[69]

Part of the change included the establishment of ground PGM units consisting of a number of battalions: the standing army Meitar Battalion, reserve battalions, and the designated David's Sling unit, which, as stated, came under the direct command of the commander of the Mafhash and was later transferred to the artillery corps.

In 1986, another unit was established within the framework of the PGM array development and, along with the Moran Battalion, was attached to the David's Sling unit. In 1991, due to financial constraints, this unit was converted into a reserve unit. But the Gulf War altered the picture and the unit changed entirely, was removed from the David's Sling unit, and came under the command of the 35th Brigade. The new commander, Tal Russo, said of this period: "The entire development was the result of two processes: one, the decision to establish a new unit and change its primary designation; two, the flow of money from Central Command and the Mafhash.[70]

A second major element in PGMs developed in the IAF, which employed other types of PGMs (a combination of anti-radiation missiles, such as AGM-78 Standard ARM, and television-guided missiles, such as an early version of the Popeye missile) against Syrian SAM batteries in Operation Artzav 19 in 1982. In the following years the IAF also developed the ability to conduct wide-scale anti-AFV attacks from the air.

Summary of the Test Case

The IDF's change in approach to PGMs and UAVs began before Shomron (who, it will be remembered, as commander of a regional command had experience in operating UAVs) and continued after Barak. Be that as it may, these two chiefs of staff had the greatest influence on the shape of the change, the budget for its development and replenishment, and the formulation of its operating concept.

Shomron countered the opposition of armor commanders who regarded the downsizing of armor's ORBAT as a grave mistake and as the price to pay for developing PGMs. He channeled budgets from tank acquisitions and the Lavi aircraft project, whose eventual closure was due in no small part to his efforts: the development of PGM capability, the establishment of new units, and the initial tests of the concept designed to derive maximum benefit from the new intelligence-fire capabilities.

Barak pursued the budgeting, promotion, and development of the weapons and their operational concept. Developing the concept required a series of exercises and tests on an unprecedented scale. The internal resistance to PGMs that had been quite intense under Shomron seems to have abated during Barak's tenure.

The case illustrates the need for passing the torch between chiefs of staff during a major change of direction in force design, which, like every change, has its opponents and technological and conceptual birth pangs. It is interesting to note that Shomron and Barak were paratroopers who converted to armor and commanded armored units in the Yom Kippur War (and afterward). Their wartime experiences undoubtedly had much to do with their awareness of the need to develop the ability to block enemy armor in acceptable attrition ratios when the ratio of tanks worked to the enemy's advantage.

Shaul Mofaz, Moshe Ya'alon, and the Diversion of Ground Force Design to Low-Intensity Conflict, 1998–2005

The first intifada, which caught Israel by surprise in late 1987 (see chapter 1), led to only minor changes in force design, mainly in preparation for routine security operations and the acquisition of crowd dispersal weapons. The first changes in organization that Chief of Staff Shomron carried out were the establishment of the elite Samson Unit (undercover special forces operators) and the use of mechanized infantry companies in routine security operations. When Barak became chief of staff, he increased the armored infantry's ORBAT designated for routine security operations, a direction that continued under Chief of Staff Amnon Lipkin-Shahak. By 1998 a limited designated ORBAT for operations in the Palestinian theater included the 92nd and 93rd battalions, the Bedouin patrol unit, and the Border Patrol (*Magav*), which expanded to twenty companies. In addition, Lipkin-Shahak broadened the investment in resources for the fighting in South Lebanon (see chapter 1).

The period presented here witnessed the signing of the 1993–95 Oslo Accords and the establishment of cooperative mechanisms with the Palestinians; Israel's exit from Palestinian cities; the violent events at the Western Wall Tunnel in 1996; Nakba Day 2000 and the violence that followed; and Operation Defensive Shield 2002 (see below). The period was unique in that force design became based on "limited confrontation" or "low intensity conflict" (LIC) as the leading fighting scenario.

Before examining the event in detail, we wish to note the difference between a multiyear work plan and an annual work plan. The multiyear plan determines long-range force design plans and the primary use of resources. Discussions deal in billions of shekels for the acquisition of such things as aircraft, tanks, naval vessels, and large stocks of munitions. Each year, the annual work plan is approved within the multiyear plan, and a smaller amount (generally in the order of hundreds of millions of shekels) of resources is channeled to solutions to challenges that have arisen in that year.

Chief of Staff Mofaz on the Eve of Operation Defensive Shield

As we saw in chapter 1's discussion of the identification and declaration of a change in the security situation, Chief of Staff Mofaz embarked upon a plan to strengthen the ground forces' readiness for a confrontation with the Palestinians prior to the outbreak of the second intifada in September 2000. The plan included training and the small-scale replenishment of designated weapons. However, as chapter 1 noted, the focus was on quelling armed rioting rather than engaging in urban warfare. In an update of the Idan 2005 multiyear plan and in preparation for the 2001 work plan (approximately one month after the start of the hostilities), Mofaz emphasized the continuation of the multiyear plan and pointed to the implications of his decisions on the 2001 work year.

The plan was based on preserving the orientations that Idan (the previous multiyear plan) had determined while enhancing readiness and professional aptitude in 2001, a year that Mofaz defined as "the year of readiness and competency." He placed confrontation with the Palestinians at the top of the agenda and determined that "in areas where the IDF engages in fighting, whatever it needs will be fully provided for." The budget for financing projects and activities stemming from operational necessities in the second intifada was often made available from the Kesem Hamangina (Magic Melody) plan. In 2001, 700 million shekels ($235 million) were invested in this plan. Budget increments notwithstanding, the level of competency in the standing army and reserve units suffered. The length of time allocated to training regular army units shrank (which detracted from fighting proficiency in urban warfare), and the class A reserve units engaged almost exclusively in operational duty instead of training. Things got to the point where "the severe budgetary situation forced the defense establishment to freeze several development and replenishment projects . . . whose expected operational benefit was low at any rate."[71]

In the same period, an external defense budget was used to build the barrier—made of a "smart fence" in most places and concrete walls in others—along the Green Line delineating the West Bank. In 2007, the project's estimated cost was thirteen billion shekels (about $3.85 billion). The introduction to the Idan 2006 work plan and 2002 work plan stated that the continuous confrontation in the West Bank and Gaza Strip had the nature of a low-intensity conflict but required a change of priorities in order to provide an answer for fighting requirements in the different arenas as regarded the allocation of manpower, budget, and weapons resources.[72]

In early 2002, Israel was inundated by a wave of Palestinian terror. The attacks precipitated Israeli responses. In view of the escalation, changes had to be introduced into the work plan. In February 2002, the chief of staff decided to focus on strengthening capabilities to combat terror (with an emphasis on the critical field of urban warfare). In accordance with his decision, a master plan was prepared for dealing with various elements in force design. Joint work procedures with the Shin Bet (internal security service) improved, the use of intelligence-gathering means expanded, protected wheeled vehicles were acquired, engineering equipment was procured and protected, APC protection was reinforced, protective vests against bullets were procured, military posts were reinforced, equipment was developed to neutralize explosive charges, means were devised for identifying short-range rocket fire, the headquarters of the regional brigades, the "90s battalions" (six battalions numbered 90–97) designated for low-intensity combat and the Duvdevan counterterrorism unit were beefed up, and reconnaissance battalions were established within the infantry brigades. Approval was given to the Shavit (Comet) plan in order to complete the inventory of critical weapons such as bulletproof vests, light weapons, helmets, radios, and night vision equipment at a cost of 200 million shekels (approximately $59 million).[73]

The summary of Operation Defensive Shield (March–May 2002), near the end of Mofaz's tenure as chief of staff, illustrates the key role that he played in preparing the IDF for confrontation with the Palestinians. Mofaz pointed to various areas that would be worthwhile to study and apply within the framework of the work plan and instructed the following areas to be brought to expression at the regional command, service, and branch levels: urban warfare in dense urban environments and in refugee camps (battle techniques, combat doctrine, training, the replenishment of designated weapons); the construction of an urban warfare training facility; and LIC ORBAT (reconnaissance platoons, six battalions designated for LIC, and the role of headquarters in LIC). Mofaz stressed that the recommendations had to take into account the military ability to handle a wide range of strategic threats simultaneously and not rest solely on confrontation in the Palestinian arena.[74]

During the general staff study session on Operation Defensive Shield, Mofaz emphasized the allocation of weapons and designated equipment for this type of confrontation and stressed that the changes must serve the nature of the fighting in dense urban environments. At the same time capability and competency must be maintained for operating in other fighting arenas in scenarios that Israel might face.[75]

Mofaz appears to have understood the inherent tension between his instructions to focus on force design for LIC and the need to preserve the ability to fight in a full-scale war.

Operation Defensive Shield's powerful influence on diverting force design in the direction of a confrontation with the Palestinians came to expression in a wide range of areas: education, training, training infrastructure, combat doctrine, and organization. (See conclusion to this chapter.)

Chief of Staff Ya'alon: Exploiting "Defensive Shield" to Expand the Orientation

Ya'alon assumed the position of chief of staff in July 2002, three months after Operation Defensive Shield. As commander of Central Command, he had overseen preparations for the escalation that would be termed later the "events of October 2000." Later, as deputy chief of staff, he implemented an increase in force design for the confrontation with the Palestinians. As deputy chief of staff, he had written that soldiers and units could not possibly be prepared to the same degree for every type of confrontation. The elements of the training and exercises were determined according to the priority at the particular time. The current situation was a balance between the special preparations for LIC tasks and the forces' regular training for scenarios known as high-intensity conflicts. "We must take into consideration the fact that the involvement of units in fighting in the Palestinian arena contributes significantly to their overall proficiency," he wrote. Every action demands basic planning, battle procedure, and debriefing. Furthermore, carrying out an assignment entails action under fire and decision making under pressure. Thus, if tasks are carried out as required and mistakes are corrected, a high level of fighting competency is created. When all of the above were present, preparing the force for other combat scenarios was relatively easy.[76]

But an inner contradiction lies in what Ya'alon said between "it's impossible to continuously prepare a soldier and unit to the same degree for every type of confrontation" and "when all of the above are present, preparing the force for other combat scenarios is relatively easy." The chief of staff seems to have tried to resolve the tension, but the reality that developed four years later in the Second Lebanon War proved that he erred. In an October 2002 general staff meeting, the results of the planning teams were presented and initial instructions were issued for planning for 2003. The team that studied the answer to terror and guerrilla threats came to the conclusion that the threats in the coming five years would be characterized by terrorism (a simultaneous action by a number of suicide bombers coupled with an attack on Israeli infrastructure) and the improvement of the enemy's guerrilla fighting capability. The team's basic assumption was that victory would not be gained by a single weapon or action but by a succession of tactical victories and the creation of successive tactical failures for the enemy so that the terror organizations' sense of "bankruptcy" permeated their consciousness. Therefore, the goal was to come up with solutions (for concepts, weapons, organization, and structure) that enhanced the ability to achieve a continuum of tactical victories and reduce the possibility of incurring a succession of tactical failures. The team determined that because of the cutback in available resources, the focus had to change and abilities had to be refocused on dealing with the terror and guerrilla threat and only then be adapted for the "first circle" threat: neighboring countries. The main principle was "investment in versatile capabilities for LIC and war." The other key principles were strengthening the designated arrays in various sectors; preserving and bolstering relative advantages (intelligence gathering, special operations capabilities, the IAF); enlarging the infantry, intelligence gathering, and special operations forces ORBAT; investing in weapons and protection; reducing the burden on the reservists; and accelerating the forces' mobility.[77]

In summing up, Ya'alon said that the main goal in combating terror and guerrilla activity was maintaining public and national security while creating the necessary conditions for the political echelon to make decisions and precluding the region's descent into an all-out war. An analysis of the "first circle" (Arab countries bordering Israel), he said, revealed that Israel retained a relative advantage but that deterrence must be maintained and intensified. To avoid attrition, the IDF had to attain victory as quickly as possible: "The paramount operational challenge is the threat of terror in the Palestinian arena."[78]

Opponents to Change

The opposition to change can be divided into two parts. The first came from relatively low-level echelons and focused on military terminology and the supposedly faulty concept and doctrine that the IDF developed that ran counter to the principles of war and ceded victory for the sake of limited gains.[79] Others opposed the organizational changes in the infantry (see below).[80]

The second type of opposition came from Agat at the start of the change (before the October 2000 events). Agat failed to see the need to divert designated resources to the limited confrontation.[81] This opposition eventually waned because Mofaz and Ya'alon were responsible for the IDF's success in handling the October 2000 events and Operation Defensive Shield. In other words, success gave cogency and momentum to the direction in which they were leading. Opponents of the change in force design, while making note of the price it might exact in the event of war, were relatively few. The claims that the "ground army is hollow" that had been voiced on the eve of the Second Lebanon War referred mainly to budgetary cuts in training the ground forces for war and less to the focus on LIC force design.

Results of the Change

Some of the aspects of force design in combating Palestinian terror were analyzed in detail in my book *Military Agility: Ensuring Effective and Rapid Transition from Peace to War*.[82] The following is a summary and elaboration of some of the findings.

Education and Training

The period after Operation Defensive Shield—from the end of Mofaz's tenure and into Ya'alon's—is characterized by military education programs that focused on LIC. After the operation, the commander of the 460th Brigade (Armor School), Colonel Guy Tzur, set up an improvised urban environment combat facility in the Shizafon Base in the Negev (using plywood boarding and metal angles) inside an existing mock-up of a Syrian fortified area with firing positions for tanks and Russian-made BMPs (infantry fighting vehicles). Fighting and capturing the area was the culmination of a combined arms demonstration for officer cadets from all corps. As a commander of the armor officers' course, under Tzur's command, the author of these lines prepared and implemented exercises against this objective for the cadets. The commander of the infantry officers' course, Lieutenant Colonel Boaz Amidror, said that after he took part in Operation Defensive Shield with the Gefen cadet battalion, he urged his superiors to permit the cadets under his command to conduct operational duty in the West Bank so they could gain firsthand experience in quality operations, such as night raids and arrests in a real operational environment.[83]

The corps where the greatest gap existed between the skills needed in war and the proficiencies needed in LIC was the artillery (there was only a minor need of tanks in confrontations in the West Bank and Gaza, and no need whatsoever for the artillery in this period). The integration of artillery units in LIC demanded many educational challenges: artillerymen had to become more proficient in basic marksmanship, and crew commanders and officers had to learn how to take charge of independent infantry tasks, such as manning roadblocks, making patrols, clearing rooms in urban warfare, and operating newly acquired infantry weapons. Artillery education became more basic and need based, depending on the concrete situation assessment. The solution to the loss of time in learning the artillery profession was that necessary artillery education would be completed in a short time in a comprehensive training program as part of the deployment plans for war. In the meantime, minimum artillery skills could be preserved even as more urgent and relevant proficiencies took precedence in the ongoing confrontation in the West Bank and Gaza.[84]

The Training Infrastructure

The preparation of forces for urban warfare underwent a dramatic development. Until the second intifada the IDF had very few urban warfare facilities, made up mostly of mock-up one-story-edifice villages. The lessons from Defensive Shield convinced the powers that be to set up the Training Facility for Urban Warfare at the Tze'elim Training Base in the Negev. In 2006, shortly before the Second Lebanon War, the facility—a Palestinian town replete with a casbah, eight-story buildings, and burnt-out cars—opened its gates to the units.

Combat Doctrine

After neglecting the development of a doctrine pertinent to limited confrontations (1996–2002), the IDF experienced a significant awakening between 2003 and 2006.[85] The main issue was the special language needed for fighting in the West Bank. As operations against terrorism and guerrilla activity in the West Bank and Gaza Strip continued, a new language emerged that included strategic, operational, and tactical elements. This was deemed vital, as the traditional terms for high-intensity conflicts were unsuited to the reality of guerrilla warfare.

In 2000, Gal Hirsch, the commander of the Binyamin Regional Brigade at the time, explained in detail the concept for IDF employment in the West Bank in a new combat doctrine pamphlet.[86] The main term, "low-signature action," was designed to achieve operational effects that would have a successive impact on others, such as presence, deterrence, disruption, and thwarting. Accompanying terms included "snailing" (engaging in self-protection, like a snail in his shell); maintaining the "life flow" of both Palestinians and Jewish settlers; and a "cooling approach" (area pacification). Another doctrinal pamphlet discussed various ways to contend with irregular militants in a limited conflict: "Israel's goal in war is to gain 'cognitive victory in the confrontation.'" This and related terms, such as "the theater of cognition," pervade the document. Israel's strategy in a limited conflict is referred to as "exhausting the enemy."[87] Another document contained a list of the forms of battle that characterize LIC, such as "encirclement," "scanning," and "interception."[88] The IDF journal *Ma'arachot*, volume 380–81, discussed in late 2001 the two poles of the military hierarchy: tactical and strategic. According to Raz Sagi, a battalion commander, dealing with combat doctrine, battle techniques, and exercises related to the LIC produced a new linguistic field. The terms seemed to supply the need for language adapted to the unique nature of limited conflict. Terms such as "situation containment," "signals," and "complete encirclement" created a new language that for all practical purposes was nonmilitary and incomprehensible and that transmitted indecipherable messages. Worst of all were the terms "preventative cooling," "absorbing fabric," and "snailing," which Sagi criticized as egregious professional deviations from military vocabulary.[89]

At the other end of the spectrum, Ya'alon (then deputy chief of staff) wrote that the use of new terms was absolutely necessary, "but at the same time we must be economical with their use since each new term has to be clarified, transmitted, and assimilated." He realized that if the development of special knowledge and terminology for a confrontation with the Palestinians did not take place, then borrowing from other scenarios could end up being an exercise in futility: "To ascertain that these terms were absorbed into a common language, we carried out exercises at the command and general staff levels in preparation for the confrontation."[90]

It is important to note that in 2003 and 2005, the regional commands presented their insights on the fighting in the Palestinian arena, along with selected studies by the Command and Staff College, in two large conferences at the Institute of Tactical Research and Force Employment.[91]

Unit Structure and Organization

Although the IDF's traditional approach to solving new, limited-size problems has always been the establishment of designated units—for example, the Egoz unit that operated in the South Lebanon security strip—the 1995–2006 period witnessed a departure from this model.

Between 1995 and 2001, the IDF formed a new type of infantry unit for routine security operations and established six new "limited conflict light infantry" battalions: the 90s battalions. In 2005, a meta-battalion framework was established—the Kfir Center for Force Design—designed for limited-conflict combat in the West Bank.[92] After the Second Lebanon War, the Kfir Brigade headquarters became a regular infantry brigade headquarters.

In late 2001, following staff work in the chief infantry and paratrooper officer's bureau on the infantry concept, and given the need to establish battalion headquarters for fighting in the West Bank and Gaza Strip, the chief of staff ordered the independent reconnaissance, anti-tank, and combat engineers companies of the regular and reserve infantry brigades to be grouped into reconnaissance battalions.[93]

Organizational transformation of this type means shifting a considerable part of the infantry brigades' ORBAT to limited confrontation, thus giving priority to LIC or routine security rather than focusing attention on force design considerations for war.

It is important to note that in the years before the Second Lebanon War, the ground forces went to great efforts to make the brigade (instead of the division) the core ground formation in a war scenario, but the examples we have discussed illustrate the initial diversion of attention to LIC.

Combat intelligence collection, too, underwent organizational change. Based on the lessons derived from Operation Defensive Shield, it was decided by the GHQ that the intelligence-gathering battalions would receive sector responsibility, their professional responsibility for specific areas of intelligence gathering would be canceled, and the previous organizational structure of the target intelligence unit would be disbanded. The Nesher Battalion, which was responsible for the radar array, was converted into Southern Command's combat intelligence-gathering battalion in Gaza and on the Egyptian and Jordanian borders. The Shahaf Observation Battalion was concentrated on the Lebanese border, and Central Command's Nitzan Battalion was deployed in the West Bank.[94]

Thus, we can see the strong bias in education, training, combat doctrine, and organization because of the need to change and adapt the IDF to the challenges of the confrontation with the Palestinians. As for the budget, the bulk of replenishment went to platforms and weapons for a war scenario (tanks and planes), whose cost, relative to the price of the abovementioned changes, was much greater.

Summary of the Test Case

The efforts of Mofaz and Ya'alon resulted in the IDF's victory over Palestinian terror. Not enough has been written about this success, and here we presented only the implications of force design on this success. The uncompromising quality of command at all echelons buffeted the surge in Palestinian terror against Israeli civilians—which reached intolerable levels prior to Operation Defensive Shield—to the minimal condition of "tolerable" in 2006–7.[95] The change contained all of the elements of force design, especially education and training. In the same period, the IDF continued purchasing weapons for war but educated and trained its personnel for combat in LIC. Opposition to the change was, as stated, nominal.

The problems in ground force employment that were revealed in the Second Lebanon War were the result of more than two decades (from the First to the Second Lebanon Wars) in which the IDF was primarily engaged in routine security operations along the northern border, in the security zone in Lebanon, and afterward in the West Bank and Gaza Strip.[96] This long period exacerbated the inherent danger in extended routine security periods and the impact on the (lack of) readiness for war. Two factors were involved: the adoption of routine security action patterns and norms on the one hand and, on the other, the loss of the competency required for war because of cutbacks in resources and the need to provide answers to routine security developments.[97] We may assume, then, that Mofaz's and Ya'alon's diversion of resources to force design that focused on the Palestinian arena was not very significant in the Second Lebanon War, unless the budget cuts that began at the same time as the confrontation with the Palestinians were harming training for war. The Winograd report discussed the forces' readiness for the Second Lebanon War and noted that the 2000–2006 period, when the IDF concentrated its focus on the Palestinian arena, was characterized by the continual decline in the length of training and the number of exercises and by the absence of interservice cooperation throughout the IDF. All of these factors detracted from the ability of the combat troops, and especially the commanders at the battalion, brigade, and divisional levels, because they had gone without training and exercises for a protracted period of time. In theory and practice, the basics that were needed for employment in "standard" confrontations (war) or in a confrontation with Hezbollah had been neglected.[98]

The statements of the two chiefs of staff bear witness to the fact that even as they reduced the forces' competency for war, they were aware of the inherent danger in their decisions. But awareness, it seems, was not enough.

Chapter Summary

Throughout most of the IDF's history, force design has been "evolutionary"—it has developed in relatively fixed directions over the years, increasing the ORBAT until the mid-1980s and then receding, generally due to resource constraints. Weapons renewal was carried out in accordance with French and later American foreign policy toward Israel and with Israel's development of its own defense industries. The three major shifts that were analyzed in this chapter were changes in the direction of force design from that of the preceding period. The first was in the fighting spirit; the second in the elements of force design, as PGMs and state-of-the-art intelligence gathering began challenging armor's dominant position; and the third in the type of scenario employed as a reference for force design (increasing the allocation of resources to limited confrontation combat at the expense of preparing the army for war—mainly in training).

What can be learned from a cross-case analysis?

As in any change of direction, the chiefs of staff had to face a certain degree of opposition from various quarters, but this proved relatively easy to ward off because of the consensus in the army on the need for change in the periods under discussion. None of the changes that were discussed ran counter to the instructions or policy of the political echelon (excluding perhaps the difference in approach between Prime Minister Sharett and Dayan, although Dayan was backed by Ben-Gurion and Defense Minister Lavon). Thus, the chief of staff had little need to win over the political echelon to support the change. No matter how light the opposition was, it had to be dealt with. The next chapter describes the changes that generated much more determined opposition and how the chiefs of staff coped with it.

Risk management was different in each of the cases in this chapter. In Dayan's case, strengthening the IDF fighting spirit was not a risk. One change that did entail a risk before a war will be discussed in the next chapter: the correct application of the IDF's limited armored force in that period.

The second test case—the change in orientation of force design in light of the challenge of the huge number of Arab AFVs—was a positive change in risk management and developed, in effect, a second alternative to what had been until then direct contact with enemy tanks at cannon range.

The third case presented risk taking that proved successful in the short term but exacted a costly price later. The chiefs of staff in this period realized the risk they were taking, but the combination of LIC with the Palestinians and budgetary cutbacks turned a calculated risk into a major operational problem in the Second Lebanon War.

The lesson here is that prudence is the key in risk management, even if the negative consequences of introducing the change seem minimal. Chiefs of staff should be prepared to suspend, abort, or even reverse a plan if the changing reality seems to disprove their previous thoughts. This is a formidable task, especially when the chief of staff is personally involved in and leading the change. I would suggest the appointment of powerful, independently minded subordinates who are willing to challenge the chief of staff's plan and assist in reevaluating the concept.

6

BUILDING RELATIONSHIPS WITH THE POLITICAL ECHELON IN FORCE DESIGN

The pattern of relationships between the highest-ranked military officer and the political echelon is a fundamental issue in any study on the chief of staff. It includes interpersonal relationships as well as the government's political and social constraints that weigh on the chief of staff's operational and organizational considerations. Analyzing this aspect of the chief of staff's role is a complex undertaking.

One aspect of these relationships is that of the chief of staff and the political echelon in wartime—as partly described in this book, the Sinai War, the Six-Day War, the Yom Kippur War, and the First and Second Lebanon Wars. While personal memoirs have tended to describe some of these cases in a biased fashion, the degree of public interest means that interechelon relations in wartime have been treated in greater depth than other issues in the biographies and studies on the wars. In the following cases, scholarly research describes and analyzes the relationships between the chiefs of staff and the political echelon before and during a war: Prime Minister Moshe Sharett, defense ministers Pinhas Lavon and David Ben-Gurion, and Chief of Staff Moshe Dayan in 1954–55; Prime Minister and Defense Minister Levi Eshkol and Chief of Staff Yitzhak Rabin before the outbreak of the Six-Day War (Rabin's status as chief of staff under the dovish

Eshkol forced him into a semi-ministerial performance situation until Dayan was appointed defense minister); Prime Minister Golda Meir, Defense Minister Dayan, and Chief of Staff David Elazar in the Yom Kippur War; Prime Minister Menachem Begin, Defense Minister Ariel Sharon, and Chief of Staff Rafael Eitan in the First Lebanon War; and Prime Minister Ehud Olmert, Defense Minister Amir Peretz, and Chief of Staff Dan Halutz in the Second Lebanon War.[1]

Another facet of the relationship is the chief of staff's periodical opposition to the political echelon's policies in peacetime as in the cases of Chief of Staff Mordechai Gur warning of the danger of Anwar Sadat's visit (1977); Chief of Staff Shaul Mofaz and the withdrawal from Lebanon (2000); and Chief of Staff Moshe Ya'alon and the Gaza disengagement (2005). The chief of staff's opposition to the political echelon's policy depends on two factors: his estimate of the degree of damage it will have on the army and the extent of his freedom of action given the politicians' need for legitimacy based on his approval.[2] Much has been written on the chief of staff's role in placing restraints and balances on the political echelon. One example is Dayan's efforts to curb Defense Minister Lavon's hawkish approach.[3]

A third aspect of the civil-military relationship is the chief of staff's attempt to influence the political echelon on the choice of his replacement, which has occasionally been defined as "adversarial" conduct, as in the case of Dayan's efforts to remove Haim Laskov from the promotion track to chief of staff, Moshe Levi's clumsy attempts to block Dan Shomron's appointment, and Shaul Mofaz's bid to cancel Uzi Dayan's promotion (see the book's conclusion).

The three facets of relationships briefly described above exemplify the challenge of comparison and lesson learning.[4] This chapter focuses on a fourth side in the relationship: force design. The reason for this is twofold. First, the subject has received relatively little attention in IDF history, and even less has been accorded to the chief of staff's relation with the political echelon on that issue. Second, relations between the military and political echelons over force design can be analyzed in an almost purely professional light. It is easier to isolate and analyze them compared to the analysis of interechelon disagreements and confrontations over policy or wartime decisions due to the latter's close links to domestic politics, public pressure, and international constraints. While considerations of these factors enter the debate on force design, they are generally less intense than differences over force employment policy. This chapter will focus on four test cases.

The first is the friction between Chief of Staff Yigael Yadin and Prime Minister and Defense Minister David Ben-Gurion over the size of the army in the early fifties. When Ben-Gurion ordered Yadin to cut back on manpower and reduce the budget, Yadin countered that a relatively large standing army was needed to guarantee Israel's security. The ensuing argument led to Yadin's resignation. This case is unique because it is the only one that resulted in a chief of staff leaving office of his own volition over a budgetary issue.

The second case deals with Chief of Staff Moshe Dayan's attempt to enlist Ben-Gurion to his side in the conceptual struggle with General Haim Laskov and Colonel Meir Zore'a on the manner of armor employment before the Sinai War. This instance describes Laskov's efforts to garner Defense Minister Ben-Gurion's support of his position and the counter-response by Dayan, who tried to enlist the political echelon in wielding his authority over recalcitrant senior officers. The importance of the case is that even a powerful chief of staff like Dayan was unable to impose his will on a doctrinal issue when another key member of the general staff held an opposing idea.

The third case relates to the conduct of three chiefs of staff (Mordechai Gur, Rafael Eitan, and Moshe Levi) in the struggle with defense ministers Ezer Weizman and Moshe Arens and Deputy Defense Minister Mordechai Tzipori over the establishment of the Ground Forces HQ (Mafhash). In this instance, senior military commanders assisted the chiefs of staff in preventing a change that the political echelon was determined to enforce on them. The case is special because it illustrates the various steps that both sides took to force their will on each other.

The fourth case describes an opposite situation to that in the second case, when Yitzhak Rabin, after assuming the role of defense minister, approved the Lavi aircraft project but later did a volte-face and sought to cancel it. In this instance, Defense Minister Rabin "mustered" Chief of Staff Dan Shomron, a longtime opponent of the Lavi, to assist him in revoking an earlier political decision. This case exemplifies a long-standing tradition of appointing a qualified general to the position of chief of staff because he is of the same opinion as the political echelon on a burning issue.

The analyses in these cases focus on the chiefs of staff's efforts to influence and convince the political echelon to accept their positions, and the political echelon's methods of dealing with them. Thus, they reflect a broad range of interechelon relations.

Yigael Yadin and David Ben-Gurion on the Size of the Army, 1952

Ben-Gurion appointed Yigael Yadin the second chief of staff in November 1949. Based on their joint effort in the War of Independence, when Yadin served as acting chief of staff because of Ya'akov Dori's illness, Ben-Gurion felt "love and a deep gratitude" toward Yadin, according to author Michael Bar-Zohar. "What was unique in the attitude of the 'Old Man' was that he regarded Yadin as more of a comrade than an officer under his command and sought to maintain cordial and cooperative relations with him rather than a superior-subordinate relationship."[5] Throughout this period, the state of Israel was struggling to absorb massive waves of immigrants and recover economically from the lengthy War of Independence. Economic measures at the time included the rationing of gasoline and food. Against this setting, unbridgeable differences, essentially disagreements over national priorities, divided the two men.

As chief of staff, Yadin claimed that Israel's security situation demanded the largest possible army at the highest state of readiness.[6] While Ben-Gurion was interested in building an advanced, highly trained, mobile, and powerfully armed maneuver army, "Yadin, who served as the chief of staff for three years, argued that the state's security needs, which included guarding borders and unsettled areas and defending against infiltrators, called for a large standing army that would be kept on alert for immediate action."[7]

During Yadin's tenure the number of conscripts, career soldiers, and civilian workers in the military increased from forty thousand in late 1950 to more than fifty-three thousand in late 1952 (when Yadin resigned). Ben-Gurion wanted to slash the standing army to twenty thousand—a size that Yadin's predecessor, Ya'akov Dori, had agreed to. The reserve force, too, exceeded the approved limit, so that the IDF's entire manpower came to 292,000, compared to the planned muster of 239,000. Furthermore, although the manpower increased, the weapons inventory stood at significantly less than what was needed. Thus, a situation arose in which the units were weak and additional units, which were needed, were not established.[8]

The tension between Yadin and Ben-Gurion was exacerbated by a document that Ben-Gurion had ordered Shalom Eshet, the head of the general staff planning department, to draft in October 1952. The document stressed the need to drastically downsize the IDF's payroll and demonstrated that in view of the available equipment and its level of maintenance, as well as the number of commanders, no more than 50 to 60 percent of the present manpower was operable. Given Eshet's criticism of the army's management, Yadin informed Ben-Gurion that this assessment of the balance of power between the IDF and the Arabs in the War of Independence, which formed the basis of his estimate for the future, was utterly mistaken and that the document failed to reflect his [Yadin's] or the general staff's views on most of the points.

The main difference over the manpower size of conscripts and career personnel revolved around the intelligence assessment. While the intelligence department in the operations branch (Agam) perceived "a manifest unwillingness on the part of the Arab states to engage in military actions against Israel," Yadin suspected that given the presence of a large Egyptian force in Sinai and the Gaza Strip and the absence of a permanent Israeli presence in the Negev (Israel's vast, sparsely populated southern desert), a second round of fighting was very likely to break out in the near future in the form of an Egyptian surprise attack, which therefore had to be planned for. Ben-Gurion seems to have thought otherwise, and this was another point of disagreement that contributed to the rift between them.

Yadin's dour assessment also characterized his approach during the War of Independence, when he sharply opposed Ben-Gurion's proposals to concentrate forces on certain fronts while thinning out forces on others. At the end of the war, he struggled to forestall the army's reduction, urging alternative ways to bridge the gap between the required manpower, as he saw it, and the limited budget that the government and the person at the head of it proposed. In the spring of 1949, prior to his official appointment as chief of staff, Yadin suggested levying civilian tasks on the army.[9] Both Ben-Gurion and the general staff vetoed the idea, with Ben-Gurion writing to Yadin in October 1949:

> We cannot allow spending money on national security beyond what is absolutely necessary. We believe it neither possible nor desirable to lower the army's standard of living, let alone economize on its equipment. Only by putting a cap on the size of manpower serving in the army and maintaining a strict regimen of belt tightening can we alleviate the burden of the military budget. . . . The army must subsist on the minimum of the minimum.[10]

Despite the opposition, and in order to justify the large-scale manpower, Yadin endeavored to integrate the IDF into the civilian economy in tasks related to infrastructure development, medicine, welfare, and education. As soon as he assumed office in November 1949, he announced an "IDF emergency regime" to prepare it for war. These measures remained in effect until early May 1950, at which time he requested an extension to October. Putting the army on a permanent war footing raised the cost of its upkeep and rendered long-term building impossible.

Yadin's insistence on maintaining the largest possible mobilized army stemmed from his limited confidence in the reserve component. Despite the impression that Yadin had adopted the Swiss army's system of reservists, it was actually Dori and his supporters who formulated the principles of Israel's reservist structure. Yadin had grave misgivings about the logic in creating this structure because of the time needed to mobilize the reservists in an emergency.[11] Thus, during his tenure the standing army ballooned to two and a half times the size of what Ben-Gurion had established in 1949.

Over the years, Ben-Gurion and other military figures presented various proposals to Yadin for downsizing the standing army. In December 1951, Ben-Gurion suggested whittling down the conscripted manpower by five thousand and using the money saved to increase and improve the mechanization and armament of the remaining force and to expand Israel's military industries, Nahal (military training combined with the establishment of new kibbutzim), and the Gadna program (pre-enlistment youth preparation for military service). Again, Yadin rejected the proposal.

In March 1952, Yadin wrote to Ben-Gurion about "the quantitative-qualitative shortcomings in manpower that are increasing to frightening dimensions."[12] Expecting a sharp decline in the number of conscripts in the coming years, in July 1952 Yadin explained to the government the need to stretch compulsory service from two years to two and a half years. The law was passed in August.

The army's routine expenses accumulated under Yadin's management to amounts that overtaxed the state's financial capability. Israel's economic crisis had forced it to adopt an emergency plan of draconian cutbacks in security outlays in February 1952.

As the 1952–53 work year approached, the IDF submitted a budget proposal for 70 million Israeli lira (IL), while the amount approved came to only IL58 million (approximately $138 million and $114 million respectively). The IDF continued to operate in a business-as-usual mode even as it overstepped the budget. The new finance minister, Levi Eshkol, who came to office in September 1952, reached an agreement with Ben-Gurion on cutting back IL10 million from the defense budget, following which Ben-Gurion ordered Yadin to trim routine expenses:

> The state's defense does not rest solely on the army. . . . It is both impossible and detrimental to act without forethought and calculated risk. The state cannot assume the present burden of the defense budget. . . . Approximately 10 million Israeli lira had to be slashed from the defense budget, not based on earlier calculations but on calculations that have guided the budgeting. The number of career personnel and civilian workers can be reduced and the cutbacks made in reservists, the Nahal can be put to better use.[13]

The situation deteriorated to the point of crisis. Yadin postponed taking immediate steps and continued to run the army as though the defense budget stood at 70 million Israeli lira. He even demanded an additional 10 million lira, which he received, but due to inflation, changes in the exchange rate, and the rise in the cost of living, the IDF still lacked one million lira for routine maintenance until the end of the work year, in March 1953.

The main expense was salaries. In late October 1952, Shimon Peres, the acting director-general of the defense ministry, wrote to Ben-Gurion that "unless you take urgent action to alter the situation, the workers won't receive their take-home pay this month and we won't be able to guarantee food and oil next month."[14] But Yadin kept to the course that he believed correct and asked for additional sums.

On November 20, 1952, he informed Ben-Gurion that since the treasury had not transferred additional money, the supply branch had ceased delivering certain goods to the army. Again, he raised the idea of increasing the army's use for civilian purposes in order to reduce maintenance costs. But Ben-Gurion, who was attentive to the finance minister, denied the chief of staff's request and demanded that Yadin implement explicit cutbacks. Yadin sent him five letters on November 23, including an introductory letter that accompanied the four others; an official letter of resignation; and a letter in which he set forth the reason for his resignation, stating that "you ignored all of the proposals . . . and by doing so you have decided my fate and the unavoidable step that I must take." Another letter presented Yadin's trenchant arguments, paragraph by paragraph, against Ben-Gurion's proposals for cutbacks. In the final letter the chief of staff revealed the personal reason for his resignation—his feeling that Ben-Gurion had lost trust in him. Ben-Gurion tried to convince Yadin not "to break up their partnership" and was even ready to appoint Yadin defense minister, but on the matter of the military budget he refused to budge. Yadin too stood his ground, and his resignation was accepted.[15]

Summary of the Test Case

The personal relations between Ben-Gurion and Yadin were excellent and the differences of opinion were businesslike. While Yadin perceived a large standing army and high level of readiness as vital for fulfilling his responsibility as chief of staff, Ben-Gurion saw the bigger picture and had to reduce the military budget given the young state's financial straits. He was naturally aware of the danger of an Egyptian surprise attack that headed Yadin's agenda, but he also realized that the cost of the readiness for such a scenario would have a detrimental effect on the IDF in both the short and the long run. The attempts by the two men to convince each other seem to have taken place in a relatively limited forum and never reached the public through the media.

Yadin waged a futile attempt to have the IDF assigned civilian tasks despite opposition in the army and Ben-Gurion's unassailable refusal to step back from his demands to cut manpower. Ben-Gurion's patience in the face of Yadin's adamant refusal to carry out his instructions was probably linked to the special personal relationship between them or to Ben-Gurion's difficulty in finding a worthy replacement for Yadin.

This is the only case in Israeli military history when the chief of staff resigned on the grounds of budgetary issues, although military-political controversies over finances have often captured prime-time news since this event. It attests to the chief of staff's overriding sense of responsibility to Israel's security, although the ultimate responsibility lies with the political echelon.

Moshe Dayan and David Ben-Gurion on the Use of Armor before the Sinai War, 1956

A conceptual debate over the use of armor prior to the Sinai War arose between Chief of Staff Moshe Dayan, who argued that armor in its current state was incapable of holding a key place in the IDF fighting concept, and Haim Laskov (the Armored Corps commander and former deputy chief of staff and head of Agam) and Meir Zore'a (the Armored Corps deputy commander), who contended that armor would be the deciding factor in attaining victory. This issue, a seemingly internal army debate, is the focus of our attention because of Prime Minister and Defense Minister David Ben-Gurion's involvement in it.

The Laskov-Zore'a approach called for the merger of nearly all the armored battalions into armored brigades, while the other approach envisioned the merger of most of the battalions (but less than what Laskov and Zore'a wanted) into armored brigades, with some of the lower-quality battalions being subordinated to the regional commands. Another distinction between the approaches was the increased allocation of manpower and other means to armor rather than to the infantry, as Laskov requested upon his appointment to Armored Corps commander and in a reversal of his previous view.[16] The debate seems to have been over the centrality and autonomy of armor. It should be noted that relations between Laskov and Dayan were stormy and probably played their part as well in the following discussion.

In this test case, Laskov sought the prime minister–defense minister's support for his position, while the chief of staff also tried to enlist Ben-Gurion to his side in the complex organizational-resource struggle (against the two senior commanders whose opinions Ben-Gurion valued highly). Dayan did this mainly by convening a large, senior-level roundtable discussion in which, according to historian Amiad Brezner, "he appears to have hoped that Ben-Gurion, who until now had supported the establishment of armor as one of the IDF's main forces, would be persuaded by general opinion in the meeting and openly back Dayan's concept of armor employment."[17] Ben-Gurion played a major role in the professional discussion, as the roundtable was preceded by his unprecedented initiative that intensified the debate, as he explained to the general staff in July 1956:

> From perceiving [armor] as the weak link in our chain of weapons . . . I did something quite unexpected, I asked General Laskov, the deputy chief of staff, to assume command of armor. . . . I am very pleased to say that he agreed. He will soon be the head of the Armored Corps HQ and his status will be like that of the commanders of the navy, air force, and regional commands.[18]

On July 24 a general staff meeting reviewed the same issue but left it unresolved.[19] Brezner wrote that "an operational discussion on armor employment" was held on September 1 (the Sabbath, generally not a work day except for operational issues), chaired by Dayan and with Ben-Gurion in attendance and thirty-eight officers taking part.[20] According to Dayan, the discussion was designed "to determine armor's employment doctrine."[21]

Dayan opened by stating that the question regarding the fighting and organizational concept arose after the Armored Corps Headquarters was set up and put forward its proposal. This matter was brought up for discussion in a general staff roundtable meeting as well as in a number of smaller general staff meetings, Agam forums, and with him. The decisions ran counter to Armored Corps' HQ concept and proposal. Following this, the commander of the Armored Corps' HQ spoke with the defense minister and voiced his objection to the decisions, and it was decided to convene a meeting in which various concepts would be presented. The defense minister, Dayan said, would chair the meeting and sum up the main points in order to determine the manner of fighting, which would be followed by a decision on the organizational structure.[22]

Regarding Ben-Gurion's presence in the meeting, Mordechai Naor claimed that Dayan came to the meeting with his mind already made up. Aware that most of the senior officers were of a like mind regarding armor's role on the battlefield, he felt it important that Ben-Gurion hear and finally accept the justification of his opinion. The other side's position on armor was presented by only three officers: Laskov, Zore'a, and Herzl Shafir. According to documentation, there were only ten officers besides Dayan, who spoke at length, and Ben-Gurion, who asked questions, and from the minutes it appears that most of them supported Dayan.[23]

Zore'a justified the argument not to divide the tanks by claiming that it was the cause of the French failure against the Germans in the Second World War, stating, "If I had [enough] tanks I would turn the entire IDF disproportionately into an armored force and the balance would come from the artillery." His opponents, led by Dayan, charged that armor's main ORBAT was not expected to increase significantly in the near future and therefore it was impossible to radically alter its employment concept. All of the commanders backed Dayan's position: Uzi Narkis, the assistant head of Agam; Yitzhak Rabin, commander of Northern Command and representing Mahad's position; Asaf Simhoni, commander of Southern Command; Amos Horev, chief ordnance officer; and Amos Messer, the head of the planning and organization department in Agam.

Dayan attacked those who sided with Laskov. More than once a volley of laughter erupted when the chief of staff emphasized yet again how ludicrous the proposals were. Laskov was very tense, and Zore'a lashed back a number of times.[24] Zore'a admitted: "The truth is there were exchanges of guffaws between the camps during the entire meeting and their [our opponents'] aim was 'to make mincemeat out of us.'"[25] After the positions were presented, Dayan summed up his opponents' armor concept, asserting that it was based on a larger-than-available number of tanks and it failed to take the IDF's needs into account, the first of which was preserving the infantry ORBAT. He also stated: "No one [among the general staff officers] has gone through a special armor school or has fought with armor in the past or has more experience than anyone else in this room." He recalled the 27th Brigade's field exercise and the deplorable state of maintenance in the armored forces. Dayan turned directly to Laskov and Zore'a and said that "establishing the Armored Corps HQ and [improving] its fighting [capability] is more than a personal task, the entire army is involved."[26]

Ben-Gurion frequently interrupted the discussion with questions. Some were of a technical nature such as the range and penetration capability of tank shells, and others were an attempt to undermine the basic assumptions that the speakers' arguments were based on. His longest interruption dealt with two subjects: first, the armor command's need to prepare the troops through basic training and command them in intense, short-term, combined arms actions; second, the likelihood that Gamal Abdel Nasser would initiate a war in the north (Syria) to draw the IDF's attention in that direction and then make his move in the south.[27] Ben-Gurion's questions show that his concept stemmed from the possibility of a multifront war where the enemy would make maximum use of its armor and thus force the IDF to allocate most of its tanks to defensive operations. This approach was closer to Rabin's position than to Laskov's, Zore'a's, or even Dayan's, which held that the main armor's ORBAT had to be employed offensively (each camp according to its modus operandi).

In the end, Dayan softened his criticism of armor's concept. Brezner, the Armored Corps historian, claimed that the reason was that Laskov and Zore'a altered their tone because they supported Dayan's offensive doctrine (but not based on infantry brigades). Be that as it may, Brezner wrote, "The main reason was probably his impression of Ben-Gurion's direction of questioning. Finally, unlike Dayan's expectations at the start of the discussion, Ben-Gurion did not sum up the main points of the meeting or deliver any concluding statements."[28]

Most scholars (Brezner, Naor, and Motti Golani) believe that Ben-Gurion decided not to take sides so as not to offend the opposing party, and that he tried to moderate the differences in approach to seemingly simple technical matters such as channeling two hundred men to armor. In practice, he continued his consultations in the following days and requested that Zore'a prepare a summary of the unresolved points. This document was submitted to Ben-Gurion the following day (September 2), with a copy to Dayan. On September 3, Ben-Gurion called Dayan to a private meeting to discuss the document and said that he agreed with Dayan's approach. On September 9, Laskov met with Ben-Gurion and again explained his concept. Ben-Gurion informed Laskov in no uncertain terms that he rejected his position but tried to mitigate the decision. The next day's entry in the prime minister's private diary reads: "I also instructed Moshe Dayan to reach a decision on Haim's [Laskov's] demands." Dayan wrote to Ben-Gurion that he realized that the differences of opinion, on manpower at least, were quite small—only a matter of an additional two hundred men—and the Armored Corps would be able to increase its communications, reconnaissance unit, armor school, corps headquarters, and other needs. Ben-Gurion concluded: "I do not see myself an authority to decide on these matters, and you must see this letter as my final statement on the Armored Corps issue." He sent Laskov a copy of his letter to Dayan and added a few personal remarks: "I think the differences are few and minor and we should consider the matter settled. As a good soldier, accept the chief of staff's decision."[29]

On September 25, the chief of staff's bureau circulated a doctrinal summary that included slight changes in the original document. Laskov, ever the loyal trooper, submitted to the chief of staff's authority.

Summary of the Test Case

Formidable professional disagreements, poor interpersonal relationships that hampered the reconciliation of differences, and the defense minister's appointment of Laskov as commander of the Armored

Corps HQ brought the chief of staff to the realization that he would have to convince the defense minister to retract his support of armor's independence and that the most effective way to do so would be to demonstrate the opposition within the IDF. To accomplish this, a general debate was held in which the defense minister served as judge. This is an example of a situation in which the chief of staff enlisted the defense minister to impose the chief of staff's will on the high command after the formal internal process failed. This is only one example of the difficulties chiefs of staff sometimes have with their general staffs. Later, Laskov, as chief of staff, failed to have his plan accepted to establish the division as a permanent body in the IDF organizational structure and not as a task-designated body only in wartime.

If the chief of staff expects to "recruit" senior commanders to implement a major change in force design, he must invest a prodigious amount of time and energy in convincing them of its efficacy and necessity. Generals are not easily persuaded or ordered.

Mordechai Gur, Rafael Eitan, and Moshe Levi on the Establishment of the Mafhash, 1977–84

Establishing the Mafhash (second version of a Ground Forces HQ—see introduction and glossary) in October 1983, while disbanding the Armored Corps HQ and subordinating the armor, infantry, combat engineers, and artillery officers from the chief of staff to the Mafhash commander, is undoubtedly the deepest organizational change that the IDF ever carried out.

The inauguration of the Mafhash was the culmination of a decade-long process that began after the Yom Kippur War, but the main progress took place between 1977 and 1984.[30] Many individuals took part in its development, but for our purposes we will focus on two defense ministers (Ezer Weizman and Moshe Arens), three chiefs of staff (Mordechai Gur, Rafael Eitan, and Moshe Levi), and a number of major generals (Israel Tal, Shmuel Gonen, Yossi Peled, Moshe Bar-Kochva, and Dan

Shomron). Gur was outspoken in his opposition to the Mafhash and did all he could to prevent its establishment. Eitan also opposed the change but refrained from voicing his position publicly. In practice he dithered over the decision. Levi agreed to carry out the change (apparently a condition for his appointment to the office) and, despite various internal obstacles, the Mafhash came into being on his watch.

This chapter does not deal with the contents of the change (whether the establishment and organization of the Mafhash was the right thing to do or the justification in delegating authority and responsibility of ground force design). Rather, it looks at the ways in which the chiefs of staff operated vis-à-vis the political echelon in rejecting or delaying the Mafhash's establishment or in changing its essence.

The need to free the general staff from its involvement in the development of the ground forces began as early as 1953.[31] The solution was the Armored Corps HQ, which made huge strides in upgrading the IDF's armor capability and contributed inestimably to victories in the Sinai, Six-Day, and Yom Kippur Wars, achieving them in large part by an approach that put the tank in the epicenter of ground fighting and elevated its dominance in the development of the land battle. However, the fly in the ointment of the tank's overascendency was revealed in the Yom Kippur War. According to Avraham Tamir, "What clinched the decision to build the ground forces by a central headquarters were the Yom Kippur War and its lessons. This war proved beyond a shadow of doubt the bankruptcy in the IDF's structure of twelve corps."[32] From the Yom Kippur War to the period that this section deals with (1977–84), it has been repeatedly stated by observers that the Yom Kippur War exposed the shortcomings of intercorps cooperation. In April 1975, Chief of Staff Mordechai Gur ordered General Gonen to examine the possibility of setting up a headquarters for building the ground combat corps (infantry, armor, artillery, and combat engineers) without canceling the chief officer headquarters of the corps and without establishing a "ground army." According to a document that was apparently written by Dan Shomron, "It quickly turned out that Gonen's proposal was unfeasible: not only would the headquarters not save manpower, it would be an additional bureaucratic level between the corps and the chief of staff." According to Shomron, Gur vetoed the proposal, claiming on principle that "the ground battle is the decisive element, and a war is not managed by contracting it out to others." According to Shomron, instead of establishing the Mafhash, Gur decided to set up the planning branch (Agat), expand the doctrine and training branch (Mahad) and turn it into a general staff branch, and establish three new corps: combat intelligence, the adjutant, and logistics (in effect the planning branch already existed and Mahad was subordinate to Agam).[33]

In October 1975, the proposal was rejected for several reasons: the proposed headquarters would oblige the general staff to engage in greater coordination between the corps and regional commands; it would inhibit intellectual and doctrinal pluralism; it would cause the general staff to lose control over manpower; and, above all, the shortcomings that Gonen had pointed to could be surmounted even without a special headquarters.[34]

It should be noted that in Israel's situation immediately after the Yom Kippur War, with a chief of staff who strongly opposed the headquarters and a teetering government, the idea would have been impossible to advance.

The Period of Chief of Staff Mordechai Gur and Defense Minister Ezer Weizman (June 1977–April 1978)

This period is characterized by a struggle between the new defense minister, Ezer Weizman, who tried to force Gur (three and a half years into his role) to set up the Field Forces HQ, and Gur, who was determined to prevent it.[35] The Field Forces HQ was supposed to have command of all the ground forces in wartime as well as their force design. The Mafhash (Ground Forces HQ), on the other hand, was intended to deal solely with their force design, while the regional commands would be in charge of their operational employment. The first discussion was based on Gonen's 1975 proposal.

Gur held a three-day conference with Defense Minister Weizman and the entire senior staff. At the end of the three days, the chief of staff presented the minister with his reasons for rejecting the plan. Weizman did not yield easily and continued pressing for the establishment of the Field Forces Headquarters. Gur reputedly told the minister that he would never agree to changes in the IDF's structure as long as he was the chief of staff and would recommend the same to his successor.[36]

When Weizman realized that salvation would not come from within the IDF, he tried a different tack: setting up an external committee and appointing an external commander from the reserves and with the rank of major general to the new body—Israel Tal. On August 8, 1977, the defense minister ordered Tal to examine the organization and structure of the ground forces according to national security needs for the 1980s. Tal was also instructed to recommend changes and updates in the force's units, competency, and organization. Additional orders were to single out the implications of the recommended organization of the security establishment in general and the general staff in particular. The criteria that the analysis was based on, and the conclusions and recommendations that were derived from it, were that administrative and military efficiency would improve the system's functioning.[37]

Tal's wide-ranging proposal, which included the establishment of the Field Forces Headquarters for ground force employment in war, not just force design and other changes (see below), triggered, as expected, across-the-board opposition. Gur claims that when Weizman broached the idea, he [Gur] told him about Gonen's work and was firmly against it:

> I elaborated on my argument but I perceived that the minister, for his own reasons, was determined to establish the Field Forces Headquarters. Because of this I suggested that if the decision is made, it would be advisable to delegate its implementation to General Israel Tal (Talik), who for years had been in favor of setting up the headquarters, and who was most knowledgeable on the subject and had amassed all of the relevant material on it. Be that as it may, I made it clear that the work was liable to be

fruitless because I remained adamantly opposed to the change and would recommend as such to the next chief of staff, at least in the first year of his tenure.[38]

On November 4, Tal met with Gur and presented the main points of the plan for establishing the headquarters. Gur replied to Tal that the flaws in his plan were greater than its benefits and that he had no intention of taking major steps. Gur later wrote, "I assumed responsibility for increasing and strengthening the IDF's assault 'teeth'—throughout the army and its corps—and this we did. I don't intend to waste manpower, time, and resources creating a sterile headquarters devoid of responsibility in war. I was ordered to organize and train the force down to the smallest detail, and I have no intention of transferring this responsibility to anyone for better or for worse. With due respect to his [Tal's] effort, I made it clear that I won't deal with this issue (my schedule is already overloaded) and invest time and energy on a matter that I don't intend to implement."[39]

Tal, who was subordinate to the defense minister, completed the study in December. The following are his main recommendations for organizational changes:

A. The general staff will continue to be both the supreme command and the general staff of the ground forces regarding their employment.

B. The chief officers of the corps as part of Agam and logistics branches of the GHQ will be canceled (excluding the chief medical officer, the chief of military police, the chief of military intelligence, and the head of civil defense). In their place the following designated commands will be established:
   • "The Ground Forces HQ" (Mafhash) will be subordinate to the chief of staff and responsible for building the ground forces.
   • The "Logistics Command," subordinate to the chief of logistics, will have responsibility for designing and maintaining the logistics units of the ground forces.

C. The ground forces will be organized in a uniform pattern as permanent divisions (i.e., not as task-designated divisions).[40]

Tal's report also recommended changes in the structure of general staff branches and the defense ministry. After the report's publication, the general staff discussed it in a series of meetings.

It should be noted that Weizman's idea to appoint Tal as commander of the Field Forces Headquarters had the support of many security figures, among them Yitzhak Rabin, who said, "[It must be] the person best suited for setting up the headquarters and running it in a way that best enhances the quality of the ground forces. Not wishing to offend any of the generals serving in the IDF today, that person is Major General Israel Tal."[41] Nevertheless Tal's appointment generated opposition in the GHQ apparently (among other reasons) because of some of the generals' apprehension that Tal would be a candidate for promotion to chief of staff. Gur himself was foremost among the opponents of Tal's appointment. Public opinion was divided.[42] After Gur's retirement in 1982 and after Weizman was no longer in the government, the former chief of staff discussed the attempts to pressure him to establish the Ground/Field Forces Headquarters:

SPEAKER: The preliminary question is how much the government can force the military echelon to make a substantial change in its structure. To the best of my knowledge, the defense minister initiated this plan, and the public sensed that the chief of staff was being unruly or purposely delaying it. So, to what extent can the government determine the army's structure?

GUR: When Weizman became defense minister, he wanted to make all kinds of drastic changes to demonstrate his leadership. For example, he'd say: "It's settled! Do it right away! Bring in the ground forces' combat corps—this'll show that there's action and change." I said, "Do you want me to introduce changes? Then this will have to go through the process of discussion that is customary in the IDF in cases like this. We'll have to weigh all the arguments and counterarguments. And if in the end you still believe it's still a good idea, then we'll prepare another series of discussions because this is a serious matter." And Ezer [Weizman] gave up on it. . . . Now this has gone public only because of Ezer's behavior. It could have remained inside the IDF and never gotten out; but it has. The fact is, he [Weizman] didn't steamroll the restructuring through. You asked if he tried to force his position on me. If he had, you would have heard about it loud and clear. I wouldn't have allowed the decision to be made on my watch. There would've been a flurry of talks, and then I'd have brought the matter before the government. In other words, if the minister had tried to force a reorganization of the army, I would've informed the government, because the government is the supreme commander of the army, and I would have seen this as the right thing to do on principle. I would never have allowed the issue to pass easily, because I can recall very few examples in Israel's history where the government forced organizational rethink on the IDF. I would never have permitted this to pass quietly, but the government can, of course, force its will on the army and it could happen if the matter reached a discussion at this level.[43]

In 1981, Weizman wrote that Gur had been the chief of staff for quite some time while he [Weizman] was a still a rookie defense minister, and that he hoped they could work together but knew it wouldn't be easy. "Gur received a battered army after the Yom Kippur War. He did a fantastic job rehabilitating it in his own way, but not everyone liked his style. Still, I couldn't help admiring his part in patching up the wounds. Gur had a free hand with my predecessor Shimon Peres . . . who gave the chief of staff almost complete free rein. Gur received me correctly as the defense minister. He tried to put me in my place, and I tried to put him in his. The hidden struggle between the civilian and military echelons ended, as I saw it, with my victory, as it should in a democracy."[44]

Regarding the Mafhash, Gur seems to have been the winner. In his analysis of the structural realization of the Mafhash, David Shalom summed up Gur's attitude toward the idea of establishing the Ground Forces HQ as a rigid organizational roadblock before the proposed restructuring. Some say Gur personified the inherent conservatism of the organization and confirmed the fear that the IDF was the same as any other bureaucratic organization. According to some observers, all the changes that began during Gur's tenure were forced on him, paradoxically, by the echelons below him. For four years Gur was unable to fix the bugs in the conservative machine. He rejected Tal's plan for the Field Forces Headquarters, charging that a large headquarters was unnecessary because it would serve as a partition between the chief of staff and the ground forces, which comprise the main strength of the IDF. It is hard to believe that this was the only reason. The relationship between Tal and Gur turned ugly, with the former seeing the latter as a charlatan and Gur regarding Tal as a stick-in-the-mud.[45]

The Period of Chief of Staff Rafael Eitan and Defense Minister Ezer Weizman (April 1978–May 1980)

At least one of Weizman's calculations in choosing Rafael "Raful" Eitan as chief of staff was Eitan's agreement to establish the Field Forces Headquarters. Following the 1977 political upheaval, when the Likud party replaced Labor's nearly thirty-year hold on government, expectations rose that the new leadership would clear away the cobwebs. Weizman and Mordechai Tzipori (deputy defense minister) agreed that if they won the election, they would enter the defense ministry and fast-track the Field Forces Headquarters issue. When they were faced with replacing the chief of staff, Weizman asked Tzipori to hold talks with a number of generals. Eitan supported the establishment of the headquarters. The understanding was clear: if he became chief of staff he would bring the Field Forces Headquarters into being.[46]

Under pressure from Weizman, Eitan had to pursue the staff work while he essentially changed Tal's proposal from the Field Forces Headquarters to the Mafhash, that is, a headquarters responsible solely for force design.

Various officers expressed their opposition to the Mafhash in their attitude toward preparations for the general staff meeting that was scheduled for July 1978 and that would be chaired by the chief of staff shortly after he assumed office. The prevailing negative atmosphere worked in Eitan's favor to persuade Weizman to back down from his single-mindedness to set up the headquarters.[47] The main staff branches whose authorities were fated to be trimmed were manpower, logistics, doctrine and training, and R&D, whose chiefs were naturally against the proposed move.

The head of manpower wrote:

I fail to see a pressing need for establishing the headquarters. The problems presented have suitable solutions without creating this headquarters. The solutions are efficient and can improve the current combat doctrine, R&D, training, and force design. On the other hand, the IDF after implementing the proposed organizational changes will be complicated and a genuine nightmare to run effectively, with lines of coordination and operation that are ambiguous, confusing, and disjointed to the point of being unmanageable beyond control. The sorry state of manpower calls for greater balance at the general staff level. The Field Forces Headquarters will have greater authority than what the services have today. Actually, a superfluous intermediate level will be created that muscles in between the general staff and the regional commands in areas that belong to the manpower branch and that weakens the regional commands in these areas. . . . I find no need or room for setting up the Field Forces Headquarters.[48]

The head of the logistics branch expressed a similar position.[49] The head of the doctrine and training branch (Mahad) put forward an alternative proposal: the deputy chief of staff would be appointed concurrently to commander of the Field Forces and in this capacity would be the commander of the chief officers of the ground corps. He would be assisted by Mahad and the R&D directorate.[50]

The head of the R&D directorate wrote:

> I agree with the deputy minister's decision that there's no justification for the addition of an intermediate operational echelon between the supreme command and the ground arenas. . . . This factor [alone] invalidates the idea for the headquarters. . . . The establishment of two separate headquarters for the ground forces and their logistics is not an alternative to the ground army and will contribute nothing to the improvement of ground force design.[51]

Aman, the air force, and the navy were not intended to be directly affected by the process, but they opposed it for other reasons.[52] Since the chief officers of the corps, mainly the ground forces corps, realized that their staff officer status would be truncated, they came up with various arguments to minimize the damage. The deputy commander of the Armored Corps HQ favored the move but proposed that the headquarters be based on the Armored Corps HQ "with its befitting infrastructure and wealth of experience."[53] The chief combat engineer officer supported the establishment of the headquarters but also recommended retaining the chief of staff's links to the chief officers of the corps.[54]

The chief artillery officer was against the new headquarters, arguing that "the establishment of the Field Forces Headquarters in the proposed framework will nullify the corps' overall responsibility for building and training the ORBAT without delegating responsibility to a body that serves the corps' interests. . . . For these reasons I stand opposed to the current proposal to establish the Field Forces Headquarters."[55]

Given the internal IDF opposition, Weizman backed down. On August 14, 1978, the defense minister summed up the issue and decided that the proposal "would be put on ice" for many reasons, including the fact the IDF had recently gone through a major rotation of senior officers that only strengthened the need to freeze the proposal at that point. Another reason was that the Egyptian-Israeli peace initiative was currently underway and the juxtaposition of the peace process and discussions on a major structural revamp of the army and security establishment was undesirable.[56]

A few months after the postponement, the deputy chief of staff, Major General Yekutiel Adam, signed a document that effectively put an end to the Field Forces Headquarters episode.[57]

The plan was frozen due to the peace agreement with Egypt, in which Weizman was closely involved as defense minister, but Weizman promised to return to the restructuring initiative after the Camp David talks. A year after his failure to convince chiefs of staff Gur and Eitan to set up the Field Forces Headquarters, Weizman reiterated his demand with a coordinated public statement—which Chief of Staff Eitan agreed with—to set up a limited version of the Field Forces Headquarters to be known as the Ground Forces HQ (Mafhash), also headed by Tal. This declaration later turned out to be hollow. The proposal that Tal submitted to Weizman and Eitan in August 1978 remained in storage for over a year.

On November 29, 1979, Weizman, Eitan, and Tal convened a press conference in which they explained the idea behind the Mafhash: "We have decided to set up a unified headquarters for the ground corps—armor, infantry, artillery, and combat engineers, minus the signal corps—that will include the ground forces R&D department and combat doctrine department connected to these corps." Eitan announced that the Mafhash was designed as an organizational—not a combat—framework, and there would be no difference in the functions of the regional commands or general staff branches as originally proposed. The new headquarters would be the supreme headquarters of the four main ground corps. The deputy chief of staff, as head of Agam, would coordinate the new HQ work with the regional commands. The new HQ would be placed in the combat echelons like the armor headquarters had been (as a wartime division/field corps HQ).[58] Acting under the defense minister's instructions, the chief of staff continued the staff work.[59] After the November 26 general staff discussion, the office of the chief of staff issued the following orders:[60]

A. The Mafhash will include armor, artillery, infantry, engineers, ground R&D, and combat doctrine departments attached to these corps.

B. Staff work will be carried out by General Tal and Agat. Its goal will be to determine costs and manpower relative to the present situation and budgetary constraints in the coming and following work years. . . . Staff work will be completed by the start of the 1980 work year (late March 1980).

C. After completing the staff work a general staff discussion will be convened.

D. The basic structure of the general staff and its branches will remain as they are. However, assignments and resources will be cut to the point of canceling, merging, or transferring department-level staff bodies so as to avoid duplication.

The chief of staff ordered Agat and a select establishment team headed by Tal to begin work on the Mafhash and finalize the HQ's structure, organization, functions, and installations, plus the work procedures with the corps, regional commands, and general staff branches, as well as the headquarters' work plan and schedule for the 1980–81 work year beginning on April 1, 1980.

After the discussion, Agat published a designated document that served as the basis for talks that were held by the head of Agat with the general staff branches, the regional commands, the corps, and the establishment team.[61] The reference point in Agat's talks and the internal discussions in the establishment team was Tal's proposal for "designating and organizing the ground forces," that is, creating the Field Forces Headquarters.

Weizman tried to secure the changes by gaining their approval in the Knesset's Foreign Affairs and Defense Committee (the subject was presented jointly by Weizman, Eitan, and Tal on December 11, 1979) and government approval in the State Security Cabinet (also known as the Ministerial Committee on National Security Affairs) on January 7, 1980.[62] None of this helped.

Although Weizman decided to establish the HQ, preparations proceeded at a snail's pace. All discussion on the matter remained in a state of limbo until Tal's team completed the staff work. Upon its completion, the general staff resumed talks, and this time, as before, they were marked by sharp differences of opinion. Various proposals were finally crystallized, including some new ones. The series of talks, however, culminated with Weizman's resignation on May 25, 1980.

Following this the entire enterprise went into retreat. The suggestion to postpone the plan was interpreted by parties outside the army as an attempt to cancel it altogether. The chief of staff, who was no longer under the authority of the now-defunct defense minister, turned to Prime Minister Menachem Begin, now also acting as defense minister, to shelve the establishment of the Field Forces Headquarters to an unspecified date. Tal regarded the postponement as an expression of no confidence. He stopped showing up at his office in uniform, and rumors were rife that he would submit his resignation if the HQ remained indefinitely on hold. It did not take much for the plan to be all but forgotten, even though it went through all the formal stages for final approval. Its demise, however, was blocked at the very last minute by the intervention of the former generals who were members of government: Yigael Yadin, Ariel Sharon, and Mordechai Tzipori, who, although not a member of government, had taken part in discussions in the State Security Cabinet. Under their insistence, the prime minister–defense minister, who leaned toward the chief of staff's view, was forced to send the plan back to the State Security Cabinet for further discussion.[63]

The Period of Chief of Staff Rafael Eitan and Deputy Defense Minister Mordechai Tzipori (May 1980–August 1981)

Between May 1980 (when Weizman was already out of office) and August 1981, with Prime Minister Menachem Begin acting as defense minister, the dominant figure in the political echelon dealing with the establishment of the Mafhash was Deputy Defense Minister Mordechai Tzipori.

The tide turned after Weizman's resignation as an increasing number of voices in the army spoke in favor of adopting the plan. Several reasons were behind this turnaround, but the clincher was the economic one. Tzipori claimed that the outlay for establishing the headquarters would not exceed IL15 million ($7.2 million; as opposed to Eitan's estimate of hundreds of millions of Israeli lira) and that in the long run, the creation of the Field Forces Headquarters would, paradoxically, prove to be a great savings. Even before the cost was brought up, various organizational steps had been taken in the IDF to scotch the plan. These steps ran completely counter to the plan to establish the HQ in the format approved by the defense ministry, the State Security Cabinet, and the Foreign Affairs and Defense Committee. It did not go unnoticed that after Weizman's departure, the IDF decided not to set up the headquarters but to proactively oppose the idea.[64]

The Begin-Eitan relationship was marked by a strong chemistry and perhaps also by the prime minister's dependency on the battle-scarred veteran. Therefore, Begin was uncomfortable about forcing the plan on the chief of staff. Unlike Begin, Tzipori waged an open struggle against Eitan and those officers who, according to Tzipori, had blocked the change. Tzipori blamed the power struggles among the senior officers for preventing the restructuring of the IDF, and he did everything in his power to induce the IDF to set up the Field Forces Headquarters.[65]

Thus, while the chief of staff wanted to conclude the affair within the IDF, the deputy defense minister torpedoed the move by shifting the decision onto the State Security Cabinet. By then, however, most of the committee members had little background in security matters, so it is difficult to believe that a professional decision would be made.

The entanglement over the creation of Field Forces HQ in this period reflects the complex relations between the defense ministry and the general staff. Senior figures defined the debate as a power struggle and clash between two camps over prestige, with Tzipori at the head of one camp and Eitan at the other. This situation exposed a flawed decision-making system in the security establishment. The vacated defense minister portfolio spawned confusion in the domains of authority in numerous key bodies. It generated uncertainty over the decision making taking place in the political and military spheres, while the polemic between the sides grew more and more audible to the public ear. The doubt continued until Ariel Sharon was appointed defense minister. Sharon seems not to have taken too deep an interest in the organizational transformations in the IDF and instead invested his efforts in the newly established national security unit and in strategic planning.

An example of Eitan's attempt to stall the decision is his beefing up Mahad with more manpower, under the command of Major General Uri Simhoni, who was "fully aware that if the reorganization plan materialized, Mahad would lose its authority to the Field Forces Headquarters. . . . This is just one small example of the steps that were taken to block the restructuring and stonewall its implementation."[66] Shalom summed up Eitan's conduct in the establishment of the Mafhash, noting that Eitan, too, a Weizman appointee, was far from enthusiastic about Tal's plans. In marathon discussions he avoided expressing his opinion. He did not want the HQ established, although he never said so. He knew that its inception was likely to swallow up much of the chief of staff's powers. If the plan materialized, the commander of the HQ would be the real supreme commander of the IDF, and the chief of staff would be a coordinator between the different services and commands.

Eitan adopted a policy of deliberately delaying the execution of the plan and endorsement of the recommendations. But he changed his view in accordance with external exigencies. When he felt obligated to the defense minister, he even expressed his support of the plan. The shifts in his position may have arisen from a tactical move of slowly strangling the idea into a comatose state. But Eitan had no intention to

self-destruct or curtail his own authorities, because of the new powerful body in the making with the potential to replace him. He prudently
planned his steps to sink and bury the idea.[67]

According to Shomron, when Eitan brought Tal's recommendations
for the new framework before the general staff for a comprehensive
discussion, two possibilities were raised: the "expanded" view (Tal's
proposal) and the "limited" view (a concept of a chief officer of a corps
with the rank of major general). Shomron wrote, "There was a consensus that the HQ had to be formed, even if only in the 'limited' version, but in practice the chief of staff withheld its implementation for
an unspecified length of time."[68] Again the general staff expressed its
opposition to the establishment of the Field Forces Headquarters. The
staff meetings became exercises in wasted energy. "Everyone could
see that Eitan was playing for time, simply to put off a decision. He
fiddled with his watch while committee members set forth their arguments and summed up the speakers' main points with a terse 'We'll let
you know later.'"[69] Curiously, neither Eitan nor Tzipori mention the
Mafhash's birth pains in their autobiographies.[70]

The Period of Chief of Staff Rafael Eitan and Defense Minister Ariel Sharon (August 1981–April 1983)

In this period, the staff work on the Mafhash was relegated to the back
burner due to Sharon's disinterest and, as noted, Eitan's aversion. In
the wake of the First Lebanon War in the summer of 1982, both men
were replaced.

The Period of Chief of Staff Moshe Levi and Defense Minister Moshe Arens (April 1983–September 1984)

It is widely agreed that Defense Minister Moshe Arens appointed
Moshe Levi chief of staff on condition that Levi set up the Mafhash.[71]
Given the double failure of the previous defense minister, the
domineering Weizman, in his dealings with chiefs of staff Gur and

Eitan, Arens's method seems elementary, if not obvious. Although a number of factors merged to produce conditions convenient for the establishment of the Mafhash, internal IDF opposition simmered unabated.

Shalom writes that people in a crisis are less sensitive to their own values and in this psychological state are amenable to reform and change. This approach matches the four main events that affected the creation of the Mafhash: (1) the Yom Kippur War; (2) Weizman and Arens assuming the role of defense minister (the former's departure having impacted in the reverse direction); (3) the IDF's redeployment in the Negev after the Egypt-Israel Peace Treaty of 1979; and (4) the consequences of the First Lebanon War (1982) and the appointment of a new chief of staff (Levi).

We may assume that those events had various affects: the criticism of the IDF following the Yom Kippur War and the conclusions of the Agranat Commission Report motivated Israel's military leadership to seek organizational solutions; the entry of a defense minister eager to introduce changes influenced the security establishment under his command to adopt certain of his ideas; the redeployment in the Negev from Sinai created an abundance of organizational opportunities in such areas as resources, strategic concepts, and innovative ideas; and the war in Lebanon and its results were an incentive to finalize the renewal process in light of the criticism leveled at the IDF and the expectations for changes within.[72]

As for Arens, Shalom believed that the new defense minister's background as a member of the Foreign Affairs and Defense Committee biased his decision. As a committee member, Arens had expressed his overall satisfaction with the "steps that were being taken for the IDF's revitalization and renewal." The committee held several meetings on the matter and called many witnesses, including former chiefs of staff and people who had been involved in the effort. According to Arens, these hearings strengthened the awareness of the need for the Mafhash. Arens realized what had to be done and the Mafhash's absolute necessity.[73]

As soon as Arens stepped into the role of defense minister, he instructed Chief of Staff Levi to work out a plan of action for establishing the Mafhash. Arens reached this decision after talking with senior commanders, listening to their opinions, and gaining the impression that even those who had been dead set against the Mafhash had changed their minds since the war in Lebanon. His decision to implement the restructuring was final. The IDF would be issued the plan without another general staff discussion on the subject. His determination was unshakable; the days of dithering were over. In his words:

> During Weizman's tenure the internal IDF opposition had prevented him from advancing the Mafhash. In my case I made the decision and we got down to brass tacks. We didn't let the project drag on and spend our time treading water; in fact, I made this a condition for the appointment of the chief of staff. Had any other modus operandi been taken, if the chief of staff had entered his role with a new set of discussions on the establishment of the Mafhash, it probably would have never come into being.[74]

Arens's explanation is revealing: "I brought up the question of the Mafhash with Levi. I told him I intended to establish the HQ and that if he disagreed, he should say so now. He gave his word that he would have the Mafhash established and so he was appointed chief of staff."[75]

However, as David Ivry, the deputy chief of staff in this period, pointed out, in reality Arens did not fully fathom the difference between the establishment of the Field Forces Headquarters that was supposed to have command over all the ground forces and the Mafhash that only had command of force design.[76] Arens seems to have agreed without genuinely understanding the real significance of the ostensibly minor change—a change that in practical terms made all the difference in the world and enabled Levi to accept Arens's condition and carry out the move.

From Levi's side, things looked different. When Levi was the commander of Central Command he had opposed the idea. As the newly instated chief of staff he wanted to secure as broad a consensus as possible for renewal and to calm the apprehension in his camp. Thus, he adopted a foot-dragging tactic in any discussions and decision making that would obligate him. His fear of dissension and confrontation with generals undoubtedly drove him to cut corners and tolerate redundancies in order to avoid painful clashes and reproach. This course undoubtedly determined the development and future shape of the new HQ.

On the day that Dan Shomron was appointed Mafhash commander, Levi said: "We've spent eight years discussing the shape of the Mafhash . . . it's impossible to know the HQ's shape before it's established. That's why I decided on a faster track . . . setting up the HQ whose modus operandi will develop only after it begins functioning." Levi added, "The integration of the ground corps is the first tier in the design of the Ground Forces HQ on the path to building the Field Forces HQ." It seems that he wanted to develop the HQ and gradually expand its areas of authority. While this goal was not stated outright, in reality the rate of the Mafhash's implementation depended on the general staff's decisions and especially on the chief of staff himself. Still, the Mafhash was planned to develop in stages and at the rate of "weeks or at the most a couple of months."[77]

It is important to note that in this period, the IDF was engaged in continuous fighting in Lebanon, with the major organizational transition taking place under turbulent security conditions. Levi opposed Tal's earlier proposal of a full-fledged command that would both prepare and employ the forces. Levi insisted that the Mafhash could not be an additional command because the IDF was based on a general staff and regional commands. Furthermore, he said that there was no scenario in which all ground forces would be employed by one HQ.[78]

Levi wrote:

The decision to establish the Mafhash was made in 1983, when the IDF was still in Lebanon and had just withdrawn from Beirut and deployed along the Awali River. During the discussion the idea was raised that the IDF needs the Mafhash, but not now, not while it's deployed in Lebanon and engaged in combat. I repudiated this charge and decided to authorize the establishment of the Mafhash.[79]

From the little that Levi spoke about the matter, we can gather that he realized that intercorps cooperation had to improve.[80] In an article that was released immediately upon the completion of his tenure, he wrote that the need to coordinate the structure and organization of the ground corps was clear; there was no longer any room for their separation. The war in Lebanon was an additional catalyst for implementing changes in view of developments in the combined arms battlefield and the assimilation of complex technological systems.[81]

In a 1985 address, Levi supported the Mafhash's autonomy vis-à-vis the general staff: "The ground HQ should have its own shoulder patch. It cannot be called the 'ground HQ' and wear the 'general staff' patch."[82]

In the June 20, 1983, general staff discussion, the chief of staff summed up the principles in establishing the Mafhash: "Our gaze has to be on the future and not on wars of the past." He determined that:

1. The Mafhash staff must be strong and authoritative.
2. It is better to establish a chief armor officer's headquarters rather than an Armored Corps HQ. The chief armor officer will be a brigadier general, not a major general, and will not participate in general staff meetings.
3. The Mafhash will be set up in stages and will gradually receive its resources and areas of responsibility.[83]

Despite the chief of staff's summary, internal opposition to the Mafhash still raged. In a general staff discussion on November 21,

1983, Mahad decided that Agat's proposal would weaken the general staff, because the R&D department would be disbanded, the combined arms combat doctrine department would be scaled back, and the proposal that the Mafhash would be given control over the training budgets was incompatible with the general staff's responsibility for training the regional commands. Instead of removing responsibility from the doctrine and training branch, Mahad argued, the Mafhash should receive the responsibilities that the corps headquarters currently had, that is, solely in the professional domain. The head of Mahad, Major General Yossi Peled, charged that the Mafhash was incapable of coping with all of the problems while operating full time as the Ground Forces HQ before a decision was made to establish it as a full service. The chief armor officer staunchly opposed any damage to the combat corps that had done an excellent job in developing the IDF's combat doctrine and had contributed to its victories. He agreed that the IDF had a problem with the combined arms battle, and therefore he was not averse to the establishment of the Mafhash, but he believed it was unnecessary "to pay" for it by hurting the general staff rather than by introducing additional manpower standards. Major General Amnon Lipkin-Shahak believed that the Mafhash could be of benefit, but he was unconvinced that its establishment was of top priority, especially in consideration of the resources that would have to be allocated. He also feared the damage that would be caused to the existing corps. Shomron, who was designated to be the Mafhash's first commander, stressed that even though the decision had been made to establish the headquarters, it was not too late to reverse course and revoke the decision.[84]

On the other hand, Peled, the head of Mahad, wrote that "the Mafhash eroded the authorities of Mahad. [Nevertheless] I saw [it] as the answer to a real need."[85] It is difficult to know his true position since Peled seems to have been struggling for extended responsibilities in the field of training even after the establishment of the Mafhash. Only in 1992 was the responsibility for instruction development transferred from Mahad to the Mafhash.

Shomron, the Mafhash commander, expressed a third perspective. After Levi was appointed chief of staff (following which Major General Avigdor Ben Gal resigned, after turning down Levi's offer to be the commander of the Mafhash), Arens persuaded Shomron, who was also considering retirement, "to continue his military service with the express promise that he would receive responsibility for establishing the Mafhash and would be appointed deputy chief of staff immediately at the conclusion of his posting as Mafhash commander."[86]

Shomron was not only in favor of the Mafhash, he even held a maximalist position of a full ground service. As a champion of renewal, in this sense he had enthusiastically supported the idea for a long time. Levi and Shomron finalized the framework of activity and responsibilities of the new HQ a few days before Shomron stepped into the new role. They agreed that "the Mafhash would deal with ground force design, the development of combat doctrine, weapons acquisition, manpower screening and allocation in the ground forces, and education and training." We can infer from their mutual understanding that the new HQ would have greater responsibility than what they first thought. It would, in effect, receive its authority in areas taken from Mahad and the chief officers of the ground corps. Shomron's order of the day stated: "The Mafhash will be responsible for ground force design. [It will receive] the powers from various elements that currently deal with force design so that better use can be made of the available resources."[87]

Later, as the chief of staff, Shomron published an article entitled, "The Mafhash: The Basis for the Development of the Ground Forces," in which he laid out in detail the paramount importance of the Mafhash in its first years.[88] Even under Shomron's command, the final staff work for the establishment of the Mafhash had been a rough ride, with internal opposition still vocal. The chief officers of the corps did not take part in the initial discussions on the Mafhash's framework for the chief of staff's approval. Shomron was concerned that deep conflicts of interest would frustrate the completion of the plan in the short time that the chief of staff had allotted. All of the corps commanders, especially the chief armor officer and chief infantry and paratrooper officer, objected to any change and had still not grasped the fact that the decision to establish the Mafhash was final. They remained contrarian and contentious, and on more than one occasion the arguments became raucous shouting matches.[89]

On December 18, 1983, the Mafhash was officially inaugurated. Yet even after its establishment the bickering continued. "The chief officers of the corps knew how to exploit the rancor and tension between Shomron and the chief of staff and wield their connections on the general staff to gain resources and manpower that the Mafhash was unable to provide," Ze'ev Drori recounted.[90] Yitzhak Mordechai, the chief infantry and paratrooper officer, said: "Levi may have given support, but not responsibility, powers and resources, which created great friction and enabled the ground corps to bypass the Mafhash staff."[91] Levi's biographer claims the opposite, that Levi put his full weight behind the Mafhash and that his move to subordinate all of the corps to the branches (the ordnance and logistics corps to the logistics branch; human resources, the women's corps, the education corps, and the military police corps to the manpower branch) was designed, among other reasons, to neutralize the ground corps' opposition to the Mafhash.[92]

Summary of the Test Case

Discussions on the Mafhash went on for seven years, from Weizman's tenure as defense minister to the HQ's establishment. This was a complex, hard-fought process that witnessed the struggle between two defense ministers and a deputy defense minister and three chiefs of staff. An analysis of the moves of chiefs of staff Gur and Eitan vis-à-vis Defense Minister Weizman reveals the different strategies employed by the sides.

On the political side, we see the formation of a committee from outside the IDF and the proposal to appoint a commander (Tal) from outside the army (Tal was a retired major general) and the stipulation of the appointment of the chief of staff (Eitan) on his willingness to establish the Mafhash; the transfer of the issue to the Knesset's Foreign Affairs and Defense Committee (in order to receive government approval for "strengthening" the IDF); and finally a joint press conference to announce the decision. While the defense ministers' insistence on implementing the decision over the years seems to have been closely tied to the shortcomings in the Yom Kippur War, political considerations cannot be ruled out, such as demonstrating leadership, as Gur noted, as well as personal considerations, such as the struggle between Tzipori and Eitan.

On the military side, attempts were made to put off the realization of the political echelon's intention by dragging out staff work, enlisting internal opposition to reinforce the chief of staff's position relative to the political echelon, and bolstering those bodies in the IDF whose authority stood to be curtailed because of the establishment of the Mafhash. Gur based his proactive opposition on claims that the ORBAT expansion was the main thing, not organizational transformation, and that he had no intention of surrendering his responsibility for ground force employment as the Field Forces Headquarters version envisioned. Eitan seems not to have believed in the need for the Mafhash, nor was he an expert in the staff work required for implementing the change; therefore, he opposed it passively. Levi carried out the plan, but only in its watered-down version that did not threaten the status of the chief of staff as the operator of the ground forces. When Levi was forced to carry out the decision, which went against his previous position as a commander of a regional command, he did so while scaling down the internal opposition and waiting until the feisty Armored Corps commander, Moshe Bar-Kochva, was promoted to commander of Southern Command. In addition, he strengthened Mahad under Yossi Peled despite the transfer of some of its responsibilities to the Mafhash, while preserving the friction that had developed between the corps commanders and its first commander, Dan Shomron, and others due to the whittling down of the newly established Mafhash's responsibilities.

The story of the Mafhash illustrates a rather similar pattern of action by the three chiefs of staff, forced by the political echelon to carry out a change that they opposed. The lesson to be drawn for the political echelon is that when asking the IDF to make a substantial organizational reform (like the one that has been raised in recent years to build a new Missile Arm in addition to the IAF), a long and consistent effort is essential.

Dan Shomron and Yitzhak Rabin on the Lavi Jet Fighter, 1985–87

The fourth test case deals with Defense Minister Yitzhak Rabin's opposition to the Lavi jet fighter project and the backing that he received from Chief of Staff Dan Shomron to revoke the previous defense minister's decision on behalf of the project.

In early 1980, despite opposition from Chief of Staff Rafael Eitan and the IAF commander, David Ivry, to the initial proposal for a relatively small aircraft, Defense Minister Weizman decided in favor of developing the jet fighter.[93] Eitan and Ivry preferred American-made aircraft and supported improvements in the Israeli-produced Kfir. Later, Eitan agreed to the IAF's proposal to install an upgraded American engine in the Lavi, which would entail an increase in the cost and changes in its designation from a relatively low-priced attack plane to an expensive multitask jet fighter. The main challenge facing the Lavi was that the entire cost would be subsumed within the defense budget.

The main proponent of the Lavi project was Defense Minister Moshe Arens, a former senior figure in the aircraft industry who replaced Ariel Sharon (Weizman's replacement). In 1984, Arens successfully convinced the Americans, who had been against the project since its inception, to allow Israel to funnel $250 million a year in US financial aid toward the plane's development.

In August 1985, Defense Minister Rabin, Chief of Staff Levi, and the commander of the IAF, Amos Lapidot, examined the project's status and found that the overall cost (development and production of 210 aircraft by the end of the twentieth century) would come to $2.5 billion, a figure far above the price of acquiring F-16s. Rabin recommended continuing the development but only under the following conditions: (1) American assistance for the project would continue; (2) at least half of the production would be carried out in the United States; and (3) the scope of financing the series production would not exceed $550 million a year.

The United States asked Israel to look for alternatives, claiming that Israel lacked the economic capability to carry out the project without additional American aid and that such assistance would not be forthcoming. Therefore, any deviation from the Lavi budget would have to come from the defense budget, at the price of other replenishment plans. However, even while discussion was taking place, the project progressed. Between 1984 and 1986 development continued, and the unveiling ceremony of the first prototype took place in July 1986.

Levi and the IDF supported the process until early 1986, when it became obvious that the necessary cutback in the defense budget, approximately $600 million, would not be a one-time affair. Levi conditioned the continuation of the Lavi's development on "finding budgetary sources outside the defense budget."[94]

In July, an Israeli newspaper article revealed that the IDF would have to demand an annual addition of hundreds of millions of dollars for the defense budget, approximately 15 percent higher than the current budget. The need for the additional funding stemmed from the estimate that the present IDF budget was insufficient to provide answers to the expected threats from the Arab armies. "Even if the money needed for the Lavi project is removed from the defense budget, it will still fall short by about $100 million a year for the IDF's basic needs," *Ha'aretz* reported.[95] The next day, the chief of staff informed military correspondents, "From the data that we collected in preparation for the IDF's multiyear work plan, it turns out that even if the necessary funds for the Lavi project do not come from the defense budget, it will still be only a partial lifeline to the IDF's budgetary requirements."[96]

Shomron opposed the project at a relatively early stage based on his understanding and his plans for developing the ground forces (see chapter 5 on changes in the direction of force design). He had been articulating his misgivings about the project since 1985, when he was deputy chief of staff and had received the support of the head of Agat, Aviyhu Ben Nun.[97] In February 1987, two months before his appointment to chief of staff, Shomron's three main arguments against the project's continuation were clarified. The economic argument was that the project's financial strain on the defense budget was so heavy that it would leave the IDF no flexibility for planning and implementing the multiyear plan. Continuation of the Lavi would prevent the security establishment from investing more time, human resources, and finances in areas no less crucial on the future battlefield. The operational argument posited that the continuation of the project would prevent the IAF from procuring more advanced aircraft at a later date. A final argument held that the continuation of the Lavi project would cause direct and critical damage to the force design of the ground forces, thus rendering them incapable of achieving victory in the next war.[98]

In the wake of the article, Shomron was dressed down by Prime Minister Yitzhak Shamir. Dov Zakheim, the American deputy under secretary of defense and senior government representative to Israel, recalled that to the best of his knowledge Shomron, as deputy chief of staff, had a powerful influence on the cabinet members delegated with security matters and that a leak of his anti-Lavi position was a significant matter.[99] On April 19, 1987, Shomron was inaugurated chief of staff, and the following excerpt appeared in a *Ha'aretz* newspaper article a month later:

> Will Chief of Staff Dan Shomron have to submit his resignation if the government overrides his recommendations and warnings and continues with the development of the Lavi at the expense of the IDF's budget? This is not a rhetorical question. Whoever listens to Shomron, as the ministers have on several occasions, knows that the chief of staff honestly believes that if the cost of the Lavi's development and production comes from the defense ministry's coffers, the IDF will go hopelessly bankrupt. Other IDF development plans will die out. The ground forces could very

well atrophy. When the air force receives the Lavi in the 1990s, it will be unprepared for the future battlefield. The qualitative gap between us and the Arab armies will narrow significantly and take several years to repair.[100]

The clash over the project also brought great tension to the relationship between the new chief of staff and Ivry, now general manager of the defense ministry and also now one of the Lavi's advocates. On July 13, 1985, the defense minister had approved the chief of staff's work plan for the acquisition and absorption of 150 to 200 F-16 fighter aircraft. Ivry, the deputy chief of staff at the time and a former IAF commander, argued that the work plan had already been approved and could not be reopened. Prime Minister Rabin agreed to let Shomron change it.[101]

As stated, Rabin approved the continuation of the project in August 1985 but seems to have changed his mind in mid-1986. The explanation, as he admits, was the reassessment of priorities due to the cutbacks in the defense budget.[102] The defense ministry comptroller's report and the staff work in Agat may have contributed to his change of heart.[103] It is important to mention as the background to Rabin's decision that Israel was close to bankruptcy and experiencing mushrooming inflation in this period. In early 1987, Rabin agreed to the American proposal to look into alternatives to the Lavi. Zakheim wrote that the IAF commander, Major General Amos Lapidot, who supported the Lavi project, was told to cooperate with the Americans on the matter "on Rabin's orders."[104]

Rabin's problem was that his turnaround on the Lavi encountered wide opposition by individuals such as Yitzhak Shamir, the alternate prime minister in the coalition government, Foreign Minister Shimon Peres, and ministers Arens, Sharon, David Levy, and others. Other supporters of the project were Ivry (previously the chairman of Israel Aerospace Industries), Lapidot, Menachem Eini (project head in the defense ministry), and persons in Israel Aerospace Industries.

Rabin enlisted to his side Shomron as deputy chief of staff and various members of the general staff, such as the commander of the navy,

Avraham Ben Shoshan, who stated in an interview on July 24, 1987, that "as long as the Lavi is on the table, there's no chance that we'll negotiate with the American shipyards about construction of the Israeli navy's future vessels."[105] The general staff's main proponent for canceling the project was Major General Aviyhu Ben Nun, the head of Agat, who had been appointed IAF commander that year. In a five-hour cabinet meeting on June 1, Shomron presented his reasons for discontinuing the project. Rabin also encouraged the defense industries that were not tied to the project (Tadiran, Rafael, and others) to oppose it, because it compromised the development of other weapons.[106] Rabin leveraged the chief of staff's stance and the opposition of members of the general staff to advance his new position in the face of significant opposition. Rabin still did not sum up his opposition in the present round of government meetings, but in the meantime took an unprecedented step. In the past he had forbidden the generals to publicly express their opinion on the Lavi and other issues without prior approval. This time Rabin granted across-the-board permission to speak: "Generals, officers, the heads of the defense industries, workers committees; everyone was allowed to voice his opinion of the Lavi," journalist Ze'ev Schiff reported.[107]

At the last minute, Rabin managed to enlist Moshe Nissim, the finance minister and Likud party member, and Foreign Minister Peres. On August 30 the government decided by a twelve to eleven vote (with one abstention) to cancel the Lavi project. In response, Arens (now a minister without portfolio) resigned.[108]

Summary of the Test Case

This case illustrates a situation in which Chief of Staff Shomron, who had swum against the current because of priority considerations even before his appointment to chief of staff in 1985–86, and who had opposed Defense Minister Rabin's position, became a central figure in the midst of the process with the ability to influence the political echelon, especially when Rabin reversed his opinion and pressed to have the Lavi project canceled. Shomron's position on the Lavi undoubtedly benefited him and led to Rabin appointing him chief of staff. Arens, who later became defense minister and Shomron's superior, wrote that he held no grudge against him for making what he (Arens) felt was a great mistake. It seems that Shomron's public esteem as the commander of the Entebbe operation (the July 4, 1976, liberation of hostages by an Israeli commando operation in Uganda) was a major factor in his ability to get his ideas into the civilian sphere.

Chapter Summary

This chapter focused on a specific area of civil-military relations—the issues surrounding force design. It presented a wide range of relations: the resignation of a chief of staff because of disagreement with the defense minister; a chief of staff's attempt to enlist the defense minister to his side in an internal IDF debate, when the defense minister had no interest in playing the role that the chief of staff was scripting for him; the various methods that three chiefs of staff employed not to implement a change that the political echelon demanded, while the political echelon also employed various methods to persuade them to implement the change; and a case in which the chief of staff's position helped the defense minister to reverse an earlier political decision that the government wanted to see implemented. Each case also described other internal issues about the chief of staff's conduct, such as the difficulty in making essential changes when a powerful general staff member stood in opposition, as in the case of Dayan and Laskov, or the chief of staff's reliance on his prestige as a war hero, as in the case of Shomron and the Lavi.

CONCLUSIONS

In view of the extensive literature that deals with the IDF's rich history, its wars, battles, and soldiers, it is surprising to discover a major gap in comparative research on Israeli military studies. For example, one would search in vain for comparative works on the performance of commanders and headquarters or the development of IDF combat doctrine and force design. This book is primarily a comparison of the chiefs of staff according to certain criteria, but I hope that it will also serve as a precursor to the type of research that the IDF sorely lacks and other military establishments can benefit from.

Each of the twenty-one chiefs of staff (as of 2020, and not including current officeholder Aviv Kochavi) who have led the IDF in a wide range of actions should have an authoritative comprehensive biography devoted to him (and each of them should review his own tenure in writing). This book's aim has not been to evaluate the chiefs of staff's successes or failures but to look at their conduct in one or more of the six aspects that were chosen for the study. Lest any misunderstanding exist, there are other aspects that beg for future research.

The challenging role of the chief of staff demands profound knowledge in a vast range of fields, as well as the ability to manage and command at a level that allows him to serve as the highest authority on an endless number of matters. He must be gifted with a sharp instinct for identifying change and he must emanate the authority to generate processes, deal with internal and external opposition, and display sangfroid in tense situations. Those who are appointed chiefs of staff have been meticulously screened during their military careers in the multitude of posts they have filled and are expected to discharge all the abovementioned qualities to the highest degree possible, if only because of the rigorous selection process. Since the role of chief of staff is so critical, professional duty calls for a serious study on it so that the IDF can learn and correct itself.

This book presumes that a critical analysis of these aspects of conduct can improve a chief of staff's performance by his awareness of the range of behaviors that his predecessors exhibited in coping with various situations, often similar to those he is facing.

Précis of Each Chapter's Insights

Chapter 1 dealt with the chief of staff's role in identifying a change in the security situation, declaring it, and initiating the necessary action. It concluded that the greatest assistance to the chief of staff in identifying a shift in reality is the wide range of operational and strategic challenges that he faced in his previous roles and the learning mechanisms that he devised to meet the developing challenges. In cases where rapid change is demanded, such as the shift from routine security to war, announcements and written communiqués have to be backed by practical steps that unite the entire army behind the new war reality. This can be accomplished, for example, by mobilizing the reserves, activating plans with code names that relate to a wartime situation, or removing safety constraints on the use of weapons that are applied in routine security.

Chapter 2 sought to establish a criterion for a chief of staff from the ground forces gaining familiarity with the air force's plans so that he can engage in a professional discussion with the IAF commander (and vice versa for a chief of staff from the air force regarding ground force plans). This knowledge is of paramount importance because the GHQ is the only real joint HQ in the IDF. The chief of staff from the ground forces must be able to shift priorities when plans go awry in aerial fighting. Given the fluctuations in the geopolitical, operational, and technological environment, the chief of staff should not only be knowledgeable in the air force modus operandi and its plans but also play an active role in developing the aerial combat concept. Taking this understanding one step further, the chief of staff needs to acquire greater knowledge in a wide range of areas, from cyber and space to lawfare. This requires the senior military echelons to promote generals with the potential to be future chiefs of staff to positions in various branches and fields of expertise that they are unacquainted with.

Chapter 3 discussed the dynamics that led to the loss of trust between the chief of staff and the commander of a regional command during fighting. The factors in such an imbroglio included the following:

- A preexisting gap in basic approaches and concepts—if these gaps are not aired before the war, they will almost certainly explode in a crisis of trust during the fighting
- Preexisting knowledge gaps on the eve of a war including the lack of a common professional language
- Gaps in expectations that emerge during the fighting, such as the level and pace of performance
- Inaccurate reporting, requests flowing in at an unprecedented rate or manner, changes in force employment that deviate from what was previously agreed on by the chief of staff without updating him
- Gaps stemming from staff work prepared by the two echelons
- The chief of staff's belief that the regional commander has lost control of his subordinates
- Occasionally, the intervention of senior commanders from outside the standard chain of command in a manner that exacerbates the trust gap

The solution should include the methodical interechelon development of knowledge between the political echelon and the general staff, regional command, and services in peacetime. Leaders should insist on the resolution of differences, which can be done in a discreet manner in periods of peace before they turn into a public display of a "war of the generals." This clarification, while absolutely necessary as it may be, is still not enough. Once a confrontation erupts in a new strategic context, interechelon gaps will surface. The answer that the book proposes is learning forums for dealing with the above-mentioned conditions. These thinking forums will not focus on the question of "what to do" (which is reserved for other forums) but on the expectations from the regional command echelon, the identification of obstacles in relaying knowledge, the source of information gaps, and such. Another element that can help in bridging the gap between the chief of staff and the regional commander lies in the role of the "deputy regional commander" (and other shadow roles held by members of the general staff) that Chief of Staff Gabi Ashkenazi added after the Second Lebanon War in order to avoid the need (quite likely based on past experience) to appoint "a representative of the chief of staff" to the command in the midst of the fighting. The person filling this role is a former general who is agreed upon by the chief of staff and the commander of the regional command, service, or branch and who will aid in mediating between echelons as the situation requires.

Chapter 4 described the pattern of action that repeats itself after a crisis and contains its own logic based on Israel's and the IDF's needs. This pattern homes in on improving the army's proficiency level through education and training, manpower enhancement, increasing or maintaining ORBAT that was seen as falling short of the number needed in the confrontation, and halting the introduction of organizational changes that can destabilize the system when it is focused on rehabilitation from the crisis. A major byproduct of this focus is the decrease, and sometimes the total cessation, of the development of new ideas for the future. Recovery from the two historical crises seems to have taken a decade in each case. In this light, the book recommends setting up mechanisms that enable the cultivation of new ideas so that an army after crisis can get back on track to the future from this "back to basics" rehabilitation period as quickly as possible.

Chapter 5 presented three cases of change in force design that illustrated different forms of process management. The takeaway insight for the future lies in the realm of risk management, the main point being that when focusing on a scenario or enemy, contingency plans for closing gaps in a low priority scenario must be made. The larger the gap that is expected to develop, the more comprehensive the answer must be. As part of this planning, the time span that an army needs to return to competency and preparedness for the low priority scenario should be carefully decided.

Chapter 6 sketched four patterns of action that chiefs of staff have taken in dealing with the political echelon: resignation because of an unbridgeable disagreement; harnessing the political echelon to the chief of staff's needs; foot-dragging in the implementation of the political echelon's instructions; and the political echelon's recruitment of the military echelon for its purposes. The chief of staff's ability to influence the political echelon depends a great deal on his public persona compared to that of the political echelon at the time.

Additional Aspects of the Role of Chief of Staff

In addition to the test cases that illustrate different aspects of the chief of staff's performance, the study has raised a number of issues that should be noted before discussing the integrated analysis.

The Chief of Staff as a Public Figure Who Represents the Entire IDF

This book opens by noting the role that the chief of staff institution plays in Israel and its wider implications—from the establishment of basic public norms to deterrence of enemies, as in Prime Minister

Menachem Begin's warning, "Watch out, Assad . . . Yanush [Avigdor Ben-Gal] and Raful [Rafael Eitan] are coming."[1]

In Israeli polls, the IDF scores far higher on public trust than other public institutions. The degree of trust in the chief of staff as the representative of the IDF has an incalculable effect on his ability to amass solidarity in defense of the country. Be that as it may, like the rest of the IDF (and many other institutions) in recent years, the chief of staff has been the target of an increasing volley of public criticism, especially with respect to judicial or public investigating committees, which is of great importance as long it relates to professional matters. But this exposure causes significant damage when it spills over to the personal arena and maligns the chief of staff's character, motives, or political positions. The most politically controversial area—events in the West Bank and Gaza Strip—is fertile ground for chief of staff bashing, and a large part of the public apparently considers the army the main tool of the old "establishment" that is blocking long-needed political changes (as this public perceives them) on the Palestinian issue.

An early example of public criticism is the scorching that Dan Shomron received on his command of the IDF in the first intifada, when he became the object of vilification by government ministers and Knesset members from the right, from the left, from the West Bank settlers, and from members of the left-wing "Peace Now" Movement, as well as from right- and left-wing journalists (who accused Shomron of ignoring cases of abuse in the Israeli-controlled territories).[2] After the funeral of the soldier Avi Sasportas in May 1989, young thugs tried to overturn the chief of staff's car.[3]

Another example is the jeer of "Nazi chief of staff," leveled at Dan Halutz prior to the Gaza Strip disengagement in 2005.[4] A relatively new case is the attitude of the media, the public, and certain government ministers to the statements and declarations by Chief of Staff Gadi Eisenkot to the shooting of a wounded terrorist by an IDF soldier in Hebron in March 2016.

The chief of staff should not be immune to criticism, but using his status for gaining public attention to those who criticize him is liable to corrode the institution whose importance, as noted, is immense. The real damage to national security is reprehensible.

Appointing the Chief of Staff and the Chief of Staff's Influence on the Choice of a Successor

Although each chief of staff appointment is made in a particular context composed of many variables, these considerations can roughly be divided into three periods. The first is the Ben-Gurion period. David Ben-Gurion preferred veterans who had served in the British army and the Hagana, as well as officers affiliated with Mapai (his political party), instead of Palmach veterans and soldiers associated with Mapam (the rival political party). This period witnessed the appointments of Yigael Yadin, Mordechai Maklef, Moshe Dayan (a Palmach veteran himself who nevertheless sacked the Hagana "old-timers"), Haim Laskov, Tzvi Tzur, and Asaf Simhoni (a potential candidate whose life was cut short in an airplane accident).

The second period can be termed the "military sectors" period, a preference for armor corps officers, such as Haim Bar-Lev and David Elazar after the Six-Day War, followed by a preference for paratrooper commanders: Mordechai Gur, Eitan, Moshe Levi, Shomron, Ehud Barak, Amnon Lipkin-Shahak, Shaul Mofaz, and Moshe Ya'alon.

The third period, the current one, is characterized by a "clean" choice of senior commanders who are best suited to the IDF's particular needs at the time (which is not to detract from the suitability of the previous chiefs of staff)—Halutz, Ashkenazi, Yoav Galant (a candidate), Benny Gantz, Eisenkot, and Kochavi—when one criterion for the post is the candidate's proximity to the prime minister. Based on this division, Yitzhak Rabin's appointment to chief of staff seems to fit the last period, since he cannot be pigeonholed in the other categories.

The political echelon's degree of control over the IDF has been studied at great length. This book describes two coexisting patterns: the appointment of the chiefs of staff and the extension (or not) of their tenures. Many chiefs of staff were appointed and their tenure lengthened or shortened depending on their willingness to carry out government policy. Regarding the ethics of selecting a chief of staff, an Israeli scholar has written that "a candidate's suitability for realizing the policy is always a major, if not decisive, factor. Its importance is so great that it justifies the acceptance of certain drawbacks in a candidate."[5]

There is no shortage of examples. Yadin resigned after his falling-out with Ben-Gurion over cutbacks; Laskov ended his role after three years for several reasons, a main one being friction with the proactive deputy defense minister Shimon Peres; Levi was appointed because he agreed to establish the Field Forces Headquarters/Mafhash; Shomron's opposition to the Lavi project was a key factor in his appointment to chief of staff; by Halutz's own admission, one of the reasons for his appointment to the post was his consent to carry out the Gaza disengagement.[6]

On the other hand, a danger exists in choosing a chief of staff on the basis of the political echelon's policy at the time of the appointment or even the expectation that the chief of staff will remain subordinate to particular officeholders—whereas in reality, the political constellation can change during his tenure. For example, Halutz stepped into his post when political leaders with rich military backgrounds stood at the helm—Prime Minister Ariel Sharon and Defense Minister Shaul Mofaz—and he entered the Second Lebanon War under the government of Prime Minister Ehud Olmert and Defense Minister Amir Peretz, both of whom had limited experience in military affairs. Another example is the five-year tenure of Eitan under Defense Minister Ezer Weizman, Deputy Defense Minister Morechai Tzipori, and Defense Minister Sharon. Under these circumstances, and with an eye to the future, the political echelon should appoint the chief of staff by taking into account his role as the leader of a major national institution rather than the executor of a particular policy.

As stated, an important element in the relationship between the political and military echelons is the chief of staff's influence on the choice of his successor. In some cases the chief of staff tried to convince the political echelon that his deputy was ill fitted to be the chief of staff

(Moshe Dayan regarding Laskov; Levi regarding Shomron; Mofaz regarding Uzi Dayan). In other cases the chief of staff tried to have his candidate chosen as his successor, as in Chief of Staff Levi's attempt to promote Amir Drori to deputy chief of staff by means of short-term posts on the general staff, in a bid to oust Shomron.[7] Another example is Chief of Staff Lipkin-Shahak's fast-track advancement of Mofaz from commander of Southern Command to the head of Agat for eighteen months followed by his promotion to deputy chief of staff (this came after another potential candidate, Nechemia Tamari, was killed in a helicopter crash).[8] In other instances (see chapter 4) the main consideration in choosing the chief of staff was his not having fought in a war that was perceived as a failure (Gur after the Yom Kippur War and Ashkenazi after the Second Lebanon War).

The Chief of Staff's Schedule

The introduction stated that one of the primary functions of the chief of staff is determining the IDF's agenda. A chief of staff who wants to introduce a change usually gets down to business as soon as he assumes office. This phenomenon is seen with many chiefs of staff: Moshe Dayan narrowing the hierarchical gap between the general staff and the field echelons and pushing devotion to mission accomplishment; Lipkin-Shahak defining activity in the Lebanese arena as combat rather than routine security; Mofaz leading the organizational changes known as IDF 2000; and Halutz introducing organizational changes in 2005–6. But more is needed than just an early start. The chief of staff who wishes to introduce significant changes must apportion a large part of his time to the effort (see Gur and Ashkenazi on training reorganization, Shomron and Barak on PGMs, and Eisenkot on the Gideon multiyear plan).

Given the concentration of the chief of staff's (and political echelon's) attention to force employment, which puts both echelons to the test relatively quickly, most of the chief of staff's time is diverted to this area and less to force design (which entails organizational changes).

In this context, the chief of staff's ability to arrange his schedule, taking into account the time he must spend on things like visits to units, operational debriefings, and meetings with the political echelon, also depends on external circumstances such as the daily security situation. Time management is of the essence for two reasons: first is the actual time that the chief of staff spends on the issues dear to his heart; second is the message that he conveys to the entire IDF regarding his priorities (see Gur's focus on training after the Yom Kippur War or Dayan's focus on building self-confidence in the forces before the Sinai War). The army soon identifies which areas the chief of staff relegates to the back burner. According to Major General (res.) Shlomo Gazit, the former head of Chief of Staff Dayan's office, Dayan stated that:

> As the commander responsible for twenty or thirty different areas, I could allocate my time to, say, twenty of them, and then devote to each of them 5 percent of the total amount of time. Even then I would be hard pressed to spend 5 percent on effective input. On the other hand, I can develop a different approach and organize an efficient staff run by a deputy or head of the staff. Each staff knows how to arrange the entire 100 percent of the area under its responsibility. . . . I then choose one or two areas to concentrate the lion's share of my energy on and thus do my maximum to revolutionize those areas.[9]

The appointments of suitable subordinate commanders and effective staff officers are fundamental tools in the chief of staff's ability to create the time needed to focus on matters most important to him.

An Integrated Analysis: The Role of the Chief of Staff in a Complex System and the Conditions That Aid in Success

The chief of staff's unique role puts him in two different worlds. Above him is the multiparty political echelon that by its nature is permanently under political constraints. Israel's government system based on a co-alition of parties makes it difficult for the defense minister, who represents the government in relations with the chief of staff, to reach an agreement or crystallize a position on a given problem. Under these circumstances, the chief of staff needs to bridge the gap informally but very practically. (The IDF's attempt to use the 2002 strategy document to introduce order into this appears in the introduction to this book.) An example of attempting to close the coherency gap in the national security concept is the IDF strategy document that Chief of Staff Eisenkot published "bottom up" in 2015 because the political echelon never released a "top down" national security strategy document. In this case an enormous burden falls on the chief of staff, while his staff (see following) finds it difficult to support him.

The echelon below the chief of staff is the general staff, a C2 body and an advisory body, made up of overburdened officers, some of them serving in multiple roles, like the IAF commander who is both the air adviser and the commander of a service/command. In this light, the general staff officers are less suited to the chief of staff's needs than the officers on the divisional, regional command and service staffs to their commanders' needs. This suitability gap stems from two factors: first, the relatively limited experience of most general staff officers in working with the political sphere—a situation that prevents the chief of staff from receiving their help in this domain; and second, the large number of functions that the chief of staff must fulfill in directing force design and force employment and the wide range of expertise needed for their successful realization. Thus, a situation develops where on average (for the sake of illustration) half the time half the members of the general staff are irrelevant to the issues on the agenda. This is apparent in the composition of the participants in discussions, which sometime changes substantially according to the issue at hand.

This book makes it clear that the myriad roles that the chief of staff is expected to perform are beyond the capacity of one person. The Americans realized this and divided the role of "commander of the armed forces" between the chairman of the joint chiefs of staff (who is responsible for force design and advises the president on general matters of armed forces employment) and the combatant commanders (who are in charge of theaters of operations and are directly subordinate to the president). The situation in Israel, where the chief of staff alone is directly subordinate to the political echelon, is different. This book offers certain insights that may assist the chief of staff in carrying out his work.

The Chief of Staff's Personal Experience

The first element is building the chief of staff candidate's firsthand experience by having him serve in roles that provide the largest repertoire of knowledge that he will need.[10] For example, potential candidates should be given roles (from brigadier general level and up) in a wide range of fighting arenas. Until the 1980s, these were Sinai and the Golan Heights. In the 1973 Yom Kippur War, Elazar's rich experience in the north was offset by his near-total unfamiliarity with Sinai, where space and time dimensions in force employment were vastly different from the Golan. The IDF paid the price for this shortcoming. In recent decades, the main arenas are in the north, especially the Hezbollah threat and the Palestinian theater in the West Bank and Gaza Strip. The candidate's familiarity with a range of theaters by having served as division commander or regional command's chief of staff or commander is critical for his successful performance in the future.

Understanding the political echelon demands more than the "fair measure" that Halutz mentioned. Therefore, another role of great value is the prime minister's military secretary, although some feel that the role "politicizes" the officeholder.

The chief of staff must acquire in-depth knowledge of Aman in order to understand its paramount position in the IDF. An intelligence background will also gain him direct contact with the political decision makers and, equally important, enable him to evaluate intelligence assessments and deal with Aman's powerful influence on the political sphere.

A chief of staff from the ground forces must be familiar with the air and sea services and also with communications and cyber organizations through his previous roles. He should be well versed in their operational and force design plans, have firsthand knowledge of their units from having visited them, participate in their conceptual discussions, and tour their test sites. All of this will provide him with an invaluable background, within time constraints, of the other services' development of concepts and ways of thinking that will assist him in future decision making.

The importance of the role of the deputy chief of staff, the senior IDF staff role, cannot be overstated, especially in cases when the person filling the role did not serve as a branch head or the commander of a service (which includes force design). It must be noted that personal experience, for all its value, contains the danger of overreliance on it and the possibility that the chief of staff will ascribe too much value to his experience that brought him to his current position. Therefore, two more areas (which I explore below) are of prime relevance: the appointment of supplementary role players and the chief of staff's proactive learning.

The Appointment of Supplementary Role Players

The second element is the appointment of assistants to supplement the chief of staff's knowledge gaps and challenge his ideas. Two examples: Halutz appointed Major General Moshe Kaplinsky to complement his lack of experience with ground forces, although the desired result seems not to have been achieved in the Second Lebanon War; and Eitan appointed Moshe Levi deputy chief of staff to assist him in staff work, an area he had little experience in. From the test cases it is difficult to identify officers whose job was to challenge the chief of staff's thinking, but there were periods when brigadiers or major generals did just that. Most periods had their "troublemakers" on the general staff who opposed the chief of staff's views in various areas. Some notable examples are Laskov's disagreement with Dayan on armor employment, Sharon's opposition to Bar-Lev on the defense of Sinai, and Moshe Bar-Kochva's criticism of Shomron in the first intifada. Invariably, the oppositionist's opinion proved invaluable for the IDF's functioning.

The Chief of Staff's Proactive Learning on the Basis of Processes and Mechanisms for Knowledge Development

The third element that can assist the chief of staff in carrying out his role is building a storehouse of learning processes and mechanisms for knowledge development adapted to the broad spectrum of topics he deals with. Given the scope of the challenges and the pace of change, the chief of staff spends a great deal of his time interpreting the implications of the change and studying the relevancy of the IDF's plans, concepts, and capabilities.

This book has presented different learning mechanisms that the chiefs of staff employed for concrete problems. Examples are "the operational discussion on armor employment" that Dayan convened in September 1956 that brought dozens of armor officers and the prime minister–defense minister together; Elazar's thinking group in the Yom Kippur War that included Deputy Chief of Staff Israel Tal, Eli Zeira, the head of Aman, and his predecessor Aharon Yariv, as well as Rehavam Ze'evi and, when necessary, Benny Peled, the IAF commander; Mofaz's Forward Drive exercise in April 2000 before the confrontation with the Palestinians; Ya'alon's thinking forum and the establishment of the role of assistant on thinking matters; and Gantz's tours of the Golan Heights in order to grasp the problem up close.

General staff war games are an important tool for testing concepts and plans. The chief of staff's role is to identify the problem or knowledge gap that the learning process or war game will focus on and, of equal importance, the concept or approach to be tested. These mechanisms are not alternatives to formal situation assessments, presentations of plans for approval, and the like, but they are crucial supplementary aids for the chief of staff. Moreover, when he wants to generate a basic change in military organization, these mechanisms are several times as important because the standard method of staff work generally inclines its participants—members of the general staff—to reach a consensus that translates into only minor changes in the system. The defense minister has to be integrated into these processes so that a coherent multiechelon concept can be formed.

The Defense Minister as a "Conversation Partner"

The last element needed to help the chief of staff fulfill his role is having the defense minister as a conversation partner. By the nature of his office, the defense minister is expected to contribute his knowledge and insights to the interechelon discourse and, following this, issue instructions.

The defense minister is supposed to share the chief of staff's burden of responsibility. In addition, the chief of staff should be able to consult and converse freely and straightforwardly with the defense minister on the broad range of issues on his agenda. This was the case in the talks between Dayan and Prime Minister–Defense Minister Ben-Gurion on the transfer of collective settlement conscripts from the defense of the settlements to assault units when Dayan faced opposition from the leaders of the Kibbutz Movement. Elazar's ability to consult with Defense Minister Dayan on the problematic behavior of Shmuel Gonen in the Yom Kippur War contrasts with Halutz's lack of a defense minister partner on the problem with Udi Adam in the 2006 Second Lebanon War. The candid dialogue between Elazar and Dayan in the Yom Kippur War enabled the chief of staff to challenge Dayan's opinions on, for example, the withdrawal to the mountain passes in Sinai. Rabin's collapse in the days leading up to the Six-Day War may have been linked to the fact that Prime Minister–Defense Minister Eshkol was not such a partner, and Ben-Gurion as an alternative merely undermined Rabin's confidence. Rabin was not pleased with Dayan's appointment to defense minister a few days before the war, and Dayan appears not to have been a conversation partner for

Rabin, but he does seem to have shared the burden of responsibility for defense, which lightened the load on Rabin's shoulders.

The awareness of these factors and the steps that need to be taken to implement them will go far in assisting the chief of staff in his demanding role.

As stated in the introduction, this book provides groundbreaking research in a broad field that calls for further study. It is my intention that the ideas presented in this book will contribute to military organizations other than the IDF as well. I hope that it will stimulate further comparative research on the role of senior commanders and their interplay with subordinates and superiors.

APPENDIX A: TENURES OF IDF CHIEFS OF STAFF

Dates	Chief of staff	Major engagements	Major conceptual changes	Main HQs and units mentioned in the book
June 1947–November 1949	Ya'akov Dori	War of Independence: the Hagana vs. local Arab militias (November 1947–May 1948); the IDF vs. Egyptian, Syrian, and Jordanian forces (and others) (May 1948–March 1949)	From fighting local Arab irregular forces to fighting state armies	—
November 1949–December 1952	Yigael Yadin	—	The reserves as a solution to budget constraints	—
December 1952–December 1953	Mordechai Maklef	—	—	—
December 1953–January 1958	Moshe Dayan	Reprisal operations: raids on Egyptian and Jordanian military posts and camps in the West Bank and the Gaza Strip aimed at forcing them to suspend support of Palestinian terrorists (Fedayun) (1953–56) Sinai War against Egypt (1956)	Building an offensive ethos; debate over armor's role	Southern Command; 38th Div.; 77th Div.; Seventh Brigade; Paratrooper Brigade; Unit 101

(*continued*)

Dates	Chief of staff	Major engagements	Major conceptual changes	Main HQs and units mentioned in the book
January 1958– January 1961	Haim Laskov	—	Mechanized combined arms warfare	—
January 1961– January 1964	Tzvi Tzur	—	—	—
January 1964– January 1968	Yitzhak Rabin	Conflict with Syria over Jordan River water sources (1964–67); Six-Day War against Egypt (in Sinai), Jordan (Jerusalem and the West Bank), and Syria (Golan Heights) (1967)	Preemptive air strike	IAF; Southern Command
January 1968– January 1972	Haim Bar-Lev	War of Attrition; Israel vs. Egypt along the Suez Canal (1968–70)	Relapse from combined arms to armor-based warfare	—
January 1972– April 1974	David Elazar	Yom Kippur War against Egypt (in Sinai), and Syria (Golan Heights) (1973)	—	Southern Command; IAF; 162nd Div.; 143rd Div.; 252nd Sinai Div.; 210th Div.
April 1974– April 1978	Mordechai Gur	Operation Litani in Lebanon against the Palestine Liberation Organization (PLO) in South Lebanon (1978)	"Return" to combined arms warfare	Mafhash; Tze'elim training base
April 1978– April 1983	Rafael Eitan	Operation Peace in Galilee against the PLO and Syrian forces in Lebanon (1982) (later called the First Lebanon War)	—	IAF; Mafhash; 162nd Div.
April 1983– April 1987	Moshe Levi	Staged withdrawal from Beirut to the security zone in South Lebanon (1985)	—	Mafhash

Dates	Chief of staff	Major engagements	Major conceptual changes	Main HQs and units mentioned in the book
April 1987– April 1991	Dan Shomron	First intifada: against Palestinian uprising in the West Bank and Gaza Gulf War; Iraqi Scud missiles hit Israel (1991)	Beginning of precision-guided munitions against masses of armored fighting vehicles	Mafhash; Moran, David's Sling stand-off fire units; 162nd Div.; 252nd Div.
April 1991– January 1995	Ehud Barak	—	Systemic concept of stand-off precision capability	162nd Div.; 252nd Div.
January 1995– July 1998	Amnon Lipkin-Shahak	Fighting with Hezbollah intensifies in the security zone in Lebanon	Defining routine security operations as combat in the security zone in Lebanon	Northern Command; Galilee Div.; Egoz Unit
July 1998– July 2002	Shaul Mofaz	Withdrawal from Lebanon (2000) Second intifada: against Palestinian armed uprising in the West Bank and Gaza (2000–2004) and Operation Defensive Shield in the West Bank (2002)	Shift of force design focus to winning the war against Palestinian terror	Central Command; Judea and Samaria Div.; Kfir Brigade
July 2002– June 2005	Moshe Ya'alon	Continued counterterrorism in the West Bank and Gaza	Counterterrorism theory regarding the Palestinian arena; airpowerbased EBO in war	Central Command; Judea and Samaria Div.; Kfir Brigade
June 2005– February 2007	Dan Halutz	Disengagement from Gaza (2005); Second Lebanon War against Hezbollah (2006)	Airpower-based EBO in war	Northern Command; Galilee Div.; Ga'ash Div.; 162nd Div.; 98th Div.; Netiv Ha'esh Div.
February 2007– February 2011	Gabi Ashkenazi	Operation Cast Lead against Hamas in Gaza (2008–9)	"Back to basics" regarding maneuver capabilities after the Second Lebanon War	—

(continued)

Dates	Chief of staff	Major engagements	Major conceptual changes	Main HQs and units mentioned in the book
February 2011–February 2015	Benny Gantz	Operation Protective Edge against Hamas in Gaza (2014)	"Deterrence operations" against Hamas in Gaza	Northern Command; Bashan Div.; Ga'ash Div.; Netiv Ha'esh Div.
February 2015–January 2019	Gadi Eisenkot	The "Campaign between Wars" mainly against Hezbollah and Iran	"Campaign between wars" mainly against Hezbollah's arms buildup	—
January 2019–present	Aviv Kochavi	Operation Guardian of the Walls against Hamas in Gaza (2021)	—	—

APPENDIX B: PRIME MINISTERS, DEFENSE MINISTERS, AND GENERALS

Year	Prime minister	Defense minister	Chief of staff	GHQ-level generals mentioned in the text in relation to specific events
1948	David Ben-Gurion	David Ben-Gurion	Ya'akov Dori	Yigael Yadin (Agam)
1949	David Ben-Gurion	David Ben-Gurion	Ya'akov Dori	Yigael Yadin (Agam)
1950	David Ben-Gurion	David Ben-Gurion	Yigael Yadin	—
1951	David Ben-Gurion	David Ben-Gurion	Yigael Yadin	—
1952	David Ben-Gurion	David Ben-Gurion	Yigael Yadin	—
1953	David Ben-Gurion	David Ben-Gurion	Mordechai Maklef	Moshe Dayan (Agam)
1954	David Ben-Gurion/ Moshe Sharett	David Ben-Gurion/ Pinhas Lavon	Moshe Dayan	—
1955	Moshe Sharett	Pinhas Lavon/David Ben-Gurion	Moshe Dayan	—
1956	David Ben-Gurion	David Ben-Gurion	Moshe Dayan	Meir Amit (Agam) Asaf Simhoni (S. Command) Haim Laskov (Armored Corps)

(*continued*)

Year	Prime minister	Defense minister	Chief of staff	GHQ-level generals mentioned in the text in relation to specific events
1957	David Ben-Gurion	David Ben-Gurion	Moshe Dayan	—
1958	David Ben-Gurion	David Ben-Gurion	Haim Laskov	—
1959	David Ben-Gurion	David Ben-Gurion	Haim Laskov	—
1960	David Ben-Gurion	David Ben-Gurion	Haim Laskov	—
1961	David Ben-Gurion	David Ben-Gurion	Tzvi Tzur	—
1962	David Ben-Gurion	David Ben-Gurion	Tzvi Tzur	—
1963	David Ben-Gurion/ Levi Eshkol	David Ben-Gurion/ Levi Eshkol	Tzvi Tzur	—
1964	Levi Eshkol	Levi Eshkol	Yitzhak Rabin	—
1965	Levi Eshkol	Levi Eshkol	Yitzhak Rabin	—
1966	Levi Eshkol	Levi Eshkol	Yitzhak Rabin	
1967	Levi Eshkol	Levi Eshkol/ Moshe Dayan	Yitzhak Rabin	Motti Hod (IAF)
1968	Levi Eshkol	Moshe Dayan	Haim Bar-Lev	—
1969	Levi Eshkol/ Golda Meir	Moshe Dayan	Haim Bar-Lev	—
1970	Golda Meir	Moshe Dayan	Haim Bar-Lev	—
1971	Golda Meir	Moshe Dayan	Haim Bar-Lev	—
1972	Golda Meir	Moshe Dayan	David Elazar	—
1973	Golda Meir	Moshe Dayan	David Elazar	Israel Tal (Dep. CoS and Agam) Shmuel Gonen (S. Command) Benny Peled (IAF) Eli Zeira (Aman) Haim Bar-Lev Ariel Sharon (143rd Div.)
1974	Golda Meir/ Yitzhak Rabin	Moshe Dayan/ Shimon Peres	David Elazar/ Mordechai Gur	—
1975	Yitzhak Rabin	Shimon Peres	Mordechai Gur	—
1976	Yitzhak Rabin	Shimon Peres	Mordechai Gur	—

Year	Prime minister	Defense minister	Chief of staff	GHQ-level generals mentioned in the text in relation to specific events
1977	Yitzhak Rabin/ Menachem Begin	Shimon Peres/ Ezer Weizman	Mordechai Gur	—
1978	Menachem Begin	Ezer Weizman	Mordechai Gur/Rafael Eitan	—
1979	Menachem Begin	Ezer Weizman	Rafael Eitan	—
1980	Menachem Begin	Ezer Weiz- man/Men- achem Begin	Rafael Eitan	—
1981	Menachem Begin	Menachem Begin/Ariel Sharon	Rafael Eitan	—
1982	Menachem Begin	Ariel Sharon	Rafael Eitan	—
1983	Menachem Begin/Yitzhak Shamir	Ariel Sharon/ Menachem Begin/Moshe Arens	Rafael Eitan/ Moshe Levi	Yekutiel Adam (Dep. CoS) Moshe Levi (Dep. CoS) David Ivry (IAF) Dan Shomron (S. Command) Yehoshua Sagi (Aman)
1984	Yitzhak Shamir	Moshe Arens/ Yitzhak Rabin	Moshe Levi	David Ivry (Dep. CoS) Dan Shomron (Mafhash/ Dep. CoS) Yossi Peled (Mahad)
1985	Shimon Peres	Yitzhak Rabin	Moshe Levi	—
1986	Shimon Peres/ Yitzhak Shamir	Yitzhak Rabin	Moshe Levi	—
1987	Yitzhak Shamir	Yitzhak Rabin	Moshe Levi/ Dan Shomron	Ehud Barak (Dep. CoS) Amnon Lipkin-Shahak (Aman) Giora Romm (Dep. Agam) Amram Mitzna (C. Command) Yitzhak Mordechai (S. Command) Yossi Peled (N. Command) Shmuel Goren (COGAT) Amos Lapidot (IAF) Moshe Bar-Kochva

(continued)

Year	Prime minister	Defense minister	Chief of staff	GHQ-level generals mentioned in the text in relation to specific events
1988	Yitzhak Shamir	Yitzhak Rabin	Dan Shomron	Ehud Barak (Dep. CoS) Amnon Lipkin-Shahak (Aman) Giora Romm (Dep. Agam) Amram Mitzna (C. Command) Yitzhak Mordechai (S. Command) Yossi Peled (N. Command) Shmuel Goren (COGAT) Amos Lapidot (IAF) Moshe Bar Kokhba
1989	Yitzhak Shamir	Yitzhak Rabin	Dan Shomron	—
1990	Yitzhak Shamir	Yitzhak Rabin/ Yitzhak Shamir/ Moshe Arens	Dan Shomron	—
1991	Yitzhak Shamir	Moshe Arens	Dan Shomron/ Ehud Barak	—
1992	Yitzhak Shamir/ Yitzhak Rabin	Moshe Arens/ Yitzhak Rabin	Ehud Barak	—
1993	Yitzhak Rabin	Yitzhak Rabin	Ehud Barak	—
1994	Yitzhak Rabin	Yitzhak Rabin	Ehud Barak	—
1995	Yitzhak Rabin/ Shimon Peres	Yitzhak Rabin/ Shimon Peres	Ehud Barak/ Amnon Lipkin-Shahak	—
1996	Shimon Peres/ Benjamin Netanyahu	Shimon Peres/Yitzhak Mordechai	Amnon Lipkin-Shahak	Shaul Mofaz (Dep. CoS) Matan Vilnai (Dep. CoS) Amiram Levin (N. Command) Amos Malka (Mazi)
1997	Benjamin Netanyahu	Yitzhak Mordechai	Amnon Lipkin-Shahak	—
1998	Benjamin Netanyahu	Yitzhak Mordechai	Amnon Lipkin-Shahak/ Shaul Mofaz	—
1999	Benjamin Netanyahu/ Ehud Barak	Yitzhak Mordechai/ Moshe Arens/ Ehud Barak	Shaul Mofaz	Moshe Ya'alon (Dep. CoS) Uzi Dayan (C. Command) Yitzhak Eitan (C. Command) Shlomo Yanai (Agat)

Year	Prime minister	Defense minister	Chief of staff	GHQ-level generals mentioned in the text in relation to specific events
2000	Ehud Barak	Ehud Barak	Shaul Mofaz	Moshe Ya'alon (Dep. CoS) Uzi Dayan (C. Command) Yitzhak Eitan (C. Command) Shlomo Yanai (Agat)
2001	Ehud Barak/ Ariel Sharon	Ehud Barak/ Binyamin Ben-Eliezer	Shaul Mofaz	—
2002	Ariel Sharon	Binyamin Ben-Eliezer	Shaul Mofaz/ Moshe Ya'alon	—
2003	Ariel Sharon	Shaul Mofaz	Moshe Ya'alon	—
2004	Ariel Sharon	Shaul Mofaz	Moshe Ya'alon	—
2005	Ariel Sharon	Shaul Mofaz	Moshe Ya'alon/ Dan Halutz	—
2006	Ariel Sharon/ Ehud Olmert	Shaul Mofaz/ Amir Peretz	Dan Halutz	Moshe Kaplinsky (Dep. CoS) Gadi Eisenkot (Amatz) Udi Adam (N. Command) Eliezer Shkedi (IAF)
2007	Ehud Olmert	Amir Peretz/ Ehud Barak	Dan Halutz/ Gabi Ashkenazi	—
2008	Ehud Olmert	Ehud Barak	Gabi Ashkenazi	—
2009	Ehud Olmert/ Benjamin Netanyahu	Ehud Barak	Gabi Ashkenazi	—
2010	Benjamin Netanyahu	Ehud Barak	Gabi Ashkenazi	—
2011	Benjamin Netanyahu	Ehud Barak	Gabi Ashkenazi/ Benny Gantz	—
2012	Benjamin Netanyahu	Ehud Barak	Benny Gantz	Yair Golan (N. Command) Aviv Kochavi (Aman) Yair Naveh (Dep. CoS)
2013	Benjamin Netanyahu	Ehud Barak/ Moshe Ya'alon	Benny Gantz	—
2014	Benjamin Netanyahu	Moshe Ya'alon	Benny Gantz	—
2015	Benjamin Netanyahu	Moshe Ya'alon	Benny Gantz/ Gadi Eisenkot	—

(continued)

Year	Prime minister	Defense minister	Chief of staff	GHQ-level generals mentioned in the text in relation to specific events
2016	Benjamin Netanyahu	Moshe Ya'alon/ Avigdor Lieberman	Gadi Eisenkot	—
2017	Benjamin Netanyahu	Avigdor Lieberman	Gadi Eisenkot	—
2018	Benjamin Netanyahu	Avigdor Lieberman/ Benjamin Netanyahu	Gadi Eisenkot	—
2019	Benjamin Netanyahu	Benjamin Netanyahu/ Naftali Bennett	Gadi Eisenkot/ Aviv Kochavi	—
2020	Benjamin Netanyahu	Naftali Bennett/ Benny Gantz	Aviv Kochavi	—

NOTES

Preface to the English Edition

1. A prodigious amount of documentation is available for some of the chiefs of staff for various reasons (David Elazar—the Yom Kippur War; Yitzhak Rabin—as prime minister; Moshe Dayan—his own documentation and comprehensive research). Other chiefs of staff (Ya'akov Dori, Mordechai Maklef, Haim Laskov, Haim Bar-Lev, Rafael Eitan, Dan Shomron, and Moshe Ya'alon) each have only one book written about them, and the period of each one's command has been only partially researched. And for still other chiefs of staff (Tzvi Tzur, Shaul Mofaz, Moshe Levi, Amnon Lipkin-Shahak, Gabi Ashkenazi, and Benny Gantz), relevant material is extremely limited. Regarding Ehud Barak, several books have been written, but documentation of his term as chief of staff is quite limited.
2. The television series *The Chiefs of Staff*, directed by Tor Ben Mayor and produced by Zvi Shefi, traces all of the chiefs of staff and was first screened in March 2017 on Israel's Channel 1, http://www.iba.org.il.
3. For examples, see Thomas E. Ricks, *The Generals: American Military Command from World War II to Today* (New York: Penguin Books, 2013); and John Keegan, *Churchill's Generals* (London: Cassell, 1991). Also see David T. Zabecki, ed., *Chief of Staff: The Principal Officers Behind History's Great Commanders*, vol. 1, *Napoleonic Wars to World War I* (Annapolis, MD: Naval Institute Press, 2008).

Glossary and Abbreviations

1. For explanations of J5 and J8, see Joint Chiefs of Staff sites "J5 Strategic Plans and Policy," https://www.jcs.mil/Directorates/J5-Strategy-Plans-and-Policy, and "J8 Force Structure, Resource, and Assessment," https://www.jcs.mil/Directorates/J8-Force-Structure-Resources-Assessment, both retrieved November 1, 2020.
2. For explanations of J3 and J7, see Joint Chiefs of Staff sites "J3 Operations," https://www.jcs.mil/Directorates/J3-Operations and "J7 Joint Force Development," https://www.jcs.mil/Directorates/J7-Joint-Force-Development, both retrieved November 1, 2020.

Introduction

1. The term "army" here means the IDF as a whole, while the term "ground forces" will be used to describe the land component of the IDF.
2. Basic Law: The IDF, April 9, 1976, amended July 15, 1976. Note the wording: "The supreme commander *in* the IDF" and not the supreme commander *of* the IDF. This appears in the original GHQ order 2.0101—General Headquarters roles.
3. Supreme Command Order 2.0101—General Headquarters. The Supreme Command's orders that deal with the general staff's functions and coordination and with the professional staff are defined in much greater detail than those of the chief of staff and describe the exact functions of the aforementioned staff officers. Furthermore, an examination of the role of the generals on the general staff, relative to the professional officers subordinate to them, shows that the further down the rank one goes, the clearer and more detailed are the descriptions of the roles.
4. *IDF Strategy: Trends and Basic Ideas for Force Design and Employment* (Amatz-Tohad, 2002), 141.
5. *IDF Strategy* (General Staff, Office of the Head of Amatz, 2015).
6. Dan Halutz, *At Eye Level* (Tel Aviv: Yediot Achronot-Hemed, 2010), 298. Halutz stresses the multifacetedness of the role of chief of staff but within the framework, as I see it, of political understanding.
7. Emanuel Wald, *The Curse of the Broken Vessels: The Twilight of Israeli Military and Political Power, 1967–1982* (Jerusalem: Schocken, 1987), 163–69. Regarding the surfeit of power in the chief of staff institution, see

also Avraham Rotem, *Self-Criticism in the Castle* (Tel Aviv: Ma'arachot and the Defense Ministry, 2007), 168–69.

8. The Knesset, Foreign Affairs and Defense Committee, "IDF Multiyear Gideon Plan: Special Report of the Subcommittee on Security Conception and Force Buildup," unclassified version, September 2017.

9. Anita Shapira, *From Firing the Head of the Hagana's National Staff to Dismantling the Palmach: Issues in the Struggle for Security Leadership, 1948* (Tel Aviv: Kibbutz Hame'uchad, 1985).

10. Supreme Command Order 2.0101—General Headquarters.

Chapter 1

1. Hanoch Bartov, *Dado: 48 Years and 20 Days*, expanded edition, vol. 1 (Or Yehuda: Dvir, 2002), 254–65.

2. Bartov, *Dado*, 263.

3. Bartov, *Dado*, 265.

4. Meir Finkel, *Military Agility: Ensuring Rapid and Effective Transition from Peace to War* (Lexington, KY: University Press of Kentucky, 2020), 31–33.

5. Shimon Golan, *War on Yom Kippur* (Ben Shemen: Modan and Ma'arachot, 2013). For the list of discussions, see p. 27. Chapter 1 contains the most comprehensive description of the alert.

6. Bartov, *Dado*, 273.

7. I would like to thank Sam Bronfeld for the calculation. All amounts in dollars will be in 2019 US dollar equivalents.

8. Israel Tal, *National Security: Few Against Many* (Tel Aviv: Dvir, 1996), 166.

9. Bartov, *Dado*, 280–81.

10. Ze'ev Drori, *Dan Shomron: Subtle Leadership* (Rishon Lezion: Yediot Achronot, 2016), 361–62.

11. Interview with Yitzhak Mordechai, cited in Drori, *Dan Shomron*.

12. Drori, *Dan Shomron*.

13. Drori, *Dan Shomron*.

14. Drori, *Dan Shomron*.

15. Shimon Golan, "The Beginning of the First Intifada as Reflected in Discussions at the Defense Minister and General Staff Levels, December 9, 1987–January 26, 1988," Warfighting Doctrine, History Department, February 2016: 15.

16. Golan, "The Beginning of the First Intifada," 16.
17. Haim Levenberg, "The IDF versus the Intifada, First Book: Surprise and Awakening," (Amatz, History Department, 2002), 36–37.
18. Levenberg, "IDF versus Intifada," 21–27.
19. Levenberg, "IDF versus Intifada," 45.
20. Levenberg, "IDF versus Intifada," 57.
21. Levenberg, "IDF versus Intifada," 63.
22. Levenberg, "IDF versus Intifada," 93.
23. Levenberg, "IDF versus Intifada," 105–12.
24. Yossi Peled, A Military Man (Tel Aviv: Sifriat Ma'ariv, 1993), 322.
25. Drori, Dan Shomron, 385.
26. Moshe Bar-Kochva, "The Intifada Fiasco and the Need for a Contingency Plan," Netiv 93 (1991): 46–52.
27. Ze'ev Schiff and Ehud Ya'ari, Intifada (Jerusalem: Schocken, 1990), 109.
28. Interview with Ehud Barak, Tel Aviv, July 26, 2017.
29. Golan, "The Beginning of the First Intifada" 122; Schiff and Ya'ari, Intifada, 109.
30. Chief of Staff's Office, "IDF Routine Security Meeting—March 1995—Chief of Staff Summary, MS 3108–22," April 27, 1995.
31. Moshe Tamir, War Without a Sign (Tel Aviv: Ma'arachot, 2005), 24–25.
32. Brigadier General Tamir Yadai, interviewed by Major Ayalon Peretz and Major Shachar Lahav, in "The Voice of Heroism: 30 Years for the Establishment of the Security Zone in Lebanon, 15 Years since the Withdrawal from Lebanon," personal interviews of cadets in the Command and Staff Course with IDF combat commanders in Lebanon, 1985–2000. The Center for Military Studies, the Interservice Command and Staff College, 2016: 185–89.
33. Brigadier General Effi Eitam, interviewed by Major Yair Zukerman, "Voice of Heroism," 33–39.
34. Yadai, "Voice of Heroism."
35. Moshe Kaplinsky, interviewed by Major Natan Jamber and Major Shay Kedem, "Voice of Heroism," 330–32.
36. Telephone interview with Nitzan Nuriel, February 7, 2017.
37. Eitam, "Voice of Heroism," 36.
38. Tamir, War Without a Sign, 172.

39. Ze'ev Elron, historical review within the framework of "A Decade of Learning Initiative, Main Trends in Force Building as Reflected in the Multiyear Plans from Mirkam to Tefen, 1991–2011," November 2013, 22.

40. Eitam, "Voice of Heroism," 37.

41. Based on unpublished manuscript by Amira Shachar, "The History of the Merkava Tank," 134–36.

42. Ohad Laslau, "From Routine Security to Guerrilla Warfare: Change in the Operational Concept in South Lebanon and Its Realization, 1992–1998" (IDF History Department, 2017).

43. Eyal Berelovich, "The Development of the IDF's Border Defense Concept, 1948–2016," Dado Center Publications, January 2017: 50–54.

44. Amos Harel and Avi Issacharoff, *The Seventh War: How We Won and Why We Lost the War with the Palestinians* (Tel Aviv: Yediot Achronot-Sifrei Hemed, 2004), 348.

45. Harel and Issacharoff, *Seventh War*, 59.

46. Moshe Ya'alon, *The Longer Shorter Way* (Tel Aviv: Yediot Achronot-Sifrei Hemed, 2008), 90.

47. Yigal Eyal, *Ebb and Tide: The Second Intifada—Multifront Confrontation, 1996–2004* (Ground Forces Command/Doctrine Department, 2015), 15–16.

48. Eyal, *Ebb and Tide*, 58–59.

49. Eyal, *Ebb and Tide*, 60–61.

50. Eyal, *Ebb and Tide*, 70.

51. Ya'alon, *The Longer Shorter Way*, 90.

52. Eyal, *Ebb and Tide*, 72.

53. Gal Hirsch, *Defensive Shield: An Israeli Special Forces Commander on the Front Line of Counterterrorism* (Jerusalem: Gefen Books, 2016), 151–58.

54. Report of the Commission to Investigate the Lebanon Campaign (Winograd Commission), Final Verdict, vol. I, 2008, 297 (hereafter cited as *Winograd Report*).

55. Halutz, *At Eye Level*.

56. Halutz, *At Eye Level*, 381.

57. Shimon Golan, "The Second Lebanon War: Decision Making at the Strategic Level" (IDF History Department, 2014).

58. Golan, "The Second Lebanon War"; *Winograd Report*, 298; GHQ Situation Assessment of July 13–14.

59. Interview with Major General Sami Turgeman, Glilot Base, Tel Aviv, April 18, 2017.

60. Golan, "The Second Lebanon War."

61. Halutz, *At Eye Level*, 386.

62. Halutz, *At Eye Level*, 386.

63. Halutz, *At Eye Level*, 406.

64. Hirsch, *Defensive Shield*, 260.

65. Hirsch, *Defensive Shield*, 264.

66. Hirsch, *Defensive Shield*, 270.

67. Hirsch, *Defensive Shield*, 275.

68. Hirsch, *Defensive Shield*, 366.

69. For details, see Finkel, *Military Agility*, 93–125.

70. Shaul Yardeni and Gal Oren, "The Air Force: The Mental Shift from Routine Security to War," in *Insight and Action*, vol. 2 (Amatz-Tohad-the Conceptual Lab, 2008), 135–42.

71. *Winograd Report*, 295–96.

72. Northern Command Situation Assessment, July 26, 2006.

73. Text of the chief of staff's authorization of the division's plans, August 3, 2006.

74. *Winograd Report*, 314–15.

75. Finkel, *Military Agility*, 124–25.

76. Interview with Benny Gantz, Tel Aviv, June 20, 2017.

77. Arik Bender, "Gantz on Syria: Growing Instability in the Golan Heights Sector," *NRG*, June 5, 2012.

78. Interview with Major General Yair Golan, Tel Aviv, July 3, 2017.

79. Yoav Zeitun, "As Gantz Sees It: The Battles in Syria on the Golan Heights Border," *Ynet*, November 4, 2012.

80. Amir Oren, "Gantz Has Decided to Establish a New Regional Division on the Golan Heights to Block Attacks from Syria," *Ha'aretz*, July 10, 2013.

81. Interview with Gantz, June 20, 2017.

82. Ben Caspit, "Towards Confrontation: The IDF of 2016 Is Going Through the Most Dramatic Change Since Its Founding," *Ma'ariv*, April 20, 2014.

The organization of divisions is defined as such in the document, "The IDF 2025—Vision and Intentions of Action," August 2013.

83. Interview with Major General Tamir Heyman, Hakirya Base, Tel Aviv, April 18, 2017.

84. Gili Cohen, "Head of Aman: 'Syria Has Become the Center of Global Jihad That Threatens the Entire Region,'" *Ha'aretz*, July 24, 2013.

85. Telephone interview and email correspondence with Brigadier General (res.) Ofek Buchris, March 24, 2017.

86. Interview with Golan, July 3, 2017.

87. Interview with Gantz, June 20, 2017.

88. Interview with Gantz, June 20, 2017.

89. Interview and correspondence with Buchris, March 24, 2017.

90. Interview with Turgeman, April 18, 2017.

Chapter 2

1. Testimony of Major General Motti Hod, IAF commander, on the activity of the operation center in the Six-Day War, November 14, 1969 (testimony continued on November 27 and December 16, 1969), 3. IDF and Defense Establishment Archives website: http://www.archives.mod.gov .il/Exhib/sixdayswar/mhod/Pages/default.aspx.

2. Testimony of Hod, November 14, 1969, 8.

3. Testimony of Hod, November 14, 1969, 19.

4. Testimony of Hod, December 16, 1969, 14–17.

5. Ran Ronen, *Hawk in the Sky* (Tel Aviv: Yediot Achronot, 2002), 172.

6. Conversation with Brigadier General (ret.) Shaike Bareket, head of the IAF's intelligence branch before and during the Six-Day War, May 4, 2017.

7. Ami Gluska, *Eshkol, Give an Order: The IDF and Israeli Government on the Road to the Six-Day War, 1963–1967* (Tel Aviv: Ma'arachot, 2004), 91.

8. Gluska, *Eshkol*, 193.

9. Ze'ev Lachish, "The Air Force in War: A Calculated Risk?" in *The Six-Day War: Cathedra of Commanders and Scholars*, ed. Effi Meltzer. Summary of the "Issues in Israel's Security" Seminar (Reut: Israel Galili Center of Defense Studies and the Israel Society for Military History, in association with Tel Aviv University, 1996), 83–90, cited on 87.

10. Danny Shalom, *Like Thunder on a Clear Day* (Rishon Lezion: Ba'aveer, Aviation Publications: 2002), 95.

11. Shalom, *Like Thunder*.

12. Yemima Rosenthal, ed., *Yitzhak Rabin, Prime Minister of Israel: Anthology of Documents of His Life*, vol. 1, *1922–1967* (Jerusalem: State Archive, 2005), 458.

13. Rosenthal, *Yitzhak Rabin*, 482.

14. Shimon Golan, *War on Three Fronts* (Tel Aviv: Ma'arachot, 2007), 116.

15. Yitzhak Rabin and Dov Goldstein, *Service Notebook*, vol. 1 (Tel Aviv: Sifriyat Ma'ariv, 1979), 147. (This section is missing in the English version of this book: Yitzhak Rabin, *The Rabin Memoirs* [Boston, Little, Brown and Company, 1979]).

16. Rabin and Goldstein, *Service Notebook*, 187. (Rabin, *Rabin Memoirs*, 104.)

17. Ezer Weizman, *Skyward, Earthbound* (Tel Aviv: Sifriyat Ma'ariv, 1973), 261. (This paragraph is missing in the English version of this book, *On Eagles' Wings: The Personal Story of the Leading Commander of the Israeli Air Force* [London: Weidenfeld and Nicolson, 1975], 215.)

18. Testimony of Yitzhak Hofi, head of the operations department, in Golan, *Three Fronts*, 77.

19. Gluska, *Eshkol*, 260.

20. Golan, *Three Fronts*, 169.

21. Shmuel Gordon, *30 Hours in October, Fatal Decisions: The Air Force at the Outset of the Yom Kippur War* (Tel Aviv: Sifriyat Ma'ariv, 2008), 443–45.

22. Gordon, *30 Hours*, 143.

23. Benny Peled, *Days of Reckoning* (Ben Shemen: Modan, 2004), 406–7.

24. Shaul Bronfeld, "From the Electronic Summer of 1970 to the Winter of 1973: The Story of the Loss of Air Supremacy," *Bein Hakatavim* 11–12 (June 2017): 143–74.

25. In loft bombing the planes release the bombs a few kilometers from the target, thus minimizing the risk from anti-aircraft cannons and SAMs. This could be done by the F-4 Phantoms with their advanced bombing computers.

26. Testimony of Lieutenant General David Elazar before the Agranat Commission, Session 74, February 17, 1974. IDF and Defense Establishment

Archives website: http://archivesdocs.mod.gov.il/Agranat2/dado/74/index.html.

27. Golan, *War on Yom Kippur*, 146–50.
28. Golan, *War on Yom Kippur*, 252.
29. Golan, *War on Yom Kippur*, 331.
30. Golan, *War on Yom Kippur*, 334.
31. Testimony of Elazar, February 17, 1974.
32. Golan, *War on Yom Kippur*, 93–107.
33. Shimon Golan, *Israel's War in Lebanon, 1982* (Ben Shemen: Modan, Ma'arachot, and the IDF History Department, 2017), 116.
34. David Ivry, "A Chapter on the SAM Array in Lebanon in the Spring of 1981: The Complexity of Processes" (unpublished memoir, updated by the author in August 2009).
35. Ivry, "SAM Array."
36. Interview with Major General (ret.) David Ivry, Museum Towers, Tel Aviv, February 20, 2017.
37. Golan, *Israel's War in Lebanon*, 130.
38. Shimon Golan, "The Strategic-Operational Planning for the First Lebanon War" (IDF, History Department, 2017), 214–15.
39. Golan, "Strategic-Operational Planning," 364.
40. Golan, *Israel's War in Lebanon*, 346–52.
41. Golan, *Israel's War in Lebanon*, 356–57.
42. Golan, *Israel's War in Lebanon*, 356–57.
43. Rafael Eitan and Dov Goldstein, *Raful: A Soldier's Story* (Tel Aviv: Sifriyat Ma'ariv, 1985), 213.
44. Rafael Eitan, *The Fourth Parachute Got Open* (Tel Aviv: Yediot Achronot and Hemed, 2001), 215, 212.
45. It should be noted that the previous general staff exercise was in January 2002. Halutz was the IAF commander in it and the exercise focused on the West Bank and Gaza.
46. Halutz, *At Eye Level*, 211.
47. Halutz, *At Eye Level*, 278.
48. Halutz, *At Eye Level*, 299.
49. Halutz, *At Eye Level*, 320.
50. Halutz, *At Eye Level*, 387.
51. Halutz, *At Eye Level*, 280.

52. Halutz, *At Eye Level*, 258, 280.
53. Graph of main events of 2004—Order No. 3, Ground Forces Command/ Operations Department, September 2004.
54. Graph of main events of 2005—Order No. 3, Ground Forces Command/ Operations Department, December 2005.
55. Graph of main events of 2006—Order No. 2, including Budgetary Assembly, Ground Forces Command/Operations Department, July 18, 2006.
56. Halutz, *At Eye Level*, 350.
57. Ohad Laslau, "Development of the Operational Concept for the Lebanese Theater," Dado Center Publications, 2015, 76.
58. Dan Halutz, "Airpower as a Decision Variable," *Studies in National Security* 2 (July 2001): 91–100.
59. The learning process the IDF conducted on the EBO is described in detail in my following book on the IDF GHQ.
60. *Winograd Report*, 274.
61. Halutz, *At Eye Level*, 350.
62. Laslau, "Operational Concept," 72.
63. Halutz, *At Eye Level*, 350–51.
64. Correspondence with Colonel (ret.) Boaz Cohen, May 2, 2017.
65. *Winograd Report*, 276.
66. Halutz, *At Eye Level*, 351.
67. *Winograd Report*, 257.
68. Laslau, "Operational Concept," 78. Sami Turgeman, head of operations division/Amatz, makes the same claim.
69. Correspondence, Cohen, May 2, 2017.
70. Interview with Major General (ret.) Udi Adam, Tel Aviv, May 30, 2017.
71. Halutz, *At Eye Level*, 375.
72. Halutz, *At Eye Level*, 376.
73. Interview with Major General Roni Numa, Tel Aviv, May 11, 2017.
74. General Staff Situation Assessment, July 18, 2006.
75. Correspondence, Cohen, May 2, 2017.
76. *Winograd Report*, 250.
77. Halutz, *At Eye Level*, 402.
78. Halutz, *At Eye Level*, 432.

Chapter 3

1. *Winograd Report*, 309.
2. IDF Strategy (General Staff, Office of the Head of Amatz, 2015), 27–28.
3. Ohad Laslau, "Pathology in the Chief of Staff-Supreme Headquarters Interface," Dado Center Publications, 2012.
4. Amos Carmel, *The Victory General: Asaf Simhoni* (Tel Aviv: Yediot Sfarim, 2009), 285.
5. Uzi Narkis, *A Soldier of Jerusalem* (Tel Aviv: Defense Ministry Publications, 1991), 160.
6. Carmel, *Victory General*, 307.
7. Carmel, *Victory General*, 292.
8. Amiad Brezner, *Gallant Chargers: Developments and Transformations in Israeli Armor from the End of the War of Independence to the Sinai Campaign* (Tel Aviv: Ma'arachot, 1999), 329–30.
9. Uri Ben Ari, *Forward Charge! The Path of the Armored Corps' Struggle* (Tel Aviv: Ma'arachot, 1998).
10. Brezner, *Gallant Chargers*, 392.
11. Carmel, *Victory General*, 304–5.
12. Cited in Motti Golani, *There Will Be War in the Summer: Israel on the Road to the Sinai Campaign, 1955–1956*, vol. 2 (Tel Aviv: Ma'arachot, 1997), 413.
13. Dov Tamari, "The Battle between Operational Thinking and Tactical Logic," *Ba'shiryon* 6 (October 1999): 12–17.
14. Golani, *War in the Summer*, 413.
15. Carmel, *Victory General*, 314–16.
16. Golani, *War in the Summer*, 417.
17. Carmel, *Victory General*, 317.
18. Moshe Dayan, *Diary of the Sinai Campaign, 1956* (London: Sphere Books, 1966), 90.
19. Mordechai Bar-On, *Challenge and Struggle: The Road to the Sinai Campaign, 1956* (Beer Sheva: Ben-Gurion University Publications, 1991), 301.
20. Golani, *War in the Summer*, 456–515.
21. Carmel, *Victory General*, 348. Quote from the diary of the chief of staff's office. Carmel added, "Sharp expressions such as these were excised from the diary over the years."

22. Colonel [res.] Yehuda Wallach, "Armor Assault That Bypasses Dayan," interview by Benny Michalson and Shaul Nagar, *Shiryon* 6 (October 1999): 28–29.

23. Golani, *War in the Summer*, 466.

24. Carmel, *Victory General*, 348.

25. Carmel, *Victory General*, 348–49.

26. Bartov, *Dado*, 223.

27. Bartov, *Dado*, 290.

28. Golan, *War on Yom Kippur*, 293–94.

29. Golan, *War on Yom Kippur*, 293–94.

30. Golan, *War on Yom Kippur*, 383.

31. Golan, *War on Yom Kippur*, 396.

32. Golan, *War on Yom Kippur*, 413.

33. Golan, *War on Yom Kippur*, 483–84.

34. Golan, *War on Yom Kippur*, 384.

35. Golan, *War on Yom Kippur*, 502.

36. Golan, *War on Yom Kippur*, 536.

37. Golan, *War on Yom Kippur*, 593–602.

38. Here Dayan recalls the events on the eve of the Six-Day War when, as an ex–chief of staff and minister, he considered commanding Southern Command "alongside" General Yeshayahu Gavish, the commander of Southern Command at the time.

39. Golan, *War on Yom Kippur*.

40. Golan, *War on Yom Kippur*, 613.

41. Golan, *War on Yom Kippur*, 613–14.

42. Halutz, *At Eye Level*, 314.

43. *Winograd Report*, interim report (April 2007), 44–47.

44. *Winograd Report*, interim report (April 2007), 59–60.

45. *Winograd Report*, interim report (April 2007), 47.

46. Interview with Brigadier General (res.) Alon Friedman, chief of staff, Northern Command, Glilot Base, March 26, 2017.

47. Laslau, "Development of the Concept," 77.

48. *Winograd Report*, interim report, 55–57; Halutz, *At Eye Level*, 375.

49. Laslau, "Development of the Concept," 78.

50. Laslau, "Development of the Concept," 82; interview with Turgeman, April 18, 2017.

51. Halutz, *At Eye Level*, 381.

52. Record of the command's situation assessment, July 12, 2006.

53. Interview with Friedman, March 26, 2017.

54. Halutz, *At Eye Level*, 385.

55. Interview with Numa, May 11, 2017. According to the IDF History Department's research on the Second Lebanon War, this occurred on the morning of July 15 and not on July 13. This is apparently due to a mistake by Halutz or Numa or a History Department typo.

56. Report of the general staff design forum, July 15.

57. Golan, *Second Lebanon War*, 89.

58. Golan, *Second Lebanon War*, 124.

59. *Winograd Report*, 81.

60. Golan, *Second Lebanon War*, 141.

61. *Winograd Report*, 88.

62. *Winograd Report*, 250.

63. Interview with Adam, May 30, 2017.

64. Halutz, *At Eye Level*, 388.

65. Colonel Boaz Cohen, "Change of Direction: Northern Command Presents Inquiries to the Chief of Staff" (presentation of the inquiry team headed by the Northern Command operations officer, Northern Command Inquiry: Northern Command's Mission Accomplishments, November 2006).

66. Halutz, *At Eye Level*, 398.

67. Halutz, *At Eye Level*, 400.

68. Halutz, *At Eye Level*, 406.

69. Halutz, *At Eye Level*, 408.

70. Halutz, *At Eye Level*, 409.

71. Halutz, *At Eye Level*, 411–12.

72. *Winograd Report*, 366.

73. Interview with Friedman, March 26, 2017.

74. *Winograd Report*, 371.

75. Cohen, "Change of Direction."

76. *Winograd Report*, 303.

77. Correspondence with Cohen, May 2, 2017.

78. *Winograd Report*, 310.

79. Halutz, *At Eye Level*, 433.

80. Halutz, *At Eye Level*, 448.

81. Halutz, *At Eye Level*, 450–51.

82. Halutz, *At Eye Level*, 452. The head of the operations division/Amatz, Sami Turgeman, who participated in the authorization of the plans, stated in an interview that he completely understood Halutz's feelings in this event and Adam's anger since Zukerman made no effort to point out at the start of his statement that he was about to present something other than what had been agreed on with Halutz the day before.

83. Amos Harel, "The First Dismissal: The Chief of Staff Appointed Kaplinsky as His Representative in the North," *Ha'aretz*, August 10, 2006.

84. *Winograd Report*, 309.

85. Halutz, *At Eye Level*, 400.

86. Interview with Turgeman, April 18, 2017.

Chapter 4

1. Dani Dor and Yehuda Schiff, *The Story of Israel's Chiefs of Staff* (Tel Aviv: Ma'ariv, 2002), 143.

2. Moshe Dayan, *My Life* (Jerusalem: Idanim, 1976), 687.

3. Avraham "Bren" Adan, *On Both Banks of the Suez Canal* (Jerusalem: Idanim, 1979), 325.

4. Peled, *A Military Man*, 192.

5. Motta Gur, *Chief of Staff* (Tel Aviv: Ma'arachot, 1998), 75.

6. Gur, *Chief of Staff*, 18.

7. Gur, *Chief of Staff*, 120.

8. Herzl Shafir, "The Yom Kippur War: Facts, Attitudes, and Evaluation, with an Emphasis on Force Design," Supreme Command Study Day, Thirty Years after the Yom Kippur War, October 8, 2003 (Amatz-Tohad, History Department), 63–84.

9. Rabin, *Service Notebook*, vol. 2, 505. Again, the paragraph is missing from the English edition (page 290).

10. Motta Gur, "Lessons from the Yom Kippur War and the Force Design That Followed," National Security College, February 17, 1986.

11. Wald, *Broken Vessels*, 142–43.

12. Uzi Eilam, *Eilam's Arc: How Israel Became a Military Technology Powerhouse* (Tel Aviv: Yediot Achronot, 2009), 224.

13. Iftach Spector, *Loud and Clear* (Tel Aviv: Yediot Achronot, 2008), 296.

14. Gur, *Chief of Staff*, 21–22.

15. Gur, *Chief of Staff*, 115.

16. Wald, *Broken Vessels*, 143–44.

17. Gur, *Chief of Staff*, 23.

18. Gur, *Chief of Staff*, 144.

19. Shlomo Gazit, *Critical Junctures: From the Palmach to the Head of Aman* (Rishon Lezion: Yediot Achronot-Hemed, 2016), 226.

20. Gazit, *Critical Junctures*, 227–28.

21. Gur, *Chief of Staff*, 21–22.

22. Gur, *Chief of Staff*, 116.

23. Gur, *Chief of Staff*, 352.

24. Peled, *A Military Man*, 193.

25. Avigdor Kahalani, *The Way of the Fighter* (Tel Aviv: Steimatzky, 1989), 197.

26. Kahalani, *The Way of the Fighter*, 203.

27. Natke Nir, *The Wounded Officer Who Returned to the Battlefield* (Tel Aviv: Yediot Achronot-Sifrei Hemed, 2010), 254–55.

28. Gur, *Chief of Staff*, 18.

29. Elhanan Oren, "Operation Litani March 1978" (Agam-Mahad, History Department, 1998), 151.

30. *Winograd Report*, 396.

31. Meir Finkel, "The Second Lebanon War: Military Failure, Political-Security Success," *Ma'arachot* 466–67: 42–48.

32. Yaara Meitlis, "The Chief of Staff: Military Correction Yes—Rehabilitation No," Channel 7, February 7, 2008.

33. Maya Bengal, "The Former Chiefs-of-Staff Salute Gabi Ashkenazi," special for *Ma'ariv*: "Four Chiefs-of-Staff Who Served before Ashkenazi Embrace Him as a Comrade in Arms, Thank Him for His Contribution and Wish Him the Best for the Future," *NRG*, February 14, 2011.

34. Amos Harel, "Chief of Staff Gabi Ashkenazi Takes His Leave from President Shimon Peres," *Ha'aretz*, February 7, 2011.

35. Alex Fishman, "The IDF Changes Orientation: The Security Agenda on the Way to the Voting Booth," *Strategic Update* 8, no. 4 (January 2006).

36. Amir Rapaport, "The IDF and the Lessons of the Second Lebanon War," *Studies in Mideast Security and Policy Studies* 85 (December 2010): 16.

37. Chief of Staff's Office, "General Staff Workshop for Formulating the 2012 Tefen Multiyear Plan—Chief of Staff Summary," September 2, 2007.
38. Elron, "Main Trends."
39. Hanan Greenberg, "A Revolution in the IDF: Soldiers to Serve Two Years in 2010," *Ynet*, February 13, 2006.
40. In 2015, service for men was shortened to thirty months.
41. *Winograd Report*; Halutz, *At Eye Level*.
42. Amnon Miranda, "Ashkenazi to Members of Parliament: What Happened in the War Won't Be Repeated," *Ynet*, March 28, 2007.
43. Hanan Greenberg, "Training Cancellations—Only with the Chief of Staff's Approval," *Ynet*, April 1, 2007.
44. Amos Harel, "Division Commanders' Course to Open Today," *Ha'aretz*, May 27, 2007.
45. Chief of Staff's Office, "General Staff Workshop."
46. Rapaport, "The IDF and the Lessons," 15–16.
47. Conversation with Colonel (res.) Zohar Ya'akobi, Ayelet Hashahar, September 7, 2017.
48. Giora Eiland, "The Conclusion of Chief of Staff Gabi Ashkenazi's Tenure: An Evaluation," *Mabat Al*, no. 242 (February 2011), Institute for National Security Studies.
49. Rapaport, "The IDF and the Lessons," 27–28.
50. Nurit Gal, "Who Moved My Powers of Authorization?" *Ma'arachot* 420–21 (2008): 80–85.
51. Gal, "Who Moved My Powers?" The retrieval of the changes included the original names of the organizations. Thus, the Technological-Logistics Branch, which had become the Logistics, Medical, and Centers Branch in 2006, returned to being the Technological-Logistics Branch, and the Human Resources Branch of 2006 reverted back to being the Manpower Branch.
52. Rapaport, "The IDF and the Lessons," 9–11.
53. Rapaport, "The IDF and the Lessons," 11.
54. Interview with Ilana Dayan on Army Radio during the fundraising telethon events, 2008.
55. Eiland, "Conclusion of Ashkenazi's Tenure."
56. The numbers are hard to judge. Each side provided different numbers of military troops and civilians.

57. Avi Issacharoff and Amos Harel, "Cast Lead: The Fighting in Gaza Was a Slight Improvement over the Flaws of the Second Lebanon War," *Ha'aretz*, January 12, 2009.

Chapter 5

1. Ze'ev Elron, *Toward the Second Round: Transformations in the IDF and the Change in the Security Concept That Wasn't, 1952–1955* (Ben Shemen: Modan and Ma'arachot, 2016), 385–93.
2. Dov Tamari, *The Armed Nation: The Rise and Fall of the Reserves' Phenomenon* (Tel Aviv: Modan and Ma'arachot, 2017), 264.
3. Sagi Turgan, *In the Rifle Sight: The Change in the IDF's Fighting Spirit, 1953–1956* (The Center for Military Studies—Command and Staff College, 2014).
4. Sagi Turgan, *I'll Never Be a General* (Jerusalem: Yad Ben Zvi, 2017), 68–72.
5. Moshe Dayan, "Military Activity in Peacetime," *Ma'arachot* 118–119 (April 1959): 54–61.
6. Moshe Dayan, *Story of My Life* (Jerusalem: Idanim, 1976), 111–13. In the English edition—*The Story of My Life* (New York: Warner Books, 1977)—the text is abridged, with essential details missing.
7. Ariel Sharon with David Chanoff, *Warrior*, hardcover in English (New York: Simon and Schuster, 2005), 83–84; Ariel Sharon, "Retaliatory Activity—That's How We Were and That's How We Did It" (lecture, Sapir College, Sderot, inauguration of the "Black Arrow" battle memorial, March 20, 2003).
8. Aryeh Avnery, *Retaliatory Raids: IDF Actions behind Enemy Lines on All Fronts*, vol. 1 (Tel Aviv: Sifriyat Madim, 1970), 15–17.
9. From archives and additional documents. General staff meeting in the defense minister's office, July 27, 1954. Israel State Archives 636.56, file no. 7, 622.
10. Israel State Archives 636.56, file no. 7, 623.
11. Avnery, *Retaliatory Raids*, 19–22.
12. Ze'ev Drori, "The Military Level's Impact on Security Escalation," in *Black Arrow: Gaza Actions and Israeli Policy in the 1950s*, ed. Motti Golani (Tel Aviv: Ma'arachot, 1994), 137.
13. Dayan, *Story of My Life*, 113; Dayan, "Military Activity in Peacetime," 54–61.

14. Dayan, *Story of My Life*, 147–48.

15. Meir Amit, *Head to Head: A Personal Look at Big Events and Secret Episodes* (Or Yehuda: Hed Artzi, 1999), 39–41.

16. Shabtai Teveth, *Moshe Dayan: A Biography* (Jerusalem: Schocken, 1971), 400. The English version—*Moshe Dayan* (Jerusalem: Steimatzky's Agency together with Weidenfeld and Nicolson, 1972), 217—does not present all the details.

17. Dayan, *Story of My Life*, 114; Teveth, *Moshe Dayan*, 388–89 (Teveth, *Moshe Dayan*, English version, 207–8); Avnery, *Retaliatory Raids*, 19–22.

18. Dayan, *Story of My Life*, 179.

19. Dayan, *Story of My Life*, 220–21.

20. Dayan, *Story of My Life*, 160–61.

21. Ze'ev Elron, "The IDF Paratroopers: From the War of Independence to the Sinai Campaign," in *1948: Studies at the Jerusalem School on War, Army and Society*, ed. Alon Kadish (Ben Shemen: Modan, 2015), 387.

22. Drori, "Military Level's Impact," 134–37.

23. Teveth, *Moshe Dayan*, 387–88 (English version, 207).

24. Dayan, *Story of My Life*, 145.

25. Rosenthal, *Yitzhak Rabin*, 157.

26. Elron, "IDF Paratroopers," 77.

27. Dayan, *Story of My Life*, 117.

28. Examples of disagreement between Lavon and Sharett can be found in the latter's personal diary: Moshe Sharett, *Personal Diary 1954* (Tel Aviv: Sifriyat Ma'ariv, 1978), 445–47.

29. Sharett, *Personal Diary 1954*, 672.

30. Sharett, *Personal Diary 1954*, 676.

31. Sharett, *Personal Diary 1954*, 806.

32. Mordechai Bar-On, *The Gates of Gaza: Israel's Road to the Suez and Back, 1955–1957* (New York: St. Martin's Press, 1994), 71–72.

33. Bar-On, *Gates of Gaza*, 73.

34. Dayan, *Story of My Life*, 178.

35. Bar-On, *Gates of Gaza*, 73–74.

36. On the merger, see Michael Bar-Zohar, *The Paratroopers Book* (Tel Aviv: Levin-Epstein, 1969), 84; Uri Milstein, *The History of the Paratroopers*

from the War of Independence to War in Lebanon (Tel Aviv: Schalgi Publishing House, 1985), 248–49.

37. Dayan, *Diary of the Sinai Campaign*, 66.

38. Dayan, *Story of My Life*, 353.

39. Moshe Dayan, "From Stage to Stage," *Ma'arachot* 33 (1959): 52.

40. David Ben-Gurion, "On the Paratroopers" (speech at a conference of commanders of the Paratrooper Brigade, April 25, 1957), in *Uniqueness and Purpose: Speeches on Israel's Security*, 3rd edition (Tel Aviv: Ma'arachot and Defense Ministry Publications, 2011), 298–99.

41. On the material element, see the beginning of chapter 5.

42. Drori, *Dan Shomron*, 221.

43. Drori, *Dan Shomron*, 250.

44. Drori, *Dan Shomron*, 254.

45. Drori, *Dan Shomron*, 311.

46. Drori, *Dan Shomron*, 242.

47. Dan Shomron, "The Commander of the Mafhash, Ground Forces and Combined Arms Battle" (lecture to cadets, National Security College, 1984), cited in Drori, *Dan Shomron*, 272.

48. Amos Kovach and Smadar Witteboon, *Insights from the Development and Force Design of the Tamuz Array* (Rafael-Mechtzav, 2017), 39–40.

49. "Summary of the Future Battlefield Project," National Security College, July 27, 1986.

50. Interview with David Ivry, February 20, 2017.

51. Shomron, "Commander of the Mafhash," 273.

52. Drori, *Dan Shomron*, 241.

53. Drori, *Dan Shomron*, 282.

54. Drori, *Dan Shomron*, 282.

55. Dan Shomron, interview, *Romach* 3 (July 1986): 1–4.

56. Benny Beit-Or, interview, 2016, cited in Drori, *Dan Shomron*, 311.

57. "The Misgav Plan: Updated Assumptions and Instructions," General Staff/Agat/Planning Department, November 1988.

58. Interview with Ehud Barak, June 26, 2017.

59. Ze'ev Bonen, *Rafael from Laboratory to Battle* (N.D.D. Media, 2003), 52.

60. Interview with Barak, June 26, 2017.

61. Meir Finkel, *The Israeli General Staff: Its Learning Methods, Planning Processes, Organizational Rationale* (Ben Shemen: Modan and Ma'arachot, 2020), 255–72.

62. "Summary of the Future Battlefield Project." The lecture in slightly different versions was published under the title "The IDF: Today, Yesterday, and Tomorrow," *Ma'arachot—Hirhoorim Vi'iroorim* 7 (January 1987): 3–22. The publication notes that the text is based on Barak's statements in memory of the late Major Amitai Nahman, Kibbutz Givat Haim Ihud, October 31, 1986.

63. "Summary of the Future Battlefield Project."

64. Elron, "Main Trends," 13–14.

65. Tal, *National Security*, 225–26.

66. Brigadier General Ran Goren, "The Participation of the Air Force in the Ground Battle in the Age of PGM," *Ma'arachot—Hirhoorim Vi'iroorim* 8 (November 1988): 3–6.

67. Interview with Barak, June 26, 2017.

68. Anshil Pfeffer, "IDF Reveals Tamuz Missile," *Ha'aretz*, August 1, 2011.

69. *IDF Strategy: Trends and Basic Ideas for Force Design and Employment* (Amatz-Tohad, 2002), 80–81.

70. The unit's heritage book, 2008.

71. Elron, "Main Trends," 35–37.

72. Elron, "Main Trends," 40.

73. Elron, "Main Trends," 41.

74. Chief of Staff's Office, "Initial Summary of Operation Defensive Shield—Chief of Staff's Summary," May 19, 2002.

75. Chief of Staff's Office, "Defensive Shield, General Staff Forum Learning Session—Chief of Staff's Summary," June 2, 2002.

76. Moshe Ya'alon, "Preparing the Force for a Limited Confrontation," *Ma'arachot* 380–81 (2002): 24–29.

77. "2007 Multiyear Committee: Terror and Guerrilla Activity," undated presentation (latest possible date: September 2002). Cited in Elron, "Main Trends," 43.

78. General staff workshop on the 2007 multiyear plan, chief of staff's summary, cited in Elron, "Main Trends."

79. Raz Sagi, "The Dangerous Language of the Limited Confrontation," *Ma'arachot* 380–81 (2001): 54–55; Yehuda Wagman, "Limited

Confrontation: The Failure," in *Limited Confrontation: An Anthology*, ed. Hagai Golan and Shaul Shai (Tel Aviv: Ma'arachot, 2004): 251–98.

80. Boaz Zalmanovich, "Clarification and Comment on Givati Reconnaissance Battalion Training," *Machatz* 14 (April 2004): 18.

81. Eyal, *Second Intifada*, 15–16.

82. See Finkel, *Military Agility*, 54–66.

83. Interview with Boaz Amidror, April 23, 2017.

84. Captain Nir and Major Yoav, "Flexibility in Force Design and Its Employment in a Limited Confrontation: The Artillery Corps as a Test Case," *Ma'arachot* 401 (May 2005): 58–61.

85. Erez Weiner, "From Confusion to Clarity: The Development of a Combat Doctrine against Irregular Forces, 1996–2004," *Ma'arachot* 409–10 (December 2006): 4–19.

86. "Low Signature Activity," (IDF, Amatz-Tohad, 2000).

87. Shmuel "Samu" Nir, "Victory and Warning in a Limited Confrontation," *Zarkor* 9 (Amatz-Tohad, April 2003).

88. Shmuel "Samu" Nir, "The Limited Confrontation: An Anthology of Articles," *Zarkor* 7, July 2002.

89. Sagi, "Dangerous Language," 54–55.

90. Ya'alon, "Preparing the Force for a Limited Confrontation," 24–29.

91. "Studies on the Combat Doctrine in a Limited Confrontation," First Annual Conference of the College for the Study of Tactics and Force Employment, November 2003, Command and Staff College; "Studies on the Limited Confrontation and Command and Control in the Information Age," Second Conference of the College for the Study of Tactics and Force Employment, November 2005, Command and Staff College.

92. *The Story of a Brigade: The Kfir Brigade—The First Years*, Association of Kfir Brigade Fighters, City of Afula, 2011.

93. Zalmanovich, "Clarification and Comment," 18. See also Boaz Zalmanovich, "The Tactical Unit for Fighting in a Limited Confrontation: The Idea, Testing Process, and Experimenting," *Ma'arachot* 405 (February 2006): 28–33.

94. Dani Asher, "Combat Intelligence Collection—The Observer before the Camp: The Combat Intelligence Gathering Branch and Its Legacy," Northern Command intelligence branch, July 2013.

95. For a description of the decline in the scope of terror, see Ya'alon, *The Longer Shorter Way*, 137.

96. This included the inability to capture the town of Bint Jbeil; the inability to stop rocket fire; major losses in the final two days of the war; damage to armor; the inability to cross Wadi Saluki; and the failure to supply units operating only a few kilometers from Israel's border with food and water.

97. For more on this subject, see Meir Finkel, *Military Agility*, chapter 2, "The Effect of Prolonged Routine Security Operations on Wartime Capabilities."

98. *Winograd Report*, 273, 277.

Chapter 6

1. For more on Eshkol and Rabin, see Gluska, *Eshkol*, 282.

2. Yagil Levy, "Military Contrarianism: The Chief of Staff's Opposition to the Political Level," *Military and Strategy* 5, no. 2 (September 2013): 35–51.

3. Dayan, *Story of My Life*, 140: "On more than one occasion I had to dissuade him from ordering military actions that seemed wrong to me."

4. Levy, "Military Contrarianism."

5. Michael Bar-Zohar, *Ben-Gurion*, vol. 2 (Tel Aviv: Am Oved, 1977), 943–44.

6. Elron, *Second Round*, 27. See additional sources there.

7. Yitzhak Greenberg, *Calculation and Power: The Defense Budget from War to War, 1957–1967* (Tel Aviv: Defense Ministry Publications, 1997), 37–38.

8. Elron, *Second Round*, 32–33.

9. Yadin's statements in a limited general staff meeting, in Yitzhak Greenberg, *Fighting Nation: Laying the Foundations of the Reserve Array, 1949–1950* (Beer Sheva: Ben-Gurion Heritage Center, Ben-Gurion University of the Negev, 2001), 18.

10. Ben-Gurion's letter to Yadin, October 27, 1949, in *David Ben-Gurion: The First Prime Minister, Selected Documents (1947–1963)*, ed. Eli Shalitiel (Jerusalem: Israel State Archives, 1997), 95–96.

11. Elron, *Second Round*, 45.

12. Elron, *Second Round*, 47. Letter quoted: the chief of staff to the defense minister, Manpower Branch, March 17, 1952.

13. Ben-Gurion's letter to Yadin, September 4, 1952, in Shalitiel, *David Ben-Gurion*, 103–4.

14. Letter from the acting general manager of the Defense Ministry to the defense minister, "The Defense Budget for 1952–1953," October 19, 1952, in Elron, *Second Round*, 51.

15. Bar-Zohar, *Ben-Gurion*, 945.

16. Elron, *Second Round*, 360–61.

17. Brezner, *Gallant Chargers*, 325.

18. General staff meeting in Prime Minister Ben-Gurion's office in Jerusalem, July 19, 1956, in Golani, *There Will Be War in the Summer*, vol. 1, 215n22.

19. Brezner, *Gallant Chargers*, 325–31.

20. Brezner, *Gallant Chargers*, 325–31.

21. Dayan, *Story of My Life*, 223.

22. General staff meeting, No. 19/56 (minutes), September 1, 1956 (Sabbath), CZO 32/847/1962, 1.

23. Mordechai Naor, *Laskov: Fighter, Human Being, Friend* (Jerusalem: Keter, 1988), 254. Bar-Lev told his biographer that Dayan's general attitude was different—he did not want to forcibly impose his opinions on his subordinates but to persuade them through discussions; see Carmit Gai, *Bar-Lev: A Biography* (Tel Aviv: Am Oved, 1998), 94–95.

24. Naor, *Laskov: Fighter*, 256.

25. Interview with Meir Zore'a, cited in Hanoch Patishi, *Major General Meir Zore'a: A Biography* (Tel Aviv: Hakibbutz Hame'uchad, 2013), 172.

26. General Staff Meeting, September 1, 1956.

27. General Staff Meeting, September 1, 1956.

28. Brezner, *Gallant Chargers*, 330.

29. Naor, *Laskov: Fighter*, 257.

30. Researched by David Shalom, *The Mafhash as Re-organization* (Jerusalem: Hebrew University of Jerusalem, 1987); Tzachi Segev, "The History of the Development of the Mazi," Doctrine Department, *Zarkor* 13 (April 2010); Ze'ev Elron, "The Organization of the Mafhash and Mazi" (draft for comments), (Tohad, History Department, 2014).

31. For a review up to 1977, see Elron, "The Organization."

32. Interview with Avraham Tamir, cited in Shalom, *Mafhash as Re-organization*, 12.

33. Deputy Chief of Staff Major General Dan Shomron, "The Mafhash: A New Array of the Ground Branches," undated, probably late 1983 or early 1984. Cited in Elron, "The Organization."

34. Elron, "The Organization," 19; Segev, "History of the Development," 23.

35. The reasons for Weizman's attempts are unclear since he did not elaborate on them in his memoirs, but we may assume they were a combination of political needs and his lessons from his roles in the IDF.

36. Drori, *Dan Shomron*, 259.

37. Mafhash establishment team, "The Field Forces Headquarters: Designation, Structure and Organization," February 1980.

38. Gur, *Chief of Staff*, 294–95.

39. Gur, *Chief of Staff*, 294–95.

40. Israel Tal, "Ground Forces: Designation and Organization," December 1977.

41. Interview with Rabin in the Israeli daily *Davar*, December 21, 1979, cited in Shalom, *Mafhash as Re-organization*, 16.

42. Shalom, *Mafhash as Re-organization*, 15–17.

43. Minutes: "The philosophy behind the organization and structure of the IDF and thoughts of the future." Participants: Lieutenant General (res.) Motta Gur, chief officer of the combat engineers, chief artillery officer, commander of the Armored Corps, head of the doctrine and training branch. National Defense College, IDF and Defense Ministry, February 24, 1982, 8–9.

44. Ezer Weizman, *The Battle for Peace: Personal Observation* (Tel Aviv: Idanim, 1981), 27.

45. Shalom, *Mafhash as Re-organization*, 28.

46. Shalom, *Mafhash as Re-organization*, 13.

47. "Various Positions on Ground Force Designation and Organization prior to the Chief of Staff Discussion," reports from National Defense College for fifth graduation class, 1977–78, released July 1978.

48. "Various Positions on Ground Force Designation," 3–5.

49. "Various Positions on Ground Force Designation," 11.

50. "Various Positions on Ground Force Designation," 14.

51. "Various Positions on Ground Force Designation," 50.

52. "Various Positions on Ground Force Designation," 16–18.

53. "Various Positions on Ground Force Designation," 19.

54. "Various Positions on Ground Force Designation," 21.

55. "Various Positions on Ground Force Designation," 23.

56. The Mafhash establishment team, "Field Forces Headquarters," 1–2.

57. Deputy Chief of Staff's Office (Major General Yekutiel Adam), "Reorganization of the Ground ORBAT," November 1, 1978. See document, "Colonel Emanuel Wald to Deputy Chief of Staff, Changes in Ground Organization and Structure," May 5, 1983.

58. Shalom, *Mafhash as Re-organization*, 20.

59. The Mafhash establishment team "Field Forces Headquarters," 1–2.

60. Chief of Staff's Office (MN-2-16334), December 1, 1979.

61. Chief of Staff's Office (MN-2-8329), December 9, 1979.

62. Shalom, *Mafhash as Re-organization*, 33.

63. Shalom, *Mafhash as Re-organization*, 34.

64. Shalom, *Mafhash as Re-organization*, 24–25.

65. Shalom, *Mafhash as Re-organization*, 24–25.

66. Shalom, *Mafhash as Re-organization*, 30.

67. Shalom, *Mafhash as Re-organization*, 24–25, 29.

68. Dan Shomron, "The Mafhash: The Basis for the Development of the Ground Forces," in *The War on Terror and Israel's Security Policy, 1979–1988*, ed. Ze'ev Klein (Tel Aviv: Ma'ariv and Revivim, 1988), 183–89.

69. Drori, *Quiet Leadership*, 259–60.

70. Eitan and Goldstein, *A Soldier's Story*, 213; Aryeh Krishak, *On a Direct Line: Mordechai Tzipori* (Tel Aviv: Yediot Achronot, 1977).

71. Interviews with Moshe Arens over a period of several years (for example: Segev, "History of the Development," 2010).

72. Shalom, *Mafhash as Re-organization*, 12.

73. Shalom, *Mafhash as Re-organization*, 25. Interview with Arens, 2016. Arens stressed the importance of his participation (as committee chairman) in the Foreign Affairs and Security Committee on the decision for establishing the Mafhash.

74. Shalom, *Mafhash as Re-organization*, 36.

75. Moshe Arens (defense minister), "Renewal of the National Agreement on Security," in Klein, *War on Terror*, 141–47.

76. Interview with Ivry, February 20, 2017.

77. Shalom, *Mafhash as Re-organization*, 41.

78. Moshe Levi, "From Lebanon to the Future Battlefield," in Klein, *War on Terror*, 150–65.

79. Levi, "From Lebanon to the Future Battlefield," 155.

80. Chief of Staff's Office, Supreme Command Office, opening statement to the 13th Graduating Class of the National Defense College, September 8, 1985. MN-00183–341, October 10, 1985.

81. Levi, "From Lebanon to the Future Battlefield," 150–65.

82. Moshe Levi, "Employing the Army in an Emergency, the Strategic Concept" (lecture, National Defense College, July 17, 1985), MN-00135–341, August 18, 1985, 21.

83. Drori, *Dan Shomron*, 261.

84. Elron, "The Organization," 12–13.

85. Peled, *A Military Man*, 272.

86. Drori, *Dan Shomron*, 260. Based on an interview with Arens.

87. Shalom, *Mafhash as Re-organization*, 34.

88. Shomron, "Mafhash: The Basis for the Development," 183–89.

89. Drori, *Dan Shomron*, 263.

90. Drori, *Dan Shomron*, 268–69.

91. Interview with Yitzhak Mordechai, in Drori, *Dan Shomron*, 269.

92. Conversation with Benny Michelson based on his unpublished biography of Chief of Staff Moshe Levi.

93. For a review of the development process and discussions on the Lavi, see Brigadier General Y., "The Lavi Project—Decision Making 1980–1987," *Ma'arachot* 341 (1995): 26–35.

94. Levi, "From Lebanon to the Future Battlefield."

95. Reuven Pedhatzur, "The IDF Will Ask for an Additional 15% for Its Budget" *Ha'aretz*, July 31, 1986.

96. Statements of the chief of staff in an article by Reuven Pedhatzur, "Even if the Lavi Project Is Not Funded by the Security Budget, the IDF Will Still Lack Money," *Ha'aretz*, August 1, 1986.

97. Ze'ev Klein, "The Lavi Aircraft," in Klein, *War on Terror*, 178–82.

98. Zvi Elush, "Not at Our Expense," *Yediot Achronot*, February 13, 1987.

99. Dov Zakheim, *Flight of the Lavi: Inside a U.S.-Israeli Crisis*, English edition (Washington, DC: Brassey's, 1996), 87.

100. Ze'ev Schiff, "The Chief of Staff's Involvement in the Lavi Episode," *Ha'aretz*, June 24, 1987.

101. Drori, *Dan Shomron*, 317–18.
102. Yitzhak Rabin, "Toward a Different Security Concept," in Klein, *War on Terror*, 171–77.
103. State Comptroller, 37th Annual Report, "The Lavi Project—Decision Making"; Brigadier General Y., "The Lavi Project."
104. Zakheim, *Flight of the Lavi*, 179.
105. Reuven Pedhatzur, "The Commander of the Navy: The Continuation of the Discussion on the Lavi Delays a Decision on Replenishment," *Haʾaretz*, June 24, 1987.
106. Zakheim, *Flight of the Lavi*, 243.
107. Zeʾev Schiff, "The Lavi Episode."
108. Moshe Arens, *War and Peace in the Middle East* (Tel Aviv: Yediot Achronot, 1995), 11–12.

Conclusions

1. Prime Minister Menachem Begin, 1981, speech on the eve of elections and with tension on the Syrian border mounting.
2. Minister Yitzhak Modaʾi went so far as to insinuate that the chief of staff should resign because of his failure to crush the Palestinian uprising. See Schiff and Yaʾari, *Intifada*, 129.
3. Schiff and Yaʾari, *Intifada*, 166.
4. Halutz, *At Eye Level*, 332.
5. Asa Kasher, "The Ethics in Appointing the Chief of Staff," *Keevoonim* 23 (October 21, 2010): 21.
6. Halutz, *At Eye Level*, 294.
7. Drori, *Dan Shomron*, 288–89.
8. With the support of Defense Minister Yitzhak Mordechai, Matan Vilnai's rival.
9. Shlomo Gazit, "Moshe Dayan and the IDF," in *Facing Hostile Borders: The Army and Security in Israel's First Decade*, ed. Mordechai Bar-On. (Modi'in, Macabim, Reut, Effi Meltzer, and the Israel Galili Center of Defense Studies, 2017), 167–78.
10. This section elaborates on the basic proposal in Kasher's article, "The Ethics in Appointing a Chief of Staff."

BIBLIOGRAPHY

Books in Hebrew

Adan, Avraham "Bren." *On Both Banks of the Suez Canal*. Jerusalem: Idanim, 1979.

Amit, Meir. *Head to Head: A Personal Look at Big Events and Secret Episodes*. Or Yehuda: Hed Artzi, 1999.

Arens, Moshe. *War and Peace in the Middle East*. Tel Aviv: Yediot Achronot, 1995.

Association of Kfir Brigade Fighters. *The Story of a Brigade: The Kfir Brigade— The First Years*. Association of Kfir Brigade Fighters, City of Afula, 2011.

Avnery, Aryeh. *Retaliatory Raids: IDF Actions behind Enemy Lines on All Fronts*. Vol. 1. Tel Aviv: Sifriyat Madim, 1970.

Bar-On, Mordechai. *Challenge and Struggle: The Road to the Sinai Campaign, 1956*. Beer Sheva: Ben-Gurion University Publications, 1991.

Bartov, Hanoch. *Dado, 48 Years and 20 Days*. Vol. 1, expanded edition. Or Yehuda: Dvir, 2002.

Bar-Zohar, Michael. *Ben-Gurion*. Vol. 2. Tel Aviv: Am Oved, 1977.

———. *The Paratroopers Book*. Tel Aviv: Levin-Epstein, 1969.

Ben Ari, Uri. *Forward Charge! The Path of the Armored Corps' Struggle*. Tel Aviv: Ma'arachot, 1998.

Ben-Gurion, David. "On the Paratroopers." Speech at a conference of commanders of the Paratrooper Brigade, April 25, 1957. In *Uniqueness and Purpose: Speeches on Israel's Security*. 3rd edition. Tel Aviv: Ma'arachot and Defense Ministry Publications, 2011.

Bonen, Ze'ev. *Rafael from Laboratory to Battle*. Tel Aviv: N.D.D. Media, 2003.

Brezner, Amiad. *Gallant Chargers: Developments and Transformations in Israeli Armor from the End of the War of Independence to the Sinai Campaign*. Tel Aviv: Ma'arachot, 1999.

Carmel, Amos. *The Victory General: Asaf Simhoni*. Tel Aviv: Yediot Sfarim, 2009.

Dayan, Moshe. *Story of My Life*. Jerusalem: Idanim, 1976.

Dor, Dani, and Yehuda Schiff. *The Story of Israel's Chiefs of Staff*. (Tel Aviv: Ma'ariv, 2002).

Drori, Ze'ev. *Dan Shomron: Subtle Leadership*. Rishon Lezion: Yediot Achronot, 2016.

———. "The Military Level's Impact on Security Escalation." In *Black Arrow: Gaza Actions and Israeli Policy in the 1950s*, edited by Mottti Golani. Tel Aviv: Ma'arachot, 1994.

Eilam, Uzi. *Eilam's Arc: How Israel Became a Military Technology Powerhouse*. Tel Aviv: Yediot Achronot, 2009.

Eitan, Rafael. *The Fourth Parachute Got Open*. Tel Aviv: Yediot Achronot and Hemed, 2001.

Eitan, Rafael, and Dov Goldstein. *Raful: A Soldier's Story*. Tel Aviv: Sifriyat Ma'ariv, 1985.

Elron, Ze'ev. "The IDF Paratroopers: From the War of Independence to the Sinai Campaign." In *1948: Studies at the Jerusalem School on War, Army and Society*, edited by Alon Kadish. Ben Shemen: Modan, 2015.

———. *Toward the Second Round: Transformations in the IDF and the Change in the Security Concept That Wasn't, 1952–1955*. Ben Shemen: Modan and Ma'arachot, 2016.

Finkel, Meir. *The Israeli General Staff: Its Learning Methods, Planning Processes, Organizational Rationale*. Ben Shemen: Modan and Ma'arachot, 2020.

Gai, Carmit. *Bar-Lev: A Biography*. Tel Aviv: Am Oved, 1998

Gazit, Shlomo. *Critical Junctures: From the Palmach to the Head of Aman*. Rishon Lezion: Yediot Achronot-Hemed, 2016.

———. "Moshe Dayan and the IDF." In *Facing Hostile Borders: The Army and Security in Israel's First Decade*, edited by Mordechai Bar-On. Modi'in, Macabim, Reut, Effi Meltzer, and the Israel Galili Center of Defense Studies, 2017.

Gluska, Ami. *Eshkol, Give an Order: The IDF and Israeli Government on the Road to the Six-Day War, 1963–1967*. Tel Aviv: Ma'arachot, 2004.

Golan, Shimon. *Israel's War in Lebanon, 1982*. Ben Shemen: Modan, Ma'arachot, and the IDF History Department, 2017.

———. *War on Three Fronts*. Tel Aviv: Ma'arachot, 2007.

Golani, Motti. *There Will Be War in the Summer: Israel on the Road to the Sinai Campaign, 1955–1956*. Vols. 1 and 2. Tel Aviv: Ma'arachot, 1997.

Gordon, Shmuel. *30 Hours in October, Fatal Decisions: The Air Force at the Outset of the Yom Kippur War*. Tel Aviv: Sifriyat Ma'ariv, 2008.

Greenberg, Yitzhak. *Calculation and Power: The Defense Budget from War to War, 1957–1967*. Tel Aviv: Defense Ministry Publications, 1997.

———. *A Fighting Nation: Laying the Foundations of the Reserve Array, 1949–1950*. Beer Sheva: Ben-Gurion Heritage Center, Ben-Gurion University of the Negev, 2001.

Gur, Mordechai. *The Chief of Staff*. Tel Aviv: Ma'arachot, 1998.

Halutz, Dan. *At Eye Level*. Tel Aviv: Yediot Achronot-Hemed, 2010.

Harel, Amos, and Avi Issacharoff. *The Seventh War: How We Won and Why We Lost the War with the Palestinians*. Tel Aviv: Yediot Achronot-Sifrei Hemed, 2004.

Ivry, David. "A Chapter on the SAM Array in Lebanon in the Spring of 1981: The Complexity of Processes." Unpublished memoir, last updated August 2009.

Kahalani, Avigdor. *The Way of the Fighter*. Tel Aviv: Steimatzky, 1989.

Klein, Ze'ev, ed. *The War on Terror and Israel's Security Policy, 1979–1988*. Tel Aviv: Ma'ariv and Revivim, 1988.

Krishak, Aryeh. *On a Direct Line: Mordechai Tzipori*. Tel Aviv: Yediot Achronot, 1977.

Lachish, Ze'ev. "The Air Force in War: A Calculated Risk?" In *The Six-Day War: Cathedra of Commanders and Scholars*, edited by Effi Meltzer. Summary of the "Issues in Israel's Security" Seminar 1996. Reut: Israel Galili Center of Defense Studies and the Israel Society for Military History, in association with Tel Aviv University, 1996, 83–90.

Milstein, Uri. *The History of the Paratroopers from the War of Independence to War in Lebanon*. Tel Aviv: Schalgi Publishing House, 1985.

Naor, Mordechai. *Laskov: Fighter, Human Being, Friend*. Jerusalem: Keter, 1988.

Narkis, Uzi. *Soldier of Jerusalem*. Tel Aviv: Defense Ministry Publications, 1991.

Nir, Natke. *The Wounded Officer Who Returned to the Battlefield*. Tel Aviv: Yediot Achronot-Sifrei Hemed, 2010.

Patishi, Hanoch. *Major General Meir Zore'a: A Biography*. Tel Aviv: Hakibbutz Hame'uchad, 2013.

Peled, Benny. *Days of Reckoning*. Ben Shemen: Modan, 2004.

Peled, Yossi. *A Military Man*. Tel Aviv: Sifriat Ma'ariv, 1993.

Rabin, Yitzhak, and Dov Goldstein. *Service Notebook*. Vol. 1. Tel Aviv: Sifriyat Ma'ariv, 1979.

Ronen, Ran. *Hawk in the Sky*. Tel Aviv: Yediot Achronot, 2002.

Rosenthal, Yemima, ed. *Yitzhak Rabin, Prime Minister of Israel: Anthology of Documents of His Life*. Vol. 1, 1922–1967. Jerusalem: State Archive, 2005.

Rotem, Avraham. *Self-Criticism in the Castle*. Tel Aviv: Ma'arachot and the Defense Ministry, 2007.

Schiff, Ze'ev, and Ehud Ya'ari. *Intifada*. Jerusalem: Schocken, 1990.

Shachar, Amira. "The History of the Merkava Tank." Unpublished manuscript.

Shalom, Danny. *Like Thunder on a Clear Day*. Rishon Lezion: Ba'aveer Aviation Publications, 2002.

Shalom, David. *The Ground Forces HQ (Mafhash) as Re-organization*. Jerusalem: Hebrew University of Jerusalem 1987.

Shalitiel, Eli, ed. *David Ben-Gurion: The First Prime Minister, Selected Documents, 1947–1963*. Jerusalem: State Archives, 1997.

Shapira, Anita. *From Sacking the Head of the Hagana's National Staff to Dismantling the Palmach: Issues in the Struggle for Security Leadership, 1948*. Tel Aviv: Kibbutz Hame'uchad, 1985.

Sharett, Moshe. *Personal Diary 1954*. Tel Aviv: Sifriyat Ma'ariv, 1978.

Spector, Iftach. *Loud and Clear*. Tel Aviv: Yediot Achronot, 2008.

Tal, Israel. *National Security: Few Against Many*. Tel Aviv: Dvir, 1996.

Tamari, Dov. *The Armed Nation: The Rise and Fall of the Reserves' Phenomenon*. Tel Aviv: Modan and Ma'arachot, 2017.

Tamir, Moshe. *War without a Sign*. Tel Aviv: Ma'arachot, 2005.

Teveth, Shabtai. *Moshe Dayan*. Jerusalem: Steimatzky's Agency together with Weidenfeld and Nicolson, 1972.

———. *Moshe Dayan: A Biography*. Jerusalem, Schocken, 1971.

Turgan, Sagi, *I'll Never Be a General*. Jerusalem: Yad Ben Zvi, 2017.

Wagman, Yehuda. "Limited Confrontation: The Failure." In *Limited Confrontation: An Anthology*. Edited by Hagai Golan and Shaul Shai. Tel Aviv: Ma'arachot, 2004.

Wald, Emanuel. *The Curse of the Broken Vessels: The Twilight of Israeli Military and Political Power, 1967–1982*. Jerusalem: Schocken, 1987.

Weizman, Ezer. *The Battle for Peace: Personal Observation*. Tel Aviv: Idanim, 1981.

———. *Skyward, Earthbound*. Tel Aviv: Sifriyat Ma'ariv, 1973.

Winograd Commission Report. Interim report of the Committee for Investigating the Lebanon Campaign, April 2007.

Winograd Commission Report, Final Verdict. Report of the Committee for Investigating the Lebanon Campaign, 2008.

Ya'alon, Moshe. *The Longer Shorter Way*. Rishon Lezion: Yediot Achronot-Sifrei Hemed, 2008.

Books in English

Bar-On, Mordechai. *The Gates of Gaza: Israel's Road to the Suez and Back, 1955–1957*. New York: St. Martin's Press, 1994.

Dayan, Moshe. *Diary of the Sinai Campaign, 1956*. London: Sphere Books, 1967.

Finkel, Meir. *Military Agility: Ensuring Effective and Rapid Transition from Peace to War*. Lexington, KY: University Press of Kentucky, 2020.

Hirsch, Gal. *Defensive Shield: An Israeli Special Forces Commander on the Front Line of Counterterrorism*. Jerusalem: Gefen Books, 2016.

Keegan, John. *Churchill's Generals*. London: Cassell, 1991.

Ricks, Thomas E. *The Generals: American Military Command from World War II to Today*. New York: Penguin Books, 2013.

Sharon, Ariel, with David Chanoff. *Warrior*. New York: Simon and Schuster, 2005.

Zabecki, David T., ed. *Chief of Staff: The Principal Officers Behind History's Great Commanders*. Annapolis, MD: Naval Institute Press, 2008.

Zakheim, Dov. *Flight of the Lavi: Inside a U.S.-Israeli Crisis*. Washington, DC: Brassey's, 1996.

Articles in Hebrew

Bar-Kochva, Moshe. "The Intifada Fiasco and the Need for a Contingency Plan." *Netiv* 93 (1991).

Bender, Arik. "Gantz on Syria: Growing Instability in the Golan Heights Sector." *NRG*, June 5, 2012.

Bengal, Maya. "The Former Chiefs-of-Staff Salute Gabi Ashkenazi." Special for "Ma'ariv: Four Chiefs-of-Staff Who Served prior to Ashkenazi Embraced Him as a Comrade in Arms, Thank Him for His Contribution and Wish Him the Best for the Future." *NRG*, February 14, 2011.

Bronfeld, Shaul. "From the Electronic Summer of 1970 to the Winter of 1973: The Story of the Loss of Air Supremacy." *Bein Hakatavim* 11–12 (June 2017).

Caspit, Ben. "Towards Confrontation: The IDF of 2016 Is Going through the Most Dramatic Change since Its Founding." *Ma'ariv*, April 20, 2014.

Cohen, Gili. "Syria Has Become the Center of Global Jihad That Threatens the Entire Region." *Ha'aretz*, July 24, 2013.

Dayan, Moshe. "Military Activity in Peacetime." *Ma'arachot* 118–19 (April 1959): 54–61.

Eiland, Giora. "The Conclusion of Chief of Staff Gabi Ashkenazi's Tenure: An Evaluation." *Mabat Al*, no. 242 (February 2011).

Elush, Zvi. "Not at Our Expense." *Yediot Achronot*, February 13, 1987.

Finkel, Meir. "The Second Lebanon War: Military Failure, Political-Security Success." *Ma'arachot* 466–67 (September 2016).

Fishman, Alex. "The IDF Changes Orientation: The Security Agenda on the Way to the Voting Booth." *Strategic Update* 8, no. 4 (January 2006).

Gal, Nurit. "Who Moved My Powers of Authorization?" *Ma'arachot* 420–21 (September 2008).

Goren, Ran. "The Participation of the Air Force in the Ground Battle in the Age of PGM." *Ma'arachot—Hirhoorim Vi'iroorim* 8 (November 1988).

Greenberg, Hanan. "A Revolution in the IDF: Solders to Serve Two Years in 2010." *Ynet*, February 13, 2006.

———. "Training Cancellations—Only with the Chief of Staff's Approval." *Ynet*, April 1, 2007.

Halutz, Dan. "Airpower as a Decision Variable." *Studies in National Security* 2 (July 2001).

Harel, Amos. "Chief of Staff Gabi Ashkenazi Takes His Leave of President Shimon Peres." *Ha'aretz*, February 7, 2011.

———. "Division Commanders' Course to Open Today." *Ha'aretz*, May 27, 2007.

———. "The First Dismissal: The Chief of Staff Appointed Kaplinsky as His Representative in the North." *Ha'aretz*, August 10, 2006.

Issacharoff, Avi, and Amos Harel. "Cast Lead: The Fighting in Gaza Was a Slight Improvement over the Flaws of the Second Lebanon War." *Ha'aretz*, January 12, 2009.

Kasher, Asa. "The Ethics in Appointing the Chief of Staff." *Keevoonim* 23 (October 21, 2010).

The Knesset, Foreign Affairs and Defense Committee. "IDF Multiyear Gideon Plan—Special Report of the Subcommittee on Security Conception and Force Buildup." Unclassified version, September 2017.

Levy, Yagil. "Military Contrarianism: The Chief of Staff's Opposition to the Political Level." *Military and Strategy* 5, no. 2 (September 2013).

Miranda, Amnon. "Ashkenazi to Members of Parliament: What Happened in the War Won't Be Repeated." *Ynet*, March 28, 2007.

Nir, Captain, and Major Yoav. "Flexibility in Force Design and Its Employment in a Limited Confrontation: The Artillery Corps as a Test Case." *Ma'arachot* 401 (May 2005).

Oren, Amir. "Gantz Has Decided to Establish a New Regional Division on the Golan Heights to Block Attacks from Syria." *Ha'aretz*, July 10, 2013.

Pedhatzur, Reuven. "The Commander of the Navy: The Continuation of the Discussion on the Lavi Delays a Decision on Replenishment." *Ha'aretz*, June 24, 1987.

———. "Even If the Lavi Project Is Not Funded by the Security Budget, the IDF Will Still Lack Money." *Ha'aretz*, August 1, 1986.

———. "The IDF Will Ask for an Additional 15% for Its Budget." *Ha'aretz*, July 31, 1986.

Pfeffer, Anshil. "IDF Reveals Tamuz Missile." *Ha'aretz*, August 1, 2011.

Rapaport, Amir. "The IDF and the Lessons of the Second Lebanon War." *Studies in Mideast Security and Policy Studies* no. 85 (December 2010).

Raz, Sagi. "The Dangerous Language of the Limited Confrontation." *Ma'arachot* 380–81 (December 2001).

Schiff, Ze'ev. "The Chief of Staff's Involvement in the Lavi Episode." *Ha'aretz*, June 24, 1987.

Tamari, Dov. "The Battle between Operational Thinking and Tactical Logic." *Ba'shiryon* 6 (October 1999).

Wallach, Yehuda. "Armor Assault That Bypasses Dayan." Interview by Benny Michalson and Shaul Nagar. *Shiryon* 6 (October 1999).

Weiner, Erez. "From Confusion to Clarity: The Development of a Combat Doctrine against Irregular Forces, 1996–2004." *Ma'arachot* 409–10 (December 2006).

Y., Brigadier General. "The Lavi Project—Decision Making 1980–1987." *Ma'arachot* 341 (June 1995).

Ya'alon, Moshe. "Preparing the Force for a Limited Confrontation." *Ma'arachot* 380–81 (December 2002).

Zalmanovich, Boaz. "Clarification and Comment on Givati Reconnaissance Battalion Training." *Machatz* 14 (April 2004).

———. "The Establishment of Special Forces in the Low Intensity Conflict." *Ma'arachot* 369 (February 2000).

———. "The Tactical Unit for Fighting in a Limited Confrontation: The Idea, Testing Process, and Experimenting." *Ma'arachot* 405 (February 2006).

Zeitun Yoav. "As Gantz Sees It: The Battles in Syria on the Golan Heights Border." *Ynet*, November 4, 2012.

IDF Internal Documents (Main Sources)

Asher, Dani. "Combat Intelligence Collection—The Observer before the Camp: The Combat Intelligence Gathering Branch and Its Legacy." Northern Command Intelligence branch, July 2013.

Berelovich, Eyal. "The Development of the IDF's Border Defense Concept, 1948–2016." Dado Institute Publications, January 2017.

Chief of Staff's Office. "Defensive Shield." General Staff forum learning session. Chief of Staff Summary, June 2, 2002.

———. "Employing the Army in an Emergency, the Strategic Concept." Chief of Staff lecture at the National Defense College, July 17, 1985. MN-00135–341, August 18, 1985, 21.

———. General Staff workshop for formulating the 2012 Tefen multiyear plan. Chief of Staff Summary, September 2, 2007.

———. "IDF Routine Security Meeting, March 1995." Chief of Staff Summary, MS 3108–22, April 27, 1995.

———. Initial Summary of Operation Defensive Shield. Chief of Staff Summary, May 19, 2002.

———. Opening statement to the 13th Graduating Class of the National Defense College, September 8, 1985. MN-00183–341, October 10, 1985.

Command and Staff College. "Studies on the Combat Doctrine in a Limited Confrontation." First Annual Conference of the College for the Study of Tactics and Force Employment, Command and Staff College, November 2003.

———. "Studies on the Limited Confrontation and Command and Control in the Information Age." Second Conference of the College for the Study of Tactics and Force Employment, Command and Staff College, November 2005.

Elron, Zeʼev. "Main Trends in Force Building as Reflected in the Multiyear Plans from Mirkam to Tefen, 1991–2011." Historical review within the framework of "A Decade of Learning" Initiative, November 2013.

———. "The Organization of the Mafhash and Mazi" (draft for comments). Tohad, History Department, 2014.

Eyal, Yigal. *Ebb and Tide: The Second Intifada—Multifront Confrontation, 1996–2004*. Ground Forces Command/Doctrine Department, 2015.

General Staff/Agat/Planning Department. "The Misgav Plan: Updated Assumptions and Instructions." General Staff/Agat/Planning Department, November 1988.

Golan, Shimon. "The Beginning of the First Intifada as Reflected in Discussions at the Defense Minister and General Staff Levels, December 9, 1987–January 26, 1988." Amatz-Tohad, History Department, February 2016.

———. "The Second Lebanon War: Decision Making at the Strategic Level." IDF, History Department, 2014.

———. "The Strategic-Operational Planning for the First Lebanon War." Amatz, History Department, 2017.

Gur, Mordechai. "Lessons from the Yom Kippur War and the Force Design That Followed." National Security College, February 17, 1986.

IDF Strategy. General Staff, Office of the Head of Amatz, 2015.

IDF Strategy: Trends and Basic Ideas for Force Design and Employment. Amatz-Tohad, 2002.

Kovach, Amos, and Smadar Witteboon. *Insights from the Development and Force Design of the Tamuz Array*. Rafael-Mechtzav, 2017.

Laslau, Ohad. "Development of the Operational Concept for the Lebanese Theater." Dado Center Publications, 2015.

———. "From Routine Security to Guerrilla Warfare: Change in the Operational Concept in South Lebanon and Its Realization, 1992–1998." IDF History Department, 2017.

———. "Pathology in the Chief of Staff-Supreme Headquarters Interface." Dado Center Publications, 2012.

Levenberg, Haim. "The IDF versus the Intifada, First Book: Surprise and Awakening." Operations Branch, History Department, 2002.

Mafhash/Establishment Team. "The Field Forces Headquarters: Designation, Structure, and Organization," February 1980.

National Security College. "Summary of the Future Battlefield Project." National Security College, July 27, 1986.

Nir, Shmuel "Samu." "The Limited Confrontation: An Anthology of Articles." *Zarkor* 7 (July 2002).

———. "Victory and Warning in a Limited Confrontation." *Zarkor* 8 (April 2003).

Oren, Elhanan. "Operation Litani March 1978." Agam-Mahad, History Department, 1998.

Segev, Tzachi. "The History of the Development of the Mazi." Doctrine Department, *Zarkor* 13 (April 2010).

Shafir, Herzl. "The Yom Kippur War: Facts, Attitudes, and Evaluation, with an Emphasis on Force Design." Supreme Command study day, thirty years after the Yom Kippur War. Amatz-Tohad, History Department, October 8, 2003.

Supreme Command Order 2.0101—General Headquarters.

Tal, Israel. "Ground Forces: Designation and Organization." Internal report, December 1977.

Turgan, Sagi. *In the Rifle Sight: The Change in the IDF's Fighting Spirit, 1953–1956.* Center for Military Studies, Command and Staff College, 2014.

Yadai, Tamir. "The Voice of Heroism: 30 Years Establishment of the Security Zone in Lebanon, 15 Years since the Withdrawal from Lebanon." Interview by Ayalon Peretz and Shachar Lahav. Personal interviews of cadets in the Command and Staff Course with IDF combat commanders in Lebanon, 1985–2000. The Center for Military Studies, the Interservice Command and Staff College, 2016.

Yardeni, Shaul, and Gal Oren. "The Air Force: The Mental Shift from Routine Security to War." *Insight and Action* 2 (Amatz-Tohad-the Conceptual Lab, 2008).

Author's Interviews (Alphabetical by Name)

Interview with Major General (ret.) Udi Adam, May 30, 2017.

Interview with Colonel (res.) Boaz Amidror, April 23, 2017.

Interview with Lieutenant General (ret.) Ehud Barak, July 26, 2017.

Conversation with Brigadier General (ret.) Shaike Bareket, May 4, 2017.

Telephone interview and electronic correspondence with Brigadier General (res.) Ofek Buchris, March 24, 2017.

Correspondence with Colonel (ret.) Boaz Cohen, May 2, 2017.

Interview with Brigadier General (res.) Alon Friedman, March 26, 2017.

Interview with Lieutenant General (ret.) Benny Gantz, June 20, 2017.

Interview with Major General Yair Golan, July 3, 2017.

Interview with Major General Tamir Heyman, April 18, 2017.

Interview with Major General (ret.) David Ivry, February 20, 2017.

Conversation with Colonel (res.) Benny Michelson, February 22, 2017.

Interview with Major General Roni Numa, May 11, 2017.

Interview with Brigadier General (res.) Nitzan Nuriel, February 7, 2017.

Interview with Major General Shlomo (Sami) Turgeman, April 18, 2017.

Conversation with Colonel (res.) Zohar Ya'akobi, September 7, 2017.

PHOTO CREDITS

ABOUT THE AUTHOR

Brigadier General (res.) Dr. Meir Finkel is the current head of research and former director of the Dado Center for Interdisciplinary Military Studies/IDF-J3 (2014–19), as well as the former director of the Ground Forces Command's Concept Development and Doctrine Department (2007–13). He served for twenty years in the armored forces and took part in operations in the security zone in Lebanon, Gaza, and the West Bank. As a colonel, he commanded an armored brigade during the Second Lebanon War (2006). He is the author of *On Flexibility: Recovery from Technological and Doctrinal Surprise on the Battlefield* (Stanford University Press, 2011) and *Military Agility: Ensuring Rapid and Effective Transition from Peace to War* (University Press of Kentucky, 2020). His book *The Israeli General Staff: Its Learning Methods, Planning Processes, Organizational Rationale* was published in Hebrew in 2020. Finkel holds an MA in Neurobiology and PhDs in evolutionary biology, political science, and prehistoric archaeology. He is an active researcher in the last three fields.

INDEX

Note: The letter f following a page number denotes a figure; the letter t denotes a table.

Adam, Udi, 51–52, 54, 94, 98, 102–3, 157, 277
  relationship with Halutz, 123–43
Adam, Yekutiel, 195, 243
Adan, Avraham, 114, 139, 147, 154, 196
Agam (general staff branch), 2, 5, 10, 21,
  27, 29, 67, 73, 78, 89, 113, 118, 223,
  228–30, 235, 237. *See also* general
  staff branch
  deputy head of, 24, 26
  head of, 4, 10, 65, 69, 74, 104–5, 148,
    174, 178, 181–82, 185, 244
  splitting of, 4
Agat (planning branch), 9, 64–65, 149,
  163, 253, 259–61, 271. *See also*
  planning branch
  establishment of, 4, 156, 235
  and establishment of Mafhash, 244
  in first intifada 42–43
  in second intifada, 210
Agranat Commission (post–Yom Kippur
  War), 20, 147, 152–53, 249
  on moving bases closer to borders, 21
  on need to establish Mafhash, 249–50
  ramifications, resignation of generals,
    147, 152–53
air force. *See* IAF
air supremacy, 64, 76–77, 80–81, 83

al-Assad, Bashar, 55, 58, 268
Aman (intelligence directorate), 6, 17,
  49, 60–61, 147, 152–53, 167, 206,
  242, 274, 276. *See also* intelligence
  directorate
  and civil war in Syria, 58, 61
  establishment of, 2–3
  in first intifada, 23–25, 29
  in First Lebanon War, 83–84
  in security zone in Lebanon, 36–37
  before Yom Kippur War, 19–20, 22–23
Amatz (operations branch), 4, 64–65, 89,
  96, 163–65
  establishment of, 4
  in Second Lebanon War, 49–50, 62,
    128–30, 135
Amidror, Boaz, 211
Amir, Amos, 84–85
Amit, Meir, 104–5, 112, 181
Arafat, Yasser, 41
  statehood declaration of, 43, 45
Aran, Zalman, 72
Arens, Moshe, 18, 221, 233, 262
  on establishment of Mafhash, 248–55
  and Lavi project cancellation 257–61
armor, debate over employment of (1956),
  228–33

Armored Corps HQ, 5, 104, 154–55, 229, 231, 233–34, 242, 252
army. *See* ground forces
Ashkenazi, Gabi, 145–46, 171–72, 266
army rehabilitation and, 157–69

Bahar, Yossi, 165
Barak, Ehud, 11, 27, 173
criticism of, regarding first intifada, 31–32
developing PGM capabilities, 192–93, 195, 198–204
perceiving first intifada, as deputy chief of staff, 29, 33–34
Bareket, Shaike, 68
Bar-Kochva, Moshe, 31, 233, 256, 276
Bar-Lev, Haim, 80, 182, 269, 276
during Elazar-Gonen tensions, 119–22
on Operation Moked knowledge, 70
Bar-On, Mordechai, 110–11, 188–89
Bartov, Hanoch, 114
Bar-Zohar, Michael, 222
Bashan Regional Division, 55, 58
Basic Law: The IDF, 7
Begin, Menachem, 245, 268
Begin-Eitan relationship, 246
Beit-Or, Benny, 193–94, 197
Ben Ari, Uri, 106, 108–9, 113
Ben Nun, Aviyhu, 259, 261
Ben Reuven, Eyal, 133
Ben Shoshan, Avraham, 260–61
Ben Yehuda, Rani, 165
Ben-Basat Committee, 161
Ben-Besht, David, 165
Ben-Gal, Avigdor (Yanush), 268
Bengal, Michael, 104
Ben-Gurion, David, 10–12, 18, 182–84, 187–89,191–92, 217, 219, 269, 277
arguing about army size with Yadin, 221, 222–28
on armor employment, 228–33
backing Dayan on changes in human resources, 101, 105, 108, 110–13
and Unit 101, 179
Beqaa Valley air battle (1982) , 81–82, 84–86

"beyond-the-line-of-sight" intelligence systems, developing, 192–93
Bint Jbeil affair (2006), impact of, 134–35
Binyamin Brigade, 45
Biran, Ilan, 29
Blue and White alert (1973), 18–22
Blue Bird plan, 72
Brezner, Amiad, 229, 231–32
Brodet Committee, 160
Buchris, Ofek, 56, 58–59
Burning Steel plan, 43–45

C2 (command and control), 11, 52, 54, 83, 90, 94, 96–98, 113, 126, 131, 141, 194, 197, 200, 202, 273
C4I, 53, 164–65
development of, 4
directorate of, 6
campaign between the wars, 7
Central Command, 4, 203, 215
commander of, 25–26, 34, 42–43, 45–46, 127, 165, 199, 208, 251
in first intifada, 23–34
force design for LIC, 204–16
in second intifada, 41–47
chief of staff (Ramatkal)
appointing, 269–71
and appointing supplementary role players, 275–76
building firsthand experience of, 274–76
chief of staff institution, 9
and choice of successor, 269–71
and minister of defense as conversation partner, 277–78
opposition to political echelon's policies, 219–22
proactive learning of, 276–77
as public figure, 267–69
researched aspects of, 14–15
role evolution, 7–12
schedule of, 271–72
significance of position, 1, 7
success of, 272–74
Churchill, Winston, 141

COGAT (Coordinator of Government Activities in the Territories), 24, 29

Cohen, Boaz, 93–94, 96–97, 135–36

command and control. *See* C2

Command and Staff College, 185–86, 194

common language, problems with
  in Second Lebanon War, 134–36
  in Yom Kippur War, 113–14

Coordinator of Government Activities in the Territories. *See* COGAT

Country Defender plan, 93

crowd dispersal assets, 27. *See also* first intifada

cyber, development of, 100

Dagan, Meir, 95

Dayan, Moshe, 219–21, 277–78
  in debate on armor employment, 228–33
  loss of trust in Simhoni , 104–13
  as minister of defense, in Yom Kippur War, 118–22
  shaping role of chief of staff, 11, 272
  transforming fighting spirit before Sinai War, 172–73, 174–92, 217
  after Yom Kippur War, 147, 152

Dayan, Uzi, 42–43, 101, 271

defense budget, 150, 196, 226, 257–60

defense minister, as conversation partner to CoS, 277–78

Depth Command, 5, 64

Dla'at outpost, incident (1994) at, 40–41

doctrine and training branch, 19, 113, 235, 241, 253. *See also* Mahad

Dori, Ya'akov, 10, 175, 222–23

Dovecote plan, 114–15

Drori, Amir, 271

Drori, Ze'ev, 255

Dugman plan. *See* Tagar/Dugman plans

EBOs (effects-based operations), 92, 166

Egoz, establishment of, 37, 214

Egypt
  Israeli attack on airfields, in Operation Moked, 66, 71–73
  SAM array, in Yom Kippur War, 74–76
  before Sinai War, 104

surprise attack, in Yom Kippur War, 114–17
  Yadin's fear of surprise attack in 1950s, 223–24, 227

Egyptian Fourth Armored Division, 79

Egypt-Israel Peace Treaty, 5, 249

890th Paratrooper Battalion, 89, 173
  combat mission assignments, 182
  Unit 101 merger with, 180, 183, 190

Eilam, Uzi, 150

Eiland, Giora, 163, 167

Eisenhower, Dwight D., 9

Eisenkot, Gadi, 64, 268–69, 271, 273
  defining chief of staff's role, 8
  as head of Amatz, in Second Lebanon War, 48–49, 89–90

Eitam, Effi, 37, 39

Eitan, Rafael (Raful), 11, 13, 63, 157, 257
  Begin-Eitan relationship, 246
  on establishment of Mafhash, 234, 240–48
  familiarity with IAF plans, 81–87, 99

Elazar, David (Dado), 60, 152, 274, 277
  familiarity with IAF plans, in Yom Kippur War, 74–81
  loss of trust in Gonen, in Yom Kippur War, 103, 113–23
  ordering Blue and White alert, 18–23

Eshet, Shalom, 223

Eshkol, Levi, 11, 69, 71–72, 219–20, 225, 277

Etgar (Challenge) plan, 148–49

Etzion Brigade, 45

"events of October 2000." *See* first intifada

F-4 Phantom, against SAM, 77, 87

Field Forces HQ, establishing, 148, 156, 235–57

Field of Thorns operational plan, 44–45

fighting spirit, enhancing, before the Sinai War, 179–82

Finkelman, Yaron, 89

Fire Stones 9 exercise, 88, 92

"first circle" analysis, 209

first intifada (1987)
  beginning of, 23–34
  force design changes following, 204–18

First Lebanon War (1982)
  Operation Artzav 19, 81–87
  research on, 34–35
force design, 15, 63–64
  development of PGM capability,
    192–204
  major changes in, 171–74, 215–18
  orientation towards LIC, 204–16
  and relations with political echelon,
    219–22
  after Second Lebanon War, 157–68
  before Sinai War, 174–92
  after Yom Kippur War, 146–57
Fortress plan, 44
Forward Drive exercise, 43–44, 47, 276
418th Ivry Missile Unit, in Blue and White
    alert, 20
440th Division Task Force, 20
460th Training Brigade, after Yom Kippur
    War, 154
Fourth Brigade, 109
Friedman, Alon, 127

Ga'ash Armored Division, 55–59, 61, 90
Gadna program, 225
Galant, Yoav, 168, 269
Galili, Yisrael, 10
Gantz, Benny, 64, 167, 269
  change of perception on Golan Heights,
    14, 18, 55–62, 276
  as head of Mazi, during Second
    Lebanon War, 133–37, 140
Gaza Strip, 5
  in first intifada, 32–33
  Israeli occupation of, 23
  in second intifada, 206, 211–16
Gazit, Shlomo, 152–53, 272
general staff branch, 63, 235, 238, 243–44.
    See also Agam
general staff meeting, 93, 105, 115, 148,
    151, 153, 156, 177
  on armor use, 229
  on first intifada, 28
  on Mafhash, 241, 252
  on second intifada, 45
GHQ (Hamatkal physical location), 2. See
    also Pit, the

Gilad, Amos, 95
Givati Brigade, 24, 182
Golan, Shimon, 74
Golan, Yair, 55, 58
Golan Heights
  change of perception on, 14, 55–62
  and Dugman plan in Yom Kippur War,
    75, 77–78, 173
  as fighting arena, 274
  preparations in Blue and White alert, 21
Gonen, Shmuel, 234–35
  on Blue and White alert, 19
  controversial rise of, 113–14
  relationship with Elazar, 101, 113–23
Gordon, Shmuel, 75–76
Goren, Shmuel, 24
ground forces (army), 4, 63–64, 99–100,
    129, 149, 163, 164–65, 205, 234,
    235–240. See also Armored Corps
    HQ; Mafhash; Mazi
  complexity of force design, 5–6
  cooperating with air force, 35–36
  culture and "DNA," 87–90
  cutback effects, 88, 90–91, 160–61
  design of, xxif
  in First Lebanon War, 81–87
  tactical echelons of, 167
  in Second Lebanon War, 87–99, 129,
    131–134
  and shift to war mentality, 52–53, 54
  in Sinai War, 190–192
  in Yom Kippur War, 74–81
Ground Forces Command, 63. See also
    Mazi
  establishment of, 6
Ground Forces Headquarters. See
    Mafhash
Gulf War (1991), 198
Gur, Mordechai (Motta), 13, 69, 220, 256
  and army rehabilitation after Yom
    Kippur War, 146–57
  on establishment of Mafhash, 235–40

Hagana, 2, 10, 189, 269
Halutz, Dan, 18, 60–61, 159, 220, 268–72,
    274–75
  on chief of staff's role, 8

crisis with Adam, during Second
    Lebanon War, 102–3, 123–43, 277
instituting organizational transfers, 164,
    172
knowledge of ground forces plans,
    before Second Lebanon War, 87–99
and war footing, in Second Lebanon
    War, 47–54
Hamas, 5, 36, 41, 167–68
Hamatkal (physical location), 2. *See also*
    Pit, the
Harel, Amos, 168
Harel, Dan, 165
Haruv Reconnaissance Unit, 154–55
Hebron Protocol, 41
Heyman, Tamir, 56, 58
Hezbollah, 35–40, 47–48, 92–99, 124, 126,
    129–31
Hirsch, Gal, 139, 165
    as Galilee Division commander, in
        Second Lebanon War, 51–52, 132,
        157, 165
    in second intifada, 45–46, 212
Hod, Mordechai (Motti), and Moked plan,
    65–74
Hofi, Yitzhak, 73
Home Front Command, 5, 18, 57
Horev, Amos, 230
HQ. *See* Armored Corps HQ; GHQ

IAF (Israeli Air Force), 5–6, 14, 65–70
    C2 method of, 90
    commander of, 49, 64–65, 67, 69–70,
        78–79, 81, 83, 85, 88–89, 92, 95, 257,
        261, 264, 273, 276
    cooperating with ground forces, 35–36
    culture of, 89, 133
    and effects-based operations, 92
    Egyptian air force, 66, 71–73
    force design model, 64, 164
    and Mafhash establishment, 242
    in Operation Artzav 19, 81, 84–85, 87
    in Operation Dugman, 74–80
    in Operation Moked, 65–74
    in Operation Tagar, 74–80
    priorities of, 99–100
    routine security and, 51–52

Icebreaker (Shoveret Kerach) plan, 93, 125
IDF (Israel Defense Forces)
    chiefs of staff, list of, 7t
    conflict terminology, 6
    fundamental mission of, 4
    history of, 2–7
    1952–53 budget, 225–26
    strategic documents of, 8
    structure of, 2–7, 3f
    intelligence directorate, 2, 17. *See also*
        Aman
internal security agency. *See* Shin Bet
intifada. *See* first intifada; second intifada
Islamic State (ISIS), 58
Israel Defense Forces. *See* IDF
Israeli Air Force. *See* IAF
Issacharoff, Avi, 168
Ivry, David, 195–96, 250, 257, 260
    as commander of IAF, in Operation
        Artzav, 19, 81–87

Jerusalem District, 177
Joint Arms exercise, before Second
    Lebanon War, 94
Judea and Samaria Division, 43–44, 45, 55

Kahalani, Avigdor, 154–55
Kaplinsky, Moshe
    as deputy chief of staff, in Second
        Lebanon War, 89, 98, 136–41, 275
    as Galilee Division commander, 37
Katyusha and other rockets, in Second
    Lebanon War, 92, 95, 131
Kesem Hamangina plan (Magic Melody),
    45, 206
Kibbutz Movement, 173
Kilshon (Pitchfork) plan, 74
Klifi, Meir, 164
Knesset Foreign Affairs and Defense
    Committee, 10, 55, 82, 161, 245, 246,
        249, 256
Kochavi, Aviv, 58, 269

Lapidot, Amos, 257, 260
Laskov, Haim, 7, 104, 112, 228
    debate with Dayan over armor's
        employment, 228–33

Laskov, Haim (*continued*)
  as 77th Division commander, in Sinai
    War, 109
  tensions with other generals, 101,
    220–21, 270
Lavi jet fighter, development of, 257–62
Lavon, Pinhas, 177–78, 187–88, 219, 220
Lebanon. *See also* First Lebanon War;
    Second Lebanon War; security zone
    in Lebanon
  defining routine security operations in,
    17–18
  withdrawal from, 35
Levi, Moshe, 145, 269–70, 275
  on establishment of Mafhash, 221,
    233–34, 248–57
  on Lavi jet fighter development, 258
  trying to block Shomron, 101, 220, 271
Levin, Amiram, 38
LIC. *See* low-intensity conflict
limited conflict light infantry battalions,
    establishment of, 214
limited confrontation doctrine, 212–13
Lincoln, Abraham, 141
Lipkin-Shahak, Amnon, 17, 60, 158, 204,
    271
  defining situation in security zone in
    Lebanon, 34–43
  as head of Aman, at outbreak of first
    intifada, 25
  on Mafhash, 253
loft bombing, 77, 80–81, 296n25
logistics branch, 2, 124, 133, 237, 241, 255
low-intensity conflict (LIC), 6, 204–5, 208
  combat doctrine of, 212–213
  military education on, 210–11
  structure and organization for, 213–15

Mafhash (Ground Forces Headquarters)
  Eitan-Sharon period, 248
  Eitan-Tzipori period, 246–48
  Eitan-Weizman period, 240–45
  establishment of, 233–57
  Gur-Weizman period, 235–40
  Levi-Arens period, 248–55
  and Yom Kippur War lessons learned,
    233–34

Magic Melody (Kesem Hamangina) plan,
    45, 206
Mahad (doctrine and training branch),
    4, 19, 113–14, 154–55, 187, 230–31,
    241–42, 247, 253–54, 256. *See also*
    doctrine and training branch
Maklef, Mordechai, 10, 173–74, 269
Malka, Amos, 39
manpower, 6, 10, 13, 24, 30, 44, 164
  branch related to, 2, 241, 255
  cutting, 225, 227, 241
  head of, 241
  increasing size of, in early 1950s,
    151–53
  before Sinai War, 182–84
Marom, Eli, 165
Marshall, George C., 9
Mazi (Ground Forces Command), 6, 63,
    136, 163–66, 171
Mei Merom (Sky High Water) plan, 93, 95,
    125–26, 128
Meir, Golda, 121, 220
  consulting Elazar, 19–20
Merkava tank
  production, 159, 196
  upgrade for operation in Lebanon,
    39–40
Messer, Amos, 230
Midras missile, as part of PGM
    transformation, 195, 202
Mirkam 2000 plan, 38
  seminar, 200–201
Mitzna, Amram, on first intifada, 26
Mizrahi, Avi, 165
Mofaz, Shaul, 11, 18, 88, 92–93, 101, 158,
    161, 220, 270–71
  on chief of staff's role, 8
  and first intifada force design changes,
    173, 204–18
  on Operation Defensive Shield eve,
    205–8
  before second intifada, 41–47, 60
Mordechai, Yitzhak, 24, 34, 255
multiyear plans, 205, 259
  Gideon, 271
  Idan, 205
  Kela, 159

Keshet, 159
Mirkam, 38, 200
Mirkam A, 201
Misgav, 197–98
Tefen, 159, 162–63

Nahal (infantrymen), 153, 173, 178, 185,
    188–89, 225–26
    and IDF offensive ability, 182–84
Nakba Day
    2000, 44–46, 47, 204
    2011, 55, 57
Nakpadon APC, in security zone in
    Lebanon, 39
Narkis, Uzi, 105
Nasser, Gamal Abdel, 104, 231
National Defense College, 195
Naveh, Yair, 55
navy, 5, 37, 50, 63, 100, 165, 194, 229, 242,
    260–61
Ne'eman, Yuval, 186
Negicha (Ramming) plan, 77
Netiv Ha'esh (Path of Fire) Reserve
    Armored Division, 56, 138
90s battalions, 207, 214
98th Division, 53
Ninth Brigade, 109
Nir, Nathan, 155–56
Nitzan Battalion, 215
Northern Command
    commander of, 13, 31, 38, 40–41,
        51–52, 55, 58–59, 60, 94, 95, 103,
        123–25
    and crisis between Halutz and
        Adam, 123–41
    dealing with civil war in Syria, 55–60
    after Second Lebanon War, 163
    in security zone in Lebanon, 33–41
Numa, Roni, 96, 127
Nuriel, Nitzan, 38
Nurit mortar fire spotting system, in
    Lebanon, 39

Officer Candidate School, 181
Olmert, Ehud, 93, 125
100th Improvised Tank Battalion,
    198

143rd Division, 116–17
162nd Division, 116
Operation Artzav 19 (1982), 19, 81–87
Operation Cast Lead (2008–9), 158
    and IDF rehabilitation, 167–68
Operation Defensive Shield (2002), 204
    combat doctrine following, 212–13
    education/training after, 210–11
    eve of, 205–8
    exploiting, 208–9
    unit structure/organization, 213–15
Operation Entebbe (1976), 156, 262
Operation Hafarperet, plan for, 85
Operation Hiram (1948), 176
Operation Horev (1949), 176
Operation Kinneret (1995), 185
Operation Litani (1978), 156–57
Operation Moked (1967)
    calculated risk during, 70
    Hod's account for, 65–66
    plan for, 65–74
    Rabin's minimal knowledge of, 68–69
    success of, 69–70
    "War over the Water," 69
Operation Olive Leaves (1955), 185
Operation Opera (1981), 87
Operation Pillar of Defense (2012), 57
Operation Protective Edge (2014), 14
Operation Valerian, plans for, 78
Operation Volcano (1955), 184–85
Operation Yoav (1948), 176
operations branch. *See* Amatz
Oranim plan, formulating, 83–84
Oren, Amir, 57
Oren, Shlomo, 46
Oslo Accords (1993–95), 24, 41, 204

Palestine Liberation Organization (PLO),
    27, 83–84
Palestinian Authority (PA), 41, 43
paratroopers, 60, 155–56, 165, 174,
    180–85, 190, 204. *See also* 890th
    Paratrooper Battalion; 202nd
    Paratrooper Brigade
Pazit UAV, as part of PGM transformation,
    193
Paztal, Gershon, 193

Peled, Benny, 149, 276
    before Yom Kippur War, 76–77
    during Yom Kippur War, 78–81, 149
Peled, Elad, 109
Peled, Matityahu, 187
Peled, Yossi, 31, 154, 256
    on initial first intifada response, 31
    on Mafhash, 253
Peres, Shimon, 159, 226, 239, 260,
    270
Peretz, Amir, 11, 125, 270
PGMs (precision-guided munitions),
    development of, 192–203
Pit, the (Hamatkal physical location),
    116, 131
planning branch, 235. See also Agat
PLO. See Palestine Liberation
    Organization
political echelon, building relationships
    with, 219–22
    arguing about army size, 222–28
    armor employment before Sinai War,
    228–33
    and force design, 219–22
    Lavi jet fighter development, 257–62
    Mafhash establishment and, 233–57
precision-guided munitions. See
    PGMs
Pundak, Yitzhak, 187

R&D directorate, 21, 150, 199, 241–44,
    253
Rabin, Yitzhak, 11, 24, 40, 148–49, 187,
    219, 230, 238, 269, 277–78
    and first intifada, 29
    on Lavi jet fighter, 221–22, 257–62
    and Operation Moked, 65–74
Rafael (company), 198
Ramatkal. See chief of staff
research and development. See R&D
    directorate
retaliatory raids before the Sinai War,
    177–91
Romm, Giora, 24, 26
routine security
    in security zone in Lebanon, change in
    definition of, 33–41
    transitioning from, in Second Lebanon
    War, 49–50
    in West Bank and Gaza Strip (see first
    intifada; second intifada)
Russo, Tal, 134, 202

Sadat, Anwar, 20, 22, 220
Sagi, Raz, 213
Sagi, Yehoshua, 83, 153
Samia, Yom Tov, 42
SAMs (surface-to-air missiles)
    in First Lebanon War, 81–87
    in Yom Kippur War, 74–80
Sayeret Matkal operations, 198
Schiff, Ze'ev, 32, 261
second intifada, time before (1999–2000),
    41–47
Second Lebanon War
    abduction attempt, 48, 126–27
    army rehabilitation following, 157–69
    changing operational/conceptual
    framework of, 49–50
    education/training/inventory emphasis
    following, 161–63
    failure to put on war footing in, 47–54
    gap in senior commanders following,
    165–66
    ground force plans before, 87–100
    ground unit cutbacks before, 160
    Halutz-Adam relationship, 123–43
    nature of crisis following, 157–59
    Operation Cast Lead following, 167–68
    organizational changes canceled,
    164–65
    return to doctrinal basics following,
    166–67
    transitions between action modes,
    49–52
security zone in Lebanon
    hostilities in, 34–41
    intelligence, 36–37
    organization, 37–38
    taking offensive during, 38–39
    weapon systems for, 35
    weapons and replenishment, 38–40
Seventh Armored Brigade, deployment
    of, 106–7

77th Division, 109
Shabak, 24. *See also* Shin Bet
Shafir, Herzl, 148, 230
Shahaf Observation Battalion, 215
Shaham, Mishael, 177
Shaham, Zonik, 107–8
Shalev, Aryeh, 153
Shalev, Avner, 118–19
Shamir, Yitzhak, 259–60
Shapira, Ya'akov Shimshon, 72
Sharett, Moshe, 187–88, 217, 219
Sharon, Ariel, 11, 13, 105, 123, 139, 176,
    179, 181, 183, 220, 245, 247, 257,
    270
  on Blue and White alert, 19
  as division commander, in Yom Kippur
    War, 114, 118–21, 123
  on Mafhash establishment, 248
  as minister of defense, during
    Operation Artzav 19, 84, 86–87
Shavit (Comet) plan, 207
Shin Bet (internal security agency), 24–25,
    29, 206
Shkedi, Eliezer, 49, 51
Shomron, Dan, 17, 60–61, 101, 155, 156,
    173, 222, 251
  on Lavi jet fighter, 257–62
  and Mafhash, 234–35, 248, 253–55
  at outbreak of first intifada, 23–34, 268
  and PGM development, 192–204
  Shoshanim war game, 83
Shoveret Kerach plan, 93
Simhoni, Asaf, relationship with Dayan,
    104–13
Simhoni, Uri, 247
Sinai War (1956), 5, 11
  armor employment before, 228–33
  Dayan-Simhoni relationship during,
    104–13
  enhancing fighting spirit before, 179–84
  expanding IDF offensive ability, 182–84
  need for change prior to, 175–78
Six-Day War (1967), 5
  "battle day" before, 69
  Operation Moked, 65–74
Sky High Water (Mei Merom) plan, 93, 95,
    125–26, 128

Skyhawks, against SAM, 77
"smart fence," developing, 206
Southern Command
  commander of, 19, 24, 34, 41–42, 47,
    60–61, 101–2, 104–5, 107, 112–18,
    142, 147, 193–94, 230, 256, 271
  in first intifada, 23–34
  in Sinai War, 104–13
  in Yom Kippur War, 113–23
Spector, Iftach, 150–51
Sreeta (Scratch) plan, 77
State Security Cabinet, 245
Suez Canal, 5, 74, 76–77, 108, 114, 119,
    139, 198
  and Blue and White alert, 19, 21
surface-to-air missiles. *See* SAMs
Syria
  civil war in, 55–58
  before and during First Lebanon War,
    82–86
  SAM array, IAF Dugman plan against,
    75–77
  "War over the Water," 69

Tagar/Dugman plans, 74–81
Tal, Israel, 39, 201, 276
  on Blue and White alert, 22
  on establishment of Mafhash, 236–38,
    243–45, 247, 255
  on Field Forces HQ, 236–38, 240
  in Yom Kippur War, 119
Tamari, Dov, 155
Tamir, Avraham, 234
Tamir, Moshe, 36
Tamuz missile, as part of PGM
    transformation, 193–95, 202
Teveth, Shabtai, 182
Tolkovsky, Dan, 65
Turgeman, Shlomo (Sami), 50, 62, 142,
    165
202nd Paratrooper Brigade, 109
210th Division, in Blue and White
    alert, 20
252nd (Sinai) Division, 5, 116
Tzipori, Mordechai, 240, 245, 256
  on establishment of Mafhash, 221,
    246–48

Tzur, Guy, 211
Tzur, Tzvi, 101, 269

UAVs (unmanned aerial vehicles), 6
    acquiring, 150–51
    as part of PGM transformation, 193–94,
        198–99, 201
    use before and during Yom Kippur War,
        79, 203–4
Unit 101, actions, 176–78, 179–80
United States
    commander in chief role in, 2
    role in Lavi project, 257–58
    tour of, influence on IDF training,
        187
unmanned aerial vehicles. See UAVs

Vilnai, Matan, 39

Wald, Emanuel, 149, 151
    on chief of staff's role, 9
Wallach, Yehuda, 107, 109, 111
War of Attrition (1967–70), 5, 54, 75
War of Independence (1947–49), 2
    force size during, 223
    IDF condition after, 174
"War over the Water," dispatchments
        for, 69
Weizman, Ezer, 65, 69–70, 221, 246, 257,
        270
    during first intifada, 25–26
    on establishment of Mafhash, 235–45,
        250, 255
    on Rabin and Moked plan, 73
West Bank
    in first intifada, 47–54
    in second intifada, 204–16
    Western Wall Tunnel events, 204
Winograd Commission report (post–
        Second Lebanon War), 48, 51, 93,
        102, 125, 128
    on absence of common language,
        135
    on conceptual gaps, 136
    on GHQ orders, 135–36

on Halutz, 96–97, 124
    after Second Lebanon War, 157–58, 216
World War II, influence of, 2

Ya'alon, Moshe (Bogie), 13, 42, 45, 88, 92,
        159, 220
    transforming IDF ground forces to LIC,
        204, 208–18
Ya'ari, Ehud, 32
Yadai, Tamir, 36–37
Yadin, Yigael, 10, 175, 187
    arguing about army size, 221, 222–28
Yanai, Shlomo, 43
Yariv, Aharon, 122, 276
Yom Kippur War (1973), 4–5
    army rehabilitation following, 146–57
    Blue and White alert prior to, 18–23
    crisis resolution formula, 148–56
    Elazar-Gonen relationship during,
        113–23
    emphasizing education and training
        following, 153–56
    force design changes following,
        192–204
    increasing manpower size following,
        151–53
    increasing number of IDF units
        following, 148–51
    and Mafhash establishment, 233–57
    nature of crisis following, 146–47
    Operation Entebbe following, 156
    Operation Litani following, 156–57
    Tagar/Dugman plans, 74–81
    "war of the generals," 139

Zahavan UAV system, as part of PGM
        transformation, 193, 202
Zakheim, Dov, 259–60
Zamir, Eyal, 162
Zamir, Zvi, 187
Ze'evi, Rehavam, 112, 116–19, 276
Zeira, Eli, 23, 152–53
    on Blue and White alert, 19
Zore'a, Meir, 221, 228, 230–32
Zukerman, Erez, 37, 138, 162